Nothing Sacred

Women Respond to Religious Fundamentalism and Terror

Edited by BETSY REED

Thunder's Mouth Press/Nation Books
New York

NOTHING SACRED:
WOMEN RESPOND TO RELIGIOUS FUNDAMENTALISM AND TERROR

Compilation Copyright © 2002 Betsy Reed
Introduction © 2002 Katha Pollitt

Published by
Thunder's Mouth Press/Nation Books
161 William St., 16th Floor
New York, NY 10038

Nation Books is a copublishing venture of the Nation Institute and Avalon
Publishing Group Incorporated.

Library of Congress Cataloging-in-Publication Data is available.

ISBN 1-56025-450-5

9 8 7 6 5 4 3 2 1

Book design by Susan Canavan

Printed in the United States of America
Distributed by Publishers Group West

Contents

Editor's Note

When Jerry Falwell blamed "the pagans, and the abortionists, and the feminists, and the gays and the lesbians . . . the ACLU, [and] People for the American Way," for bringing on the terrorist attacks of September 11, he surely had no idea that such religious-right boilerplate would get him excommunicated from polite Christian company. Most distasteful to his erstwhile friends was the notion that the events were a manifestation of divine will, as opposed to the work of barbaric evildoers inspired only by unfathomable forces of darkness. But as born-again Christians scurried to absolve their God of any responsibility for the awful acts, an idea took hold in more mainstream, secular circles that bore a subtle resemblance to Falwell's original theory: America was attacked because of its values, its freedoms, its "way of life"—because of "who we are as a people," as Hillary Clinton put it.

Many who found comfort in that thought, along with Falwell's indignant critics on the religious right, were loath to admit that the attacks had "an intimate connection with the culture war at home," as Ellen Willis writes in her essay here. What Falwell's statement inadvertently exposed was the distinct affinity between his own movement and religious fundamentalisms in other parts of the world, which share, among other things, a visceral antipathy toward feminism. This book is a more deliberate attempt to examine such parallels, looking especially at what they mean for women.

These essays (some of which appeared previously in the *Nation* or other publications) consider the ways in which Christian, Jewish, Hindu and Muslim extremists, often in the name of fidelity to sacred texts, seek to restrict women's freedoms, particularly sexual freedoms—as well as the ways women are fighting back. A recurring theme is the cross-cultural collusion of reactionary forces, such as the Vatican's insidious alliance with conservative Islamic nations—and the Bush administration—to torpedo UN treaties that would improve women's access to reproductive health care. Pieces by Laura Flanders, Rosemary Radford Ruether, Margaret Lamberts Bendroth, Barbara Ehrenreich, and others assess the considerable contributions of Christians to the history of fundamentalism—a movement that, after all, first surfaced among early 20th-century American Protestants.

While it is essential to understand that fundamentalism is not only an

Islamic phenomenon, it is equally important to recognize that feminism does not belong to the West. Muslim women's movements have long been bedeviled by the charge that women's rights are a Western concept, an affront to the authentic traditions of Islam. In fact, as Susan Muaddi Darraj notes, the history of Arab feminism is "long, layered, and impressive," and Madhavi Sunder presents a case study of the pioneering women's human rights organization Women Living Under Muslim Laws, which encourages Muslim women to define their own culture and religion. In essays documenting diverse traditions of religious extremism and women's resistance within Muslim countries, Valentine Moghadam looks at women's efforts to reform the theocracy in Iran; Karima Bennoune interviews her father, the anthropologist Mahfoud Bennoune, about the recent history of Algeria, where women have had to tread a treacherous path between violent Islamists and a corrupt secular state; and Janet Afary excavates the complicated historical and social roots of fundamentalist movements across the Muslim world.

As the Western media has focused on conflict in the Middle East, South Asia has been wracked with some of the bloodiest religious violence of recent years, with as many as 2,000 Muslims killed in Gujarat, India, by marauding mobs of Hindu fundamentalists in the spring of 2002. Arundhati Roy here delivers a scathing indictment of the Indian government's complicity in the atrocities, which included rampant violence against women. The relationship between the Indian state and religion is also a primary concern in Martha Nussbaum's essay, in which she argues that the law should strive to protect both religious liberty and women's rights.

In addition, the volume includes a number of essays reflecting a range of feminist opinion on the U.S. war in Afghanistan and on the causes and consequences of September 11. American feminists were well aware that militant, faith-based fanaticism did not begin with al Qaeda's attack on the United States. Most conspicuously, as Katha Pollitt notes in the introduction, the Feminist Majority had spearheaded a campaign against Afghanistan's brutal Taliban regime, prodding the Clinton administration to sever diplomatic ties in 1997. Yet while some feminists supported the U.S. intervention in the wake of the terrorist attacks—and all welcomed the demise of the Taliban—many were appalled by the spectacle of a right-wing administration dropping cluster bombs in the name of feminism when its only previous interest in women's rights was in suppressing them.

Elsewhere in the world, meanwhile, it is increasingly clear that the unilateral militarism of the U.S. government is likely only to aggravate the fundamentalist threat. But that knowledge has yet to spawn a visible movement with a coherent alternative agenda here in the United States. And as Charlotte Bunch observes, the perception abroad that the U.S. women's movement is lined up behind the Bush administration, however unfair, hampers efforts to build international solidarity among feminists—a crucial weapon against the global forces of reaction. So it's all the more important that women raise their voices now.

Thanks go to tireless *Nation* interns Emily Biuso, Daphne Carr, Rebecca Ruiz, and Kabir Dandona, for their creative and meticulous research assistance. For advice, support, and/or indulgence, I am grateful to Liberty Aldrich, Ruth Baldwin, Carl Bromley, Roane Carey, Liza Featherstone, Hillary Frey, Naomi Klein, Richard Kim, Katha Pollitt, Eyal Press, Ann Snitow, John Stamm, Alex Star, Katrina vanden Heuvel, and Mike Vazquez.

Introduction

Katha Pollitt

In Bangladesh, Muslim fanatics throw acid in the faces of unveiled women; in Nigeria, newly established shariah courts condemn women to death by stoning for having sex outside of wedlock. In Israel, women walking in ultra-Orthodox neighborhoods have been physically attacked for wearing sleeveless tops. In the United States, Protestant evangelicals and fundamentalists have forged a powerful right-wing political movement focused on banning abortion, stigmatizing homosexuality, and limiting young people's access to contraception and accurate information about sex. Modernity wasn't supposed to be like this. As women became better educated, went out to work and won more rights, as families became smaller and less tied to the land, as information flowed more freely, scientific and technical knowledge became more widely disseminated, and thrones and dynasties crumbled in favor of representative democracy, the natural similarity of the sexes was supposed to stand revealed, making possible new, more equal and companiable relationships between them. The same forces of progress, this view held, would cause organized religion to wither away or at any rate modulate away from dogma and authority and reaction toward a kind of vague, kindly, nondenominational spiritual uplift whose politics, if it had any, would be liberal.

In Europe that prediction has proved accurate—even in Spain and Italy, not to mention Scandinavia, the United Kingdom and the Netherlands, the churches are emptying and the once-mighty political power of Catholic and Protestant churches is on the wane. But in many other parts of the world, religion is tightening its grip. While there are many differences among the numerous movements popularly called "fundamentalist"—so many the very term is a matter of some contestation—what's clear is that in many countries and regions, antimodernist religious movements that claim to offer a return to a better, more orderly, "traditional" way of life are rapidly growing in popularity.

The subordination of women is a central feature of every variety of fundamentalist religion—how could it be otherwise if one is trying to live life through literal and simplistic readings of texts produced by ancient

ix

patriarchal societies? As a matter of fact, female subjection is a feature of most non-fundamentalist religion, too: think of the Catholic Church's intransigence on contraception, abortion, divorce, and women priests. And yet the misogyny inherent in fundamentalism has been a kind of open secret—obvious, but boring. Feminists warned about the Taliban for years; raising awareness about the regime and its extreme restrictions on women was a major project of the Feminist Majority and other groups as well. The media wasn't interested: A few years ago one female editor at the *Los Angeles Times* arranged a seminar on Afghan women for her colleagues, and not one man showed up. Women! Always complaining. Consider, by contrast, the immense global outrage when the Taliban announced it would destroy the ancient giant Buddha statues of Bamiyan as part of its attempt to eradicate everything non-Islamic from Afghanistan. Well-meaning Westerners—and those who just don't care—see fundamentalist restrictions on women as a matter of "culture" or "tradition" even when, as with the Taliban, those measures are new and imported and so unpopular they must be enforced with beatings and jail.

Before the attack on the World Trade Center, it was not hard to find articles in major magazines and newspapers that portrayed the Taliban neutrally or objectively or in a "balanced" way or even in a favorable light—for ending the rule of the warlords and bringing order to the country. Typically, Western readers were urged to be culturally sensitive and suspend judgment of its harsh practices. It was left to activists of the Revolutionary Association of the Women of Afghanistan (RAWA) to get footage of the now-notorious public execution of a woman in the Kabul soccer stadium—footage that appeared on television practically every day after September 11, when for a brief moment Afghan women held the media spotlight and it was belatedly discovered that they didn't like being confined to their houses and deprived of jobs and education after all. It was also revealed that the Taliban were not noble warriors but operators of a clerical police state, ignorant, corrupt, vicious, and sadistic, as likely to commit rapes, murders, and abductions as to prevent them.

The hatred of women that animated the Taliban was extreme to the point of mania, perhaps because their ranks were filled with young men who had grown up as orphans in the all-male world of Pakistani *madrassas* (religious boarding schools)—men who had never had real contact with women, even in their families. Some of their rules, in their obsessive and legalistic precision, remind one of the Nazi edicts against the Jews: Women were to paint their windows black so no man could see them, were not to wear white socks (the color of the Afghan flag) or shoes that made a noise and would entice men to lust. It is as if the goal was less the control of women than their erasure. Thus, under no circumstance, even to save her life in childbirth, could a woman be treated by a male doctor—but women doctors were barred from working. Women could not leave their homes without a male relative as escort, but Kabul alone had 40,000 widows: Were they supposed to sit at home and starve? It would be hard to take the suppression of women further—although our ally Saudi Arabia does its best—and it is important to remember just how barbarous and cruel the Taliban were. Yet it is also important not to use their example to obscure or deny the common thread of misogyny that connects them with Focus on the Family and the Christian Coalition, who see modern women—working mothers, sexually active singles—as the source of an immense range of social woes, or the Promise Keepers, who urged men to "take back" the leadership of their families and somehow never did include domestic non-violence in their principles of Christian manhood.

The situation of women, in mainstream politics and on the left as well, is usually seen as something apart from "real" politics, which are about wars and borders and leaders and macro-economic forces and so on. It was only within the last decade, for example, that experts concerned to reduce population growth—an area in which one would think attention to women's status was inescapable—realized that the key to smaller family size in the developing world was raising the abysmal social position of women, by providing education, employment, health care, and legal rights and by raising their status in the family. The same is true of the AIDS epidemic devastating Africa and much of Asia: If women are utterly dependent on men for survival, how can they negotiate safe sex, demand fidelity, reject predatory older men looking for uninfected young girls? Or think of war: Our image is still men fighting, women on the sidelines, with sexual assault the regrettable but politically irrelevant result of having a lot of armed and desperate men rampaging about far from wives and girlfriends. One has only to consider the role of mass rape in Bosnia, Rwanda, and the Congo to see that wartime assaults on women are profoundly political acts. Indeed, the bodies of women are one of the terrains upon which modern wars are fought—humiliating the community by destroying its "honor," breaking up families by forcing the rejection or even murder of daughters, wives, and mothers, polluting the hated ethnic group by forcing alien children upon it.

Similarly, women's bodies—what they should wear and where they can be, who can look at them or touch them, who controls their sexuality and fertility—are crucial battlegrounds for all varieties of fundamentalism. Mohammed Atta's highly sexualized obsession with women as impure and unworthy—the famous funeral instructions barring women from touching his corpse's genitals or visiting his grave are all the nuttier coming from a "martyr" who expected seventy-two beautiful virgins to entertain him in Paradise—is not characteristic only of Muslim fanatics. As the Israeli feminist Alice Shalvi details in her contribution to this volume, ultra-Orthodox Israelis regard women's hair and women's voices raised in song as an "abomination," practice strict segregation of the sexes, demand large families (while banning abortion, even where Judaism permits it), and have managed the neat trick of maintaining male dominance in marriage despite the fact that wives, often better equipped for the modern world than their yeshiva-bucher husbands, not only do all the housework and childcare but earn all the money, too. Apparently the materialist explanation of sexism has its limits! American Christian fundamentalism is obsessed with abortion—a procedure never mentioned in either Old or New Testament—and premarital virginity, although given the statistics on teenage sex, they have had to invent something called "secondary virginity" (abstinence after becoming sexual active) in order not to be preaching to empty pews.

There has been fierce debate over whether September 11 and the militant Islam behind it can be best understood as a politically motivated response to U.S. foreign policy—its support for Israel and sanctions on Iraq, as well as the larger fact of American world dominance—or, as Ellen Willis argues in her essay, primarily as a religiously motivated attack on "the West," meaning secularism, consumerism, cultural pluralism, and the emancipation of women. Probably both these positions are too simple—Islamic fundamentalism, like ultra-Orthodox Judaism, born-again Christianity and India's militant Hinduism, is connected in complicated ways with nationalism, power politics, ethnic and class antagonisms, and profound economic shifts. As Janet Afary and Fatima Mernissi point out, Islamic fundamentalism is popular among men who find themselves competing with women for jobs in a declining economy, and with women who find that modern ways have freed them for boring and pointless low-paid employment, while releasing their husbands from traditional obligations to the family. In the same way, if we look at who actually becomes a Christian fundamentalist, we will find not so many graduates of elite universities, well equipped to make their way in the Information Age, and lots of anxious workers and small business people, as well as a good many ex-alcoholics and ex-addicts and other casualties of contemporary life, who are attracted to the practical support system, emotional fellowship, and structured ideology provided by their churches.

There are those who reject the view that women are simple victims of fundamentalism and stress the agency of the women in its ranks. Yet it's hard to get around the obvious ways in which fundamentalism limits women's freedom—how freely does a woman "choose" the veil if unveiled women are beaten by the religious police or harassed with impunity by men who call them whores? You might as well say New York women "choose" not to walk topless down Fifth Avenue. It is certainly true, though, that fundamentalism is not without its rewards for certain women. All fundamentalisms express great concern and respect for family and childraising, the traditional sphere of women, and for traditional culture, of which women are typically the custodians. Then, too, like every large social movement, fundamentalism needs female cadres to carry out its mission. Thus, some women are able to use their involvement in fundamentalist activities to get more personal freedom and respect in return for policing the behavior of other women.

Like accounts of fundamentalism's appeal that stress its usefulness to people trying to ford the difficult rapids of modernity, explanations that focus on fundamentalism as a reasonable strategy for obtaining some practical goal—preschool for the kids, jobs for men, a small but safe social space for women—have the advantage of explaining why ordinary people, including those who seem to be its victims, turn to fundamentalism, yet they seem to leave out the elements of fanaticism and violence that are so striking to outsiders. Sure, modern life is unsettling and challenges to established gender hierarchies produce losers as well as winners. But Algerian fundamentalists slit the throats of school girls because women are getting too many academic posts? Christian fanatics burn down abortion clinics and try to ban the Pill as an "abortifacient" because the divorce rate is too high? Jewish settlers colonize the West Bank, putting their children in daily danger, so that the kids can grow up with grass and fresh air? When progressive writers try to understand fundamentalism, the intense satisfactions of intolerance, violence, groupthink and xiv • Nothing Sacred

the conviction that God is on your side smiting your enemies tend to drop out of the picture.

Women have been seriously marginalized in the ongoing debates about September 11, Islam, and fundamentalism generally; when it comes to Afghanistan, feminism has been little more than a flag of convenience under which the War Party is currently sailing. Afghan women, a potential source of support for democracy, modernization, and peace, have gotten a lot less out of the recently concluded Loya Jirga than the Northern Alliance and other warlords who brought nothing but ruin and backwardness on their country and who are still raping and pillaging with impunity in many parts of it. But why is the Bush administration's tepid support for Afghan women's rights surprising? President Bush is a fundamentalist! He owes one in four of his votes to the Christian right. That Afghan women have one of the world's highest maternal mortality rates is of far less interest to him than that somewhere—anywhere—in the world a woman is having a safe and legal abortion or a teenage girl is taking the Pill. As I write, the news is that, to please his fellow fundamentalists, the president is withholding $34 million from the United Nations Population Fund, on the spurious grounds, rejected by his own fact-finding team, that it funds forced abortions in China.

Nothing Sacred is a mine of valuable information, a unique sampler of perspectives. It brings to the debate a wealth of divergent views and voices that need to be heard and so far have not been: feminists inside and outside the academy, Arab and Muslim scholars, writing in publications that often do not get the attention they deserve. While there are many debates to be found in these pages, there is one thing on which all the contributors agree: The opposite of fundamentalism is feminism.

Fundamentalisms

The War on Women

Rosemary Radford Ruether

From *Conscience*, Winter 2001/2002

Several years ago, Martin Marty and others edited a prestigious series of important studies, published by Chicago University Press, on the rise of fundamentalisms across world religions. These books saw striking resemblances between the wave of fundamentalisms that were appearing in the Catholic and Protestant right in the West, in various Muslim fundamentalisms, in right-wing Judaism—particularly in Israel—and rightist forms of Hinduism, Confucianism and other Asian religions. All these movements seemed to have in common a rejection of modernity and efforts to reestablish the public role of religion, if not religious states, to counter what was seen as evil secularity, with its lack of established public values.

What the Marty books overlooked was perhaps the most striking similarity of all between these fundamentalist movements: namely their efforts to reestablish rigid patriarchal control over women and their hostility to women's equality, autonomous agency, and right to control their own sexuality and fertility. This hostility to feminism or women's autonomous agency, particularly in sexuality and reproduction, links all these right-wing groups. Consider, for example, the extraordinary diatribe of Pat Robertson, who, in a 1990 fundraising letter for a campaign to oppose a state ERA bill, opined that "Feminism makes women leave their husbands, kill their children, destroy capitalism, practice witchcraft, and become lesbians." Even the current Bush administration responded less than favorably when Jerry Falwell, backed up by Pat Robertson, suggested that the September 11 attacks on the World Trade Center and the Pentagon represented God's punishment of America for allowing the existence of such evils in this country as feminism, gays, abortion providers, and the ACLU.

The Vatican is hardly less obsessed with women's equality and reproductive rights as the epitome of evil modern secularity and the cause of civilization's decline. At the 1994 UN conference on Population and Development at Cairo, the 1995 Fourth World Conference on Women at Beijing and the five-year follow-up meetings to these two conferences, the Vatican distinguished itself by tireless efforts to oppose any language that would declare that women's rights are human rights and that women's autonomous decision-making about their own sexuality and reproduction were integral elements of such rights.

The Muslim fundamentalism that has swept not only Afghanistan with the Taliban, but has major influence in Islamic states from Algeria and Egypt to Iran and Pakistan, has made war on women the center of their campaign against modernity and what they regard as irreligion. In Afghanistan under the Taliban, women were banned from even primary school education, paid work, and virtually any public presence. Even the windows of their houses had to be blacked out lest they be viewed going about their housework by men looking in.

Why this war on women in the name of true religion? Women seem to have become the scapegoats for male fears of loss of control in society. In a world where anonymous global forces control and decide the economies of nations, control over women seems to become the place where men can imagine that they are reclaiming order against chaos, their dignity, honor, and security in a world where there is little available on the macro level. With life out of control for many men, rigid control of the women in their homes becomes the place where they can imagine that they are still in charge.

But such a war on women is totally counterproductive from the point of view of any real emergence from poverty and underdevelopment for those impoverished societies most prone to such fundamentalist takeovers. Studies have long shown that women's development is absolutely key to the betterment of society as a whole. The education of women is statistically closely linked with smaller families, better health and education of children, and emergence from poverty. An Egyptian study found that if women with no education had finished primary school, poverty would have been reduced by one-third. UN agencies have duplicated this study in several other countries.

Economic stability, political moderation, and democratic order are closely linked with higher education and public participation of women. The attack on women has every likelihood of increasing the gap between rich and poor, between the underdeveloped and the developed worlds, that fuels the anger of the fundamentalist backlash but is misguidedly channeled into attacks on women, not to mention attacks on public buildings such as the World Trade Center.

For me, one of the areas of particular concern is the potential for alliances between right-wing religious movements, one might say "ecumenical deals" of convenience between Christians—Protestant and Catholic—Jews, Muslims and others, all of whom invoke modern injustices and anxieties over loss of values to argue in favor of turning back the clock on women's emergence as equal human beings in society.

One can cite various efforts to make such alliances. In the United States, some right-wing Focus on the Family-type Protestants have long hoped for an alliance with conservative Catholics. Such an alliance has been impeded by the very different authority structure of the two religious groups and the not-too-distant memory among Catholics of the anti-Catholicism of fundamentalist Protestantism. But before September 11, George Bush, who identifies as a born-again Protestant, clearly saw the placating of conservative Catholic demands against birth control, abortion, fetal tissue use, and other such sex- and gender-related issues as the way to cement support for his next presidential election bid, having won the last time with a razor-thin majority in key states and by dubious tactics. The Bush administration courted and was photographed surrounded by smiling Catholic prelates.

Another such ecumenical deal was sought by the Vatican with conservative Muslims at the Cairo Population and Development conference in 1994. Hoping to create a common Catholic-Muslim front against birth control, abortion, women's equality, and recognition of diverse forms of the family, the Vatican adopted rhetoric that pilloried Western feminists as assaulting the cultural traditions of the third world. In this effort, the Vatican posed as a defender of cultural pluralism against Western cultural hegemony, an unlikely role given its own history as the epitome of Catholic or universalist religio-cultural hegemony.

This alliance partly fizzled because Muslims had reason to doubt the Vatican's sudden support of cultural pluralism, and also due to the somewhat different agenda of Muslims in population and development issues. Although some Muslims share a desire to subordinate women to an authoritarian male-dominated family and curb what they see as Western sexual promiscuity among women and youth, they are not against birth control either in principle or in terms of any particular method. Although generally against abortion, they adhere to a medieval Aristotelian view that the fetus is not ensouled until the 120th day of gestation and thus early abortion is not murder. Oddly enough, this is a position that was shared by medieval Catholics and was abandoned only in modern times in favor of the strangely disincarnate view of the fertilized egg as a full human being.

But such right-wing Christian and Muslim alliances against women's development and reproductive rights are still possible. Despite the horrendous treatment of women by the Taliban, George Bush recently suggested that the "Alliance against Terrorism" should not make women's rights a central issue since this would "offend Muslims."

Right-wing ecumenical deals between Catholics, Protestants, Jews and Muslims often employ rhetoric that draws on a post-modern critique of liberalism, modernity, and universalism in order to serve a reactionary, premodern agenda. One finds an appeal to cultural relativism or pluralism used to assault efforts to establish a standard of universal human rights, particularly when these explicitly include women. Post-colonial resistance to Western colonialism, which historically denigrated the traditional cultures of colonized regions such as the Middle East, Africa, and Asia, is evoked to suggest that any principles of universal human rights are examples of cultural colonialism and Western hegemonic dominance. Feminism is billed as a purely Western, and, of course, culturally decadent, movement that is foreign to the cultural traditions of Africa, Asia, and the Middle East.

Western liberals, who themselves invented and support such post-modern critiques of Western cultural hegemony, are often at a loss to respond when such principles are used against them to support premodern social patterns that subordinate women. As I have mentioned, the Vatican used exactly this kind of anti-Western rhetoric in its bid for a Catholic-Muslim alliance at Cairo. Such right-wing ecumenical deals typically feature males of both religious cultures shaking hands with each other, while women of either group are prevented from speaking for themselves. Western feminists are demonized, while women of non-Western cultures are pictured as vulnerable innocents liable to corruption from said evil Western feminists.

I had an experience of such an appeal to the myth of sacrosanct traditional culture ten years ago when I was teaching and lecturing on feminist theology in South Africa. At one of the Bantustan universities, an African Anglican priest in elegant cleric dress and speaking the Queen's English rose to declare that feminism could not be accepted in Africa "because it is against our culture." "And culture cannot be challenged," he declared in ringing tones. Earlier one of the African women had warned me about such an argument and given me a good response. I repeated her words: "Well, white racism is a part of white culture. Does that mean it can't be challenged or changed?"

This demonization of feminism as Western totally ignores the fact that for more than two decades women of Asia, Africa, Latin America, and the Middle East have been creating their own contextualized forms of feminism and speaking about their rights and demands in their own voices. This globalization of feminisms was evident at the Beijing world conference on women, where representatives of women's movements from every nation gathered and networked. This kind of networking across women's movements in every country and culture could well represent the alternative to the kinds of ecumenical deals of men against women that are being hatched by the Vatican and right-wing Protestants and Catholics.

Religion Counts is an initiative that aims at a progressive ecumenical alliance between Catholics, Protestants, Jews, Muslims, Hindus, and Buddhists that supports women's equality and reproductive rights. It met in Rome in January 1999 and issued the "Rome Statement on the International Conference on Population and Development," which sought to explore common principles on women, sexuality, and reproductive rights across the world's major religions.

The United Nations and international media too often pay attention only to right-wing or fundamentalist religion. The media typically assumes that feminist Christians or feminists in other religions are marginal and don't really represent their own religious traditions. It is right-wing men in leadership positions who are treated as the authentic spokespersons for the religious tradition. Thus conservative or fundamentalist denunciations of secularism receive disproportionate attention, reinforcing the false dichotomy of religious values versus secular lack of values put forward by religious conservatives. Religion Counts seeks to mobilize and ally the progressive voices across the religious traditions and to make these progressive voices players in public culture and decision-making. This has remained a very small initiative, but I think represents an important alternative that needs to be cultivated.

Secularity is being portrayed as a failed modern experiment that has resulted only in valueless anomie. There are in secular liberalism valuable principles that need to be vindicated, but that is subject for another time.

For the moment a key way to combat the claim that religiousness is authentically represented only by patriarchal, misogynist religious traditions is to vindicate the progressive, egalitarian principles within religious traditions themselves. This is essentially what Christian and Jewish feminisms have been doing for the last thirty years. Christian and Jewish feminists have mined their own traditions to show their potential for an egalitarian reading. Muslim feminists today are also developing a similar strategy, engaging in a prowomen, proegalitarian rereading of the core religious values. For Muslim feminists, such as Riffat Hassan, a religious scholar of Pakistani origin, the Qur'an is essentially an egalitarian scripture. Hassan and other Muslim feminists do close readings of the Qur'an to show that mistreatment of women, their segregation, imposition of the veil, and denial of education, political, and business involvement is nowhere found in the Qur'an. Rather these traditions come from the incorporation of Arab or other local customs. In some cases the arguments for women's inferiority were actually imported from Christianity.

Hassan, for example, has done her major work on the texts regarding the creation of humanity, male and female, in the Qur'an. She has shown that the Qur'an lacks the tradition of Eve's creation from Adam's rib and her sin as the cause of the Fall. These concepts do not exist in the Qur'an, which contains only the story of Genesis I of the creation of the human, male and female, equally and at the same time. The stories of Adam's rib and the apple were imported into later Islamic commentaries from neighboring Christianity and, as in Christianity, used to argue for women's inferiority and punishment. In a tradition that sees the Qur'an as the norm for what is truly Islamic, such arguments carry weight.

These more progressive and feminist voices of Islam need to be supported. These are the movements that not only can allow Western anti-Muslim bigotry to see a different, more progressive face of Islam, but also, even more important, can allow Muslim cultures themselves to embrace democratic, equal-rights agendas as compatible with Islam, rather than as humiliating Western cultural impositions. Interestingly enough, the current antiterrorist campaign, with all its gross errors, and I count our bombing war against Afghanistan as a major error, has done one thing right. It has realized that if it is to build a Western-Muslim alliance, it cannot simply demonize Islam. It needs to publicize the positive, progressive voices of Islam. Thus most Americans have probably read and heard more about the diversity of the Muslim world in the last seventy-five days than all their previous lives.

The very existence of Muslim feminist movements and their strategies for a progressive, egalitarian reading of Islam have been well-kept secrets from most Western Christians. There has now been some discussion of such movements as Women Living Under Muslim Laws and the Revolutionary Association of the Women of Afghanistan, but there needs to be much more. Progressive Muslim women's movements need to be given space to speak and develop. In the process it is important that the distortion of Western feminism be corrected. It needs to be made clear again and again that granting equal rights for women is the best way for the whole society to emerge from poverty and authoritarianism. Feminism is not about pitting women against men and children. Feminism is about men and women becoming real partners in a way that can develop their humanity to the fullest and that will allow children the best chance to flourish. It is male domination that impoverishes us all.

Fundamentalism

Karen Armstrong

From *Islam: A Short History* (The Modern Library, 2000)

The Western media often give the impression that the embattled and occasionally violent form of religiosity known as "fundamentalism" is a purely Islamic phenomenon. This is not the case. Fundamentalism is a global fact and has surfaced in every major faith in response to the problems of our modernity. There is fundamentalist Judaism, fundamentalist Christianity, fundamentalist Hinduism, fundamentalist Buddhism, fundamentalist Sikhism and even fundamentalist Confucianism. This type of faith surfaced first in the Christian world in the United States at the beginning of the twentieth century. This was not accidental. Fundamentalism is not a monolithic movement; each form of fundamentalism, even within the same tradition, develops independently and has its own symbols and enthusiasms, but its different manifestations all bear a family resemblance. It has been noted that a fundamentalist movement does not arise immediately, as a knee-jerk response to the advent of Western modernity, but only takes shape when the modernization process is quite far advanced. At first religious people try to reform their traditions and effect a marriage between them and modern culture, as we have seen the Muslim reformers do. But when these moderate measures are found to be of no avail, some people resort to more extreme methods, and a fundamentalist movement is born. With hindsight, we can see that it was only to be expected that fundamentalism should first make itself known in the United States, the showcase of modernity, and only appear in other parts of the world at a later date. Of the three monotheistic religions, Islam was in fact the last to develop a fundamentalist strain, when modern culture began to take root in the Muslim world in the late 1960s and 1970s. By this date, fundamentalism was quite well established among Christians and Jews, who had had a longer exposure to the modern experience.

Fundamentalist movements in all faiths share certain characteristics. They reveal a deep disappointment and disenchantment with the modern experiment, which has not fulfilled all that it promised. They also express real fear.

11

Every single fundamentalist movement that I have studied is convinced that the secular establishment is determined to wipe religion out. This is not always a paranoid reaction. Secularism has often been imposed very aggressively in the Muslim world. Fundamentalists look back to a "golden age" before the irruption of modernity for inspiration, but they are not atavistically returning to the Middle Ages. All are intrinsically modern movements and could have appeared at no time other than our own. All are innovative and often radical in their reinterpretation of religion. As such, fundamentalism is an essential part of the modern scene. Wherever modernity takes root, a fundamentalist movement is likely to rise up alongside it in conscious reaction. Fundamentalists will often express their discontent with a modern development by overstressing those elements in their tradition that militate against it. They are all—even in the United States—highly critical of democracy and secularism. Because the emancipation of women has been one of the hallmarks of modern culture, fundamentalists tend to emphasise conventional, agrarian gender roles, putting women back into veils and into the home. The fundamentalist community can thus be seen as the shadow side of modernity; it can also highlight some of the darker sides of the modern experiment.

Fundamentalism, therefore, exists in a symbiotic relationship with a coercive secularism. Fundamentalists nearly always feel assaulted by the liberal or modernizing establishment, and their views and behavior become more extreme as a result. After the famous Scopes Trial (1925) in Tennessee, when Protestant fundamentalists tried to prevent the teaching of evolution in the public schools, they were so ridiculed by the secularist press that their theology became more reactionary and excessively literal, and they turned from the left to the extreme right of the political spectrum. When the secularist attack has been more violent, the fundamentalist reaction is likely to be even greater. Fundamentalism therefore reveals a fissure in society, which is polarized between those who enjoy secular culture and those who regard it with dread. As time passes, the two camps become increasingly unable to understand one another. Fundamentalism thus begins as an internal dispute, with liberalizers or secularists within one's *own* culture or nation. In the first instance, for example, Muslim fundamentalists will often oppose their fellow countrymen or fellow Muslims who take a more positive view of modernity, rather than such external foes as the West or Israel. Very often, fundamentalists begin by withdrawing from mainstream culture to create an enclave of pure faith (as, for example, within the ultra-Orthodox Jewish communities in Jerusalem or New York). Thence they will sometimes conduct an offensive which can take many forms, designed to bring the mainstream back to the right path and resacralize the world. All fundamentalists feel that they are fighting for survival, and because their backs are to the wall, they can believe that they have to fight their way out of the impasse. In this frame of mind, on rare occasions, some resort to terrorism. The vast majority, however, do not commit acts of violence, but simply try to revive their faith in a more conventional, lawful way.

Fundamentalists have been successful in so far as they have pushed religion from the sidelines and back to center stage, so that it now plays a major part in international affairs once again, a development that would have seemed inconceivable in the mid-twentieth century when secularism seemed in the ascendant. This has certainly been the case in the Islamic world since the 1970s. But fundamentalism is not simply a way of "using" religion for a political end. These are essentially rebellions against the secularist exclusion of the divine from public life, and a frequently desperate attempt to make spiritual values prevail in the modern world. But the desperation and fear that fuel fundamentalists also tend to distort the religious tradition, and accentuate its more aggressive aspects at the expense of those that preach toleration and reconciliation.

Muslim fundamentalism corresponds very closely to these general characteristics. It is not correct, therefore, to imagine that Islam has within it a militant, fanatic strain that impels Muslims into a crazed and violent rejection of modernity. Muslims are in tune with fundamentalists in other faiths all over the world, who share their profound misgivings about modern secular culture. It should also be said that Muslims object to the use of the term "fundamentalism," pointing out quite correctly that it was coined by American Protestants as a badge of pride, and cannot be usefully translated into Arabic. *Usul*, as we have seen, refers to the fundamental principles of Islamic jurisprudence, and as all Muslims agree on these, all Muslims could be said to subscribe to *usuliyyah* (fundamentalism). Nevertheless, for all its shortcomings, "fundamentalism" is the only term we have to describe this family of embattled religious movements, and it is difficult to come up with a more satisfactory substitute.

One of the early fundamentalist idealogues was Mawdudi, the founder of the Jamaat-i Islami in Pakistan. He saw the mighty power of the West as gathering its forces to crush Islam. Muslims, he argued, must band together to fight this encroaching secularism, if they wanted their religion and their culture to survive. Muslims had encountered hostile societies before and had experienced disasters but, starting with Afghani[*], a new note had crept into Islamic discourse. The Western threat had made Muslims defensive for the first time. Mawdudi defied the whole secularist ethos: he was proposing an Islamic liberation theology. Because God alone was sovereign, nobody was obliged to take orders from any other human being. Revolution against the colonial powers was not just a right but a duty. Mawdudi called for a universal *jihad*. Just as the Prophet had fought the *jahiliyyah* (the "ignorance" and barbarism of the pre-Islamic period), Muslims must use all means in their power to resist the modern *jahiliyyah* of the West. Mawdudi argued that *jihad* was the central tenet of Islam. This was an innovation. Nobody had ever claimed before that *jihad* was equivalent to the five Pillars of Islam, but Mawdudi felt that the innovation was justified by the present emergency. The stress and fear of cultural and religious annihilation had led to the development of a more extreme and potentially violent distortion of the faith.

But the real founder of Islamic fundamentalism in the Sunni world was Sayyid Qutb (1906–66), who was greatly influenced by Mawdudi. Yet he had not originally been an extremist but had been filled with enthusiasm for Western culture and secular politics. Even after he joined the Muslim Brotherhood in 1953 he had been a reformer, hoping to give Western democracy an Islamic dimension that would avoid the excesses of a wholly secularist ideology. However, in 1956 he was imprisoned by al-Nasser for membership of the Brotherhood, and in the concentration camp he became convinced that religious people and secularists could not live in peace in the same society. As he witnessed the torture and execution of the Brothers, and reflected upon al-Nasser's avowed determination to cast religion into a marginal role in Egypt, he could see all the characteristics of *jahiliyyah*, which he defined as the barbarism that was for ever and for all time the enemy of faith, and which Muslims, following the example of the Prophet Muhammad, were bound to fight to the death. Qutb went further than Mawdudi, who had seen only non-Muslim societies as *jahili*. Qutb applied

---

[*]Jamal al-Din ("al-Afghani"), 1839–97: an Iranian reformer who urged Muslims of all persuasions to band together and modernize Islam to avoid the political and cultural hegemony of Europe.

the term *jahiliyyah*, which in conventional Muslim historiography had been used simply to describe the pre-Islamic period in Arabia, to contemporary Muslim society. Even though a ruler such as al-Nasser outwardly professed Islam, his words and actions proved him to be an apostate and Muslims were duty-bound to overthrow such a government, just as Muhammad had forced the pagan establishment of Mecca (the *jahiliyyah* of his day) into submission.

The violent secularism of al-Nasser had led Qutb to espouse a form of Islam that distorted both the message of the Qur'an and the Prophet's life. Qutb told Muslims to model themselves on Muhammad: to separate themselves from mainstream society (as Muhammad had made the *hijirah* from Mecca to Medina), and then engage in a violent *jihad*. But Muhammad had in fact finally achieved victory by an ingenious policy of non-violence; the Qur'an adamantly opposed force and coercion in religious matters, and its vision—far from preaching exclusion and separation—was tolerant and inclusive. Qutb insisted that the Qur'anic injunction to toleration could occur only *after* the political victory of Islam and the establishment of a true Muslim state. The new intransigence sprang from the profound fear that is at the core of fundamentalist religion. Qutb did not survive. At al-Nasser's personal insistence, he was executed in 1966.

Every Sunni fundamentalist movement has been influenced by Qutb. Most spectacularly it has inspired Muslims to assassinate such leaders as Anwar al-Sadat, denounced as a *jahili* ruler because of his oppressive policies towards his own people. The Taliban, who came to power in Afghanistan in 1994, are also affected by his ideology.** They are determined to return to what they see as the original vision of Islam. The *ulama* are the leaders of the government; women are veiled and not permitted to take part in professional life. Only religious broadcasting is permitted and the Islamic punishments of stoning and mutilation have been reintroduced. In some circles of the West, the Taliban are seen as quintessential Muslims, but their regime violates crucial Islamic precepts. Most of the Taliban ("students" of the *madrassas*) belong to the Pashtun tribe, and they tend to target non-Pashtuns, who fight the regime from the north of the country. Such ethnic chauvinism was forbidden by the Prophet and by the Qur'an. Their harsh treatment of minority groups is also opposed to clear Qur'anic

**This essay was published in 2000, before the fall of the Taliban in December 2001.

requirements. The Taliban's discrimination against women is completely opposed to the practice of the Prophet and the conduct of the first *ummah*. The Taliban are typically fundamentalist, however, in their highly selective vision of religion (which reflects their narrow education in some of the *madrassas* of Pakistan), which perverts the faith and turns it in the opposite direction of what was intended. Like all the major faiths, Muslim fundamentalists, in their struggle to survive, make religion a tool of oppression and even of violence.

But most Sunni fundamentalists have not resorted to such an extreme. The fundamentalist movements that sprang up during the 1970s and 1980s all tried to change the world about them in less drastic but telling ways. After the humiliating defeat of the Arab armies in the Six-Day War against Israel in 1967, there was a swing towards religion throughout the Middle East. The old secularist policies of such leaders as al-Nasser seemed discredited. People felt that the Muslims had failed because they had not been true to their religion. They could see that while secularism and democracy worked very well in the West, they did not benefit ordinary Muslims but only an elite in the Islamic world. Fundamentalism can be seen as a "postmodern" movement, which rejects some of the tenets and enthusiasms of modernity, such as colonialism. Throughout the Islamic world, students and factory workers started to change their immediate environment. They created mosques in their universities and factories, where they could make *salat*, and set up Banna-style welfare societies with an Islamic orientation, demonstrating that Islam worked for the people better than the secularist governments did. When students declared a shady patch of lawn—or even a noticeboard—to be an Islamic zone, they felt that they had made a small but significant attempt to push Islam from the marginal realm to which it had been relegated in secularist society, and reclaimed a part of the world—however tiny—for Islam. They were pushing forward the frontiers of the sacred, in rather the same way as the Jewish fundamentalists in Israel who made settlements in the occupied West Bank, reclaiming Arab land and bringing it under the aegis of Judaism.

The same principle underlines the return to Islamic dress. When this is forced upon people against their will (as by the Taliban) it is coercive and as likely to create a backlash as the aggressive techniques of Reza Shah Pahlavi. But many Muslim women feel that veiling is a symbolic return to the precolonial period, before their society was disrupted and deflected from its true course. Yet they have not simply turned the clock back. Surveys show that a large proportion of veiled women hold progressive views on such matters as gender. For some women, who have come from rural areas to the university and are the first members of their family to advance beyond basic literacy, the assumption of Islamic dress provides continuity and makes their rite of passage to modernity less traumatic than it might otherwise have been. They are coming to join the modern world, but on their own terms and in an Islamic context that gives it sacred meaning. Veiling can also be seen as a tacit critique of some of the less positive aspects of modernity. It defies the strange Western compulsion to "reveal all" in sexual matters. In the West, people often flaunt their tanned, well-honed bodies as a sign of privilege; they try to counteract the signs of aging and hold on to this life. The shrouded Islamic body declares that it is oriented to transcendence, and the uniformity of dress abolishes class difference and stresses the importance of community over Western individualism.

People have often used religion as a way of making modern ideas and enthusiasms comprehensible. Not all the American Calvinists at the time of the 1776 American Revolution shared or even understood the secularist ethos of the Founding Fathers, for example. They gave the struggle a Christian colouration so that they were able to fight alongside the secularists in the creation of a new world. Some Sunni and Shi'ite fundamentalists are also using religion to make the alien tenor of modern culture familiar, giving it a context of meaning and spirituality that makes it more accessible. Again, they are tacitly asserting that it is possible to be modern on other cultural terms than those laid down by the West. The Iranian Revolution of 1978–79 can be seen in this light. During the 1960s Ayatollah Ruhollah Khomeini (1902–89) brought the people of Iran out onto the streets to protest against the cruel and unconstitutional policies of Muhammad Reza Shah, whom he identified with Yazid, the Umayyad caliph who had been responsible for the death of Husain at Kerbala, the type of the unjust ruler in Shi'ite Islam. Muslims had a duty to fight such tyranny, and the mass of the people, who would have been quite unmoved by a socialist call to revolution, could respond to Khomeini's summons, which resonated with their deepest traditions. Khomeini provided a Shi'ite alternative to the secular nationalism of the shah. He came to seem more and more like one of the *imams:* like all the *imams,* he had been attacked, imprisoned and almost killed by an unjust ruler; like some of the *imams,* he was forced into exile and deprived of what was his own; like Ali and Husain, he had bravely opposed injustice and stood up for true Islamic values; like all the *imams,* he was known to be a practising mystic; like Husain, whose son was killed at Kerbala, Khomeini's son Mustafa was killed by the shah's agents.

When the revolution broke in 1978, after a slanderous attack on Khomeini in the semi-official newspaper *Ettelaat,* and the shocking massacre of young *madrasah* students who came out onto the streets in protest, Khomeini seemed to be directing operations from afar (from Najaf, his place of exile), rather like the Hidden Imam. Secularists and intellectuals were willing to join forces with the *ulama* because they knew that only Khomeini could command the grass-roots support of the people. The Iranian Revolution was the only revolution inspired by a twentieth-century ideology (the Russian and Chinese revolutions both owed their inspiration to the nineteenth-century vision of Karl Marx). Khomeini had evolved a radically new interpretation of Shi'ism: in the absence of the Hidden Imam, only the mystically inspired jurist, who knew the sacred law, could validly govern the nation. For centuries, Twelver Shi'ites had prohibited clerics from participating in government, but the revolutionaries (if not many of the *ulama*) were willing to subscribe to this theory of Velayat-i Faqih (the Mandate of the Jurist). Throughout the revolution, the symbolism of Kerbala was predominant. Traditional religious ceremonies to mourn the dead and the Ashura celebrations in honour of Husain became demonstrations against the regime. The Kerbala myth inspired ordinary Shi'ites to brave the shah's guns and die in their thousands, some donning the white shroud of martyrdom. Religion was proved to be so powerful a force that it brought down the Pahlavi state, which had seemed the most stable and powerful in the Middle East.

But, like all fundamentalists, Khomeini's vision was also distorting. The taking of the American hostages in Teheran (and, later, by Shi'ite radicals in Lebanon, who were inspired by the Iranian example) violates clear Qur'anic commands about the treatment of prisoners, who must be handled with dignity and respect, and freed as soon as possible. The captor is even obliged to contribute to the ransom from his own resources. Indeed, the Qur'an expressly forbids the taking of prisoners except during a conventional war, which obviously rules out hostage-taking when hostilities are not in progress. After the revolution, Khomeini insisted on what he called "unity of expression," suppressing any dissentient voice. Not only had the demand for free speech been one of the chief concerns of the revolution, but Islam had never insisted on ideological conformity, only upon a uniformity of practice. Coercion in religious matters is forbidden in the Qur'an, and was abhorred by Mullah Sadra, Khomeini's spiritual mentor. When Khomeini issued his *fatwah* against novelist Salman Rushdie on February 14, 1989, for his allegedly blasphemous portrait of Muhammad in *The Satanic Verses*, he also contravened Sadra's impassioned defence of freedom of thought. The *fatwah* was declared un-Islamic by the *ulama* of al-Azhar and Saudi Arabia, and was condemned by forty-eight out of the forty-nine member states of the Islamic Conference the following month.

But it appears that the Islamic revolution may have helped the Iranian people to come to modernity on their own terms. Shortly before his death, Khomeini tried to pass more power to the parliament, and, with his apparent blessing, Hashami Rafsanjani, the Speaker of the Majlis, gave a democratic interpretation of Velayat-i Faqih. The needs of the modern state had convinced Shi'ites of the necessity of democracy, but this time it came in an Islamic package that made it acceptable to the majority of the people. This seemed confirmed on May 23, 1997, when Hojjat ol-Islam Seyyid Khatami was elected to the presidency in a landslide victory. He immediately made it clear that he wanted to build a more positive relationship with the West, and in September 1998 he dissociated his government from the *fatwah* against Rushdie, a move which was later endorsed by Ayatollah Ali Khamenei, the Supreme Faqih of Iran. Khatami's election signalled the strong desire of a large segment of the population for greater pluralism, a gentler interpretation of Islamic law, more democracy and a more progressive policy for women. The battle is still not won. The conservative clerics who opposed Khomeini and for whom he had little time are still able to block many of Khatami's reforms, but the struggle to create a viable Islamic state, true to the spirit of the Qur'an and yet responsive to current conditions, is still a major preoccupation of the Iranian people.

Notes

Appleby, R. Scott (ed.), *Spokesmen for the Despised: Fundamentalist Leaders of the Middle East* (Chicago, 1997)

Armstrong, Karen, *The Battle for God: Fundamentalism in Judaism, Christianity and Islam* (London and New York, 2000)

Choueiri, Youssef M., *Islamic Fundamentalism* (London, 1990)

Fischer, Michael J., *Iran: From Religious Dispute to Revolution* (Cambridge, Mass., and London, 1980)

Gaffney, Patrick D., *The Prophet's Pulpit: Islamic Preaching in Contemporary Egypt* (Berkeley, Los Angeles and London, 1994)

Hamas, *The Covenant of the Islamic Resistance Movement* (Jerusalem, 1988)

Heikal, Mohamed, *Autumn of Fury: The Assassination of Sadat* (London, 1984)

Hussain, Asaf, *Islamic Iran: Revolution and Counter-Revolution* (London, 1985)

Jansen, Johannes J. G., *The Neglected Duty: The Creed of Sadat's Assassins and Islamic Resurgence in the Middle East* (New York and London, 1988)

Kepel, Gilles, *The Prophet and Pharaoh: Muslim Extremism in Egypt* (trans. Jon Rothschild, London, 1985)

Khomeini, Sayeed Ruhollah, *Islam and Revolution* (trans. Hamid Algar, Berkeley, 1981)

Lawrence, Bruce B., *Defenders of God: The Fundamentalist Revolt Against the Modern Age* (London and New York, 1990)

Marty, Martin E., and R. Scott Appleby (eds.), *Fundamentalisms Observed* (Chicago and London, 1991)

———, *Fundamentalisms and Society* (Chicago and London, 1993)

———, *Fundamentalisms and the State* (Chicago and London, 1993)

———, *Accounting for Fundamentalisms* (Chicago and London, 1994)

———, *Fundamentalisms Comprehended* (Chicago and London, 1995)

Mawdudi, Abud Ala, *Islamic Law and Constitution* (Lahore, 1967)

———, *Jihad in Islam* (Lahore, 1976)

———, *The Economic Problem of Man and Its Islamic Solution* (Lahore, 1978)

———, *Islamic Way of Life* (Lahore, 1979)

Milton-Edwards, Beverley, *Islamic Politics in Palestine* (London and New York, 1996)

Nasr, Seyyed Vali Reza, *The Vanguard of the Islamic Revolution, the Jama'at-i Islami of Pakistan* (London and New York, 1994)

Qutb, Sayyid, *Islam and Universal Peace* (Indianapolis, 1977)

———, *Milestones* (Delhi, 1988)

———, *This Religion of Islam* (Gary, Indiana, n.d.)

Ruthven, Malise, *A Satanic Affair: Salman Rushdie and the Rage of Islam* (London, 1990)

Sick, Gary, *All Fall Down: America's Fateful Encounter with Iran* (London, 1985)

Sidhared, Abdel Salam, and Anonshirivan Ehteshani (eds.), *Islamic Fundamentalism* (Boulder, 1996)

World Culture War

Meredith Tax

From *The Nation*, May 17, 1999

In the past ten years, nationalist, communalist, and religious fundamentalist social movements have surfaced all over the world, moving into the power vacuum created as local elites have been overwhelmed by the new global financial ruling class. The emerging struggle is not between East and West, as Samuel Huntington would have it, but within both; it is a struggle between the forces of globalization and the atavistic social movements that have sprung up to oppose it. Civilian populations, especially ethnic minorities, women and children, are caught in between. Among such movements are the Taliban in Afghanistan; the Serbian nationalist movement (and its opposing counterparts elsewhere in the former Yugoslavia); Islamic fundamentalist movements in Egypt, Algeria, and elsewhere; the Hindu communalist movement in India; the Israeli settler movement in the West Bank; and a whole range of militantly patriarchal Christian groups, from the militias to Operation Rescue, in the United States.

These movements have in common a desire for racial, ethnic, and religious homogeneity; an apocalyptic vision of purification through bloodshed; and a patriarchal view of women and the family. I call them atavistic because of the way they yearn for a mythic past, often the age of barbarism, when their nation, tribe, or religion was great. ("Atavism: *Biol.* the reappearance in an individual of characteristics of some more or less remote ancestor that have been absent in intervening generations." *American College Dictionary*). In Israel, to take one example, religious fundamentalists who believe they should control all the land that was biblical Israel's at its point of greatest territorial strength have repeatedly brought the peace process to a standstill. And in the United States, a cadre of religiously driven conservative leaders paralyzed the federal government for more than a year in their campaign against the Sixties and Sin, both exemplified by Bill Clinton.

As central to such movements as ethnic or religious homogeneity is the

23

control of women. Atavistic social movements attack feminism not only as an obstacle to such control but as part of their war on modernity itself, for, like other movements for social and political rights, feminism is inescapably secular and thus part of the project of modernity, opposed to older forms of social organization in which women's needs and voices were subsumed into a communal or religious entity represented by male elders. Even in countries where the women's movement is led by female versions of tribal elders, feminism resists being swallowed up in male definitions of the class, the nation, the community; it sticks in the craw. Add to this the threat of female sexual and reproductive autonomy, then place both in the context of a volatile world situation where local males are losing power and the family has become the last bastion of unquestioned male authority and privilege, and what have you got? A world culture war, in which feminism becomes the scapegoat for every frustration and women become the focus of every contradiction.

This war takes culturally specific forms in each country, targeting poor women, because they are most vulnerable, and feminist intellectuals and organizers, because they stir up the others. Last month [April 1, 1999] in the Bronx, Tabitha Walrond, a nineteen-year-old African-American, was tried for homicide in the death of her infant son. She had been breast-feeding him; her milk was insufficient, and he died of malnutrition. The prosecution also charged her with second-degree manslaughter and endangering the welfare of her child by failing to get him emergency medical care when his condition became acute. But Walrond was unable to get medical care for her son; she was repeatedly denied a Medicaid ID number by a city administration that has shown an unholy eagerness to get women off the welfare rolls regardless of what will happen to them and their children. Tabitha Walrond is but one example of the way American women are caught between the drive to cut government spending and release capital from all constraint on the one hand, and backlash tendencies invoking earlier, more patriarchal forms of social organization on the other.

To nationalist, communalist, and religious backlash movements, feminism, no matter how rooted in local conditions, represents the globalizing forces that are undercutting patriarchal traditions. For them, it is intrinsically foreign, a fifth column undermining their efforts at unity. This contradiction is vividly apparent in the former Yugoslavia. Relatively weak before the Yugoslav federation began to unravel, feminist groups in the various republics did their best, in the summer of 1991, to come together against war; they even attempted to stage a women's march from Zagreb to Belgrade that was supposed to "surround the generals with a wall of love" (it was stopped by Serbian troops). During the wars that ensued, when most other contacts between the former republics were broken, some feminist groups stayed in clandestine communication and developed into pacifists, helping men who were hiding from the draft and moving into the leadership vacuum left by the men's absence. Many of these activists had done advocacy for battered women before the war; they moved into work with women war victims in the belief that rape in wartime and domestic violence are part of the same continuum, enraging nationalists by refusing to focus on the ethnic motives for rape.

One of the most consistent and effective antinationalist groups in Serbia is Women in Black, who held demonstrations against Serbia's war machine every week for seven years—and every week were denounced and threatened as traitors—until the NATO bombing closed down the small amount of political space that had been available for autonomous women's activities. On their seventh anniversary, they issued a statement that read, in part: "I confess to my longtime antiwar activity...that for the entire war I crossed the walls of Balkan ethno-states, because solidarity is the politics which interests me; that I understood democracy as support to antiwar activists/friends/sisters—Albanian women, Croat women, Roma women, stateless women; that I first challenged the murderers from the state where I live and then those from other states, because I consider this to be responsible political behavior of a citizen . . . that I took care of others while the patriots took care of themselves."

Women's political activism became a point of contention in Croatia last June, during a Zagreb television panel on the status of women. One of the male participants published the following post-mortem in the government paper *Vecernji List;* his association of feminism with the foreign, and his panic at the idea of women's controlling their own sexual, reproductive, and political lives, are palpable: "These women, who speak the loudest in defending women's rights in the family, present in their personal lives a model that directly opposes that of the ideal and desirable Croatian family [that is, they are married without children, are old but unmarried, etc.]. . . . Although they oppose the laws of nature, they would like to impose laws in Parliament. Without the support they receive from abroad (in the form of promotions, money, and awards from international organizations), they are quite insignificant, and only through this support do they gain some importance."

Elsewhere, the successes of the women's movement are also seen only as symptoms of globalization, rather than as the result of an autonomous movement for female emancipation. Every gesture of solidarity, every offer of support from abroad, increases the danger that local feminists in such places will be called tools of the United States or the World Bank.

The situation is complicated by the fact that the World Bank does have an agenda for women: It wants them to have enough education to read instructions for birth control pills, to have enough freedom to work outside the home in export processing zones and to have enough money to feed themselves and their children. The World Bank has understood, in sub-Saharan Africa at least, that women keep some societies from falling apart completely, and for that reason it wishes to support their efforts at financial independence. But that does not mean it will intervene to protect them when things turn nasty. In Russia, for example, women have borne a disproportionate share of the burden of economic transition and the disappearance of social services. According to Nadia Azhgikhina of the Association for Russian Women Journalists, more than 70 percent of those fired from industrial jobs are women and only 12 percent of Russian women now have access to adequate health care.

While poor women and children are the largest group of victims in the global culture war, feminist writers, educators, and organizers are those most deliberately targeted by atavistic social movements, because they give voice to the discontent of others and describe their misery. As president of Women's WORLD, a global network of women writers fighting gender-based censorship, I hear many such cases. Take, for instance, women writers in Kosovo. Did you assume there weren't any? This, according to Sazana Caprici, editor of the Kosovo feminist literary magazine *Sfinga* (Sphinx), is part of the problem: "The Yugoslav state authorities do their best to deny not only the existence of Albanian women writers, but the very possibility of the existence of such a category of Albanian women. . . . Among Serbs [government propaganda] has created a stereotype of the Albanian woman: an uneducated woman utterly subjected to her husband's authority. . . . Albanian men, on the other hand, make use of this propaganda to reinforce their control over Albanian women. Every time women try to speak up against their inferior position, they are accused of being in the service of the state, which in Kosovo is considered a foreign occupier."

In Zimbabwe, where the Mugabe government has been arresting journalists and persecuting gays and lesbians to distract from social unrest and economic crisis, the Supreme Court has just undercut all laws protecting women, in a 5-to-0 decision that cannot be appealed. The Court ruled that, following African cultural traditions, a woman should be treated as a "junior male." The government has also targeted individual feminists. Patricia McFadden, an outspoken African feminist born in Swaziland, was subjected to a 1997 deportation campaign that may well recur when her two-year visa expires this December. She had made herself unpopular not only by defending gay rights but by calling for a new, more aggressive political direction for the women's movement. As she put it in her speech to the 1998 African Women's Leadership Institute, the African women's movement is "taking over the civic responsibilities which the state should be shouldering, and we are not critically asking ourselves whether this is our agenda or it is an imposed agenda. . . . If we continue to separate the private from the public, our Movement will die, and we will be wrapped up in welfarism and catering for everyone else's needs, and we will never reach our political goals."

Participants in the African Women's Leadership Institute made a list of terms used to describe feminists in their societies: "Lesbians, Power hungry, Emotionally deprived, Sexually frustrated, 'Beijing women,' Sexually promiscuous, Unmarriageable, Against God's plan, Castrators, Westernized, Witches, Women who want to have testicles, Elite." U.S. feminists, who have been targeted by conservatives for the last two decades, have added another term: "femi-Nazis." Twenty years of conservative attack and media stigmatization have put us in a place where even the "official women's movement," as it was called at the UN's Fourth World Conference on Women, in Beijing in 1995, has had to fight for its life, while more radical alternatives are virtually invisible.

Censorship of feminism has also become noticeable in education. The State University of New York's board of trustees, largely appointees of Governor George Pataki, led by Candace de Russy, has conducted a two-year witch hunt among teachers at SUNY New Paltz in the name of preserving standards and protecting the interests of taxpayers. Why? Because the women's studies program had a 1997 conference on female sexuality that ruffled a few feathers and was attacked in the *Wall Street Journal.* A similar right-wing campaign, spearheaded by religious groups on Long Island, resulted in a lawsuit against Nassau Community College in which the plaintiffs argued that course materials covering abortion, birth control, sexual behavior, and homosexuality were intended to influence students to reject "traditional" Judeo-Christian religious attitudes toward sexuality and adopt an antireligious ethic of "sexual pluralism." In February 1999, however, Federal District Court Judge Nina Gershon dealt a blow to creeping theocracy in the SUNY system by dismissing the case, concluding that the course materials were designed to teach about human sexuality as an academic subject, not about religion.

And at the University of Arizona, following a threat by the state legislature to cut off funding for women's studies, the administration has just polled its faculty to see how they feel about putting the warning "course content may be deemed objectionable" on some course syllabuses. The powerful grassroots Christian conservative movement regularly launches school and library censorship campaigns against any children's book that depicts an "abnormal" family (like my own *Families*), has characters with antiauthoritarian or irreverent attitudes, or even deals with magic, since fairy tales are seen as an introduction to New Age religion and Satanism.

If feminists are being targeted by reactionary movements all over the world, one might assume that progressives would leap to their defense. Unfortunately, this has not been the case. Denunciations from the right have been too often echoed on the left, from the "defense of the family" in the mid-eighties to the attacks on affirmative action and "identity politics" now. Some U.S. progressives today argue that the way to build a strong movement is to concentrate on electoral or economic issues and forget about the things that divide us. This strategy overlooks the fact that the fastest-growing sectors of the work force, not to mention the labor movement and poor people's movement, are full of women and minorities who do not check their identities at the door.

Nor can a purely domestic approach to politics work in an era of global culture war. It is wonderful to see the labor movement start to come alive again. This reborn movement, however, will only be as strong as its ability to learn from the diversity inside its ranks and to build coalitions with the international movements for human rights (including minority and gay rights), the environment, and the emancipation of women.

None of our movements will get very far unless we recognize the centrality of struggles around culture. As we can see from the former Yugoslavia, culture wars around questions such as national identity, women's roles and minority rights have a way of turning into wars of blood. The way we frame our issues now will resonate for generations. Unity in the U.S. progressive movement—not to mention survival, and our ability to defeat the antidemocratic, atavistic forces that have tied up the federal government for the past year—depends on solidarity with all those attacked by racists, zealots, and thugs, at home and abroad—whether, like Tabitha Walrond and Amadou Diallo, they are targeted merely because they are poor and black, or because, like feminists the world over, they represent a threat to patriarchal control of female sexuality and productive and reproductive capacity.

The Burden of Eve: Religious Fundamentalism and Women in Israel

Alice Shalvi

Adapted from an essay in *The Freedom to do God's Will*
(Routledge, 2002)

The beginning of the third millennium is, somewhat surprisingly, proving to be an era of increasing religious fundamentalism marked by a fanaticism that expresses itself in unprecedented civil violence. Jewish religious zealots have nowhere engaged in the kind of murderous attacks that have been perpetrated between Hindus and Muslims in India, nor have they targeted women as savagely as the Taliban did in Afghanistan. Nevertheless, in modern, democratic Israel there are distressing examples of the impact of fundamentalism, especially on women.

The tradition that governs Jewish fundamentalist thought and practice is, above all, androcentric and patriarchal, drawing a clear distinction between male and female derived from the opening chapters of Genesis. These not only describe the creation of male and female in the image of God; they also determine a biologically based distinction in functions (his, to "get bread" . . . by the sweat of [his] brow, "hers to bear children in pain"), and—alas—a hierarchical relationship: ". . . your desire shall be unto your husband, and *he shall rule over you*" (my italics).

Contemporary Jewish religious law is predicated on the Ten Commandments and their explication, interpretation, and amendment via the priestly code initially described in the Pentateuch. Subsequent codifiers produced the Mishna in the second century CE, the Talmud in the period between the second and sixth century, the Maimonidean code of the twelfth century and, finally, the sixteenth-century *Shulkhan Arukh*, which is currently considered the principal codificatory receptacle of *halakhah* (oral, or rabbinical, law).

Not only has no further code emerged that embraces the entire field of Oral Law, but that code itself has ceased to be universally accepted by all those who define themselves as Jews. The secularization and emancipation that began in late eighteenth-century Europe radically changed the face of Jewish society, dividing it into traditional and nontraditional elements, religiously observant and secular. The process of rabbinical reinterpretation continues to the present day, conducted by hundreds—even thousands—of rabbis worldwide. But these rabbis are now sectorized within different "denominations" or "streams" of Judaism, including Reform Judaism, which has almost completely abandoned *halakhic* authority, and Conservative Judaism, which is based on *halakhah*, but stresses the importance of its reinterpretation in the light of changing social norms. The *responsa* and edicts of Conservative and Reform rabbis and the practices of their respective adherents are fiercely criticized and rejected by the Orthodox and ultra-Orthodox (*haredi*) streams, who question the authenticity and deny the very legitimacy of the newer streams.

The androcentric and patriarchal nature of Orthodox and fundamentalist Judaism finds expression in Jewish theology and practice. Hebrew, which is not only the language of the Scriptures but also of prayer, is gender-inflected, lacking the neuter form. The deity is masculine; so, also, in the prayer book, is the person addressing Him. The spiritual covenant between God and His chosen people finds physical expression in the circumcision of every male child at the age of eight days. Girls—mercifully—are exempt from such physical mutilation; but this exemption has led to others that apply to Jewish females (for example, exemption from the obligation to pray three times a day) and these in turn have gradually hardened into prohibitions that confirm women's inferiority in the Jewish community and Jewish life, as conducted in the synagogue, the *Beit Midrash* (House of Study), and public life in general.

Women's Traditional Role and Social Status

The traditional roles of the Jewish woman, predicated on the earliest chapters of Genesis, are those of wife ("helpmate"), mother and homemaker—roles performed in the private, domestic domain that is considered a bastion of Jewish life and practice. Jewish women are to aspire to the ideals embodied by the family and the domestic sphere.

In legal terms, a Jewish woman is subject to the authority of a male relative, first as daughter and later as wife. Indeed, the Jewish marriage ceremony is an act of symbolic purchase (though no money needs to change hands) in which the bride becomes her husband's property, while he undertakes to provide for all her needs, including sexual satisfaction. The Hebrew word for "husband" is "owner." A woman can be released from marriage only if her husband, of his free will and being of sound mind, places in her willingly outstretched hands a *get* or bill of divorcement. In Orthodox Judaism worldwide, there have never been, nor are there at present, any women on the three-member panels of rabbinical judges that authorize (but cannot finalize) the granting of a divorce. In Israel, the rabbinical courts have sole jurisdiction over personal law and there is no option of civil marriage or civil divorce for any citizen, irrespective of the religion of which they are officially registered as members.[1]

The overriding quality desired in the traditional Jewish woman—and the one most frequently adduced by religious authorities as a justification for her exclusion from the public arena—is modesty. Woman's voice is decried by fundamentalists as an "abomination," as is woman's hair, while other parts of her body are considered inducive to lascivious thoughts in men. Thus Orthodoxy demands that married women cover their hair (or, in some extremely fundamentalist communities, shave their heads upon marriage prior to covering their baldness with a kerchief); that unmarried women and girls keep their hair neatly braided and never "disheveled" (the latter being a sign of wantonness and even prostitution); that all females wear long-sleeved garments and stockings at all seasons and that their clothing never reveal the contours of their bodies. There is, however, no demand to conceal the face, though cosmetics are frowned upon.

While Judaism has no practice comparable to purdah, in Orthodox circles women are customarily expected to stay away from the company of men, even when the latter congregate in a private home. At all times they are expected to speak softly, avoid boisterous behavior of any kind, and above all never to raise their voices in song except when there is no possibility whatever of their being heard by a man. According to rabbinic law, a man and woman (other than a married couple) may not be alone together in a closed room. Marriages are frequently arranged by the parents or acquaintances of the couple; courtship is brief and there are (albeit increasingly infrequent) cases in which the bride and groom first meet only days before the wedding and are never alone together until after the ceremony. At Orthodox weddings, men and women do not mingle, there is no mixed dancing and, when space allows, the sexes celebrate in separate rooms. Ultra-Orthodox men will not shake hands with women, nor sit beside them, even in public vehicles.

In the synagogue, Orthodox women are concealed behind a *mehizah*, a dividing screen designed to make them invisible to the eyes of male worshippers. Frequently, they are relegated to an upper room or gallery where, in many cases, they are not only not seen, but are also prevented from seeing (and, in some cases, even from hearing) what is going on in the service.

The traditional role of *materfamilias* that Jewish women are expected to fill has in recent years, especially in Israel, become a kind of "maternal imperative," the motto of which seems to be "the more, the better." Ultra-Orthodox women pride themselves on bearing as many as fourteen or fifteen children; in this they are comparable to earlier generations of women, although now the children more frequently survive, creating an enormous burden in terms of time and money. In 1999, the Israeli media reported cases in which fundamentalist rabbis provided fertility pills to childless women or to those who here having problems in becoming pregnant once more after having borne "too few" children.

Such rabbis forbid the use of contraception and cessation of pregnancy, sometimes even in cases where medical opinion has indicated that pregnancy might prove physically incapacitating or fatal to the mother. Paradoxically, the rabbinical edict in such cases goes counter to *halakhah*, which permits and even prescribes abortion if the mother's life is at risk and which at all times, even during labor or delivery, gives the mother's life precedence over that of the unborn child.

The trauma of the Holocaust and the loss of six million Jewish lives have cast such a profound shadow over contemporary Jewish society that it is comparatively easy to induce guilt in any woman who fails to do her utmost to replace the lost generation. In Israel, the threat of being outnumbered by the hostile surrounding countries or by the indigenous Arab population provides another impetus. Needless to say, multiple births and the consequent duties of mothering also serve to keep women securely confined to their households.

Despite this confinement, Orthodox—and particularly ultra-Orthodox—women continue the long-established tradition of women being income earners, often even the primary income earners in the family, in order to enable their husbands to engage in full-time Torah study—an occupation that is considered the fulfillment of the most important of all commandments, since it teaches one to obey the other commandments. Whereas in the past it was often difficult to combine or reconcile income earning with the demands of modesty and separation of the sexes, modern technology has facilitated such a combination; women can and do use telephones, facsimile machines, computers, and other electronic devices in order to work from home. Not only can working hours then be flexible and consistent with the demands of family, but—ironically—the degree of technical knowledge and skills required has resulted in women being far better educated than their menfolk, whose studies are still confined primarily, even solely, to ancient texts whose contemporary relevance is questionable. Nevertheless, these women would be the first to maintain that what they are doing is as naught in terms of spiritual or religious value compared to what their husbands are doing. Their pride is precisely in that they are enabling that study to take place undisturbed and uninterrupted by material concerns and the exigencies of everyday family responsibilities.

※ ※ ※

Enlightenment, emancipation, the steady ascendancy of the non-Orthodox movements, the "liberation" of secular women (both Jewish and non-Jewish), together with other aspects of modernity, have all had a dual impact on Jewish orthopraxis and fundamentalism. On the one hand, modernity has weakened the Orthodox hold over the Jewish community. On the other, it has aroused a (not unexpected) absolutist intensification of the practices that distinguish the Orthodox, ultra-Orthodox and fundamentalist sectors from the rest of society—a reaction that expresses itself in ever more severe attacks on the various phenomena that characterize modernity.

Zionism and the establishment of an autonomous "Jewish state" in 1948 constituted the major challenge to Orthodoxy in the twentieth century, engendering (perhaps inevitably) conflicts between religious tradition and modernity, between the determination to establish a democratic mode of government that promised equality of opportunity, reward, and status to *all* its citizens, "irrespective of race, creed, or sex" (in the words of the Declaration of Independence), and the dictates of traditional Judaism.

The majority of the pioneers who came from Europe to reclaim the land of Israel were secularists who had quite deliberately shaken off the shackles of religion, together with other aspects of what they considered to be ghettoized, effete qualities of diaspora life; similarly, secular Jews today constitute the majority of Israeli citizens. However, there is and has always been an overriding desire to maintain certain basic Jewish principles and practices that are considered fundamental to ensuring the Jewishness of the state—a state in which 17 percent of the citizens are Muslim or Christian Arabs.

Thus, Saturday is the official Sabbath, or day of rest, and the Jewish calendar determines public holidays; Hebrew is the official language; and observance of *kashrut* (dietary laws) marks all public institutions. Yet all this does not suffice for the Orthodox and, especially, the ultra-Orthodox sectors of Israeli society, many of which quite clearly favor the establishment of a quasi-theocracy in which Jewish law would take precedence over—or would at least infuse—legislation passed by a democratically elected parliament.

In order to exert maximum influence on the legislative process, various sectors within the religious community in Israel established political parties, which over time have significantly increased their representation in the Knesset (Israel's parliament), and exploited their growing electoral power by bringing pressure to bear on successive governments in order both to impede secularization and to increase the financial and material benefits extended to the Orthodox population.

The political platforms of these parties clearly aim at ensuring that Orthodox *halakhic* principles maximally determine such critical issues as "Who is a Jew?," Sabbath and Holy-day observance, and personal status (in particular, marriage and divorce). Since 1977, the fundamentalist religious parties have gained so much power that whichever majority party seeks to set up a coalition government is left with little option but to surrender to at least some of the demands made by the religious parties on whose support such governments depend.

Perhaps the most remarkable increase in power has accrued to Shas, the most recently founded of the Orthodox parties, which combines religion and ethnicity, claiming to represent the socio-economically deprived sector of Israeli society, those who immigrated from the Arab states in the early 1950s and who are still in many respects discriminated against.

Like fundamentalist groups elsewhere (e.g., the Hamas under the Palestinian Authority), Shas has won adherents by developing social and educational services that ease the burden of the poor, and they have done so by extorting subsidies and funding in return for their support of successive governments, irrespective of the political ideology of the ruling party.

Shas's educational institutions are sex-segregated from early childhood and their curriculum is extremely narrow, focusing on religious studies that are taught from a strictly fundamentalist, non-critical point of view. Nevertheless, increasing numbers of moderately religious or even wholly nonobservant families are availing themselves of these kindergartens and schools because they alone provide hot lunches, longer school days, and busing. Since poorer parents also tend to have more children, the proportion of young people attending Shas schools is constantly growing, with subsequent intellectually detrimental effects.

More damaging to the democratic mode of government to which Israel aspires is the fact that members of the Knesset from the religious parties never make a political decision without first consulting their respective "spiritual leaders," rabbis who are, of course, not democratically elected. These leaders, it should however be noted, are clearly guided by expediency and non-spiritual considerations.

Probably the most significant indication of religious control in Israel is the fact that there is no true separation of state and religion such as exists in most democratic regimes. The Knesset legislates some aspects of religious life and practice, such as Sabbath working hours, while supervision of the implementation of such legislation is in the hands of a state-appointed, state-salaried Chief Rabbinate, a Chief Rabbinical Council, local and regional religious councils and rabbinical courts, all of whose members are Orthodox males. Rabbinical courts have sole jurisdiction over personal status. Only state-recognized rabbis may officiate at weddings, if the marriage is to be officially recognized by the Ministry of the Interior (which itself has long been in the hands of representatives of one or other of the religious parties). None of the non-Orthodox streams of Judaism enjoys official status; a marriage service conducted by one of their rabbis must have an official representative of the local rabbinical council present to "legitimize" it, or it will not be recognized as valid.

Since there is neither civil marriage nor civil divorce in Israel, the Orthodox monopoly over personal status is a major factor in determining that there is neither freedom of, nor freedom from, religion in what purports to be a modern, democratic, pluralistic state. Similarly, it perpetuates women's inferior status, since it currently fails to relate positively to the essentially compassionate nature of rabbinical law regarding marriage and divorce. While in no way egalitarian, that law gradually granted women greater protection, evolving from the biblical edict, which permitted a man to unilaterally cast off a wife for a variety of reasons, to a requirement that the woman willingly accept the bill of divorcement. In addition, *halakhah* provides for a number of means, which range from the comparatively mild "demand" to the most severe—imprisonment, by which a "recalcitrant" husband who refuses to grant his wife a bill of divorcement may ultimately be compelled to do so. Unfortunately, Orthodox divorce courts have proved reluctant to avail themselves of these means. Although civil rights activists and particularly women's organizations have been actively engaged in attempting to persuade the Chief Rabbis to instruct the rabbinical courts to act in accordance with these halakhically approved remedies, there is no sign of imminent change in the attitudes or decisions of the courts. While the vast majority of recalcitrant husbands continue with impunity to harass or impose unlimited suffering on their wives rather than release them from the marriage bonds, women who similarly refuse to accept the *get* are designated "rebels" whose husbands may then even be given permission to take a second wife, while they themselves remain undivorced and therefore neither eligible for any kind of financial support or sharing of property, nor able to marry another man.[2]

※ ※ ※

Since the establishment of the state in 1948, Israeli women have enjoyed equal civil rights and have benefited from a considerable amount of enlightened legislation and legal decisions extending their rights and privileges beyond those traditionally enjoyed in *halakhah* or in the practice of Jewish communities in the Diaspora. Nevertheless, autonomy and equality do not extend to areas where religious, rather than civil, law has supremacy. Furthermore, there remains the strong influence of *minhag*, or custom, especially in the Orthodox and ultra-Orthodox communities, which supersedes civil law in the eyes of their members.

Thus, for example, schools that are under the supervision of the state-religious branch of the Ministry of Education and, even more so, those belonging to the independent ultra-Orthodox network, do not offer their female pupils the same kind or degree of Jewish studies that they consider mandatory for boys. Since the 1970s, most of the state-religious schools have become single-sex schools, as the ultra-Orthodox always were. Even those few schools that have remained co-educational segregate the sexes in separate classes. The study of Talmud, considered *de rigueur* for boys, continues to be denied to girls, except in a very few private schools accredited by the state-religious system. No government-subsidized *yeshiva*-style institutions of higher Jewish education exist for women, although a number of such institutions have been founded since the late 1990s.

With considerable difficulty and admirable determination, some Orthodox women have surmounted innumerable obstacles placed in their way by rabbinical authorities and have qualified as para-legal "pleaders" permitted to appear before the rabbinical courts in divorce proceedings. In 1999, in an historic and unprecedented move, two women graduates of one of the women's seminaries were accorded the status of "advisors" (but not *halakhic* "decisors," as men are called) in the areas of dietary laws and family purity. While these women have no official status, and they receive no payment of any kind from official sources, their status and legitimacy are assured by the numbers of Orthodox women who consult them on these two issues and who will in all likelihood eventually seek and abide by their opinions in other areas.

In accordance with the Orthodox emphasis on modesty, attempts have been made to ban the employment of women in positions that bring them into contact with male clients, such as serving as postal clerks or bank tellers. Some banks have acceded to these demands in branches located in religious areas, but the state-operated postal service has not. In at least one city with a predominantly religious population, women are required to sit at the back of buses, or, on occasion, to travel in segregated vehicles. Neighborhoods populated primarily or even solely by the orthodoxly observant prominently display notices warning women that they must comply with strict standards of what constitutes modest dress or risk being ousted or attacked. Indeed, women employees of the Ministry of Education, which is located on the border of one of Jerusalem's Orthodox quarters, have suffered verbal and physical attack for wearing short skirts or sleeveless dresses. Women who seek to pray at the Western Wall in the Old City of Jerusalem (the sole relic of the Temple that was destroyed in 70 C.E., one of Jewry's holiest sites), which is controlled by the Ministry for Religious Affairs, have been forbidden to worship there wearing prayer shawls, raising their voices or reading from a Torah scroll. They have also been physically attacked for doing so. Their appeal to the High Court, first presented in 1989, has yet to be satisfactorily resolved.

In the Orthodox community, political power, like religious authority, is vested solely in men. Apart from the National Religious Party, which was until recently comparatively moderate, none of the religious parties has ever fielded a woman candidate for election to the Knesset. Nevertheless, it is well-known that in the ultra-Orthodox community the wives of the most politically powerful rabbis exert considerable influence behind the scenes.

Clearly, the modern State of Israel is a land of innumerable contradictions and paradoxes. On the one hand, it has universal suffrage and a democratically elected parliament, but represented within that legislature are parties that openly declare their desire to replace democratic rule with a theocracy in which Jewish law will take precedence. It is one of the few countries that have had a woman prime minister; yet until 1977 ultra-Orthodox rabbis forbade the women of their communities to vote. In Israel's Supreme Court, women currently number three out of a total of fifteen judges, yet there is not a single woman judge in the rabbinical court system. Israel has a law mandating universal conscription, yet religiously observant young women may request exemption on grounds of modesty. Furthermore, married women and mothers are exempted from military service, in accordance with the importance placed on marriage and motherhood even for secular women. Israeli theaters, most of which are state or city subsidized, boast numerous outstanding women actors, and there are equally numerous fine women singers in both classical and popular entertainment. Yet religiously observant girls and women perform only before all-female audiences, while no ultra-Orthodox male will attend a performance by females. A woman's voice—like her hair—is considered an abomination!

Emancipation, freedom, and liberty are countered by reaction and repression. But there is undeniably a light at the end of the tunnel of fundamentalist oppression—a light kindled by women themselves. It is the light of learning and knowledge—for so many centuries the monopoly of Jewish males. Like their non-Jewish sisters, Jewish women have struggled against all odds to attain the scholarship that grants intellectual, and ultimately also social, authority. There are already an impressive number of women rabbis in the Reform and Conservative movements in Israel as in the Diaspora. In the opinion of many feminists, the time is not far away when there will also be Orthodox women whose halakhic authority will equal that of male rabbis, whatever title they may be accorded in place of "rabbi." Reinterpreting Jewish law and practice, collaborating with non-Orthodox women similarly concerned with the secure establishment of a democratic, pluralist, egalitarian civil society, they may well bring about a spiritual revolution that will enable a blending of Judaism with modernity, and have an ineradicable impact on the currently far too conservative quasi-secular state of Israel.

Notes

[1] Muslims and Christians come under the jurisdiction of the shariah or the ecclesiastical courts respectively.

[2] Israeli and civil law forbids bigamy, but this obstacle has been overcome by the rabbinical authorities, who cite the supremacy of *halakhah* over civil law. Jewish law permits taking a second wife if the first is unable or unwilling to accept a *get*. It is an indication of the gender-based discrimination practiced by the rabbinical courts that annually some fifteen to twenty men receive rabbinical permission to take a second wife, while in the first fifty years of statehood fewer than twenty men were coerced into granting the *get* by threat of imprisonment.

Bibliography

Adler, Rachel. *Engendering Judaism*. Philadelphia: Jewish Publication Society, 1998.

Biale, Rachel. *Women and Jewish Law: An Exploration of Women's Issues in Halakhic Sources*. New York: Schocken, 1984.

Halpern, Micah D. and Chana Safrai. *Jewish Legal Writings by Women*. Jerusalem: Urim Publications, 1998.

Hauptman, Judith. *Rereading the Rabbis*. Oxford: Westview Press, 1998.

Howland, Courtney W. "The Challenge of Religious Fundamentalism to the Liberty and Equality Rights of Women: An Analysis Under the United Nations Charter," *Columbia Journal of Transnational Law*, 271, 1997.

Plaskow, Judith. *Standing Again at Sinai*. San Francisco: Harper & Row, 1990.

The Battle For Islam

The War Against Feminism in the Name of the Almighty: Making Sense of Gender and Muslim Fundamentalism

Janet Afary

From *The New Left Review*, July-August, 1997

I. Two Feminisms[1]

In recent years, some postmodern feminists have warned us about the perils of generalizations in feminist theory that transcend the boundaries of culture and region, while feminist critics of postmodernism have argued conversely that abandoning cross-cultural and comparative theoretical perspectives may lead to relativism and eventual political paralysis.[2] As I will argue in this article, the two positions are not always as diametrically opposed as they seem to be. The militant Islamist movements which have proliferated across a wide variety of cultures and societies in North Africa, the Middle East, and Southeast Asia have propagated remarkably similar policies and doctrines with regard to gender issues. As a result, a comparative theoretical perspective that would focus on this issue is both essential and surprisingly neglected. But careful distinctions need be made between conservative discourses—both *Sunni* and *Shi'ite*—that praise women's roles as mothers and guardians of the heritage yet deny them personal autonomy, and progressive discourses on Islam that argue for a more tolerant and egalitarian view of gender roles.

In examining the gender ideologies of several fundamentalist movements, we shall see that, despite regional and cultural variations, they exhibit a significant degree of similarity. Gender relations are not a marginal aspect of these movements. Rather, an important strength of fundamentalism lies in its creation of the illusion that a return to traditional, patriarchal relations is the answer to the social and economic problems that both Western and non-Western societies face in the era of late capitalism.

A number of feminist thinkers have tried to explain the appeal of fundamentalism among the middle and lower-middle classes in the predominantly Muslim societies of the Middle East, North Africa, and Southeast Asia. Despite some significant regional variations, these studies can be divided into three groups. One group of writers has stressed the economic and political issues that have contributed to the rise of fundamentalist movements; a second group has explored the disruptive impact of modernization on the family; while a third group has argued that militant Islamist movements and organizations may indeed empower students and professional women in certain ways, though restricting their lives in others.[3] By critically examining these three approaches, we can develop a more integrated and dialectical explanation of fundamentalism, and understand why in the late-twentieth century men *and* women have become attracted to such authoritarian ideologies.

At the same time, Western readers need to become more attentive to the progressive Islamic discourses that are gradually developing in the region, voices that call for greater tolerance, diversity, and more egalitarian gender relations. In Iran a new generation of men and women, who are in opposition, are constructing feminist and democratic discourses on *Shi'ite* Islam, and are carefully and thoughtfully reinterpreting Muslim jurisprudence to arrive at more liberal perspectives on the issue of women's rights. As an Iranian historian who has followed these developments from afar, I will argue that we must map out the differences between voices of progressive women and men who, in difficult conditions, are carving out a more egalitarian discourse on Islam and gender relations, and the rhetoric of those who, under the rubric of the "sovereignty of the Muslim people" and "the struggle against colonialism and imperialism," have maintained nativist and reactionary teachings with regard to gender relations.

II. A Battle Over Terminologies or Bodies?

Scholars of the Middle East and of religious issues continue to debate the relevance of two terms "Islamism" and "fundamentalism" to a growing number of cultural and political movements that have made substantial inroads in the Middle East, North Africa, and parts of Southeast Asia. Some, such as Martin E. Marty and R. Scott Appleby, have argued for the relevance of the term "fundamentalism," not just in the context of the Middle East, but for similar ideological currents around the world, which, in the last two decades, have sought political power in the name of religion, be it Islam, Christianity, Judaism, Hinduism, Buddhism or Confucianism. Fundamentalism in this view is a late twentieth-century phenomenon, a response to the loss of identity in a modern secular world. Fundamentalism is a militant movement that accepts and even embraces the technological innovations of the West, but shuns many social and cultural aspects of modern society, particularly in the realm of the family. Fundamentalists fight for a worldview based on an ideal and imagined past, and yet this past is a carefully constructed one which often rests on unacknowledged forms of theological innovation. Fundamentalists believe they are carrying out the will of God, and are often intolerant of dissent both within and without the community of believers.[4] Others, such as John Esposito and Edward Said, have criticized indiscriminate use of the term. In Said's view, by constructing reductive notions of "terrorism" and "fundamentalism," the West has attempted to claim for itself "moderation, rationality" and a specific Western ethos.[5] Both groups of writers, however, would agree that despite significant regional and political differences among these movements, such Islamist or fundamentalist groups have called for a return to more traditional norms for women, emphasizing women's roles in procreation, the adoption of "proper *hijab*" (the Islamic dress code), and submission to patriarchal values. A few examples should suffice to establish this point.

The first dramatic reversal in women's rights took place during the Iranian Revolution of 1979 which brought to power the Islamic Republican Party (IRP). To this day, strict government enforcement of the *hijab* and periodic rounding up, fines, and imprisonment of women on charges of "improper *hijab*" continue. Despite some compromises by the government in the areas of education, divorce and marriage law, and employment, and despite the fact that women remain very active in the social and political life of Iran, holding high academic, managerial, and even political positions, Iranian women remain segregated in schools, on buses, and on beaches and are restricted in their choice of career, employment, and education. Prohibitions against dating and casual friendship between unrelated men and women remain strong, while polygamy, encouraged by the government, has increased among the urban middle classes.[6] The election in May this year by a large margin of the more moderate President Mohammad Khatami, whose support was particularly strong among women and young people, shows how frustrated Iranians have become with the harsh policies of the Islamist government, and how widespread the desire for change was after eighteen years.

In Sudan and Afghanistan fundamentalist groups have assumed control of the government and so have significant authority in imposing their views, while in Egypt, Algeria, Jordan, and Lebanon, Islamist movements remain in opposition to the government. These and other religious revivalist movements do not operate in isolation from one another. Indeed, the 1994 UN Population Conference in Cairo became the scene of a new type of alliance between the Roman Catholic Church and a host of Muslim fundamentalist groups. Both opposed any reference to abortion rights in the UN documents. Since Muslim jurisprudence has historically been tolerant of birth control methods, one wonders whether Islamist movements are learning new arguments from the Catholic Church or from Christian fundamentalist groups in the United States in their efforts to limit women's reproductive rights.[7]

There have been frequent reports of human rights violations against Sudanese women since the National Islamic Front (NIF), led from behind the scenes by the Sorbonne-educated theologian, Dr. Hasan al-Turabi, assumed power in a coup d'état in 1989. The process of Islamization and Arabization of Sudan, where the dissenting southern region of the country has a mix of Muslims, Christians, and followers of indigenous religions, and where the northern Muslim Sudanese have often embraced more tolerant Sufi expressions of Islam, is rigidly pursued. Large numbers of women in the legal and medical professions, and in the civil service have either been barred from work or placed under severe restrictions. Women who do not observe proper *hijab* are periodically rounded up, and their names broadcast on radio to further shame and humiliate them.[8]

On September 27, 1996, when the Afghan Taliban, whose activities have been backed by Pakistan and the United States, captured Kabul, their first decree was to close girls' schools and force women to stay home from work. This went far beyond the restrictions of the previous fundamentalist faction in power, the *mujahedeen*, or for that matter those of any other militant Islamist governments—including that of Iran. Similar measures were adopted in Herat and Jalalabad, which had been earlier taken over by the Taliban. Women may not leave their homes unless accompanied by a male relative, and then only with their bodies, including their faces, completely covered.[9] The fanatical government forbade surgeons from operating on members of the opposite sex, and called for stoning as the penalty for adultery. These actions prompted UN Secretary-General, Boutros Ghali, to call for a withdrawal of aid by UN agencies to Afghanistan if the Taliban did not end these extraordinary and discriminatory policies. The actions of the Taliban have provoked a deep sense of revulsion throughout much of the Muslim world. In Iran, even the militant cleric, Janati, who heads the Hezbullah Party of God, complained that the actions of the Taliban "were giving Islam a bad name."

In Algeria, the Islamic Salvation Front (FIS) won the 1991 elections but was banned by the government in January 1992 and prevented from taking power. The FIS has unleashed a campaign of terror that has killed over fifty thousand residents, and has targeted foreigners, those who attended French schools, feminists, and gays. The FIS has vowed, if it comes to power, to end women's employment, to make sexual relations outside marriage punishable by death, and to enforce the *hijab*. Since January 1992 several hundred women have been assassinated by the fundamentalists for not wearing a head scarf, for wearing Western clothing—such as jeans—for working alongside men, or for living without a male guardian in their own apartments. Many more have been stabbed, raped, or subjected to death threats for the same "violations," or for such offences as teaching boys in school and running hair salons. Algerian feminists have consistently protested these and other abuses. The regime itself has accommodated fundamentalist pressure, enacting the Family Code (1984) which allows men the right to divorce their wives for any reason, and to practice polygamy.[10] In recent years, the regime has permitted the emergence of a moderate Islamist party, the Islamic Movement of Society for Peace, which won sixty-nine seats in the controlled elections held in early June [1997]. It now holds posts in the government. Women have on occasion played a leading role in the opposition: The socialist-feminist Haroun was elected to the Assembly as a member of the Socialist Front, and is an opponent of both the regime and the integralists.

In Malaysia, the more liberal customary Malay laws dealing with marriage, divorce, and child custody have been replaced by the Islamic *Shafi'i* laws that oppose family planning policies and call for punishment in cases of "wilful disobedience by a woman of any order lawfully given by her husband." Religious law has once again sanctioned the marriage of young girls without their consent, and accepted repudiation of wives by husbands with impunity.[11]

Persecuting the Opposition

In Bangladesh, a state which was originally dedicated to the ideals of secularism and socialism during the period immediately after its independence from Pakistan in 1971, Islam was declared the state religion in 1988. Fundamentalist clerics, with backing from the government, have issued a *fatwah* (religious decree) calling for the death of the feminist Muslim writer and poet Talisma Nasrin. She is the author of a popular novel, *Shame* (1993), in which she recounts the killing of Hindus by Muslim fundamentalists, and she has been accused of calling for the reform of the *Qur'an*.[12]

Even in predominantly Muslim societies where feminists have made some inroads, these gains have to be defended from continuous attack. Many literary works are denied publication in Egypt on the grounds that they violate religious, sexual, or moral taboos. At the plenary session of the 1993 annual conference of the Middle East Studies Association in North Carolina, Egyptian feminist writer and physician Nawal el-Saadawi announced that fundamentalists in both Egypt and Algeria had threatened to kill her. Saadawi's organization, the Arab Women's Solidarity Association, was banned by the Egyptian government in 1991 as a move to appease the fundamentalists. Some of her books remain banned in Egypt.

Other secular intellectuals have similarly been persecuted. In late 1995, Dr. Nasr Abu-Zeid, an Egyptian professor, was ordered to divorce his wife—also a university professor—because his writings smacked of "apostasy."[13] In Pakistan the respected poet and social campaigner Akhtar Hamid Khan known for his lifelong support of family planning, education, and employment for impoverished women, was threatened with execution by both the government and the *ulama*. The 1979 *Hudud* Ordinance declared all sex outside marriage unlawful, practically eliminating the distinction between rape and extra-marital sex. It also sanctioned the flogging of accused women. Despite her promises, Benazir Bhutto, who was reelected premier in 1993, did not during her abbreviated term of office take any major steps to reform laws that deny women's rights.[14]

In recent years, Turkish women have campaigned around the issue of domestic violence and helped to create shelters for battered women. They have formed consciousness-raising groups, and have discussed the limitations of legal reforms such as those introduced by Ataturk in the 1920s, and have demonstrated in the streets against sexual harassment. They have also become active in environmental issues. Additionally, feminists have set up women's coffee houses and have organized art exhibits. The Women's Library and Information Center, the first such centre devoted to feminist scholarship, was opened in Istanbul in April 1990. But Turkish feminists are extremely worried about the fundamentalist Islamic Welfare Party (RIFAH), which now heads the coalition government, fragile though that now seems, and they fear that the new government might try to dismantle Ataturk's secular reforms.[15] Followers of the Welfare Party claim to represent women's rights and direct their attacks at the objectification of women under Western-style capitalism. The fundamentalists' criticisms of pornography and prostitution, and the many free social services they provide for the community have helped to legitimize their claim that they represent issues of concern to women. Their outspoken challenge to industrial pollution has also gained them converts. A return to religious values, they insist, would solve the myriad social and economic problems of Turkish society.[16]

Palestinian women in the occupied territories became instrumental in forming decentralized popular committees once the *Intifada* was initiated in 1987. They also began to address women's issues. Debates on divorce, women's income, and greater respect for women continued to be aired during the *Intifada*. Many young women activists broke with earlier traditions of arranged and semiarranged marriages, pursuing marriages based on individual choice. Others tried to remain politically involved even after marriage. This was a new phenomenon in a movement which had historically insisted that married women must leave the political organizations and instead give "sons to the resistance," and where the birth of boys was glorified under various names such as the "Palestinian womb," the "factory of men," or the "women's *jihad*"[17]. The Palestinian community took pride in the impressive role of Hanan Mikhail Ashwari, a feminist and professor of English at Bir Zeit University, who emerged as the official spokesperson for the Palestinian delegation to the 1993 Middle East peace talks. Ashwari was elected as an independent to the Palestinian legislature in January 1996 and was subsequently appointed Minister of Education in the Palestinian Authority. The Palestinian leadership is divided, however, in its attitude towards women's rights and on women's place in the nationalist struggle. With the ascendancy of the religious right in Israel and the unravelling of the Oslo agreements, any accommodation between the Palestine Liberation Organization and the fundamentalist group Hamas would surely mean greater limits on women. Hamas projects a theocratic and sex-segregated state as its ideal vision of a Palestinian society, one which undermines the basic civil rights of, not only women, but also of Christian Palestinians who have long been active in the resistance movement.[18] The above list could continue since a number of other nations such as Lebanon, Morocco, Nigeria, Saudi Arabia, and Somalia have also experienced the growing power of fundamentalism.[19]

III. Feminist Writing on the Roots of Fundamentalism

As the political discourse of the Middle East, North Africa, and Southeast Asia became increasingly dominated by conservative Islamist arguments, a number of feminist thinkers and writers have tried to probe the contradictions of the region in an attempt to understand the underlying reasons for the growth of fundamentalism. These studies can be broadly divided into the following three categories:

The Political and Economic Explanation

Several sociologists and political scientists have discussed the rapid economic changes which have characterized the region in the period since World War II, changes which took place under secular and highly authoritarian governments.[20] Iranian sociologist Valentine Moghadam points out that in the 1960s and 1970s, improvements in health, at the start of the demographic transition in the Middle East and North Africa, led to an increasingly youthful population. At the same time, the fall in oil prices in the late 1970s, and the accompanying unemployment, increased the gap between the upper classes and the middle and lower-middle classes. A crisis of political legitimacy ensued in which the secular, authoritarian governments were attacked for corruption, continued subservience to Western powers, and especially for the propagation of supposedly immoral modernist values and institutions. This last point of contention was fueled by the growth of women's education and employment. The fierce competition of the university entrance exams, and government civil service jobs, especially affected the lower-middle classes, who were the first generation of their families to attend colleges and universities. To pacify this angry and youthful population, and also to undermine the leftist and Marxist groups, the secular governments of the region, whether Anwar al-Sadat in Egypt, or Muhammad Reza Shah Pahlavi in Iran, permitted, and sometimes encouraged, the activities of Islamist groups.[21]

Fatima Mernissi has focused on the economic and political problems that contributed to the growth of fundamentalism in North Africa.[22] She argues that the spread of fundamentalism in the last two decades has stemmed from the political and social failures of the secular, authoritarian states of the postcolonial period, states that operate within the rules of the International Monetary Fund and the interests of the imperialist powers.[23] Mernissi also traces the development of Muslim fundamentalism among the urban lower-middle classes and university students—who make up the great majority of the movements' adherents—to factors such as rapid urbanization and mass education. The sharp increase in the number of educated and employed women, the fact that most women now delay marriage until their twenties, the greater authority women experience as a result of the earnings they bring home, the greater control they have gained over unwanted pregnancies, and the higher divorce rate, have all helped produce important changes in relations between the sexes.[24] Given the limited opportunities for advanced education in most third world countries, there is great competition between men and women for university placement and processional positions, adding fuel to an already explosive situation in predominantly Muslim countries. High unemployment rates in North African countries (in Algeria, the rate is close to 40 percent) have only increased the tension. Many men, who have been stripped of their old identities as heads of households and patriarchs, find the message of fundamentalist Muslim clerics and politicians quite appealing. As Mernissi argues:

> The *hijab* is manna from heaven for politicians facing crises. It is not just a scrap of cloth; it is a division of labor. It sends women back to the kitchen. *Any Muslim state can reduce its level of unemployment by half just by appealing to the shariah, in its meaning as despotic caliphal traditions.* This is why it is important to avoid reducing fundamentalism to a handful of agitators who stage demonstrations in the streets. It must be situated within its

regional and world economic context by linking it to the question of oil wealth and the New World Order that the Westerners propose to us.[25]

In her study of the National Islamic Front (NIF) in Sudan, Sondra Hale presents a similar analysis. She argues that a variety of economic and political factors, such as the emergence of multinational corporations, the uneven nature of economic development, and emigration as a result of high unemployment, have contributed to the "socio-political/economic crises which in turn have had a profound impact on gender arrangements." The process of "romanticizing" women's role in reproduction and the insistence of the NIF that women return to the home and take care of children and husbands can be viewed as an attempt to force women out of the labor process and to create jobs for lower- and middle-class urban males, civil servants, and college instructors, in areas in which women have made significant inroads.[26]

The Economic Benefits of Getting Religion

Several writers have also pointed to the economic opportunities that fundamentalist institutions provide for believers, thus attracting women with low incomes and their families.[27] In oil-producing countries, wealthy supporters donate large sums as alms to these institutions, allowing them to engage in a wide range of charitable activities. The oil-producing countries, such as Saudi Arabia and Iran, also give large sums to these institutions in other countries, both openly and covertly. Naila Kabeer writes that in Bangladesh the fundamentalist organizations, with funding from Saudi Arabia, have established a large network of Islamic Nongovernmental Organizations (NGOs) that provide students with a wide variety of educational assistance, from scholarships and vocational training to dormitories, jobs, and medical clinics. The same organizations train Muslim clerics to run the village administration and to provide basic health care including pre- and postnatal care. These services are dispensed alongside a religious and ideological message which seeks to counter Western and modernist views. For example, the feminist literature in the West which emphasizes women's contribution to the household as a form of unpaid labor is adopted, but then a different conclusion is derived from this literature: Women, therefore, need not work outside the home because they already make substantial contributions at home.[28] Andrea Rugh points out that in Egypt the services which the private mosques provide for the community are not only more reliable than government services but also contribute to the community's sense of dignity:

> Services may include the provision of subsidised clothing and food, health care, regular educational programs (usually at the preprimary or primary level), after-school tutoring for children, religious instruction, subsidies for students, evening courses, social group activities, *Qur'an* reading sessions, and special programs for religious holidays. In poor areas, mosque representatives hand out free food, clothing, and money in exchange, as one poor woman put it, "for our wearing proper Islamic dress." Money can also be borrowed through Islamic banks in the approved "profit sharing" way where a fixed interest is not required.[29]

While these services bring new adherents, the truth remains that, despite their claims, none of the Islamist movements have been able to offer a viable solution to the overall economic problems of their societies. Decades ago, Maxime Rodinson showed in his *Islam and Capitalism* that Islamist economic policies are no alternative to capitalist development.[30] More recently, Iranian economist Sohrab Behdad has shown that if a utopian Islamic economic system ever were viable, it should have happened in Iran where every ideological, social, and economic condition was at its disposal. Instead corruption is rampant in the country, unemployment is above 20 percent, the rhetoric of "the role of the oppressed" has been shelved and "a privileged class of clergy and their cronies, their sons, daughters, and other relatives, have replaced the privileged class that the revolution uprooted".[31] Continuing this line of thinking, Valentine Moghadam has argued that since Islamist governments in Sudan, Iran, and Pakistan were unable to prevent escalating and structural unemployment, to carry out a programme of wealth distribution, or even to reduce government corruption, they have instead focused on issues of family, culture, and law as the root causes of all social and economic problems.[32]

The Cultural Explanation: Modernization and the Family

A second argument that appears in writings about fundamentalism, including those on the American Protestant fundamentalist movement, is that women should not be viewed as passive and submissive objects who are coerced or simply duped into such movements. Fundamentalism is not simply "constructed by men and imposed on women," notes Julie Ingersoll.[33] Women are drawn to these movements because of their emphasis on family, and because fundamentalist organizations demand that both women and men place a higher priority on raising children and family relations in general. We are living in a world in which the requirements of capitalist development have placed an enormous strain on married life. Husbands and wives often both work full time; there is appallingly inadequate child care; there are frequent job losses and relocations; and to make ends meet couples often work much beyond the eight-hour day. The fundamentalist message, which appeals to a much "higher" authority than corporate owners and manufacturers, falls, therefore, on receptive ears. Women who generally hold low status jobs in the capitalist market, and are overburdened with responsibility for children as well as care for the elderly, may in fact, writes Helen Hardacre, make a "conscious decision to use the fundamentalist message to secure the husband's loyalty and support of them and their children."[34]

Sociologist Deniz Kandiyoti, ethnologist Aihwa Ong, anthropologists Erika Friedl and Mary Hegland, and political scientist Cynthia Enloe have all, in their respective areas of research, emphasized the disruptive consequences of shifting gender roles in developing societies, especially changes in the family in the Middle East and Southeast Asia. They suggest that we may be witnessing a growing interest in a return to a more traditional and seemingly secure patriarchal culture of the past in both women and men.[35]

Kandiyoti, a Turkish feminist, suggests that in Asian and Middle Eastern societies a tacit intergenerational agreement, a "patriarchal bargain," has historically helped to maintain the social structure. A young bride who is deprived of inheritance rights in her father's house, acquiesces to her subservient position at the residence of her in-laws. She accepts her role and internalizes the patriarchal values because she anticipates a day when she herself may become the beneficiary of these traditions and could rule over her daughters-in-law. In the late twentieth century the process of modernization rapidly deprived this social bargain of its necessary economic foundation.[36] Once, however, the built-in insecurities of the capitalist structure and the nuclear family become more obvious—unemployment, lack of child care, or care for the elderly—both younger and older women grow more receptive to an ideology which calls for a return to the old patriarchal bargain in exchange for greater security.

Aihwa Ong probes into why many lower-middle-class women have been attracted to the Islamist movement in Malaysia. She argues that the process of modernization has had a mixed impact insofar as women are concerned. It has given them greater economic and personal freedom, with paid employment, spending money, and the power accompanying it, but it has also resulted in men abandoning their customary obligations to the family. Given the inherent instability of the capitalist economy and continued exploitation by the West, as well as the economic recessions of the last two decades, which have hit many third world countries especially hard, women who may not have long entered the labour market often finds themselves out of a job, and without the traditional support of the extended family or the community. Ong writes, "Land scarcity, widespread female wage labour, and secularization in many cases reduced men's customary obligations to be the sole supporter of their families."[37]

As Cynthia Enloe argues, "It isn't always obvious that surrendering the role of cultural transmitter or rejecting male protection will enhance a women's daily security [or] reduce her burdens."[38] The return to traditional and religious values may thus be attractive to the overworked homemaker, worker, and mother who hopes that her husband and community assume a greater share of her burden. She is also more likely to turn to the religious foundations and their networks of social support. These associations have assumed the customary role as head of the patriarchal clan. They also act as family counsellors and help to end conflicts by advising women to be more subservient to their husbands, but they also ask men to uphold their traditional obligations to the family.

Veiling as Empowerment

A third group of feminist scholars has argued that women who join militant Islamist organizations do so not only because of the economic support they gain, or the pro-family message they cherish, but also because of the alternative social and political power and autonomy they gain in the movements. By donning the veil, young lower-middle-class women may lose many individual freedoms, but they gain access to public spaces, to employment, and can become valued and powerful members of political organizations that propagate the militant Islamist ideology. When a young girl adopts the *hijab* she becomes physically restrained in certain ways. She may not be able to climb a tree or ride a bicycle so easily. But she may also face a lesser degree of sexual harassment. She may gain the right from her traditional family to finish high school and even attend the university, to seek outside professional employment, to socialize with her peers in mass organizations that promote the Islamist ideology, and even to choose her own husband in these gatherings rather than submit to an arranged marriage. Those women who become active members of militant Islamist groups also gain power over other, more secular, women. They become the guardians of morality on the streets and public spaces. They abuse and arrest more upper-class secular women on charges of improper *hijab* and are tremendously feared in the community.

The Jordanian feminist Lama Abu Odeh writes of the problem of sexual harassment and the dilemma Middle Eastern women have faced ever since they unveiled in the early twentieth century. Negotiating the streets, using public transportation, and working side by side with men in offices and factories became ordeals for unveiled women. They found that their bodies were constantly under the intrusive gaze of men. In societies where sexual harassment and molestation of women—touching, fondling, stalking, and derogatory comments—are rampant on the streets, in buses, and in work places, unveiled women often have no recourse to law or higher authorities. Even worse, they themselves are held responsible for the harassment they endure.[39] Under such circumstances, the veil can offer women a certain degree of physical protection. A veiled woman is seldom harassed in public, and if she is, she can loudly appeal to the chivalry and religiosity of the men around her who would almost certainly come to her help.

The Syrian feminist Bouthaina Shaaban who has studied the personal lives of Lebanese, Palestinian, Algerian, and Syrian women, is particularly effective in showing the appeal of Muslim fundamentalism to lower-class single women. Shaaban shows how adherence to the Islamist dress code provides a new public space for young women in traditionally segregated societies. In one case study we read about Zeinab, a single woman from a working-class district with a university education, who has joined the *Shi'ite* fundamentalist organization Amal in southern Lebanon. She explains how her activity with Amal, and her wearing of the prescribed outfit, *al-Shari*, have given her both protection and increased freedom of action. She feels safe from harassment and considers herself a productive member of society, helping to feed and shelter the poor. Above all, she has gained greater respect, power, and authority: "My father who used to be the only supreme authority in the house, never takes any decisions now concerning the family without consulting me first."[40] Zainab can stay out until eleven o'clock at night doing organizational work without her parents questioning her. She has this liberty in a society where even grandmothers cannot stay out late for fear of what the neighbors might say.

There is considerable disagreement among feminist writers on the actual liberatory potentialities that donning the veil provides. Leila Ahmed, for example, draws on a study of four hundred veiled and unveiled women at Cairo University which shows that there is a direct correlation between the *hijab* and the economic level of the female students. Those with lower-class parents are more likely to adopt the veil. She thus concludes that the veil is not a social innovation but a sign of conformity to the social class from which these upwardly mobile young women have emerged. The veil certainly saves young women from the expenses of acquiring many fashionable outfits. But joining the Islamist groups also carries "the comfort of bringing the values of home and childhood to the city and its foreign and morally overwhelming ways."[41]

While Ahmed recognizes the severe limitations that have been imposed on women in countries where fundamentalists have entered the government or gained substantial power, she nevertheless believes that the new practice of veiling serves as a transition process for lower-class women. In Ahmed's view, some of the goals of secular and upper-class Egyptian feminists, who were the first generation to demand women's entry into the universities and professional employment, are now pursued in a different ways by middle- and lower-middle-class women. The new *hijab*, in her view, marks a "broad demographic change—a change that has democratized mainstream culture."[42]

The Veil and Menial Work

Anthropologist Lila Abu-Lughod takes issue with Leila Ahmed on this point. She argues that since Islamist movements are unwilling or incapable of carrying out a serious programme of redistributing wealth, they have instead attempted to construct the illusion of equality through the imposition of the veil. She asks why "a political discourse in which morality displaces class as the central social problem is so appealing."[43]

Arlene MacLeod points to the alienating nature of the labor most women perform. Using Antonio Gramsci's concept of hegemony, she argues that, where Islamist movements oppose the state, the wearing of the veil is neither a sign of victimization and subordination, nor is it an expression of "false consciousness." Rather, it is a measure of women's alienation from modernization and its false promises. The subordinated lower classes are neither forced not completely duped into accepting regulations and restrictions. MacLeod describes the difficult lives of women who take care of their families and work for a living. She shows how demoralized these women become when they realize that the jobs they so much fought for at home are so repetitive and uncreative. Most lower-middle-class women who have entered civil service jobs find their work "boring and unchallenging," as well as "useless."[44] These ambitious women have few options but to work for the public sector which provides them with jobs, but allows them no true initiative or creativity. Thus, women suffer from a gender division of labor which assigns them to low-status jobs, a class division which limits them to repetitive and boring work, and an economic straightjacket which obliges them to work outside the home in a culture which sees women's primary role to be in the home. Women who lack viable and tangible alternatives and who have come to view Western women as sex objects because of the popular media, have, therefore, turned to traditional alternatives to gain some measure of control over their lives.[45]

MacLeod speaks of the veil as a conscious symbol of resistance in an Arab society where women work outside the home. But choice involves having access to information and real options. MacLeod says nothing about the fundamentalist message that male sexuality is by nature "uncontrollable," that women "induce" inappropriate male sexual behavior. Likewise, she glosses over the vast unemployment and the pressures of women to return to the home so that more jobs are opened for men. The questions remain: To what extent does the wearing of the *hijab* empower young students and professional women? What does it mean if you choose your own husband but are then denied the right to divorce, to child custody, or to a fair share of the property you and your husband have acquired during your marriage? How free is a woman who goes to the university and seeks employment but is then deprived of a choice of a career by her husband? How much autonomy does a veiled woman have when the very acceptance of the veil means approval of gender segregation, and the admission that a woman is first and foremost a sexual object? What does it mean when the burden of avoiding sexual harassment is placed on women, while men are seen as impulsive creatures with little or no control over their sexual desires? Further, what kind of freedom is this when governments sanction homophobia and severely persecute homosexuals?

These and other questions indicate that while young unmarried women may gain some control over their lives through wearing the *hijab*, or find temporary solutions to the problems of sexual harassment and other issues facing them in modern society, donning the *hijab* is by no means a serious step toward resolution of these problems. In the late twentieth century, emancipation for women means the free exercise of body and mind, ending degrading traditions that limit women's choices, and enabling women to pursue alternative lifestyle. There can be no emancipation when women are deemed inferior and different beings by virtue of their biology.

IV. A New Feminist Discourse on Islam in Iran

While feminist issues are more easily articulated in a progressive, democratic, and secular society, the serious efforts of feminists who live under Islamist regimes and hope to bring about a more egalitarian society cannot be dismissed because they are not expressed in a secular discourse. In contrast to countries such as Algeria, where fundamentalists are in violent opposition, or in Afghanistan, where extreme fundamentalists have only recently assumed power, the fundamentalist government in Iran has been in power since 1979. As a result of popular disillusionment with the system, a new and democratic discourse on Shi'ite Islam is gradually and painstakingly taking shape within the opposition. The most well-known advocate of this new school is the German-educated philosopher and theologian Dr. Abd al-Karim Surush. A former IRP ideologue, he is now regularly harassed by Hezbullah goons. Surush peppers his pleas for a more democratic and tolerant interpretation of Muslim jurisprudence before hundreds of enthusiastic university students with references to European thinkers such as Immanuel Kant, Karl Popper, and Erich Fromm.[46]

But it is the Iranian women's journal *Zanan* that has taken up the even more difficult task of developing a new feminist interpretation of Shi'ite Islamic laws and is aided in this by a group of progressive educators, lawyers, and theologians, both women and men.[47] *Zanan*, which began publication in 1991, is edited by the feminist Shahla Sherkat and is part of a growing

effort by women writers, filmmakers, academics, artists, and other professional women, who have reclaimed some of the rights and organizations that
they had developed before the 1979 Revolution. By Western standards
Zanan, which could be shut down by the government at any time, is a
curious publication. There are regular features that would appear in a popular women's magazine on such topics as food, diet, health and exercise,
fashion, family psychology, science, and medicine. But *Zanan* is also a literary and cultural magazine with an explicitly feminist agenda. There are
detailed reviews of films, poems, and short stories produced by Iranian
women. Recent books by and about women are regularly featured. There
are also translations of classic feminist essays by authors such as Mary Woll-
stonecraft, Virginia Woolf, Charlotte Perkins Gilman, Evelyn Reed, Nadine
Gordimer, Alison Jaggar, and more recent articles by contemporary feminist
writers from the U.S. magazine *Ms* in which feminist perspectives and politics are defined and explicitly defended.[48] *Zanan* regularly features original
sociological studies on working women and is trying to start the first shelter
for battered women in the country.

Rereading the *Qur'an*

But, more importantly for our purposes, the journal has embarked upon a
meticulous reexamination of the *shariat* in light of feminist issues. The
shariat is the code of laws, close to 1,400 years old, which determines what
actions of the *ummah* (community of believers) are regarded by God as
obligatory, recommended, neutral, objectionable, or forbidden. The Twelve
Shi'ite jurisprudence practiced in Iran is derived from the *Qur'an,* the Traditions attributed to the prophet Muhammad, and the accounts attributed
to the Twelve Shi'ite Imams. In contrast to most Sunni schools, *Shi'ism*
gives greater recognition to the authority of living *mujtahids,* legal and theological scholars, whose training has qualified them to render judgment on
contemporary issues.[49] There is a long-standing tradition of reading and
reinterpreting both the *Qur'an* and the accounts attributed to Muhammad
and various imams in the light of contemporary social and political realities.
Feminist theologians and legal scholars who have entered these debates
demonstrate a remarkable familiarity with such arguments. While many
Qur'anic laws on women and family call for a more conservative regulation
of gender relations, others can be found that uphold the matrilineal and
matrilocal traditions of pre-Islamic Arabia of the seventh century C.E.[50] In

deconstructing the text and reexamining the narratives which form Islamic jurisprudence, feminist scholars also employ a series of reputable and acknowledged strategies to their advantage. Qur'anic verses and narratives that suggest a more egalitarian treatment of women are highlighted. Those which call for restrictions on women's actions are reinterpreted. Often a word has multiple meanings and a less restrictive synonym can be adopted. Since stories attributed to the prophet Muhammad (*hadiths*) and many of those attributed to the imams (*ravayats*) were not written down until much later, a chain of reporters known as *isnad* exists for each account. The strength of a narrative is based on the reliability of the transmitters of that story, much like the task of footnotes in Western scholarship. A weak link, a reporter with a reputation for unreliability, could weaken the entire chain and make the story suspect.[51] As the following two examples demonstrate, feminist scholars showed that they could use such strategies to buttress innovation, just as fundamentalist theologians had done.

In an essay entitled "Man: Partner or Boss?," Shekufeh Shokri and Sahereh Labirz argue that Islam does not privilege men over women because of their biology and that, therefore, it is not "sexist." The only distinction that can be found among Muslims in the *Qur'an* is between the pious and the impious. To prove their point they turn to chapter 49/verse 13 of the *Qur'an* which says: "O mankind, surely We have created you from a male and a female and made you tribes and families that you may know each other. Surely the noblest of you with Allah is the most pious of you. . . ."[52] Having argued that God privileges only the most pious and knowledgeable human beings, the two writers conclude that "If a woman were more knowledgeable and more scholarly than a man," surely she would be regarded in higher esteem in God's eyes. They then return to an earlier verse in the *Qur'an* (chapter 4/verse 34) which says, "Men are *custodians* [*qavuamun*] of women, with what Allah has made some to excel over others, and with what they spend out of their wealth."[53] This verse is commonly used by conservative male theologians to argue that God has elevated men over women. The feminist theologians tackle this verse from several different angles. They argue that a better translation for the word "custodian" is "initiator in affairs." The word "custodian" implies that women are minors whose affairs should be regulated by men, but "initiators in affairs" points to a man's responsibility to provide for his family without, it is claimed, having the parallel degrading view of women. The authors then present the more audacious argument that because of numerous changes in present-day society such as women's education and employment, and their participation in politics, economics, and even war, new and more egalitarian interpretations of Islamic doctrines must be adopted. Finally, they conclude that Article 1105 of the Iranian civil code, which designates husbands as heads of households and establishes an unequal conjugal relation between husband and wife, is contrary to Islamic doctrine. Since the *Qur'an* recognizes only piety as a matter of hierarchy, not gender or race, the Iranian civil code which purports to base itself on Islamic doctrines is in fact un-Islamic and inaccurate and should be changed. [54]

In another article, entitled "Women as Justices of the Court," Mina Yadgar Azadi writes that chapter 33/verse 33 in the *Qur'an* which reads, "And stay in your houses and display not your beauty like the displaying of the ignorance of yore . . . "[55] has been used to argue that women should not hold the prominent social position of a judge. Azadi rebuts the interpretation of this verse in three different ways. She argues that the verse addresses only Muhammad's wives and not other women. Further, even if it were addressing all women, it should at most be considered a recommendation not an obligation upon women, since no religious scholar has ever ruled for women's seclusion at all times. Finally, she argues that if this verse were indeed carried out, women of all professions, including teachers, nurses, and doctors, would be prohibited from working. Hence, why invoke the verse when the debate is about reinstating women as judges in Iranian courts, but not at other times?[56]

These and other arguments may not seem radically egalitarian from a secular feminist perspective, but they have an impact on the public as well as many clerics. The state, after all, draws legitimacy for its conservative patriarchal politics from the same sources. Women have now entered the debate and have proven knowledgeable about minute theological issues. They have become capable of demonstrating ambiguities and multiple meanings in Qur'anic verses and other texts, and are trained as theologians in major religious centers. These facts are in some ways more significant than the substance of the argument. They mean that feminist theologians and legal experts have to be taken seriously and that they have opened a breach in conservative ideology at a time when there was popular dissatisfaction anyway with the heavy-handed patriarchy of the Islamist regime.

Indeed theology is not the only male-dominated domain in which Iranian feminists have made some inroads. They have also been active in politics. In spring 1996, the fifth round of elections to the parliament resulted in the election of Fa'ezeh Hashemi, the former President's daughter. Hashemi, who was elected with over 850,000 votes, apparently received the highest number of votes of any candidates from Tehran, though official tallies subsequently demoted her to second place. An accomplished athlete in a variety of fields including riding and water-skiing, Hashemi, who is in her late thirties, is unlike anything the Islamic Republic of Iran propagates as the image of the subservient Iranian woman. She founded the Iranian Federation of Women's Sports, and heads the country's Olympic Committee. She is married to a psychologist and is pursuing an advanced degree in international law. In a recent interview, Hashemi admitted that most family responsibilities, including the care of their two children, were shouldered by her husband, and that she was not even aware of current food prices in the market. What she is aware of is the bias against women in society and in public television, where working women are always demonized and homemakers are presented as obedient women who serve tea. Hashemi wants new legislation that would address the unequal treatment of women under the law, that would push for greater education for women, more participation in top-level management positions, and more involvement in national sports. This last issue caused a great brouhaha when Hashemi called for the construction of bike paths in Tehran for the use of both men and women. Several leading clerics issued *fatwahs* against women cyclists, claiming that the sight of such women out and about in Tehran would be too erotic. While the degree of Hashemi's commitment and her ability to bring about these reforms remain to be seen, she has received much support from *Zanan* and other women's publications.[57]

The May 1997 election of President Muhammad Khatami may strengthen the voices of women like Hashemi and journals such as *Zanan* which supported him. Khatami, who speaks three languages and teaches university courses on Islamic reform movements, was Minister of Culture and Islamic Guidance from 1982 to 1992. He was ousted from that position because he gradually adopted a more moderate view on social and cultural issues and would not strictly enforce the censorship laws. Khatami is certainly not an opponent of the government. He was one of four candidates—out of 238—who were handpicked by the Council of Guardians and allowed to run for election. Nevertheless, he was allowed to do so only two weeks before the elections, in order to give a greater semblance of democracy to the process. The clerical establishment which runs the government, and the grand ayatollahs all backed the Speaker of the Parliament, Ali Akbar Nateq Nouri, who was expected to win with a comfortable majority. Once Khatami campaigned on a platform of curbing censorship, fighting fanaticism and calling for greater tolerance on social and cultural issues, his candidacy was embraced by much of the public. Of 33 million eligible voters, 29 million (88 percent) voted, an unprecedented number in Iranian elections. Twenty million votes (70 percent) went to Khatami, who did equally well in cities and in villages. Word of mouth that Khatami would adopt a more liberal stance on gender relations and that he wished to remove the severe censorship on the media and the ban on satellite dishes, and that he advocated a more tolerant interpretation of Islam, one that "was opposed to oppression and coercion," brought women and young people on to the street to vote for him in overwhelming numbers.

Following the elections, Fa'ezeh Hashami demanded that Khatami show his gratitude towards the women who helped elect him by appointing women to his cabinet—a request he was to respond to—while others have called for wide-ranging reform of laws that deprive women of rights, especially in matters of divorce and custody of children. It remains to be seen whether the new president is willing and able to carry out such reforms, or if his opponents in government—who include most members of Parliament, and who harassed him and his supporters during the election—will prevail. Even so, the vast majority of Iranians voted for a change and to an end of the strict rule of the Islamist government which can no longer claim a public mandate.

V. Toward A New Politics

As has been argued in this article, the emergence of Muslim fundamentalism is a complicated phenomenon stemming in part from the crisis of capitalist development and modernization in the third world. Muslim fundamentalism has been difficult to confront, not only because in the seminaries and in the mosques it has an organization with ample financial backing and, at times, state support, but also because the fundamentalists speak to many urgent economic, social, and cultural needs.

At least three sets of illusions have fueled the intensity with which some women and men in the region have embraced the fundamentalist cause:

1. That an Islamist economy would remove the country from

the orbit of the IMF and the imperialist powers; provide the necessary health and social services that corrupt, authoritarian governments have all but ignored; solve the problems of high unemployment and underemployment; and offer the male heads of households both better educational opportunities and a more generous income for their families.

2. That the "higher" authority of religion would slow down the capitalist and modernist onslaught on the private domain; that an Islamist government would bring back traditional social relationships, the collective and personal loyalties and obligations which maintained the cohesiveness of the community; and that the old patriarchal bargain could be reinstated, enabling women to devote their time and energy to their families and also feel secure about their husband's loyalty and support.

3. Finally that the veil and self-imposed rules of chastity would empower women; solve the persuasive problems of sexual harassment and molestation on the streets and in the workplace; and thus pose an alternative to the much-maligned Western and secular model of feminist empowerment.

The way to challenge such illusions is not to move away from a progressive feminist agenda. Feminism is the response of fundamentalism, which is why fundamentalists have waged a war against feminism. But to be more effective, a new feminist politic must become indigenous to the region and permeate both the economic and ideological domains. To prevent the Islamists from driving a wedge between middle- and upper-class advocates of women's rights and others, including working-class and rural woman, feminists ought to pursue a three-pronged policy in conjunction with educators, journalists, the democratic Left, labor, and other grassroots activists.

1. Modernization without grassroots democracy or autonomy for the fledgling institutions of civil society, rapid economic development and high productivity without concern for workers' welfare and care of the environment, and increased integration of women into the capitalist economy without providing alternative institutions that

would shoulder women's traditional responsibilities to their homes and communities, have contributed to the growth of fundamentalism everywhere. One answer, therefore, is to call for a lessening of the burdens of the overworked mother and homemaker. A shorter working week that would allow more time for families; improved health care and working conditions; reduction in environmental pollution; high quality and affordable child care centers, such as those in France and Japan that are used by all classes; and facilities for the care of the elderly would be essential steps in this direction. It is important that feminists put forward such issues at a time when their opponents seek to portray them as part of a rich Westernized elite having nothing to say to ordinary women.

2. Equally important is for advocates of women's rights to call for a feminist education, one that aims at the empowerment of young girls and social awareness among young boys from the elementary schools to the college and university levels. Such a feminist education ought to be pursued, insofar as political conditions permit, in both Muslim countries and in exile communities across Europe and the United States. Ever since the late nineteenth century, intellectuals in exile have had a profound impact on political and ideological movements in their home countries in the Middle East and North Africa, and feminists need to take more advantage of such opportunities. Pedagogical strategies that focus on global and comparative feminist perspectives, that show the pervasive and systematic abuse of women in all cultures and throughout history, and also elaborate on the global struggles for women's rights, offer the greatest possibility of success. To avoid the charge by fundamentalists and others that feminism is a tool of imperialist governments, a feminist education should begin with a comparative view that focuses on the subordinate role of women in all major religions (not just Islam), move on, for example, to a discussion of the chastity belts that the European Crusaders forced on their wives when they went off to fight Muslims in the eleventh to thirteenth centuries, and continue with a discussion of European witch-hunts by the Catholic Church, up through the job discrimination, sexual violence, and

the abusive relationship that so many women in the West face today. After such an introduction, it would be more acceptable to speak of issues that affect the lives of women who live under Muslim law, issues such as women's poor health and diet, lack of exercise, denial of women's sexuality and reproductive rights, unfair divorce laws, lack of common property in marriage, cruel custody laws that tear young children from their mothers, and the need for legal, cultural, and religious reforms. Such debates must enter the mainstream through textbooks, storybooks, newspaper columns and cartoons, television and radio shows, as well as films and plays.

3. The work of individuals and institutions that are dedicated to developing an indigenous expression of Muslim feminism must be encouraged. This includes individuals such as Fatima Mernissi of Morocco who, together with a number of colleagues, is working on a project entitled "Humanist Islam" that plans to publish verses from the *Qur'an and Traditions of the Prophet* that are sympathetic to women's rights.[58] It also includes journals such as *Zanan* in Iran and *al-Raida* in Lebanon, or institutions such as [the International solidarity network] Women Living Under Muslim Laws, and the U.S. organizations The Association for Middle East Women's Studies, and Sisterhood Is Global.[59] A more progressive and feminist interpretation of Muslim law is gradually gaining ground through the collective efforts of these and other individuals and institutions. Such developments are an important step toward undermining fundamentalism. They should be supported by secular feminists, although the latter should never give up their own right to address all major issues confronting women, including religion.

These and other efforts by feminists offer hope for an alternative future for the region, one in which emancipatory rather than reactionary politics might come once again to the fore. This time, however, in their alliance with other progressive movements, women must never again subordinate their own demands or organizational independence to nationalist, leftist, or democratic political parties.

Notes

1 A version of this article was presented at the 1997 annual meeting of the American Historical Association in New York. I am grateful for many helpful comments and suggestions by Kevin Anderson, Robin Blackburn, Sondra Hale, Valentine Moghadam, Claire Moses, Rayna Rapp, and especially Nikki Keddie on various drafts of this article.

2 For the first view, see Linda J. Nicholson, ed., *Feminism / Postmodernism,* London 1990, pp. 1-16, and Judith Butler and Joan W. Scott, eds., *Feminists Theorize the Political,* London 1992; for the second view, see Nancy C. M. Hartsock, "Foucault on Power: A Theory for Women?," in Nicholson, *Feminism / Postmodernism,* pp. 157-75, and Caroline Ramazanoglu, ed., *Up Against Foucault,* London 1993.

3 I would like to stress that these three categories are not mutually exclusive, and that some authors have utilized two or all three approaches. My classification here is based on the authors' emphases.

4 See Martin E. Marty and R. Scott Appleby, eds., *The Fundamentalism Project: Fundamentalisms Observed,* Vol. I, Chicago 1991, pp. IX-X. Bernard Lewis prefers the term "fundamentalism" because use of the terms "Islamic" or "Islamist" to identify such movements implies that "this is what the Islamic religion and civilization is about". See "Unentretien avec Bernard Lewis," *Le Monde,* 16 November 1993; see also Henry Munson, Jr., *Islam and Revolution in the Middle East,* New Haven 1988, pp. 3-4, and Nikki Keddie's forthcoming essay "Women, Gender, and Fundamentalism," which she kindly shared with me.

5 See Edward Said, *Culture and Imperialism,* New York 1993, p. 375-7. See also John Esposito, "Secular Bias and Islamic Revivalism," *Chronicle of Higher Education,* 26 May 1993, p. 44. I have used the terms "fundamentalism" and "Islamism" for the conservative movements, but not the term "Islamic," leaving space for other more democratic interpretations of Islam to be discussed later.

6 For a summary of these policies, see Nayereh Tohidi, "Gender and Islamic Fundamentalism: Feminist Politics in Iran," in C. Mohanty, A. Russo and L. Torres, eds, *Third World Women and the Politics of Feminism,* Bloomington 1991, pp. 251-65; Azadeh Kian, "Gendered Occupation and Women's Status in Post-Revolutionary Iran," *Middle East Studies,* vol. 31, No. 3, July 1995, pp. 407-21. For the more recent reforms in family law, see Shala Haeri, "Obedience Versus Autonomy: Women and Fundametalism in Iran and Pakistan," *The Fundamentalist Project: Fundamentalisms and Society,* No. 2, 1993,

pp. 181-213; and N. Ramazani, "Women in Iran: The Revolutionary Ebb and Flow,",in *U.S.-Iran Review: Forum on American-Iranian Relations,* vol. I, No. 7, October 1993, pp. 8-9.

7 On contraceptive methods in pre-modern Arab societies, see B. F. Musallam, *Sex and Society in Islam,* Cambridge, 1989. On the debates at the Cairo conference, see "Vatican Seeks Islamic Allies in UN Population Dispute", *New York Times,* 18 August 1994, p. 1.

8 See Ali A. Abbas, "The National Islamic Front and the Politics of Education," *MERIP,* September-October 1991, pp. 23-5; *Women Living Under Muslim Laws (WLUML)* , 6 July 1992; Manahil A. Salam, "Islamic Fundamentalist Rule is a Setback to Women's Progress in the Sudan," paper presented at the Purdue Women's Symposium, Fall 1995.

9 See Elaine Sciolino, "The Many Faces of Islamic Law," *New York Times,* 13 October 1996, p. 4. Fred Halliday, "Kabul's Patriarchy with Guns," *The Nation,* 11 November 1996, pp. 19-22. For a discussion of the mujahedeen's opposition to female education, see Valentine M. Moghadam, *Modernizing Women: Gender and Social Change in the Middle East,* Boulder 1993, pp. 207-47.

10 See "Algeria Again at the Crossroads," *Middle East International,* 24 January 1992, p. 3; *Le Nouvel Observateur,* 15 January 1992; Anis, "Un homosexuel algérien à Paris," *Le Monde,* 22 June 1996, p. 15; Karima Bennoune, "Algerian Women Confront Fundamentalism," *Monthly Review,* vol. 46, No. 4, November, pp. 26-39.

11 Maznah Mohamad, "Islam, the Secular State and Muslim Women in Malaysia", *WLUML,* Dossier 5/6, 1989, pp. 13-19.

12 See "Man sukut nakhvaham kard," *Kayan* (London), 6 January 1993; Naila Kabeer, "The Quest for National Identity: Women, Islam and the State of Bangladesh," in Deniz Kandiyoti, ed., *Women, Islam and the State,* Philadelphia 1991, pp. 115-43.

13 *Al-Jadid,* No.2, December 1995, pp. 16-17.

14 See *WLUML,* 27 October 1992; "Pakistani Crusader vs. the Mullahs," *New York Times,* 10 August 1992. See also Paula R. Newberg, "The Two Benazir Bhuttos", *New York Times,* 11 February 1995, p. 5.

15 See "Turkish Women and the Welfare Party," *Middle East Report (MERIP),* Spring 1996, pp. 28-32.

16 See Nukhet Sirman, "Feminism in Turkey: a Short History," in *New Perspectives on Turkey,* vol. 3, No. 1, Fall 1989, pp. 1-34.

17 See Rosemary Sayigh, "Palestinian Women: Triple Burden, Single Struggle,"

Palestine Profile of an Occupation, London 1989; Islah Jad, "From the Salons to the Popular Committees, Palestinian Women, 1919-1989," in Jamal R. Nassar and Roger Heacock, eds., *Intifada: Palestine at the Crossroads,* New York 1990; Rita Giacaman and Penny Johnson, "Palestinian Women: Building Barricades and Breaking Barriers," in Zachary Lochman and Joel Beinin, eds., *Intifada: The Palestinian Uprising Against Israeli Occupation,* Boston 1989, pp. 155-69.

18 This point was eloquently discussed by a long time Palestinian activist Rabab Abduladi at the 1993 meeting of the Association for Middle East Women's Studies at Triangle Park, North Carolina.

19 For example, see "For Another Kind of Morocco: An Interview with Abraham Serfaty," *MERIP,* November-December 1992, pp. 24-27.

20 Moghadam, *Modernizing Women;* Saad Eddin Ibrahim, "Anatomy of Egypt's Militant Islamic Groups," *International Journal of Middle East Studies,* vol. 12, No. 4, 1980, pp. 423-53.

21 See Moghadam, *Modernizing Women,* p. 137.

22 Fatima Mernissi, *Beyond the Veil: Male-Female Dynamics in Modern Muslim Society,* Bloomington 1987, second edition.

23 Fatima Mernissi, *Doing Daily Battle: Interview with Moroccan Women,* New Jersey, 1989, pp. 3-4.

24 Mernissi, *Beyond the Veil,* pp. VII-XV.

25 Mernissi, *Islam and Democracy: Fear of the Modern World,* Workingham 1992, p. 165.

26 Sondra Hale, "Gender, Religious Identity, and Political Mobilization in Sudan", in V. Moghadam, ed., *Identity Politics and Women,* Boulder 1994, pp. 145-66.

27 "Women Regain a Kind of Security in Islam's Embrace," *New York Times,* 27 December 1992.

28 Kabeer, "The Quest for National Identity," pp. 134-5.

29 Andrea B. Rugh, "Reshaping Personal Relations in Egypt," in *The Fundamentalist Project: Fundamentalism and Society,* p. 164.

30 Maxime Rodinson, *Islam and Capitalism,* Austin 1978 (first edition, 1966).

31 See Sohrab Behdad, "A Disputed Utopia; Islamic Economics in Revolutionary Iran," *Comparative Studies in Society and History,* vol. 36, No. 4, October 1994, p. 810.

32 Moghadam, *Modernizing Women,* p. 167.

33 See Julie J. Ingersoll, "Which Tradition, Which Values? 'Traditional Family Values' in American Protestant Fundamentalism," *Contention,* vol. 4, No. 2, Winter 1995, p. 93. See also Helen Hardacre, "The Impact of

Fundamentalisms on Women, the Family, and Interpersonal Relations," *The Fundamentalism Project,* pp. 129-50.

34 Hardacre, "The Impact of Fundamentalisms on Women," p. 142.

35 The two essays by Hegland and Friedl appear in N. Keddie and B. Baron, eds., *Women in Middle Eastern History,* New Haven 1991. Others will be cited below.

36 D. Kandiyoti, "Bargaining with Patriarchy," *Gender and Society,* vol. 2, No. 3, 1988, pp. 274-90.

37 Aihwa Ong, "State Versus Islam: Malay Families, Women's Bodies, and the Body Politic in Malaysia," *American Ethnologist,* vol. 17, No. 2, May 1990, p. 269. For a recent reaction by progressive Malay women such as Sisters in Islam, see "Blame Men, Not Allah, Islamic Feminists Say," *New York Times,* 10 October 1996, p. 4.

38 Cynthia Enloe, *Making Feminist Sense of International Politics: Bananas, Beaches, and Bases,* Berkeley 1989, p. 55.

39 See Lama Abu Odeh, "Post-Colonial Feminism and the Veil: Thinking the Difference," *Feminist Review,* No. 43, Spring 1993, pp. 26-37.

40 Bouthaina Shaaban, *Both Right and Left Handed,* Bloomington 1991, p. 85.

41 Leila Ahmed, *Women and Gender in Islam: Historical Roots of a Modern Debate,* New Haven 1992, pp. 222-3.

42 Ibid., p. 225.

43 Lila Abu-Lughod, "Movie Stars and Islamic Moralism in Egypt," *Social Text,* No. 42, Spring 1995, p. 53.

44 See Arlene Elowe MacLeod, "Hegemonic Relations and Gender Resistance: The New Veiling as Accommodating Protest in Cairo," *Signs,* vol. 17, No. 3, Spring 1992, p. 546.

45 Ibid., p. 555.

46 Surush's writings appear regularly in the *Kiyan.* Judith Miller, who has visited the offices of *Kiyan* in Tehran and has interviewed scores of other progressive writers and clerics, writes that "despite what Iran has endured, it remains a vibrant society—far more than it ever was under the Shah and more so than any of its Arab neighbors." She suggests that an "Islamic reformation" may very well be part of Iran's future. See her *God Has Ninety-Nine Names,* New York 1996, p. 431. Arguments similar to those of Surush have also been raised by the Syrian writer Muhammad Shahrur who has been greeted enthusiastically by many secular Arab intellectuals. See Dale F. Eickelman, "Islamic Liberalism Strikes Back," *MESA Bulletin,* vol. 27, no. 2, December 1993, pp. 163-7.

47 I should point out that in recent months the Western media has paid much attention to the army of mujahedeen that sits on the border between Iran and Iraq, and includes many women in its officer corps. Some Western analysts have suggested that the mujahedeen represent a progressive and feminist alternative to the government of the Islamic Republic. See for instance Barry Iverson, "Women's Army Takes on the Mullahs," *The Sunday Times,* April 27, 1997, p. 19. The mujahedeen are, however, highly discredited in the eyes of many Iranians—both inside and outside the country—because of their authoritarian and indeed cultist Islamist beliefs, and because they are fully maintained by Iran's arch enemy, Saddam Hussein.

48 For two recent examples see a selection of Jaggar's *Feminist Politics and Human Nature in Zanan,* no. 26, Mehr/Aban 1374 / Fall 1995, pp. 48-51; and "What is Feminism," in *Zanan,* no. 28, Farvardin 1375 Spring / 1996, pp. 2-3.

49 For a discussion of the shariat and sources of the Islamic law under Shi'ism see Arthur Goldschmidt, *A Concise History of the Middle East,* Boulder 1983, pp. 93-9; and Said Amir Arjomand, *The Shadow of God and the Hidden Imam,* Chicago 1984.

50 For further discussion on this issue, see Ahmed, *Women and Gender in Islam,* pp. 41-78.

51 Goldschmidt, *A Concise History of the Middle East,* p. 95.

52 *The Holy Qur'an,* Colombus 1991, p. 979. Here and below, I have slightly modified the English translation for greater clarity.

53 Ibid., pp. 199-200.

54 See "Man, Partner or Boss ?" in *Zanan,* No.2, 1992, p. 27.

55 *The Holy Qur'an,* p. 808.

56 See "Women as Judges," *Zanan,* no. 4, Ordibehesht 1371 / Spring 1992, pp. 20-26, and *Zanan,* no. 5, Khordad & Tir 1371 / Summer 1992, pp. 20-26. See also the essays by Mehrangiz Kar.

57 For a recent interview with Hashemi, see *Zanan,* no. 28, Favardin 1375 / Spring 1996.

58 See the interview with Mahnaz Afkhami in the Summer/Fall 1996 issue of the Lebanese journal *al-Raida,* pp. 13-18.

59 The most recent publication of Sisterhood Is Global is a handbook *Claiming Our Rights: A Manual For Women's Human Rights Education in Muslim Societies,* Bethseda, Maryland 1996.

"A Disease Masquerading as a Cure": Women and Fundamentalism in Algeria

Karima Bennoune

An interview with Mahfoud Bennoune

My father, Mahfoud Bennoune, was raised in a devoutly religious Sunni Muslim peasant family in the mountains of northeastern Algeria. Serving in the Algerian resistance to French colonial rule, he spent over four years as a prisoner of war during the war of independence that raged from 1954–1962. In his most recent book, *Les Algériennes: Victimes d'Une Société Néopatriarcale,* he writes of how deprivation of freedom in French prison reminded him of the condition of many Algerian women and deepened his concern with women's issues.[1] After independence he went abroad to study, obtaining a Ph.D. in anthropology from the University of Michigan. He retired from the University of Algiers in 1994 but has continued to fight fundamentalism, armed only with his pen and his voice.

The lack of attention paid to Algeria in the United States is demoralizing for secular intellectuals like my father. Muslim fundamentalist crimes against Westerners are of interest, but not those much more numerous offenses against their own people. At least one hundred Algerians were killed in June 2002 alone and as many as one thousand since the beginning of the year. A June 28 attack by fundamentalists on a bus in a suburb of the capital, Algiers, killing thirteen, generated virtually no comment in the U.S. media. While little space is devoted to recounting these events, less still is given to attempts at making any sense of them. This excerpt from a much longer interview is a small effort to rectify this situation by recording the views of one academic who, like many in the Muslim world, has risked his life to offer a humanist perspective.

I. Algeria

Karima: What does the term "fundamentalism" mean to you? There are other terms that are used sometimes like "Islamism" or "religious extremism." What terminology is used in Algeria to refer to these phenomena?

Mahfoud: In Algeria the term in Arabic used most often is either *"Al Islamiyoun"* which is "the Islamists," or *"Al Usuliyoun"* which is "the fundamentalists." Some nonfundamentalist Muslims object to the term "Islamism" because they see it as derogatory of Islam. Prior to the emergence of the Islamic Salvation Front (FIS), they called them "the brothers," which actually is derived from the Muslim Brotherhood of Egypt. What is really meant by "fundamentalism" in this context is the use of Islam to promote a political project that is highly retrograde and extremely conservative. It is anti-woman, anti-rationalism, anti-science. In Algeria, the fundamentalists think the only period of Muslim history that is truly Islamic is that during the time of Muhammad and the rule of the first four caliphs. Then Muslims became un-Islamic.

K: The specific organizational roots of the contemporary Algerian fundamentalist movements really date to the 1970s. Why?

M: The early fundamentalists in Algeria came from middle-class backgrounds. Their movement took the form of reaction to land reform and the radicalization of the socialist workers management in industry. Specifically, the state decided to promote land reform, limiting the Algerian landlords' property to twenty hectares. The rest would be bought by the state and distributed to peasants who were organized in cooperatives. The leader of the fundamentalists at the time, Soltani, issued a *fatwah* declaring land reform un-Islamic. According to him, prayer performed on nationalized land would not be accepted by God. They joined an alliance with petty intellectuals and landlords who financed them.

Internationally, at the end of the seventies you had the invasion of Afghanistan by the Soviet Union, the emergence of the New Right in the West, the advent of post-modernism and the rejection of the Enlightenment, and especially the collapse of socialism as an alternative. Within this framework, after the death of Boumedienne,[2] the fundamentalists thrived and widened their base.

K: As we watch the crystallization of fundamentalist movements from the seventies to the nineties, what's happening in Algerian society in terms of the struggle over the status of women?

M: The question after independence was how to put an end to polygamy and how to resolve the problem of inheritance within the framework of the new Algerian state, whose constitution guaranteed women equality with men. Under colonial rule, marriage, divorce, and inheritance were regulated by the shariah and decided by special religious courts. The judges of these courts were trained by the French within the Islamic tradition and appointed by the French state. So we did not enjoy the separation of church and state because the French secular state did not apply the same rules to the Jews, the Protestants, and the Catholics as to the Muslims. After independence, the clerics and religious conservatives decided they would not agree to resolve these issues until the political tide turned against women. Legal reform in the political climate of the sixties and early seventies would have been favorable to women. But the clerics blocked reform until 1984. Meanwhile, women who had participated in the independence movement were pushed back home and their representation in politics fell. In 1962, the first Algerian constituent assembly had 10 women deputies out of 196 deputies, which gave it one of the highest proportions of women in a national assembly in the world, higher than in France or Sweden at the time. But this shrank to 2 deputies in the second national assembly, then to none between 1965 and 1982.

K: What happened in Algeria in the 1980s that made the fundamentalists' offer of an "Islamic solution" seem attractive to a broader sector of the population?

M: One factor is the authoritarianism of the Boumedienne era, and the corruption that existed under Boumedienne, though not to the degree as under Chadli's regime.[3] Then in the eighties, Chadli annulled the progressive reforms that were carried out during the sixties and seventies. The private sector was promoted and the public sector was dismantled completely. The regime even split the sixty-six public corporations, which carried out the development of the country in the sixties and seventies, into 472 minicorporations. This came during the period when, around the world, big mergers were taking place giving rise to huge multinational companies. The atomization of these public corporations, coupled with the cancellation of progressive social programs, led to disenchantment with socialism, but also to disenchantment with capitalism. And, therefore, it sort of became inevitable that the only way out seemed to be what they call "the Islamic solution."

K: What was happening to Algerian women while this "reform" was occurring in the 1980s?

M: 1984 saw the adoption by the national assembly of the family code. This code implemented *shariah* law in its most reactionary form concerning the marital status of women, putting women at the mercy of their husbands. It was pushed by the government, in alliance with the religious right and the fundamentalists. From a social and political point of view, government corruption and increasing political despotism pushed many young people toward the fundamentalists. They were suggesting that the only way out is to go back to our values and to the greatness of a past which is mythical, an illusion. They started attracting some middle-class, blocked youth, but especially those young people who had no educational or vocational training prospects, no job prospects and no housing prospects. Those are the ones that furnished the future shock troops of the fundamentalists. However, the leadership was provided by middle classes who professionally were blocked too. They were financed by the landlords and some conservative merchants.

K: October 1988 seems to have been a significant turning point.

M: On October 5, 1988, young people from popular quarters began demonstrating and attacking luxurious shops, and, especially the Riyad al Feth shopping mall, which was seen as representing consumerism within the context of an underdeveloped country. It became a demonstration against the symbols of the state and lasted for five days.

K: How did the state react and how did the fundamentalists step in and capitalize on that response?

M: Hundreds of Algerians were rounded up by the military and police, and they were atrociously tortured. The president declared a state of siege and ordered the army to shoot at random at young people demonstrating. The estimates of the number killed varied from five hundred to seven hundred. The fundamentalists at that point had been on the decline because the Bouali terrorist movement, which started attacking the state and the gendarmerie back in the eighties, was completely decapitated, and its leaders were put in jail. So the fundamentalists at that time were quite discouraged. But in the wake of the unrest, Chadli brought them into the picture. What we have to stress here is that the slogans the young people used in October '88 were asking primarily for good education and jobs. What they obtained afterwards was fundamentalism and the IMF-sponsored reduction of social spending and the loss of various jobs, which is a paradox.

K: In the climate of despair that followed, fundamentalism absolutely mushroomed within the country. How do we then get from the October uprising to the late eighties period and ultimately the triumph in the 1990 municipal elections of the Islamic Salvation Front?

M: By October 10, 1988, before the end of rioting, Chadli called in the leaders of the Islamists, and he struck a deal with them. Within the FLN itself various groups sympathized with the fundamentalists. But also Chadli and the ruling group in the military knew that the only way they could cope with the Islamists was by out-Islamizing them, co-opting their slogans and their program and implementing it themselves. When you try to out-Islamize the Islamists, you open the door for them. This led to legalization of the fundamentalists, especially the FIS, in violation of Algeria's constitution which prohibited parties based on religion. (The promotion of political pluralism in Algeria included support of the parties with state funds.) The fundamentalists were also helped by the unpopularity of the Chadli government, due in particular to his wild liberalization, and the FLN.[4] People thought then that the only way out was the Islamists. Therefore their numbers inflated very rapidly. Instead of the democratic forces demanding that Chadli, who was responsible for the bankruptcy of the state, resign, they accepted him as the father of Algerian pluralism and democracy. The fundamentalists, knowing his unpopularity, established their political party. But they never stopped denouncing democracy as blasphemy and insisting that there is no pluralism in Islam.

K: That reminds me of the Algerian joke that fundamentalist democracy means one man, one vote, one time. But, seriously, I remember visiting Algeria in this period and for the first time seeing a woman in a *chador*. What happened to women in the late eighties and early nineties as fundamentalism gained in strength?

M: Women were subjected to intimidation and verbal aggression, and sometimes actual violence, to pressure them to stay where they "belong," at home, and to veil. Publications, books, articles, newspapers, radio programs, and sermons in mosques were all attacking the emancipation of women. The fundamentalists wanted to kill the whole idea, rejecting its proponents as "the daughters of colonialism" or "the daughters of General Massu," a French general responsible for much brutality during the war. They wanted to discredit the women's movement completely.

K: One of the stories I remember from this period, when the FIS was

legally allowed to operate, was about fundamentalist teachers asking children in their classes to report whether or not their mothers and sisters veil
or wear bathing suits to the beach.

M: There were many fundamentalist teachers. They often tried to pressure children to denounce their parents—whether they drink alcohol,
whether their mothers go out without the veil, whether they listen to
Western music. The school system played a major role because of its control
by the religious right. The official mosques also played a tremendous role in
the promotion of this Islamic agenda and the attack on women's rights.

K: What did FIS governance in the municipalities look like between 1990
and 1992?

M: The first thing the FIS did was to change the names of the city halls
to Islamic municipalities. They imposed gender segregation; women had to
enter from one side and men from the other. They banned concerts and
mixed swimming on beaches. They used the city halls and provincial councils as an infrastructure to promote their own agenda.

K: There is a contradiction here, it seems to me. The fundamentalists are
an essentially anti-modernist movement in substantive ideology. On the other
hand, they engaged in many projects that may be described as modernist—
organizing a political party, participating in elections and governing municipalities. How ought we to understand this contradiction?

M: It is very simple. They accept technology but reject science because
science is premised on doubts. For them, technology is a means to an end
and does not raise philosophical questions regarding the origin and evolution of the world. Biology and anthropology were denounced to me by
Abassi Medani[5] himself, as alien, as a catastrophe for Muslims. They went as
far as rejecting psychoanalysis as a Jewish plot by Freud, socialism also
because Marx was Jewish and sociology because its founder Durkheim was
a Jew. At the university where I used to teach, the fundamentalists wrote on
the wall that these three figures were Jews, and that psychoanalysis,
socialism, and sociology have to be banned as such because they are a plot
against Islam. The fundamentalists are organized in the modern fashion with
parties but their central committee is called *majlis al shura*, which is a religious council. In Islam there is a notion of *alem* or theologian, which is a
status acquired through learning and work in the community. The fundamentalists said we do not need these theologians. Any Muslim who can read
the Qur'an in Arabic can understand it by himself. This allowed them to

interpret the Qur'an as they wished. They said there are four loyalties they would have to break: loyalty of the Algerian to the past, because this past is un-Islamic; loyalty to the nation-state for the same reason; and loyalty to the family since the family did not teach Islamic fundamental values to the child. And you have to break with all your friends who are not Islamic enough. Even though confession is not an Islamic practice, a militant must also confess to an emir, a political leader within his cell, who would help him resolve his own inner contradictions. This operated as a sort of brainwashing, which has nothing to do with Islam, and created what I call a *homo Islamicus fundamentalis* or extremist militant. You are dealing with a sect that deemed all the rulers apostates. They denounced all forms of the nation-state, its secular laws, and its rulers which they call *pharaohs*, who rule without God's law. For them, the modern state and democracy is equated with blasphemy and secularism, and leads to the denunciation of Islam.

K: The Western media always implies the fundamentalists took up arms only after the interruption of the electoral process by the military in January 1992 [when the Islamists were poised to win]. Could you talk about the phenomenon of fundamentalist violence prior to the cancellation of the second round of legislative assembly elections?

M: For the fundamentalists it was very clear that the Algerian state became un-Islamic and had to be Islamized, that Algerians became almost impious and have to be reconverted to Islam. There are two ways they could be reconverted, either by persuasion, if possible, if not through *jihad,* by force. This goes back even to Sayyid Qutb[6] who declared that *jihad* is allowed against the nation-state to establish an Islamic state. In order to prepare Mujahideen, throughout the eighties when they were underground, the Algerian fundamentalists organized sports and cultural associations and summer camps. They were actually training Algerians in guerrilla warfare. Therefore, they were already psychologically and militarily prepared to carry out their struggle against the state. And by the early eighties, the various fundamentalist movements in Algeria were recruiting Algerians, and sending them to Afghanistan to fight on the side of the Mujahideen against the Soviet Union. They were recruited by the fundamentalist parties and associations which were underground at the time, financed by Saudi Arabia and helped by France and the United States. That is where the terrorists of the early nineties came from. Between six hundred to nine hundred Algerians who had some combat experience in Afghanistan fighting the Soviet Union came back to Algeria after the withdrawal of the Soviet Army. They provided the nucleuses of the future terrorist groups of the FIS in the countryside after the cancellation of the elections.

K: Are there specific incidences of violence by the fundamentalists, prior to the cancellation of the elections, which you can mention?

M: There were women who were killed and some students.[7] There was also the attack by a group of fundamentalists in El Oued on November 25, 1991, one month before the legislative elections, that ended with the massacre of eleven soldiers. This was carried out by Tayyeb al Afghani, an Algerian who had been in Afghanistan. He was actually the head of the city council of El Oued as an elected FIS official. But what is criminal is that Chadli's government did not reveal the El Oued attack to the population before the elections.

K: It seems to me that the real tragedy of Algeria in the last few decades is the lack of good alternatives. What people essentially had before them in the elections was a choice between Scylla and Charybdis, between two monsters. What choice did Algerians really have?

M: The regime of Chadli was pro-West, antisocialist, profundamentalist. It used religion and the fundamentalists to undermine the left. Chadli also created a state which was completely paralyzed by corruption, corruption which was denounced by the fundamentalists. Therefore these corrupt rulers of the state on the one hand and the fundamentalists on the other took Algerian society and squeezed it between them and to this day, this is the Algerian tragedy. As an old woman said, between the thieves, that is the corrupt state officials and the army officers, on the one hand, and the killers, that is the fundamentalists, on the other, if I have to choose between them, I would rather coexist with the thieves. At least they will not kill me, and they will not tell me how to dress, what to do and what not to do. It is not a good choice to have to make.

The state originally promoted gender mixing in schools, and its policy was based on the idea that through the education of women, their status would improve. But, at the same time, within that state there were social forces that worked to prevent the kind of secular, rationalist education that would free Algerians from religious prejudices. So, there are some tremendous contradictions. But, for the fundamentalists, the question of women is very simple. They attributed all the evils of Algerian society to the debauchery of women whom they saw as the prostitutes of the modern postcolonial situation.

K: With hindsight, how do you view the cancellation of the second round of national assembly elections in January 1992?

M: Most of the associations, the foundations and some of the non-Islamic parties agreed that elections had to be cancelled, because otherwise the dictatorship of the FIS would be much worse than that of the mullahs of Iran. During the campaign, during the elections, the fundamentalists used a slogan: "'No charter, no constitution,' said God, said the Prophet." The day after the first round of elections a FIS representative said Algerians have to get ready to wear different clothes and change their lifestyles. In addition, there was evidence the fundamentalists tampered with the elections in the city halls they controlled. One million voters never received their voting cards and therefore could not vote. They knew that certain categories of society would not vote for them and therefore did not send those cards from the city halls. Taking all this into consideration, it seemed obvious that the elections had to be cancelled. Everybody believed, at least among politicized women and men, and in the trade unions, that they had to stop them or otherwise we would have a civil war.

K: Even understanding the nature of the fundamentalist movements in Algeria, the Islamic Salvation Front in particular, as an international lawyer I remain uncomfortable with the idea that a military can put an end to an electoral process. As you yourself said, one of the reasons not to go to the second round of elections was to avoid a civil war. But since 1992 widespread violence between the armed fundamentalist groups and the forces of the state has claimed the lives of an unknown number of Algerians—perhaps between fifty and one-hundred thousand.

M: Actually the cancellation of elections helped the FIS a great deal to influence international public opinion. But you have to put the cancellation in context, which is never done. The trade unions, some of the women's groups, some of the NGOs were calling for it. Muhammad Boudiaf, who founded the FLN back in 1954 and was in exile in Morocco, was brought in as provisional head of state. He was given the authority to prevent civil war and to identify and implement a policy to resolve the crisis. He called upon the FIS, the FLN, and other parties to join him in this. Boudiaf realized that without addressing the causes that generated this crisis there was no way out. So he decided to: 1) cleanse the state of corruption, 2) put the military out of politics and 3) organize elections within a pluralist framework. With his dynamism and integrity, he became so popular, especially among women, youth, and even with some former fundamentalist supporters, that he was assassinated in June 1992. He was shot on live television by one of his guards, an army officer of the secret service. After his assassination, his policies were abandoned by the generals, and the present crisis of terrorism and counterterrorism escalated. If we do not address the causes underlying the crisis we cannot get out of the crisis, but since we did not, we are stuck. This is the rub.

K: Can you talk a bit about what has happened, particularly to women, in the decade of despair in Algeria: 1992 to 2002?

M: There were many hideous crimes committed against women, justified by fundamentalist ideology. For example, the fundamentalist armed groups went back to an old Qur'anic verse which allowed Muslims to have what they call *zaouj al muta* or temporary marriage. So, with this justification, many hundreds of women were taken hostage by the fundamentalist armed groups, especially in the countryside, and subjected to a kind of slavery. They had to cook and wash and were sexually abused. After they are impregnated, they are often killed in an atrocious way. Other women who defied the fundamentalists were also killed. In one instance a high school student who was abducted in Boufarik in 1994 was used as a terrible example to try to stop students from going to schools. The fundamentalists wanted to impose a general strike against schools. They cut her throat and hanged her in a tree in front of the high school of Boufarik. There are lists of hundreds of women who were murdered. Within my own family, I had a cousin who was killed, shot many times, in front of his wife and eight children. His youngest daughter, five years old, became mentally ill because she was covered with his blood.

K: Why do you think there has been this doubt in the international community at times about whom is doing the killing in Algeria, when within the country there seems to be much more clarity?

M: There are multiple factors, including the clumsy and ignorant way, grotesque way, the Algerian government dealt with international public opinion, such as the barring of foreign journalists from coming into the country. But more than that the government did not present and implement a strategy capable of redressing the economic and social issues, eliminating corruption and defeating the fundamentalists in an efficient, legal, transparent way. This led to suspicion of the military and the Algerian generals. There *were* gross violations of human rights by the state, without any doubt.

But not on the same level as the killings, the assassinations, rapes, burnings, the suffering that was inflicted by the fundamentalists, all in total contradiction with the laws of war in Islam.[8] How could somebody come to you and declare a group of people, Muslims, as un-Islamic and go as far as justifying the killing of children, old people, the putting of bombs in airports and streets?

II. Algeria and Beyond

K: Algeria's terrible decade coincided with the heyday of globalization. What is your view of globalization's relationship to fundamentalism?

M: Fundamentalism is a by-product of globalism and the spread of capitalism and exclusion, because these trends create despair, and despair pushes people to become victims of groups who sell them some crazy ideas as solutions. "Islamic solution" is nonsensical, as is the global market fundamentalist solution, which is impoverishing and excluding people. And the latter actually creates the conditions for the growth of more fundamentalism of a political nature. On the one hand, you have the global markets, on the other hand, fundamentalism, conservatism, or fascism. Just like in Algeria, democracy then is caught in the middle of these forces.

K: In light of all this, where do we start to look for solutions? How can the situation of women in Algeria today be improved facing these forces of religious fundamentalism on the one hand and market fundamentalism on the other?

M: I am very hopeful as far as this is concerned. In Algeria, women have resisted fundamentalism despite torture, killing, intimidation. They never gave up trying to work, study, and go out, and they succeeded. Today they are the majority of our students. Over fifty percent of students in the universities are women, which is remarkable. Sixty percent of the successful baccalaureate candidates are women. In the high school population, women represent fifty-six to sixty percent. In the labor force, there are more and more women. But these successes are thwarted by the fact that Algeria today has the highest rate of unemployment in the world. Just over forty-five percent of its labor force is unemployed and the proportion of the unemployed among women is seventy-six percent. Therefore, women are faced with a situation where wages have declined, jobs do not exist, and when they are employed by the private sector, they are exploited and discriminated against. This is the future struggle. I just learned that they have created a new ministry of women's affairs in Algeria. There are also four women in the new cabinet, named in June. But I do not expect anything from the current government, which is backed by the military, because they have so far avoided addressing the causes underlying the Algerian impasse. Therefore, the struggle goes on, more suffering will go on, but the women of Algeria today are determined to keep on struggling to improve their conditions.

K: How did Algerians react to the atrocities of September 11?

M: Well, Algerians knew more than anybody else, except the Afghans, about the hideous crimes of fundamentalist terrorism. They thought that while Algerians were victims of this form of terrorism, the Western powers, including the United States, were working with these fundamentalists and accepting their representatives in their own capitals, including Washington. In Algeria, every year since 1993, we had the equivalent of the victims of September 11 in the country, that is, victims of the fundamentalists. So, the Algerians deplore deeply what happened in the World Trade Center and the indiscriminate and hideous nature of that crime. At the same time, some add a comment, saying that maybe this will teach the U.S. officials a lesson that they should not play with a snake. It may turn around and bite you. There is also another lesson they want the U.S. officials to take into account. You cannot indiscriminately use force and bomb anywhere else in the world. You actually obtain the same results as terrorism, but from a plane high up where you do not see the impact. The Western powers want to believe that terrorism has no causes, but is like evil come from the devil. It has no historical roots, and therefore you have to isolate it and kill it, like you kill the devil. Terrorism, whether al Qaida, or bin Laden or the GIA[9] in Algeria has historical roots, has causes.

K: There are some who might try to co-opt your criticism of Muslim fundamentalists as a justification for their own negative views of Islam as a whole, their Islamophobia.

M: This thesis is based on ignorance. To reduce the Muslim religion which produced fantastic spiritual traditions, poetry, Sufism, and mystical philosophy and has a plural nature—there are all sorts of Islams—and to confuse it with fundamentalism, is a huge mistake. No one can condone Islamophobia. Fundamentalism is a universal phenomenon. It is not only the Muslims who have fundamentalism, but also the Christians, Jews, Hindus. All these fundamentalisms and all of this fanaticism have to be opposed. To confuse Christianity with Christian fundamentalists, Judaism with Zionists or the Jewish fundamentalists, or Hinduism with the Hindu fundamentalists or Islam or Islams with fundamentalism is ridiculous. Any religion in the world, especially the major religions of the world, can be used to promote the liberation of human beings, freeing them from alienation and oppression. But at the same time every religious tradition can be used to foster and promote highly alienating, oppressive policies.

K: What do you have to say to those progressives in the West who do not want to criticize the Muslim fundamentalists because of this Islamophobia, or who simply do not understand what a threat these forces pose to their own societies but instead read them as representatives of the downtrodden?

M: It is true that fundamentalism is a by-product of globalization. It is an attempted cure. It is considered by the fundamentalists as a cure, but it is a disease masquerading as a cure. A disease cannot be used to cure societies. Fundamentalism cannot promote internationalism, brotherhood, toleration, understanding, or cooperation between peoples and cultures. Fundamentalism promotes narrow-mindedness, narrow identities, exclusions, frustrations, and hate. Its essence is based on the premise that some people are more religious than others, are superior to others and that you have to kill other people because of their beliefs. You cannot really think that people responsible for this kind of behavior can defend the oppressed and promote human freedom. They cannot. What we must understand is that religions have to be respected. But these religions have to tolerate and coexist with other people who have other beliefs and other values. The fundamentalists do not. Human rights, women's rights, freedom, equality, justice, all those things are very universal. No value whatsoever is relative and can be an excuse for discriminating or committing injustice.

K: Could you talk about the ways in which religious fundamentalism in the West impacts Muslim fundamentalism? President Bush recently said, in response to the Pledge of Allegiance controversy, that "this [the U.S.] is a nation that values its relationship with the Almighty." How does this kind of discourse interact with fundamentalism in the Muslim world?

M: A French philosopher, Régis Debray, called it recently "the return of God." Everybody is speaking about God and this God is almighty, and he knows everything and justifies everything. What is happening is very dangerous. Because of my own experience with the fundamentalists I believe the separation of the church and state represents major progress in human history. What would have happened if the United States Constitution did not guarantee freedom of religion to all the sects and remove religion from the running of the state? If they allowed a major religion or sect to interfere with the running of the state, they would have ended up by provoking permanent civil war. The separation of church and state is the only way you can promote tolerance, coexistence and democracy within a state. I am more convinced than ever now that secularism is the only way out.

K: Recently there has been a lot of organizing among Muslim conservatives and Christian conservatives to block a progressive human rights agenda in international conferences. How do you understand the relationships between the Muslim fundamentalists and Christian fundamentalists?

M: There is actually a dialectical relation between the various religious fundamentalisms around the world. You take the Muslim fundamentalism, and Jewish fundamentalism which is expressed in the form of Zionism. They actually feed each other with hatred. You take Hindu fundamentalism and Islamic fundamentalism in the subcontinent of India and exactly the same thing is happening there. You take the reaction of the Christian right in the United States and their denigration of Islam. So, within this framework then the denunciation of each other's beliefs fosters hate and more fundamentalism. Also, the fundamentalists do share a lot of values, including prejudice against science. Once I had a problem with my fundamentalist students in Algiers who did not want me to teach evolution. I tried to work out a solution with them, pointing out ways the Christians and Jews came to terms with evolution. They told me they do not want to read the literature of the infidels. The next day they brought me the literature of the Christian right in America supporting a ban on the teaching of evolution or to put creationism on the same footing. They gave it to me in Algiers, translated into Arabic, and wanted to convince me that biology and evolution are wrong because this is what even the Americans say. This fortified the Algerian Muslim fundamentalist belief in the denunciation of science.

K: How popular are your secular humanist views in Algeria and in the Muslim world?

M: Secularists existed within the nationalist movements of the past and they exist today. After the fundamentalist banning of science and reason in the middle ages, critical thinking was frowned on. But the free thinkers have been trying very hard, and there are a lot of writings, a lot of discussion within the Arab world. To understand, you have to look at what has been said and done inside the Muslim world. But who gives a damn about what the Arab Muslim press says, about what Arab intellectuals say?

K: Can you talk a bit about what difficulties and dangers you have faced personally for speaking out against fundamentalism and fundamentalist oppression of women?

M: I have difficulties talking about myself in a struggle which actually claimed the lives of thousands of people, in which many intellectuals and colleagues were murdered, even had their throats cut in front of their children. But all I can tell you is that I decided to oppose the fundamentalists because I think they are the most dangerous force within Muslim societies. I have been denounced publicly, I have been condemned to death publicly, and they openly tried to "execute" me. Between 1993 and 1997 I did not know when I went out in the morning whether I would come back alive. But I was lucky. A week before they were to kill me, I went into hiding. They found their way to my apartment and left me a message inside: "Consider yourself dead."

III. Conclusions

K: As Tolstoy asked, "What then must we do?"

M: Well, it's a very difficult question actually. You cannot give recipes for what can be done. We have to keep trying to promote hope and provide analysis of the causes of all this and the relationships between these various factors and variables, internal and external. This helps the framing of a perspective that would allow people to act in hope and figure out how to struggle for a better future.

K: The Egyptian singer Mohammed Muneer in the lyrics of a song from Youssef Chahine's "Al Maseer," the greatest antifundamentalist musical of all time, attests that "Singing is still possible." It is a song of hope in the face of extremism. After all you have lived through, both in the war of independence and in the last decade, are you still hopeful?

M: I am very hopeful and my hope is vindicated by the fact that in Algeria they killed women to try to force them to veil, but women opposed them and the majority of women and girls in Algeria today are unveiled, and they are defiant as ever to the fundamentalists. The fundamentalists are condemned to disappear because they oppose not only hope but also love.

Notes

1 Mahfoud Bennoune, *Les Algériennes: Victimes d'Une Société Néopatriarcale* (Editions Marinoor, Algeria: 1999) 10.

2 Houari Boumedienne, independent Algeria's second president, was in office from 1965 to 1979.

3 Chadli Benjedid was President of Algeria from 1979-1992.

4 FLN stands for *Front de Libération National,* Algeria's independence movement, which became the single ruling party after 1962.

5 Abassi Medani was head of the Islamic Salvation Front.

6 A leader of the Muslim Brotherhood in Egypt, executed by Nasser in 1966.

7 For an account of fundamentalist violence against women prior to 1992, see Karima Bennoune, "S.O.S. Algeria: Women's Human Rights Under Siege" in Afkhami (ed.) *Faith and Freedom in the Muslim World* (1995) 193-7.

8 For information on these laws, see Karima Bennoune, "As-Salmu 'Alaykum?: Humanitarian Law in Islamic Jurisprudence," 15 *Michigan Journal of International Law* 605 (Winter 1994).

9 *Groupe Islamique Armé* or Armed Islamic Group, one of the fundamentalist armed entities reportedly responsible for many of Algeria's atrocities in the last decade. It was formed by Algerians returned from Afghanistan.

The Two Faces of Iran:
Women's Activism, the Reform Movement, and the Islamic Republic

Valentine M. Moghadam

In her 2002 documentary film *Our Times*, Rakhshan Bani-Etemad, one of Iran's leading women filmmakers, begins by showing young people engaged in an electoral campaign to promote the reelection of reformist President Mohammad Khatami in spring 2001. Energetic, attractive, and evidently from the affluent and Westernized northern suburbs of Tehran, these young women and men are seen setting up their headquarters, designing campaign posters, distributing leaflets, cracking jokes, discussing strategy, engaging in debates with citizens on the streets, and, in one case, getting roughed up by opponents. The young women supporters, who are in their teens and early twenties, are determined, opinionated, and actively involved in the campaign. The film then cuts to a scene at a large stadium filled with Khatami supporters who are cheering, clapping, hooting, and whistling—decidedly and deliberately non-Islamic expressions—as Khatami smiles and waves from the podium. The massive participation of women in the "Youth for Khatami" campaign and in the reform movement that backs Khatami is obvious as the camera scans the crowd. In this part of the documentary, we see the Iran of modernization, democratization, and women's participation.

In the second part of the film, Bani-Etemad moves on to interview the women who nominated themselves as presidential candidates only to be immediately disqualified on the basis of sex. In a voice-over, Bani-Etemad explains that several of these women were unavailable or unwilling to be filmed; one said she would think about it, only to inform the filmmaker later that her husband would not allow her to be interviewed. The irony is apparently lost on the would-be presidential candidate, but not on the filmmaker or the audience.

Bani-Etemad focuses on the story of Arezoo Bayat, a divorced twenty-eight-year-old woman who lives with her small daughter and mother in two rented rooms of a traditional house in the southern and low-income part of Tehran. Initially, the ever-smiling, attractive, and apparently optimistic Arezoo appears to be a symbol of the advancement of women in contemporary Iran. But gradually it becomes clear that Arezoo's reasons for self-nomination have to do with the almost unbearably sad experiences of her young life. She had wanted a platform to share these experiences and to find solutions for women with similar difficulties.

Arezoo has been married and divorced twice from drug-addicted men, one of whom is in prison; in order to provide for herself, her small daughter and her blind mother, she works long hours at two jobs, both of which offer only modest salaries; at her day job in a privately owned insurance company, her boss is an ogre; she is asked by her landlady to move out because the landlady's son and his new wife need to move into the rooms; she spends three days looking for alternative housing, only to find that almost everything is way beyond her means; she is also told that landlords are reluctant to rent to a young woman without a husband or father. We see her at home at night, rubbing her aching feet. On two occasions her sweet, smiling face dissolves into tears of frustration and anger, and she declares at one point that her life has been ruined by men, adding, "I hate men." The voice-over informs us that the film crew eventually pitched in to donate enough money to allow her to put a down payment on a small house, and we see Arezoo almost deliriously happy. But when she returns to work the next day, she discovers that her boss has fired her for having been absent the previous three days. The documentary ends with the camera focused on her bewildered face, as she contemplates an awful future without a job and a home.[1]

Bani-Etemad's documentary highlights the contradictions of the status of women in contemporary Iran and allows us to observe the difference that social class makes. To a certain extent, patriarchy is in crisis in Iran, due to the increased educational attainment of women, changes in family structure, the proliferation of a lively feminist press, and the emergence of what Shahla Sherkat, editor of the well-known magazine *Zanan,* calls an indigenous feminism (*feminizm-e boomi*). Among other things, *Zanan* launched what has come to be called "Islamic feminism," whereby believing women seek greater rights based on a progressive rereading of the Qur'an and early Islamic history.

These developments have been studied extensively by expatriate Iranian feminist scholars as well as analyzed in the many women's magazines, journals, books, and films produced in Iran.[2] But patriarchal attitudes and practices still govern the lives and life-options of low-income urban women—and of course, of rural women. Thus it might be said that there are two faces of Iran. There is the superstructure of active pro-Khatami women from various social classes; a growing proportion of women enrolled in universities; a prodigious women's press; a dramatic decline in fertility; and a large number of nongovernmental organizations staffed by women. Beneath that, however, lies a socio-economic base of profound inequalities, high unemployment, low salaries, inflation, economic stagnation, corruption, and serious social problems such as drug addiction, prostitution, divorce, runaway teens, a shortage of affordable housing, domestic violence, and an alarming brain drain.

Moreover, Iran is today almost as politically polarized as it was immediately before the 1978–1979 revolution. At the root of these problems lies the failure of the social experiment of Islamization, outdated and unpopular legal frameworks, the regime's inability to ensure economic growth and redistribution, and the stubborn monopolization of economic and political power by the conservatives.

Because of the structural nature of Iran's socio-economic problems and the now five-year-long standoff between reformers and conservatives, President Bush's controversial "axis of evil" speech had little impact. While nearly all Iranians were irritated by the silly term "axis of evil" (a term that similarly antagonized nearly all Koreans), most reformists could only agree with Bush's reference to the "unelected minority dominating an elected majority." Hardliners took advantage of public dismay over Bush's words to orchestrate anti-U.S. demonstrations, such as one that took place in mid-July 2002. But that month also saw clashes by riot police and Islamic militants against antigovernment demonstrators marking the third anniversary of the regime's crackdown on Iran's student reform movement, when gangs of *hezbollah* viciously attacked pro-Khatami reformist students in their dormitories at Tehran University on the night of July 9, 1999.[3] At the anniversary demonstration, about one thousand protestors chanted slogans and demanded freedom for political prisoners in the greatest unrest in the capital for nearly a year, resulting in several arrests.

Heightening the tension, one of Iran's most prominent ayatollahs,

Jalaleddin Taheri, issued a damning indictment of the conservative clerical establishment in a public letter of resignation and called militant Islamic groups—like those that attacked student demonstrators—"mad, ignorant fascists." A group of one-hundred-twenty-five proreform members of parliament signed a letter of support praising Ayatollah Taheri's statement, as did the largest reform party, the Participation Front. In what can only be defined as a wanton defiance of the public mood, the regime banned the Iran Freedom Movement (the forty-year-old liberal political party) and sentenced several of its members to jail terms.[4] As rumors spread of an imminent ban on reformist politics altogether, the summer of discontent appeared to be getting hotter.

Women, whose votes were crucial to the election of Khatami in 1997 and in 2001 as well as to the formation of a majority reformist parliament in 2000, are strongly behind the reform movement. Prominent women parliamentarians such as Soheila Jelodarzadeh, Jamileh Kadivar, Fatemeh Rakai, Fatemeh Haghighatjoo, and Elaheh Koulai are outspoken advocates for reform and for women's rights. They have called for reform of the patriarchal civil code, which permits fathers to marry off their daughters at the onset of puberty (or as young as nine) and allows husbands to choose the domicile and to veto their wives' choice of occupation. Under the code, it is much harder for women to seek a divorce than men, and fathers are automatically granted custody of their children. Feminists have tried (but failed) to raise the minimum age of marriage for girls to fifteen and are calling for greater child custody rights for divorced mothers.

Despite disappointment over Khatami's selection of an all-male cabinet in his second term, the women parliamentarians form part of the bloc of state feminists who support Khatami, the reform movement, and women's rights. Some, such as Jamileh Kadivar, are also known as Islamic feminists, which carries with it certain contradictions. For example, in an interview during a visit to Brussels in early July 2002, Iran's advisor to the president on women's issues, Zahra Shojaie, defended death by stoning for adulterers as permissible by the shariah "to defend the inviolability of the family."[5] When Iran's top state feminist defends not only capital punishment but also the stoning to death of adulterous women, it is clear that there are serious limits to Islamic feminism and to the government's reform agenda.

For several years, Iranian academics and activists have debated the prospects for progressive social change in Iran, including democratization and women's equality.[6] It is widely acknowledged that reformers and conservatives are at an impasse, though what the near future holds is unclear. Despite the serious social problems and evidence of deep social tensions, it appears that after the crackdown on the students in July 1999, Iranians have become risk-averse and unwilling to engage in the sort of large anti-regime street demonstrations that precipitated the 1979 revolution. To be sure, the Islamic Republic of Iran has evolved from the fundamentalist nightmare that it was in the 1980s to a more open environment in which the political and cultural status quo can be openly questioned by reformists and by women's rights advocates alike. But Iran is far from a democratic country with full popular sovereignty and freedoms of press, association, and opinion; and the Conservative forces, while enjoying only about 30 percent of electoral support, are in command of the police, military, and judiciary, which they use frequently and effectively for repressive ends. Thus the reform movement has faced serious constraints on its progress. Internal disagreements over aims, strategy, and tactics also have contributed to the reform movement's setbacks and disappointments and to the political stalemate. Such disputes have arisen between the left and right wings, the radical and moderate factions, and the secular and "religious intellectuals" of the reform movement. Hardly anyone counsels direct action and open confrontation, but some have suggested mass resignations from parliament, while others urge restraint and patience. As a result, at least for the time being, the advantage appears to lie with the conservatives.

Women's Rights Activists: Issues and Divisions

A similar predicament faces the women's movement. There is, first of all, disagreement among expatriate feminist scholars as to whether a fully fledged social movement of women has emerged, as distinct from a more inchoate premovement. More to the point, it is clear that although common ground exists among women's rights activists, they are also deeply divided politically and ideologically. The lines of demarcation are secular feminists versus Islamic feminists, socialist feminists versus liberal feminists, and pro-Khatami versus independent feminists. Secular feminists are opposed to the Islamic Constitution and to the shariah-based family law and penal code, and favor the complete separation of religion from the state and legal frameworks. The major representatives of this perspective are the lawyers Mehrangiz Kaar and Shirin Ebadi and the publishers

Noushin Ahmadi-Khorasani and Shahla Lahiji, along with the vast majority of expatriate Iranian feminist scholars and activists. In contrast, Islamic feminists are not opposed to religious-based laws but seek their reform by contesting traditional and patriarchal interpretations of the Qur'an in favor of alternative interpretations, emphasizing its emancipatory and egalitarian content. The prinicipal proponent of this perspective is the magazine *Zanan*, whose editor, Shahla Sherkat, is also open to publishing articles by or interviews with secular feminists. Whereas secular feminists are generally sympathetic to the more radical faction of the reform movement, the Islamic feminists tend to be associated with the right wing or the moderate faction of the movement, and with the religious intellectuals.

Among secular feminists at least two tendencies may be discerned. In their writings and conference presentations most secular feminists use the language of liberal democracy, emphasizing political freedoms for the country and personal freedoms for women. The socialist-feminists among them, who appear to be fewer in number, also insist on social rights, including enhanced labor rights for working-class women; and they view the neoliberal alternative to the clerical economic monopoly with skepticism. No matter what their political orientation, though, women's rights activists lack the overt forms of collective action such as independent organizations and public protests that have constituted women's movements in the past, whether in Iran (e.g., 1979) or elsewhere.

Still, women's rights advocates have discussed, debated, and exchanged ideas about women's rights and the needed legal reforms through the media, especially in the pages of the women's press. Such well-known Islamic feminists as the publishers Shahla Sherkat, Mahboubeh Abbas-Gholizadeh (editor of the women's studies journal *Farzaneh*), former member of parliament Faezeh Hashemi, Azzam Taleghani (a former member of parliament who tried to run for president in 1997), and local councilor Marzieh Mortazi, along with secular feminists in Iran (e.g., Ebadi, Kaar, Lahiji and Ahmadi-Khorasani) and expatriate academics such as Nayereh Tohidi, Ziba Mir-Hosseini, and Farideh Farhi have converged and collaborated around issues such as the modernization of family law, the need for more political participation by women, support for President Khatami, integration of women's concerns into the reform movement, and ways of tackling social problems.

And yet the divergences are pronounced and some ill-feelings have emerged. The issue of laicization is one point of contention. Also divisive has been the controversy surrounding a conference on Iranian politics in Berlin in April 2000. At the conference, in which many major reformists and feminists participated, Kaar and Lahiji criticized the application of Islamic law in Iran. Later, they were prosecuted and jailed for their comments.[7] (Five men, including the well-known reformist journalist Akbar Ganji, also received jail sentences during the January 2001 trials.) Secular feminists were dismayed when prominent Islamic feminists did not come to the defense of the accused. Shahla Sherkat was reportedly sympathetic to the plight of her secular sisters, but concerned that in a climate of repression in which numerous newspapers and magazines had been closed down, the authorities would ban *Zanan* and thus a major forum for feminist views. Although at least one member of parliament expressed alarm at the sentences, there were no petitions circulated in Iran or public protests organized over the arrests. By contrast, expatriate Iranian feminists, some working within transnational feminist networks, spearheaded a major international protest campaign.

About Islamic Feminism

Despite the contradictions and inconsistencies of their stances, Islamic feminists are part of a dynamic trend among Iranian women toward the assertion of rights. In addition to their rereading of the Qur'an, they have challenged the clerical establishment by pointing to the discrepancy between the Islamic Republic's claim of having liberated women and the persistent reality of male privilege in areas such as marriage, divorce, and child custody. Islamic feminism in Iran is also part of a larger trend in Muslim countries of believing women who have parted company with Islamic fundamentalist movements.

The very emergence of Islamic feminism should be seen as a response or a reaction on the part of women who have been either disappointed with the promises of Islamic movements (like Islamic feminists in Iran, who were initially very enthusiastic about Khomeini's project) or who rejected the fundamentalist project at its inception and sought to recuperate their religion from what they regarded as a flawed or dangerous political movement (as with Morocco's Fatima Mernissi, U.S.-based Rifaat Hassan of Pakistan, U.S.-based Aziza al-Hibri of Lebanon, and the group Sisters in Islam in Malaysia). Their strategy is to engage in a feminist rereading of the Qur'an and early Islamic history, in which they highlight the emancipatory content and dispute patriarchal interpretations and cod-ifications. Certainly Islamic feminism is a more dynamic and ascendant movement and set of ideas than is Islamic fundamentalism, which appears to be on the wane as a popular movement, whether in Iran or elsewhere. Islamic fundamentalism seems to have exhausted its possibilities and prom-ises, while its violence has repulsed many Muslims. In many countries, including Iran, Muslims are searching for alternative ways to live without compromising either their religious identity or their human rights. Many Muslim scholars are also engaged in a kind of religious reformation, some of which is Qur'an-centered and some of which addresses issues such as Islam and democracy, Islam and human rights, and Islam, science, and philosophy—which are the concerns of the "religious intellectuals" in Iran. Islamic feminism in Iran and elsewhere has arisen on the cusp of this new alternative formulation and religious reformation.

If Islamic feminism is part of the emerging feminist movement in Iran, we should also view it as part of global feminism—the social movement and dis-course of women around the world for empowerment, equality, and social change. It is telling that former member of parliament Faezeh Hashemi (and daughter of former president Ali Akbar Hashemi Rafsanjani) defined femi-nism in the following way:

> Feminism is about defending women's rights and fighting for equal rights for women and men. In this context I do believe that I have been involved in defending women's rights. There are issues which affect all of us. Even in the parliament, we may dis-agree on political issues but most women members are agreeing on most issues in relation to family law, women's education and employment. This is very encouraging, especially as I see this on a global level, where there is a global women's movement that is unstoppable, like a stream.[8]

Such statements allow one to imagine the emergence of an Islamic femi-nism of a new type in Iran, one with a hybrid "ideology"—perhaps a liberal-Muslim feminism. But it leaves unresolved the question of whether there is a cohesive social movement of women that can bring about the necessary legal and political reforms to accompany the very real social changes that have occurred in Iran.

A Moment of Truth for Women's Activism?

At least two expatriate Iranian sociologists have described women's activism in Iran as evincing a lack of interest in ideology, economic issues, or strategy. U.S.-based Iranian sociologist Ali Akbar Mahdi has argued that women have created a movement "without direction, leadership, and structure" and are asserting their identities "by peeling off layers of physical and ideological covers imposed on them" by the Islamic Republic. At the same time, according to Mahdi, this movement reveals women's "greater awareness of human rights, individual rights, individual autonomy within marriage, family independence within the kinship network, and a form of national consciousness against the global diffusion of Western values." He and Paris-based sociologist Farhad Khosrowkhavar have described the women's movement in Iran as one of the three "new social movements" (along with those of students and intellectuals) that emerged in the latter part of the 1990s.[9] These are portrayed as postideological, postclass movements—although an alternative perspective might regard them as middle-class movements of a liberal orientation.

Whether or not women's activism in Iran may be deemed a new social movement or a feminist premovement, one can certainly identify positive signs of women's activism and indicators of movement formation. First, it is clear that women in Iran have grievances concerning their second-class citizenship in both the private sphere of the family and the public sphere of the state, culture, and employment. Many young Muslim women as well as committed secular women dislike compulsory *hijab* (veiling), and there have been numerous instances of informal and spontaneous individual acts of resistance—as distinct from organized protests—against it. Many articles published in the women's press criticize the subordinate status of women in the Islamic Republic and call for the modernization of family law. Second, there is feminist leadership and activists who are well known within the country and internationally. Third, there are reports of feminist mobilizing. On International Women's Day in 2002, women's gatherings took place in a number of cities across the country, although it is not clear if these were coordinated activities.

Fourth, one can identify innovative and entrepreneurial characteristics of women's activism, such as the many feminist magazines and women's publishing collectives (e.g., *Zanan, Jens-e Dovvom, Farzaneh, Hoghough-e Zanan, Roshangaran Press,* and the new Cultural Center of Women); the legal campaigns on behalf of the rights of women and children; the emergence of Islamic feminism; academics who try to form women's studies courses or programs at their universities or write on women's topics in the women's press; the growth of nongovernmental organizations devoted to women's empowerment. The publishing collectives, NGOs, and informal networks among the women's rights activists certainly form part of the mobilizing structures that have helped to make "the woman question" and feminist politics visible in Iran. So much so, in fact, that Ayatollah Khamenei—the country's unelected clerical leader—has warned against the dangers of the "feminist tendency" and declared it to be an inappropriate solution for Muslim women.

Fifth, women activists in Iran have framed their grievances and demands in Islamic terms and have drawn from the cultural stock to press for women's rights and equality. But they also have used secular language and pointed to international conventions and standards, thus challenging the dominant political and ideological framework. They have called for the adoption of international conventions and norms such as the UN's Convention on the Elimination of All Forms of Discrimination Against Women and the implementation of the Beijing Platform for Action; they have participated in international forums such as the Beijing Plus Five meeting in June 2000; they have formed links (albeit limited) with global feminists; and they have received various kinds of support from Iranian expatriate feminists.

But there are serious obstacles, some internal and some external. In addition to the aforementioned tensions between secular and Islamic feminists, there is the problem of the limited (self-limiting?) nature of women's demands in Iran. At the moment, women's rights advocates in Iran are focused on problems in the Islamic Republic's shariat-based family law. This leaves untouched the matters of economic justice and democratization of the political structure—and it leaves these matters exclusively to the male reformists. Issues of personal and family status are certainly crucial to the well-being, dignity, autonomy, and equality of women. But equally important to women's empowerment and their ability to participate in public life are issues of civil society and citizenship, especially given the lack of interest in women's rights on the part of male reformers, as many feminists have noted. Feminists in Iran have yet to contribute to the national dialogue (if it can be called that) on the need for freedom of association and independent organizations, and on the need to redefine and institutionalize civil, political, and social rights of citizens vis-à-vis the state and the market. Independent organizing and citizen rights are feminist issues that many women's movements around the world have openly addressed. Without feminist interventions in discussions about democratization, state-citizen relations, and economic justice, Iran's reform movement is likely to result in "democratization with a male face" or a capitalist economy that is detrimental to working women's interests—as occurred in Eastern Europe after the collapse of communism and during the transition to liberal capitalism.

Last but certainly not least, the environment of repression precludes organizing of an independent and activist nature. This may be one reason why the women's NGOs in Iran are not integrated into transnational feminist networks such as Development Alternatives with Women in a New Era (DAWN), Women Living Under Muslim Laws (WLUML), the Women's Learning Partnership for Equality, Development, and Rights (WLP) or the numerous women's health and reproductive rights networks. Nor are they well connected to global civil society organizations dealing with human rights, children's rights, or the environment. Expatriate Iranian feminists are trying to rectify this and to facilitate international networking by inviting Iran-based feminists to conferences in Europe and the United States, by distributing edited volumes, calendars, and other publications of the Iranian women's press (e.g., the impressive output of Noushin Ahmadi-Khorasani), by organizing screenings of films with feminist themes, by circulating petitions protesting the mistreatment of feminist leaders in Iran, and, of course, by writing on and lecturing about Iranian women's activism.

The consequences of the Berlin conference showed, however, that international networking must be done carefully. It would be extremely counterproductive to follow the Afghan model of transnational feminist condemnations and intervention by Western governments.[10] Rather, women activists in Iran and transnational feminist leaders elsewhere should work to forge tries with each other toward mutually beneficial ends. Through dialogue and consultation regarding feminist goals, they could support women's advancement in Iran and feminist organizing globally, and further develop feminist alternatives to current economic, political, and cultural models and practices.

The social movement of women clearly has a foundation in Iran. Its informal networks, publishing collectives, and nongovernmental organizations could form the springboard for a more self-conscious and formally organized movement that could recruit members and supporters and engage in more systematic forms of collective action on behalf of women's rights and equality, so that women like Arezoo Bayat can find meaningful work, affordable housing, and a sense of empowerment. At the same time, women's organizations could build bridges with other social movements—the student movement, the intellectuals' movement, and with associations of workers and professionals—to help redefine and redirect democratic reform and economic justice in Iran. So along with the daunting obstacles, there are promising opportunities. In that sense, it is a moment of truth for women's activism in Iran.

Notes

1 The documentary was shown at the fourth conference of the Society for Iranian Studies, in Bethesda, Maryland, May 2002.

2 See Ziba Mir-Hosseini, "Women and Politics in Post-Khomeini Iran: Divorce, Veiling, and Emerging Feminist Voices," in *Women and Politics in the Third World,* ed. Haleh Afshar (London and New York: Routledge, 1996): 142-169, and "Stretching the Limits: A Feminist Reading of the shariah in Post-Khomeini Iran," in *Feminism and Islam: Legal and Literary Perspectives,* ed. Mai Yamani (New York University Press, 1996): 285-319; Nayereh Tohidi, "'Islamic Feminism': A Democratic Challenge or a Theocratic Reaction?" Kankash (no. 13, 1997) [in Persian]; Afsaneh Najmabadi, "Feminism in an Islamic Republic: 'Years of Hardship, Years of Growth,'" in *Women, Gender, and Social Change in the Muslim World,* eds. Yvonne Y. Haddad and John Esposito (New York: Oxford University Press, 1998): 59-84; Parvin Paidar, "Gender of Democracy: The Encounter between Feminism and Reformism in Contemporary Iran," Geneva: UNRISD, Democracy, Governance and Human Rights Programme Paper no. 6, October 2001; *Elaheh Rostami Povey, "Feminist Contestations of Institutional Domains in Iran," Feminist Review,* number 69 (Winter 2001): 44-7; Val Moghadam, "Islamic Feminism and Its Discontents: Toward a Resolution of the Debate," *Signs: Journal of Women in Culture and Society* (vol. 27, no. 4, Summer 2002).

3 For details on the student unrest, see articles by Ali Akbar Mahdi, Charles Kurzman, Val Moghadam, Farhang Rajaee, Kamran Dadkhah, Hamid Zanganeh, and others in *Journal of Iranian Research and Analysis,* vol. 15, no. 2 (November 1999).

4 Najmeh Bozorgmehr, "Students in Tehran Clash," *Financial Times,* July 10, 2002; Guy Dinmore, "Ayatollah Attacks Iran's Clerical Elite," *Financial Times,* July 11, 2002; Najmeh Bozorgmehr, "Iran Fears Factional Infighting May Prompt U.S. Attack," *FT,* July 20-21, 2002, p. 5.

5 Guy Dinmore, "Death by Stoning Defended in Iran", *Financial Times,* July 8, 2002, p. 5.

6 For analyses in English see articles by Gholamreza Vatandoust, Siamak Namazi, Ali Mohammadi, and Fariborz Raisdana in *Journal of Iranian Research and Analysis* (vol. 16, no. 1, April 2000) and articles by Eric Rouleau, Mark Gasiorowski, Hossein Bashiriyyeh, Abbas Abdi, and others in *Global Dialogue,* vol. 3, nos. 2-3, Spring/Summer 2001). For an excellent analysis of the reform movement and the woman question, see Farideh Farhi, "Religious Intellectuals, the 'Woman Question,' and the Struggle for the Creation of a Democratic Public Sphere in Iran, *International Journal of Politics, Culture and Society,* vol. 15, no. 2 (Winter 2001): 315-333.

7 For transcripts of the comments, see Lili Farhadpour, *Zanan-e Berlin* (The Women of Berlin), Tehran: Cultural Center of Women, 1371 (2002).

8 Cited in Elaheh Rostami Povey, "Feminist Contestations . . .," p. 63.

9 Farhad Khosrokhavar, "New Social Movements in Iran," *ISIM Newsletter,* no. 7 (2001): 17; Ali Akbar Mahdi, "Caught Between Local and Global: Iranian Women's Struggle for a Civil Society," paper presented at the CIRA annual meeting, Bethesda, MD, April 2000 (http://www.owu.edu/~aamahdi/globalization-final.doc).

10 See Val Moghadam, "Globalizing the Local: Transnational Feminism and Afghan Women's Rights," paper prepared for the Conference on Beyond September 11: Afghan Women's Prospects, Mount Holyoke College, March 7-8, 2002; and "Patriarchy, the Taleban and the Politics of Public Space in Afghanistan," *Women's Studies International Forum,* vol. 25, no. 1 (Spring 2002): 1-13.

Gender and Literacy in Islam

Leila Ahmed

From *A Border Passage: Cairo to America—A Woman's Journey*
(Farrar, Straus and Giroux, 1999)

When I arrived in the United Arab Emirates, a small country of spectacular deserts, mountains, and oases on the shallow, vivid blue Persian Gulf, it was in the middle of the most momentous transformation of its history. A few years earlier, Zayed, the sheikh of Abu Dhabi, had offered to use his oil wealth to finance education, housing, and medical treatment for all the people of the region (including neighboring emirates) that was now united under his titular leadership. And thus the people of the region, a nomadic Bedu people, were in the process of being settled; and the country as a whole was being catapulted almost instantaneously into modernity.

To provide its people with these new amenities, the U.A.E. had had to look to other countries for skilled personnel, and they looked above all to other Arab countries. By the time I got there, foreign Arabs—Egyptians, Palestinians, Syrians, Jordanians, and others—outnumbered the local Bedu population six to one. These other Arabs were architects, doctors and nurses, teachers and headmasters and headmistresses. To house this vast and, as it were, invading population, as well as the local people, cities had arisen almost overnight out of the sands. Ten years earlier there had been no constructed building in Abu Dhabi, which was now the capital, only tents and reed huts; no building other than the solitary whitewashed fortress that now stood in the middle of a city of towering high-rises.

Abu Dhabi had the air of a place conjured out of the sands overnight. Silhouettes of cranes stood against the horizon in every direction, two or three buildings going up at once alongside each other. Nearby there were still other new-looking buildings; beyond these one saw structures that were at at once new-looking and derelict. Blocks had gone up too fast. Many buildings had to be abandoned after two or three years. There was one such apartment block that I passed in my afternoon walks along the corniche: a grand blue-and-white tower that stood like a ship, with a commanding view of the sea; gleamingly new and completely uninhabitable. I would hear the sea wind that always blew here, whispering and moaning through its gaping, darkening windows and doors, whining and whistling and tugging and fidgeting as if to pick it apart.

I was often conscious in Abu Dhabi of the foreignness of all this—modern high-rises, higgledy-piggledy construction cranes, new and derelict buildings, and this invasion of other Arabs from abroad—their cultures smothering and overwhelming the local Bedu culture. All in the name of modernity and education. It often seemed like something—dream, nightmare—conjured just yesterday out of the sands, and that would any moment pass away. Left to nature, to the deft, steady workings of desert, sea, and wind, all of this surely—I'd find myself thinking—would soon disappear, the old desert simplicity once more restored. It was not an unpleasant thought.

In all of Abu Dhabi there was only one place that had its own intrinsic loveliness: the old whitewashed fortress built in the local style, with its ancient, studded wood door, beside it a cluster of sheltering palms and a small thicket of vivid, yellow-flowering shrubs.

And so I sensed even then that I was witnessing loss: the vanishing of Bedu culture, its banishment to the edges of life, its smothering by a supposedly superior culture bringing "education." I sensed this, but I didn't quite understand or trust my intuition. After all, wasn't all this—education, modernity, progress—a necessary and incontrovertible good? I don't know the answer even now. But I do believe that I was right in my feeling that I was witnessing a profoundly different—and in many ways inferior—culture.

As soon as I arrived in the country, I was placed on a committee charged with overseeing the development and reform of education throughout the Emirates. In the preceding few years schools had opened fast, without much planning, and we now had to revise and rationalize the curricula. My fellow committee members were Egyptians like me, or Palestinians. There were no locals on the committee, although we reported as a committee to the minister of education, who was from Abu Dhabi. This arrangement was typical. Advisors and advisory committees were made up of foreign Arabs, but the people who held the highest posts were local. The latter were drawn from among those few who had had a formal education—only a small handful in the country—and from among the sons of important families.

All the other members of the committee were men. In those days there were no more than three or four people in the entire country with Ph.D.'s, and I was one of them. It was this that had made it possible to appoint me, a woman, to such a high-level committee.

We began our work by polling the locals about how they wanted to see education developed. We also visited schools, observed classes, and interviewed teachers and students. I met with local women to hear how they felt about women's education. Of course I was the only member of the committee who could do this, since the local Bedu society was strictly segregated—women did not meet with men who were not relatives.

Mariam, one of the first women I interviewed, was a member of one of the ruling families. I sat waiting for her in the reception room at the women's center with my companion, Gameela, an Egyptian who had been in the Gulf for several years. She had been assigned to be my interpreter, to begin with. Gulf Arabic was scarcely intelligible to me. In the corner sat a heavy figure completely hidden in a black *'abaya*. We both assumed that this was some simple woman waiting to meet with Mariam, but she turned out to be Mariam herself. I went through the questionnaire, asking her about women and education. She was probably in her fifties, and she was non-literate.

Of course women should have the right to education up to the highest levels, she said. And of course they should be able to pursue whatever profession they wished.

What about—I asked, moving on to the next item on the questionnaire—women's role in Islam, and the requirements of Islam?

Who founded Islam? Mariam instantly retorted. A man or a woman?

Startled, my companion, who was dressed in Egyptian-style robes and a head veil of strict piety, murmured, "The Prophet Muhammad, peace and mercy be upon him!"

"Exactly!" said Mariam. "And whose side do you think he was on?"

Mariam told us she was engaged in an argument with Fatima, the principal wife of Zayed, the ruler, and with other women, as to what should be the emblem of women's centers in the Emirates. A gazelle had been proposed, partly to honor Zayed, whose emirate, Abu Dhabi, meant "father of [place of] the gazelle." Mariam wanted it to be the face of an unveiled woman, with some sign indicating that she was a doctor or engineer. A gazelle sounded like a nice idea, she said, but it associated women with animals, nonhuman creatures, and that was a dangerous thing to do.

Mariam was among the most remarkable and forthright of the women I would meet in Abu Dhabi. But all of them shared her passion about the importance of education for women and many had those same qualities of strength, directness, clarity, and secure confidence in their own vision. There was Moza, a cousin of the ruler. In her late twenties—too old to have benefited from the country's educational revolutions—she attended literacy classes until a few days before she gave birth. In fact, she had founded and endowed the Women's Adult Education Center, where she took the classes. A woman of enormous wealth, she wanted other women to be able to pursue an education. Women's centers offering literacy classes (and childcare for the women who took them) existed throughout the Emirates, many of them funded by local women.

Those qualities of resolve, spiritedness, and passion were there, too, in the new generation. Hissa was a youngster of fifteen when I met her; she had been removed from school and married off against her will when she was twelve. She appealed her case to the president through his wife Sheikha Fatima: Hissa insisted that Islam gave her the right not to be married without her consent and the right to education, and she demanded both. She won. As we strolled in the schoolyard, with its white colonnades and splashes of bougainvillea, she told me she intended to become a petroleum engineer. Hissa's story was unusual, but the schools were full of young women as spirited as she: they had every intention of going on to become engineers, architects, scientists. Few wanted to major in literature and the humanities, the subjects that girls are steered toward in other countries.

It soon became ordinary for me to encounter these extraordinary women each day, to observe the clarity and forthrightness with which they expressed their opinions and went about their lives, the sense of humor and quick laughter that they brought on their gatherings. Only a handful of local women had had formal education and, like the local educated men, they held responsible positions (though they were less public and less powerful then the men)—as headmistresses, say, or regional educational directors. It became ordinary too, then, to wait in an office or reception room and observe one of the younger, formally educated women arrive, wrapped in the black *'abaya*. Once in the privacy of an all-women's space, she would let it drop to reveal an elegant pantsuit. Naturally it was soon quite obvious to me that the local culture bred people who needed no instruction from anyone in the qualities of strength, clarity, vision, understanding, or imagination.

As the responses to our questionnaire began to come in, it quickly became evident that it was not only the women here who supported women's education. The local men, too, were overwhelmingly in favor of equal education for women. They believed that women should be able to qualify for any profession. Whatever either sex felt about segregation and about women's pursuing professional lives within segregated context, they did not want to see women held back intellectually or prevented from pursuing the professions they wished.

These views, I discovered, were not those of the committee. As we reviewed the responses and prepared to reformulate the country's educational goals, Dr. Haydar, the chair of the committee, instructed us to set aside the local people's views regarding equal education for women. The majority of our respondents were uneducated people, he pointed out; most, in fact, were illiterate. They had nice hopes and wishes about equal education for women, but their lack of education meant they didn't have the knowledge or capacity to foresee the consequences of policies in the way that educated people could. That was why they had us here, to tell them how best to develop their society rationally.

Haydar, a Lebanese who had studied in Egypt and America, was a complicated man. The notion of women's equality was deeply antithetical to him; a sneering, bitter tone crept into his words whenever he spoke of it. Invariably, his example of how things spun out of control and into destructive chaos when societies treated women as equal was America, where, I surmised, he had suffered some awful rejection. In America, he once said, they were giving women the right to serve in the army, including positions where they would have men serving under them.

"Can you imagine a pregnant woman," he said, making the gesture of a swollen belly before him, "giving orders to her soldiers!" He looked at each of us in turn, laughing a humorless, scandalized laugh. Laughter ensued from all around me. That moment has stuck with me.

If women had degrees in engineering or some such subject, he asked, would they still be willing to be the servants of society? If we, the committee, gave the locals what they wanted, the entire basis of society would be destroyed. For society depends on women's role in the family, and on their willingness to be the servants of men. Had the local people thought of such things? Of course not!

Our job was to think of these things and to plan an educational future for the country consonant with the Islamic principles on which the society—and the national constitution—was based. Haydar was, he told us, an atheist himself. (I knew no one else in the Emirates who openly declared his atheism: it was a courageous act.) But his personal beliefs were irrelevant, he insisted: it was simply his professional duty to see to it that we came up with an educational program that conformed to the principles of the country, and Islamic principles were completely clear as to the role of women.

Haydar's comments met with nods and general approval from the committee. We should begin, Haydar then proposed, by cutting down on math and science in girls' schools and substituting, say, home economics.

This appalled me, of course, and the situation seemed hopeless—I was totally outnumbered.

Brooding on the gray-faced men on the committee, who were so casually preparing to blight the hopes of the local women, and on the fact that these men were nonlocals from other Arab cultures who were now imposing the narrow, bigoted ideas of their own backgrounds, I decided to talk to Ibrahim, the director of education. He was a local and my immediate boss. He had been the person responsible for my appointment to the committee.

I knew Ibrahim was strongly in favor of equal education for women. As a boy he had attended the only school in the region before the oil boom, an English school funded by the British government. Then he had won a scholarship to England, where he earned a B.A.

He listened to what I had to say and suggested that I tell Moza and the other local women what the committee was planning. So I stopped by the Women's Center that evening and told Moza about Haydar's plan over a glass of tea. Within a week or two, the committee got a directive from above instructing us to drop this scheme. After that, I didn't much worry when Haydar came up with some similar idea. I'd listen and mildly demur—or even appear to agree—and then let one of the women know what was afoot. It always worked. I must confess that I enjoyed the bemused look on Haydar's face whenever he announced—as if despairing of these foolish, unpredictable locals—that he had got a call or a note from the minister telling him that the committee was not to do this or that. I am sure now that in appointing me to that committee, Ibrahim had hoped I would serve precisely the role that I did. I was recruited to be his ally against the stifling attitudes that had inundated the Emirates from other Arab countries.

As director of education, Ibrahim had considerable power. But he was not a member of an important family and, as these things still counted, he had to use his wits to bring about the outcomes he wanted. His superior, the minister of education, was from a prominent family and had a B.A. from Cairo; he had the power to override his decisions and accept the recommendations of our committee. He was much more ambivalent than Ibrahmi on the question of equal education for women.

The divide on this question, as I gradually came to understand, was not at all a straightforward divide between women and men. While the nonlocal Arab men on the committee were opposed to equal education, the local men as a group were not. Ibrahim, educated in England, was in favor of it—but so were others, among them the nonliterate and the barely literate, including Zayed, the president of the country and a nonliterate man, who had committed funding to men's and women's education in equal measure.

Among local men, there was a divide between those who were ambivalent about or opposed to equal education for women—mostly men educated in the Arab and primarily in the Egyptian education system—and those who supported equal education. A small minority of the latter group had been educated in the English system; the rest were nonliterate or barely literate—in other words, they were men who belonged fully to the oral, living culture of the region.

At the time the only thing clear to me was that there seemed to be something distinctly more oppressive toward women in the attitudes of nonlocal Arab men, and that the Arabic, Egyptian-inspired educational system seemed to have a perceptibly negative effect intellectually. It seemed to close minds instead of opening them up—close minds in all sorts of ways, but particularly with regard to women.

What I was observing, I realize now, was the profound gulf between the oral culture of the region, on the one hand, and the Arabic culture of literacy, on the other. Oral cultures here in the Gulf—indeed, oral cultures everywhere—are the creations of communities of men and women; they represent the ongoing interactions of these communities with their heritage, beliefs, outlook, circumstances, and so on. But the Arabic culture of literacy—a culture whose language nobody, no living community, ordinarily speaks—

clearly isn't the product of people living their lives and interacting with their environment and heritage. The Kenyan writer Ngugi wa Thiong'o has pondered the relationship between mother tongue and written language. He describes his mother tongue as the language that people used as they worked in the fields, the language that they used to tell stories in the evenings around the fireside. It was a language alive with "the words and images and with the inflection of the voices" of the people who made up his community, a language whose words had "a suggestive power well beyond the immediate and lexical meanings. Our appreciation of the suggestive magical power of language was reinforced by the games we played with words through riddles, proverbs, transpositions of syllables, or through nonsensical but musically arranged words. So we learned the music of our language on top of the content. The language, through images and symbols, gave us a view of the world."

All of Ngugi's words apply to Gulf Arabic and Egyptian Arabic and to the many varieties of vernacular Arabic, none of which currently has a written form. But Ngugi's words do not apply to standard Arabic, the only written form of Arabic that there is. Nobody in the world—except maybe academics and textbook writers—sits around the fireside telling stories in standard Arabic; no one working in a field anywhere in the Arab world speaks that language; no children anywhere play word games and tell riddles and proverbs in standard Arabic.

But if this language and its culture are not the language and culture of a living community, whose culture is it that is being disseminated by the culture of literacy that Arab governments are zealously imposing on their populations through schools and universities? Rooted in no particular place and in no living culture, from whom does this culture emanate and whose values do its texts embody? Presumably they are the values and worldviews of government bureaucrats and textbook writers and the literate elites of today, along with those of the Arabic textual heritage on which textbooks and the contemporary culture of literacy still draw. The Arabic literary heritage was produced over the centuries primarily by men: mainly middle-class men who lived in deeply misogynist societies. Perhaps it is their perspective, recycled today in textbooks and throughout the Arabic culture of literacy, that imparts to that culture its distinctly negative disposition toward women.

Whatever its sources and whoever its creators, it is, as I observed it, a sterile and oppressive culture. I remember my uneasy feeling in Abu Dhabi, as I watched Egyptians and Palestinians trained in this prevailing culture of literacy inculcate it in their young charges, that I was witnessing the tragic imposition of a sterile, inferior, bureaucratic culture on young minds—and the gradual erasure of their own vital, local culture, a culture much richer and more humane. And this was being done in the name of education.

The imposition of this culture of literacy throughout the Arab world amounts to a kind of imperialism—a linguistic and cultural imperialism conducted in the name of education, Arab unity, and the oneness of the Arab nation. Throughout the Arab world, as this Arab culture of literacy marches inexorably onward, local cultures are erased, their linguistic and cultural creativity condemned to permanent, unwritten silence. And we are supposed to applaud this, not protest it as we would if it were any other form of imperialism or political domination. This variety of domination goes by the name of "nationalism," and we are supposed to support it no matter what is destroyed in its wake.

My time in Abu Dhabi—especially my days of conversation with its women—recalled the world of my childhood.

The women of my family, too, had their own understanding of Islam, an understanding that was different from official Islam. For although it was only Grandmother who performed all the regular formal prayers, religion was an essential part of the way all the women of the house made sense of their lives. It was through religion that one pondered the things that happened, why they had happened, and what one should make of them, how one should take them.

Islam, as I learned it, was gentle, generous, pacifist, inclusive, somewhat mystical—just like these women themselves. Mother's pacifism was entirely of a piece with this sense of the religion. Being Muslim was about believing in a world in which life was meaningful, in which all events and happenings were permeated with meaning even if it was not always clear to us. Religion was above all about inner things. The outward signs of religiousness, such as prayer and fasting, might be signs of true religiosity. But they equally well might not. They were certainly not what was important about being Muslim. What was important was how you conducted yourself and how you were in yourself and in your attitude toward others, and in your heart.

What it was to be Muslim was passed on quietly—not, of course, wordlessly, but without elaborate sets of injunctions and threats and decrees and dictates about what we should do and be and believe. What was passed on, besides the general basic beliefs and moral ethos of Islam (which are also those of its sister monotheisms), was a way of being in the world. A way of holding oneself in the world—in relation to God, to existence, to other human beings. This the women passed on to us most of all through their being and presence, by the way *they* were in the world, conveying their beliefs, ways, thoughts, and how we should be in the world by a touch, a glance, a word—prohibiting, for instance, or approving. Their mere responses in this or that situation—a word, a shrug, even a posture—passed on to us, in the way that women (and also men) have forever passed on to their young, how should be. And all of these ways of passing on attitudes, morals, beliefs, knowledge—through touch and the body, in words spoken in the living moment—are by their very nature subtle and evanescent. They shape the next generation, but they do not leave a record in the way that someone who writes a test about how to live or what to believe leaves a record. Nevertheless, they leave a far more important living record. Beliefs, morals, and attitudes, impressed on us through those fleeting words and gestures, are written into our lives, our bodies, ourselves, even into our physical cells and into how we live out the script of our lives.

It was Grandmother who taught me the *fu-ha* (the opening verse of the Qur'an, and the equivalent of the Christian Lord's Prayer), along with two or three other short suras. When she took me up to the roof of our house in Alexandria to watch for angels on the twenty-seventh night of Ramadan, she recited the sura about that special night, a sura that was also about the miraculousness of night itself. It is still my favorite sura; even now I remember its loveliness.

I don't remember receiving much other direct religious instruction, from Grandmother or from anyone else. Sitting in her room, the windows opening behind her onto the garden, the curtain billowing, my mother once quoted to me the verse in the Qur'an that she believed summed up the essence of Islam: "He who kills one being"—*nafs*, self, from the root *nafas*, breath—"kills all of humanity, and he who revives, or gives life to, one being revives all of humanity." It was a verse that she quoted often, that came up in any important conversation about God, religion, those sorts of things. It represents for her the essence of Islam.

When I was thinking about all this, I happened to be reading the auto-biography of Zeinab al-Ghazali, one of the most prominent contemporary

Muslim women leaders. Al-Ghazali founded a Muslim Women's Society that she eventually merged with the Muslim Brotherhood, the "fundamentalist" association that was particularly active in the forties and fifties. Throughout her life she upheld the legitimacy of using violence in the cause of Islam. In her memoir, she writes of how in her childhood her father told her stories of the heroic women of early Islam who had written poetry eulogizing Muslim warriors and who themselves had gone to war and gained renown as fearless fighters. Musing about all this and about the difference between al-Ghazali's Islam and my mother's pacifist understanding, I found myself falling into meditation on the seemingly trivial detail that I, unlike al-Ghazali, had never heard stories about the women of early Islam, heroic, or otherwise, as a young girl. And it was then that I suddenly realized the difference between al-Ghazali and my mother and between al-Ghazali's Islam and my mothers.

The reason I had not heard such stories as a child was quite simply that back then, those sorts of stories were to be found only in the ancient classical texts of Islam, texts that only men who had studied the classical Islamic literary heritage could understand and decipher. The entire training at Islamic universities—the training, for example that Ghazali's father, who had attended al Azhar University, had received—consisted precisely in studying those texts. Al-Ghazali had been initiated into Islam and had gotten her notions as to what a Muslim was from her father, whereas I had received my Islam from my mother. So there are two quite different Islams, an Islam that was in some cases a women's Islam and an official, textual Islam, a men's Islam.

Indeed, it is obvious that a far greater gulf must separate men's and women's ways of knowing, and the ways in which men and women understand religion, in the segregated societies of the Middle East than in other societies—and we know that there are differences between women's and men's ways of knowing even in nonsegregated societies such as America. Besides the fact that women often could not read (or, if they were literate, could not decipher the Islamic texts, which require years of specialist training), women in Muslim societies did not attend mosques. Mosque-going was not part of the tradition for women of any class (that is, attending mosque for congregational prayers was not part of the tradition, as distinct from visiting mosques privately and informally to offer personal prayers, which women have always done). Women therefore did not hear the sermons that many men heard. And they did not get the orthodox (male, of course) interpretations of religion that many men got every Friday. They did not have a man trained in the orthodox (male) literary heritage of Islam telling them week by week and month by month what it meant to be a Muslim, what the correct interpretation of this or that was, and what was or was not the essential message of Islam.

Rather, they figured these things out among themselves: they figured them out as they tried to understand their own lives, talking them over together among themselves, interacting with their men, and returning to talk them over in their communities of women. And they figured them out as they listened to the Qur'an and talked among themselves about what they heard. For this was a culture, at all they of society and throughout most of the history of Islamic civilization, not of reading but of the recitation of the Qur'an. It was recited by professional reciters, women as well as men, and listened to on all kinds of occasions. There was merit in having the Qur'an chanted in your house and in hearing it chanted wherever it was chanted, whereas for women there was no merit attached to attending mosque, an activity indeed prohibited to women for most of history.

The women I knew didn't feel that they were missing anything by not hearing the exhortations of sheikhs, nor did they believe that the sheikhs had an understanding of Islam superior to theirs. Although occasionally there might be a sheikh who was regarded as a man of genuine insight and wisdom, the women I knew generally dismissed the views and opinions of the common run of sheikhs as mere superstition and bigotry. These were not Westernized women: Grandmother, who spoke only Arabic and Turkish, almost never set foot outside her home, and never even listened to the radio. The dictum that "there is no priesthood in Islam"—meaning that there is no intermediary or interpreter, and no need for one, between God and each individual Muslim— was something these women and many other Muslims took seriously as a declaration of their right to their own understanding of Islam.

The Islam I received from the women among whom I lived was part of their particular subculture: there are not just two or three different kinds of Islam, but many different ways of being Muslim. But what is striking to me now is not how different or rare the Islam in which I was raised is, but how ordinary and typical it seems to be. After a lifetime of meeting and talking with Muslims from all over the world, I find that this Islam is one of the common varieties—perhaps even *the* common or garden variety—of the religion. It is the Islam not only of women, but of ordinary folk generally, as opposed to the Islam of sheikhs, ayatollahs, mullahs, and clerics. It is an Islam that doesn't necessarily place emphasis on ritual and formal religious practice; it pays little or no attention to the utterances and exhortations of official figures. Rather, it is an Islam that stresses moral conduct and emphasizes Islam as a broad ethos, a way of understanding and reflecting on the meaning of one's life and of human life more generally.

This variety of Islam (or, more exactly perhaps, these familial varieties of Islam, existing in a continuum across the Muslim world) consists above all of Islam as essentially an aural and oral heritage and a way of living and being—and not a textual, written heritage, not something studied in books or learned from men who studied books. This latter Islam, the Islam of the texts, is quite different: it is the Islam of the arcane, mostly medieval written heritage in which sheikhs are trained; it is men's Islam. More specifically still, it is the Islam erected by that minority of men who have created and passed on this particular textual over the centuries: men who, although they have always been a minority in society as a whole, have always made the laws and wielded enormous power (like the ayatollahs of contemporary Iran). The Islam they developed in this textual heritage is similar to the medieval Latin textual heritage of Christianity—abstruse, obscure, and dominated by medieval, exclusively male views of the world. Imagine believing that those medieval texts represent the only true and acceptable interpretation of Christianity. That is exactly what the sheikhs and ayatollahs propound, and this is where things stand now in much of the Muslim world: most of the texts that determine Muslim law date from medieval times.

What remains when you *listen* to the Qur'an over a lifetime are its recurring themes, ideas, and words, its permeating spirit: mercy, justice, peace, compassion, humanity, fairness, kindness, truthfulness, charity. It is precisely these recurring themes and this permeating spirit that are for the most part left out of the medieval texts or smothered and buried under a welter of obscure and abstruse "learning." One would scarcely believe, reading or hearing the laws these texts have yielded, particularly when it comes to women, that the words *justice, fairness, compassion,* or *truth* ever occur in the Qur'an. No wonder non-Muslims think Islam is such a backward and oppressive religion: what these men made of it *is* largely oppressive. The men who wrote the foundational texts of official Islam were living in societies and eras rife with chauvinism, eras when men believed that God had made them superior to women, and that God fully intended them to have dominion over women. And yet, despite such beliefs and prejudices, here and there in the texts they created, in the details of this or that law, they wrote in some provision or condition that, astonishingly, does give justice to women. So the Qur'an's recurring themes filter through—if only now and then—in a body of law overwhelmingly skewed in favor of men.

I am sure, then, that my foremothers' lack of respect for the sheikhs was not coincidental. Generations of astute, thoughtful women, listening to the Qur'an, understood its essential themes and its faith perfectly well. And looking around them, they understood perfectly well what a travesty men had made of it.

Leaving no written legacy—written only on the body and in the scripts of our lives—this oral and aural tradition of Islam no doubt stretches back through generations, as ancient as any written tradition.

One might even argue that the oral tradition is intrinsic to Islam itself. The, Qur'an was originally recited to the community by the Prophet Muhammad. Throughout his life, and for several years after his death, it remained an aural text. Moreover, a bias in favor of the heard word, the word given life and meaning by the human voice, the human breath (*nafas*), is there, one might say, in the very language. In Arabic script, as in Hebrew, no vowels are set down, only consonants. A set of consonants can have several meanings; it only acquires a specific, fixed meaning when given vocalized or silent utterance, unlike words in European scripts, which have the appearance, anyway, of being fixed in meaning. Until life is literally breathed into them, Arabic and Hebrew words on the page have no particular meaning. Indeed, until then they are not words but only potential words, a chaotic possibility of meanings. It is as if the scripts of these languages, marshaling their bare consonants across the page, hold within them vast spaces where meanings exist in a condition of whirling potentiality until the moment that one is singled out and uttered. And so by their very scripts, Hebrew and Arabic seem to announce the primacy of the spoken, living word; they announce that meaning can only be here and now. Here and now in this body, this breath (*nafas*), this self (*nafs*) encounters the word, gives it life. Without that encounter, the word has no life, no meaning. Meaning always only here and now, in this body, for this person. Truth always only here and now, for this body, this person. Not something transcendent overarching, larger, bigger, more important than life—but here and now and in this body and in this small and ordinary life.

We seem to be living through the steady, seemingly inexorable erasure of the oral and ethical traditions of lived Islam, and the ever-greater dissemination of written Islam—textual Islam's narrower and poorer descendent. Practitioners of the older, learned Islam usually studied many texts; they knew that even in these medieval texts there were disagreements among scholars, differing interpretations of this or that sura. But today's fundamentalists, literate but often having read perhaps a single test, take it to be definitive, the one and only truth.

Thus, literacy has played a baneful role both in spreading once form of Islam, and in working to erase oral and living forms of the religion. For one thing, many of us automatically assume that those who write and who put their knowledge down in texts have something more valuable to offer than those who simply live their knowledge and use it to inform their lives. And we assume that those who interpret texts in writing—the sheikhs and ayatollahs—must have a better, truer, deeper understanding of Islam than the untutored Muslim. But the only Islam that the sheikhs and ayatollahs have a deep understanding of is their own gloomy, medieval version.

Even the Western academic world is contributing to the greater visibility and legitimacy of textual Islam and to the gradual silencing and erasure of alternative oral forms of lived Islam. For we too in the West, and particularly in universities, honor, and give pride of place to, texts. Academic studies of Islam commonly focus on its textual heritage or on visible, official institutions such as mosques. Consequently it is this Islam—the Islam of texts and of mosques—that becomes visible and that is presented as in some sense legitimate, whereas most of the Muslims whom I know personally, both in the Middle East and in Europe and America, would never go near a mosque or willingly associate themselves with any form of official Islam. Throughout history, official Islam has been our enemy and our oppressor. We have learned to live with it and to survive it and have developed dictums such as "There is no priesthood in Islam" to protect ourselves from it; we're not now suddenly and even in these new lands going to easily befriend it. It is also a particular and bitter irony to me that the very fashionableness of gender studies is serving to disseminate and promote medieval men's Islam as the "true" and "authentic" Islam. (It is "true" and "authentic" because it is based on old texts and represents what the Muslim male powers have considered to be true for centuries.) Professors, for example, including a number who have no sympathy whatever for feminism, are now jumping on the bandwagon of gender studies and directing a plethora of dissertations on this or that medieval text with titles like "Islam and Menstruation." But such dissertations should more aptly have titles along the lines of "A Study of Medieval Male Beliefs about Menstruation." For what, after all, do these men's beliefs, and the rules that they laid down on the basis of their beliefs, have to do with Islam? Just because they were powerful, privileged men in their societies and knew how to write, does this mean they have the right forever to tell us what Islam is and what the rules should be?

Still, these are merely word wars, wars of ideas that, for the present anyway, are of the most minor significance compared with the devastation unleashed on Muslim societies in our day by fundamentalism. What we are living through now seems to be not merely the erasure of the living oral, ethical, and humane traditions of Islam but the literal destruction and annihilation of the Muslims who are the bearers of those traditions. In Algeria, Iran, Afghanistan, and, alas, in Egypt, this narrow, violent variant of Islam is ravaging its way through the land.

If a day won't come
when the monuments of institutionalized religion are in ruin
... then, my beloved,
then we are really in trouble.

Rumi

Missing in Action

Amira Hass

From *Drinking the Sea at Gaza: Days and Nights in a Land Under Siege* (Metropolitan Books), which was published in June 2000, just before the start of the second Palestinian *intifada*.

The simple room was adorned with a gallery of photographs showing the men of the family. I was in the house of supporters of the Popular Front, once considered the vanguard of Palestinian secularism. The daughter-in-law who entered the room was in an advanced stage of pregnancy, held an infant in her arms, and was all of eighteen years old. "Why are there no pictures of women on the wall?" I asked her later. "That's the custom," she said. "It would be a disgrace to show their faces," she explained. "After all, men come to visit, you know."

In my years in Gaza, I almost never wrote about women's inferior position in Palestinian society and its emotional and intellectual consequences. I was hitched to the tireless hunt for breaking news, and the newsmakers were men. The IDF redeployment, Arafat's arrival—these were decidedly male events. The organization heads I interviewed were men; the military and religious leaders, the unionists, the politicians, the economists were almost exclusively men. Even most of the journalists, photographers, sources, and drivers were men. Like a skulk of foxes, we would streak after the male architects of the day's headlines and events. In the pursuit I failed to report on a compelling dynamic: in a patriarchal society such as the Gaza Strip, women's absence from public life becomes a motivational force in itself. Hidden away at home, cut off even from one another, women began to organize themselves; openly, timidly, they had begun to confront their domestic oppression, forcing it into the public and political spheres, bringing it into the light. Feminist developments and expressions had been especially prominent during the *intifada*. Women's committees, for example, set up learning centers offering classes in reading and writing and courses in sewing, juice making, and other ways to support a family. Centers like these, coupled with the sudden transformation of

121

many women into household heads while their husbands were in jail, encouraged women to speak out, come forward, and make demands of society and the men who dominated it. Unfortunately for me, a woman journalist, I arrived in the Strip at a time when this dynamic was on the wane.

I learned that the distinction between the public and private domains was carefully observed, even within people's homes. As a guest, I often felt like a *jasusa,* a collaborator, when, with a wave of his hand, a husband or a brother would order the women to make me coffee or when I, the Israeli guest, joined in a conversation about politics or work while the women were excluded. Or when I sat on the men's side of a length of cloth separating us from the women's area, or when the woman preparing the refreshments would call to her husband to pull himself away from the clouds of cigarette smoke and come get the tray, or when we'd all troop out to visit some interesting people and the women would stay behind to take care of the many children. Every so often, I'd say something about how the men sat around at home during curfew or when they were unable to work, not lifting a finger while the women did all the household chores.

In Gaza, women's absence from public life is as conspicuous and tangible as their presence at home. As a journalist, I lived most of my life outside, in the world, and realized that I actually knew very few women. Those I knew well, those who had talked to me about their lives, were awake to women's inferior status in Gaza and were part of the effort to remedy it. I would like to believe that their awareness and protest was emblematic, that Palestinian women everywhere were chafing at their constraints, but I had too few such conversations to be able to generalize.

M.H. from the Khan Yunis camp is a determined feminist active in the Popular Front. A thirty-five-year-old mother of four, she lost her job in a kindergarten when it ran out of money to pay her. M.H. grapples with her simultaneous absence and presence in public life. She is clearheaded and vocal about her pain and anger. I once heard a story about a woman who tried to make a match between her engineer son and M.H., a traditional match in which the engaged couple would not meet until their wedding. M.H. was staunchly opposed to arranged marriages but still turned the mother down politely and pleasantly. When the mother refused to give up, M.H. picked up a table, according to her delighted friends, and dropped it at the startled woman's feet. The mother fled and with her all other potential matchmakers.

At the Islamic University, where M.H. studied biology in 1985, she and her girlfriends organized a Popular Front rally commemorating the massacre at Dir Yassin in 1948. But the Islamic distaste for Communists proved stronger than the national cause and M.H. and her friends were denied permission. The rally went ahead in spite of the university's opposition, and M.H. was eventually expelled.

M.H.

As a child I dreamed of being a fighter like my father and brothers. At ten years old I already had a brother in an Israeli jail, one of the first men to be imprisoned in the seventies. My father was an officer in the Egyptian police intelligence. When the Israelis took over in 1967, they insisted that he continue working in intelligence, but he refused along with eleven other men, preferring to stay at home even though he had no work. Now they're all working for the Palestinian Authority.

So the role models were the men in my family. My mother was shut up inside the house all the time, which might be why I felt I had to resist, to get out, although I didn't really analyze things at the time. I just knew that something was wrong. Whenever my brother went outside, my mother would say that I was a girl and had to stay at home. It was always like that, all the way through school. Once I graduated and went to university, it became a little easier, though. But I was the only one of my sisters to behave this way. They said I was strange, aggressive, stubborn. I'd fight with my mother to let me join in the protests, to let me go out in the street with other kids and demonstrate.

In a way, fighting the occupation led to feminism. It also taught me to not just obey blindly. I watch my sisters obeying orders and I see their lives, which are so difficult. On the other hand, maybe it's easier for them because they don't know what it's like outside, they don't know what they're missing. Still, they're jealous of me sometimes. They ask their husbands why I can make decisions when they're not allowed to. And they ask me why our men make all the decisions. They always tell me that I'm strong but my answer is that we all possess strength.

For example, my sister complains that her husband gives all his wages to his parents. If she needs money she has to get it from them. So my sister is oppressed by her husband and her mother-in-law. Lots of women have to get permission from their in-laws as well as their husbands when they want to visit their families.

Things began to change with the intifada. *During curfews the women instead of the men went out to bring home food. When the soldiers tried to grab at the children, the older women would argue with them, even fight with them. Traditionally women are not allowed to open the door, but during the* intifada *it was the women who opened the door to the soldiers. So our society began to get used to behavior that had always been considered improper. Also, the men weren't bringing in as much money so the women were encouraged to go out and look for work, to grasp more freedom for themselves.*

And this affected relations in the family. When I was working at the kindergarten, I felt I had more of a role, that I was in a stronger position, I was listened to more. Now I'm not earning anything and my role is weaker. When I want to buy something I have to explain it to S., my husband, because he hands out the money. Now I can't make my own economic decisions and I feel ashamed and angry. S. is relatively okay, but his Middle Eastern way of dealing with things sometimes really irritates me and it makes me rebellious. If we have a decision to make, he always wins because he's the man. When I agreed to marry him, he promised that I could go on studying, that he'd share the chores at home, and that I could carry on being active in the Women's Committee. Now he complains when I'm away from the house and I have to keep reminding him of his promises. Sometimes he apologizes. Still, his attitude is different from that of most men and it's really noticeable. My mother and grandmother told me their husbands always treated them badly and stopped them from doing all kinds of things. Now I understand that my mother was always depressed, especially when she had to live with her husband's parents. They constantly meddled in the way we were brought up.

I began to think about my needs maybe after I got married. Actually, when I thought about myself before that—beyond activism at the university—I realized that I had to get married, the demands of my society made it unavoidable. I wasn't crazy about it—S. asked me three times before I finally agreed at the age of twenty-two, which is considered late.

Most of my friends waited like me, but may sister got married at sixteen. Even now, her husband overrules her on everything. He treats her like a little girl whose only job is to bring children into the world. Getting married so young means the man can remake the woman, actually brainwash her. Sometimes my sister's husband really bullies her and she runs away to our parents.

One time when she was staying at our parents' house, I convinced her not to go back home before our father spoke with her husband. Since our father's signature is on the marriage agreement, all the problems are brought to him. He was angry at her the first time she ran away and sided with her husband, ordering her to go back to him. But when her husband began hitting her, our father took her part. S. and I argued about it. He tried to rationalize the way my brother-in-law behaved, saying that the economic difficulties were making him act badly. This really upset me and we kept arguing until he got fed up and said, "Okay, your sister's not wrong and neither is her husband."

Since Oslo, the atmosphere has changed a little. There's some encouragement for women to work outside the home, but mostly in the towns, not in the refugee camps. Nothing has changed in the family, though. In fact, we've even lost ground. There's no work for men, so they escape the house, the children, and the wife. It's hard for them to deal with the family's demands when they can't even help support the household. At the same time, we women feel that we can't complain or make demands either, given the situation.

Now my one dream is to live in a house by ourselves—me and my husband and the children, without the rest of the family. That's all I want. I suppress any other dreams I might have had. When I let myself think about it I feel terribly sad that I'm satisfied to just dream about a house, not about something really for me. And then I just feel the whole sadness of our society pressing down on me and I can't think about myself.

M.H. and I left her house to walk among the tin huts and cinder-block shanties of Khan Yunis camp and she quickly covered her head with a *mandeel,* a scarf. At the university she covered herself up to the eyeballs, she told me. "Here, even if I go out covered with long pants and a long-sleeved blouse, people still call me a *safra,* a barefaced woman disobeying Islamic law, so I certainly can't go without the *mandeel.* I don't really care enough to fight for the right not to wrap up. Actually, it bothers me that people on both sides think it's so important. If the social pressure dies down, then I'll take it off."

I met H. and A. at a friend's house. H. teaches mathematics and A. works in a kindergarten run by a Hamas-affiliated charity. My friend and I waited in the doorway, watching the street. "Here they come," my friend said, spying two women sheathed from head to toe in veils and traditional dresses that thoroughly blurred the outlines of their bodies. Once inside the house, after making sure that no man could see them, the women began to peel off the layers: first they removed the veils covering their faces. I caught myself staring at their slanting eyes and long eyelashes, at their full, round mouths and smiling lips. Then they removed their gloves, pulling them from their wrists, until long, delicate fingers were exposed. When the women sat down I saw their ankles revealed beneath perfectly ordinary jeans. Perversely, in the very act of stripping off their gloves, the two women radiated sensuality and sexual self-awareness.

H.

We cover ourselves up because that's what's written in the Qur'an. Allah commanded the Prophet Muhammad to order his wives and the wives of his companions to wrap themselves in their clothes and cover their faces so no one would harm them. I've dressed like this since my wedding. Until then I wore only the mandeel, *but later, out of inner conviction, I decided to cover my whole body.*

It's not that men are so dangerous but that woman is a temptress by nature, liable to seduce a man and spoil his marital relations if she's more beautiful than his wife. So Islam commands women to conceal themselves. Also, uncovered women might encourage prostitution, because unmarried men would be tempted and feel the urge to go with women in exchange for money.

It's a fact that family relations in the West are a shambles. Families that don't observe the ways of Islam are not secure. True, not all men are weak, we can't generalize; but this prohibition is meant to protect those who are. I myself feel safer. I know that my clothing immediately sets limits for a man. I'm not angry at women who dress differently, but I hope God will guide them to behave according to Islamic doctrine.

During the *intifada,* our hostess—a secular woman—was attacked by a group of young men because she was in the street without a head covering. The incident took place far from her own neighborhood, where no one would have dared attack her, she says, "because we all know one another." The young men called her a *jasusa,* a collaborator, and demanded to look inside her purse. She refused and the enraged men began hitting her and yelling hysterically. Fortunately, a friend of her brother's happened to pass by and immediately summoned help. Word of that incident and others spread quickly, making it clear to every woman that she would be better off covering her head. When I met with H., though, she denied all knowledge of such tactics. "I haven't heard of physical coercion," she said. "I know that leaflets and graffiti spread the idea that women should dress according to the laws of Islam."

Like other devout Muslims, H. believes there is nothing to prevent a woman from entering public life—joining demonstrations, working, or studying at a university—as long as she wears traditional clothing. And there is nothing to stop a woman from working outside the home as long as she doesn't neglect her family duties. Covering her face and body, though, is a way to increase a woman's absence from public life, even when she is taking part in it. Some women consider this a source of power: they can see without being seen; strangers cannot know their identity.

H.

When I was young, I dreamed of having my own Islamic family, and I've done it. I did once think of being a doctor, but there are no medical universities here and my father didn't want me to travel abroad. I accepted his position and gave in, and I'm satisfied with my life. It's natural for every woman, when she becomes an adult, to want a good marriage. I wanted a Muslim husband because I believe in the words of the Prophet Muhammad, peace and blessings be upon him: every Muslim man who loves his wife is to treat her with generosity and graciousness. Even the Muslim man who doesn't love his wife must treat her justly. I hear of many problems in other families and am convinced that a man who is truly a Muslim will not hurt his wife. According to the Prophet Muhammad, the best Muslim is judged on the basis of his family and marital relations. The fact is that my husband irons and helps with the housework.

As for permission to leave the house, it's only natural. The Prophet Muhammad said that the wife who goes out without her husband's permission will be cursed by the angels until she returns home. When my husband was in prison, I told him I needed to leave the house to take care of all kinds of things and he gave me blanket permission to go out as long as he was in jail.

At the time of our conversation, A.'s husband was being held in a Palestinian jail with other Hamas and Islamic Jihad detainees. A. is his second wife. She agreed to marry him only after reciting the *istikhara*, the prayer of choice, in which Allah guides the supplicant toward the correct decision. "Marriage had been proposed to me once before," she said, "and I had felt a choking sensation. I didn't know what to decide. I recited this special prayer but still felt a kind of suffocation, so I said no. On the other hand, with the man I married, I also said this prayer and immediately felt serene and tranquil even though he was already married." A. recounted that it was her husband's first wife who suggested she marry him. "But why?" A. asked, and was told that the wife was ill. After a month of marriage, A. discovered that the first wife was beautiful, well-groomed, and attentive to her children. "I was angry, and my husband felt it," A. said. "I asked him why he'd married me if his wife was healthy, and he said time would tell. The truth is that in time I saw the first wife was irritable and restless and didn't care about her husband."

A young woman—a second wife—came into J.'s yard in al-Shatti camp, seeking the advice of her older neighbor. Her husband's first wife had a young son who had married a sixteen-year-old girl. One month into the marriage, the couple were unhappy and the son wanted to marry a new wife and kick the girl out of the house.

Fifty-five-year-old J. listened politely, concealing her annoyance at the interruption. "*Ya ukhti*, my sister," she said to the young woman, who kept smoothing her hair and rearranging her *mandeel* as she talked, telling us how hard it was to share the house with her husband's son and his unhappy wife. "*Ya ukhti*," J. said again. "You can't undo one mistake by making another. You were wrong to marry him off at such an early age. And to a girl so young. Don't add to your mistakes by sending her away."

The suffering of women who marry young is reflected in the divorce statistics: in 1995 approximately 39 percent of women getting divorced were between fifteen and twenty years old. Their proportion of the divorce rate has been stable for years, even as the numbers of women marrying in that age group have declined from some 30 percent in 1992 to 25 percent in 1995. On the other hand, the overall ratio of divorces to marriages has risen steadily since 1991: from 9.7 percent in 1991 to 14.2 percent in 1995, or 1,239 couples getting divorced while 8,698 couples got married.

Very young women and older women alike must cope with the demands of a society in which large families are the norm. On a routine day when I visited one of the refugee camps' UNRWA clinics, eight women had come in to ask the family-planning nurse about contraception. A few, though only twenty-two or twenty-three, already had three or four children and wanted a rest. Sometimes, the nurse told me, the women are older, forty or so, and want to stop getting pregnant because of health problems. One of that morning's patients had five daughters and no sons. The nurse was surprised. "Your husband agrees to using contraception?" The woman explained: "Yesterday we all felt bad, me and the girls. Some of them simply lay about whimpering. I announced that I'd had enough, that I was exhausted, and my husband agreed I could stop getting pregnant. So I came straight over. If his mother found out, she'd never agree." The day had been set aside for counseling only, not for fitting diaphragms, but the nurse was willing to take care of the woman right away.

"It's a problem," the nurse told me. "There's a general understanding that having too many children doesn't make sense. But the mothers-in-law insist on keeping to the old ways. The more children there are, the more secure they feel in their old age. They think there'll be someone to take care of them. And the women are afraid their husbands will take another wife if they don't have a child every year." Other family-planning departments report a growing number of inquiries about contraception. One such department is at the Women's Health Center in al-Bourij camp, the first center of its kind, offering a range of services related to women's health, from exercise classes to psychological counseling.

More than a few couples learn the hard way that having many children is not a guarantee of security in old age. There are very few places to turn in Gaza for the many children with genetic defects—marriage between first cousins is fairly common in the Strip. For children suffering from hereditary mental retardation, there are, however, the Forget Me Not Centers, a rare source of support and the brainchild of Naama al-Hilu, a groundbreaking woman who ran as a candidate of the Palestinian Democratic Union (FIDA) in the elections.

Hilu was one of fourteen women candidates. She was not elected, but two Gazan women were, out of thirty-seven representatives. In the course of her campaign, Hilu met hundreds of women and found that their chief concerns were the low level of general education among women (I know two school principals whose wives are illiterate) and polygyny. "The women demanded that we pass a law prohibiting marriage to a second wife. They demanded that we take action against the practice of forcing girls into marriage, and they complained that educated women can't find work." But the Legislative Council is unwilling to challenge the religious authorization of polygyny. As the Council begins to debate the Palestinian constitution, it apparently will not intervene in Islamic matrimonial law.[*]

A founder of the Democratic Front in the Strip (and of its pro-Oslo breakaway faction, FIDA), Hilu was imprisoned four times in Israeli jails for a total of fourteen years. Everyone in her office proudly reminds me that she was one of the first women to join the armed struggle: in 1970 she threw a grenade at an IDF unit beside her refugee camp home. In the explosion and the ensuing gunfire she lost her right hand and an eye. Early in the *intifada* she was placed on the Israelis' wanted list and eventually sentenced to four years in prison. In the two years before she was captured, though, she set up the Strip's first nursery school for mentally challenged children. Later she established an elementary school for these children and a vocational school. Her educational venture expanded, and now there are twenty-five kindergartens under her direction and thirty classes for women. At one of her campaign rallies, Yassir Abed Rabbo, a FIDA leader, spoke of Hilu's experience in the Palestinian struggle: "She has given her life for her people. Instead of being a mother, she has sacrificed herself." Even among political activists, Hilu's choice to remove herself from domestic life and not to marry is considered a sacrifice.

Motherhood is the main calling in the life of D. from al-Shatti camp. Thirty-four, she has been separated from her husband for twelve years now and has brought up her children alone. To make some money, she opened a kindergarten in her house, but during 1996 the number of children attending plummeted—the long months of closure meant that

---

[*]In 1996, Palestinian feminists set up a model parliament that debates issues related to women's status and equality. The same group organized consciousness-raising groups throughout Gaza and the West Bank and, in its parliamentary "sessions," drew up "bills" to be presented as working proposals to Palestinian lawmakers. The Gaza branch of the model parliament (closures frequently prevented joint sessions with West Bank members) drew considerable anger from religious figures when it posited that Islamic law, the shariah, is only one source of legislation among other systems, which include universal principles and international conventions. In another vote, a decisive majority of the eighty-eight members (men from various grass-roots organizations also participate) "approved" a law forbidding polygyny.

few parents could afford the NIS 20 ($6) monthly fee. I met D. at the home of her sister S., who coaxed her to speak to me without fear.

D.

Look, nothing good has happened to me in my life. Nothing good my whole life. The best thing that ever happened was when my father was allowed back into Gaza. He left the country before the war in 1967 when I was in elementary school, and then the Israelis wouldn't let him come back. He finally got a permit from Israel, but that was after my brother was killed.

I'm laughing, but it's because of the sadness of my life. Because of my tragedy. I have to bear all the responsibility for my children. This is my fate. I believe in fate. And I do have bright, healthy children. Everything comes from God, but I am suffering a great deal. I have to be mother and father to my children. It's not worth getting divorced officially. What for? Marriage is only for having children, and I have them.

When I was a child I just wanted to study. My parents destroyed my dream when they arranged my marriage. I was the best in my class, but my father decided to marry me off and my mother was too weak to object. Then I understood what a big difference there is between sons and daughters. For my own daughters I wish that they finish school and that they have good husbands and marriages, because that's what brings happiness in life.

Our society shackles our dreams. I dream of visiting London by myself, but our society would never let me do that. But I do have one dream. I'd like to own a plot of land where I'd build a model kindergarten. There'd be lots of kindergarten teachers and I'd be in charge.

S., D.'s Sister

The whole time we were growing up we saw our mother sacrificing herself. Her life is joyless, even today. Her big mistake was to raise us for the same kind of life. But now I'm beginning to learn how to take things for myself. I've signed up for a video course. And I can see that our daughters are different.

J., age fifty-five, was forced by her father to marry young and then swore she wouldn't rush her daughters into marriage. Today, one daughter is thirty and single, and J. is consumed with regret and worry. "Maybe I made a mistake. Maybe she was taken over by a jinn, a demon. Do you believe in demons?" M., a twenty-eight-year-old engineer, has called off three engagements. "Maybe a jinn got into me," she wondered. "Do you believe in demons?"

Um Ahmad

I was signed up for the ninth grade. I'd paid twenty-five liras, I remember. It was at the end of the summer and I was working in the fields. My brother-in-law has a plot of land and we were working there. I told my father I had to go to school the next day and I would only be able to work on weekends. He said no, that I was a young woman and had to bring home a little money. All that night I cried, I was so angry. It's been twenty years and I'm still angry. That's why the one thing I care about is my children's education. Look at my neighbors. One of them had a thirteen-year-old girl and wanted her to help in the house and get married. Another neighbor has a nineteen-year-old daughter who has been helping in the house since the sixth grade. Her other girl stays home when she should be in junior high. I'm angry at these people. When I sit with them, I always talk about these things, education and marriage, but they say that a twelve- or thirteen-year-old girl is only going to be a housewife anyway, so she might as well start early.

Still, our lives have improved a bit, in spite of everything. Twenty years ago, you couldn't find a mop or a bottle of bleach in the whole village— we had to kneel on the floor to wash it by hand, with a rag. Today there are lots of courses for women, so they can learn to read and write. We've got young women here who've never been to school—can you imagine? A twenty-year-old woman who doesn't know how to read and write? UNRWA organizes the courses. Sometimes we used to go to brush up a little. I'd knock on all the doors to convince the other women to come with me.

And now we've got a proper sewage system. It's much easier for women when there's a better standard of cleanliness. We didn't use to have plumbing in the house, before my husband went to prison. We didn't have a bathtub or a toilet. Sometimes I'd cook over an open fire from wood that I'd brought in from outside. My husband was constantly talking about wanting to move to another house, but it was always tomorrow, never now. When he was in prison, though, I fixed up this room and I put in a bathtub over there. I didn't ask him. I saved the money and consulted with friends. We couldn't live like that, it was impossible. I had money from sewing that I took in and UNRWA helped us with flour and things like that.

My husband is the one who decides things. I'm not ashamed to say it. When he was in prison he told me to do whatever I thought needed doing.

But now that he's out, he decides what I do. I have to take his mother to the clinic, even though he's not working. I don't argue. I'm used to not arguing. He believes he's doing the right thing when he makes decisions for me, and I do too. One day he decided I should stop smoking and I obeyed him. That was good. He still smokes, but I can't decide for him what he should do. That's the way it'll always be among Arabs—the man decides. But my husband wants our daughters to study. He's not like my father. He'd give anything for me to keep on studying. He gave me money to learn to drive, and I got my driver's license just as they took his away. During the intifada *I'd drive into Gaza City and bring home fresh vegetables for the whole neighborhood. I bought corn on the cob and cooked it. Everyone would wait for me to get home because I bought good produce and didn't take too big a profit. It felt good to be doing something.*

Awhile ago I was visiting some family in Israel. They have four sons and a daughter and they're very rich. The youngest boy had fallen out of bed and broken his arm. When he fell out of bed a second time and cracked his head, a social worker came round. They thought the parents were abusing him. I thought they should come to Gaza and see how people behave. There are women who hit their children really hard. But it's the pressure. The mothers are under so much pressure—from the economic situation and the daily grind, but mainly from their husbands and their mothers-in-law. My mother-in-law decides for all of us and I don't dare argue. What I dream of is privacy in a home of my own. My oldest son says one day he'll bring home some dynamite and blow up the house. Then we'll build a new one.

The percentage of women working outside the home is lower in the Strip than in the West Bank. A 1992 study by FAFO, a Norwegian research center, found that some 8 percent of the Strip's work-force were women, compared with 19 percent in the West Bank. The Palestinian Ministry of Planning puts the figures even lower, probably because, unlike the FAFO study, its findings do not include women who work as cleaning ladies outside their homes or as seamstresses at home. One way or the other, the low percentage results from a combination of factors: the traditional inclination to see a woman's proper place as in the home, household chores that make it hard for women to take on other work, chronic unemployment in the Strip, which prevents them from entering the workforce or relegates them to unskilled jobs, and fundamental doubts about women's capabilities.

In 1995, according to Planning Ministry figures, a workforce of 131,000 included 6,200 women, or 4.7 percent, but this was an improvement over previous years: in 1991, 2,900 women worked outside their homes out of a total workforce of 107,700, 2.7 percent. At the beginning of 1995 there had been a general drop in the number of civilian wage earners in the Gaza Strip (that is, those working in Israel, in the Strip, or for UNRWA, but not for the Palestinian security establishment); by the end of the year the number of employed persons had increased within the Strip as a whole and in the Palestinian Authority's ministries in particular, and the percentage of women had doubled. For one thing, following the advent of Palestinian self-rule, educated and well-trained women had returned from abroad. The number of clerical jobs increased, as did those in the public sector, especially in the education and health ministries. Moreover, the Palestinian Authority intentionally sought to promote women's employment. Some saw this encouragement as a welcome aspect of the struggle between the Authority—or the secular tradition of the PLO—and the Islamic opposition.*

Late in 1995 the Palestinian Ministry of the Interior issued a regulation requiring that a woman's request for a travel permit be signed by her husband, her father, or some other male guardian. Possibly the Authority hoped to appease its Islamic rivals with the new regulation (and Hamas was pleased by the legislation), although it also confirmed how deeply ingrained patriarchy is in Gazan society, even as the Authority appeared to encourage women's participation in public life. Women's organizations and female candidates for election protested. "Why didn't we need men's permission when we struggled against the occupation? Why maintain the pretense of democracy while discriminating against women?" demanded one leaflet distributed a week before the Legislative Council elections. Although increasingly disregarded after the elections, the regulation is still enforced ad hoc according to each clerk's disposition.

Ashraf, a religious man turned secular, returned to Gaza after ten years in jail and was shocked at the regression in women's status. "The women, poor things, that's not living when you can't make your own decisions." He

---

*In subsequent years, women's employment fell in tandem with the Strip's overall lack of employment due to the closures.

quickly noticed how much stronger the institution of the family had become in his absence. Research findings of the Jerusalem Media and Communication Center concur:

> Deprived of their land and the right to live independently and freely, the Palestinian family has become one of the few institutions in which the Palestinians have been able to live and act as they were accustomed to doing. The family has thus gained an enormous importance as a protector of national identity and as a maintainer of the Palestinian culture.
>
> The home and the family, "the inner circle" and domain of women, has become the only arena where men have been able freely to enforce their otherwise restricted possibilities of control and domination. The home has also become, even more than formerly, the place where the menfolks could seek shelter from psychological wounds and where they would be taken care of by the women members of the family.
>
> A big family also has meant a stronger family and a stronger community, thus the bearing of children has become a national duty which women carry out proudly.
>
> On the one hand the Israeli occupation has reinforced the traditional duties of women, while on the other hand it has led, ironically also, to the development and change of their position in society, by confronting them with situations and circumstances which women in orderly conservative patriarchal societies, such as the normal Palestinian one, would usually not have to face.

FAFO offered statistical confirmation of a conservative trend among younger women:

> Perhaps the most interesting comparison is the regular difference in attitudes between the age groups 15–19 and 20–29 year olds. On every issue, the youngest age group of women is consistently more conservative than women in their twenties. The important point lies not so much in the degree of differences but in the consistency of the differences. This suggests that there might be

a larger set of interrelated ideas about women's correct role in society that has had an impact on the young women who came of age during the last few years of the *intifada*. Stated more directly, the data seems to vindicate observations that there has been a general social retrenchment during the *intifada*, with women in their teens being most affected by new conservative ideologies.

Affirmative responses to the question of whether it was "acceptable for women to work outside the home" were divided as follows: 71 percent of females between the ages of 15 and 19 answered yes; in the 20–29 age group many more—87 percent—responded in the affirmative, as did 66 percent in the 30–39 age group and 77 percent of those between 40 and 49. And to the question of whether it was "acceptable for women to send their children to day care centers," 46 percent of the youngest females, 15–19, 59 percent of those between the ages of 20 and 29, and 58 percent of those between 30 and 39 answered yes.

Um Saber and Abu Saber are both forty years old, and their views have been influenced by emancipatory ideas, both personal and national. They live in the Nasser neighborhood of Gaza City with their seven children. Abu Majed, a friend, dropped by to talk while I was visiting them.

UM SABER: When I was a girl I dreamed of being an airline hostess or a journalist. Without a passport there was no chance of being an airline hostess, so that left journalism. Before I knew it, though, I'd signed up for advanced classes in husband, home, and children. I got married when I was fifteen years old, just a child.

ABU SABER: That was because I asked for her hand. I saw her, we met, we married, and that was it for her.

UM SABER: Thanks be to God, I'm satisfied with my life. I'm active in the Fatah Women's Committee and work to help women recognize their strength. Women should be able to say no to anything they don't like at home, instead of saying *khader*—at your service—all the time. We talk about the role of women in society, about how to educate children so they'll value peace and know right from wrong. But we still don't have a permanent place to meet and bring women together.

ABU SABER: The movement still hasn't found somewhere for the

Women's Committee. I know Um Saber has been fighting for that. She wanted to build on the land near our house, but they haven't agreed yet.

UM SABER: During the elections we campaigned for the Fatah slate. We wanted the good people to get voted in, the ones Abu Amar chose. We went from house to house; explaining how the elections worked. But we didn't campaign for the independent women candidates. We didn't know them. We hadn't heard of them, people like Rawya al-Shawwa, nor her newspaper articles. In Palestinian society, we women are cut off from what's going on outside. We're uncultured. We don't know one another.

There are things I've gotten used to. Studies are a lost cause. That was finished when I married Abu Saber. I was a girl, and there's no room in your head for learning when you're taking care of children all the time. Now I want to give my children the things I missed out on. I want my daughters to go to university, and I push them harder than I push my sons. I'm satisfied with my life, but I was angry that they married me off so early. When Abu Saber was arrested, I could have done more for the children if I'd had a profession, had a diploma.

ABU SABER: Do you know how hard it is for a woman on her own, without money and without a profession?

ABU MAJED: My wife managed. We've got a big family. When I was arrested they took care of her, but I saw with my friends how hard it was for their families. Some women worked as seamstresses while their husbands were in prison. By the time the husbands came home, their wives couldn't see, their eyes were so tired. They'd worked day and night to bring in a little money.

ABU SABER: When I got out of prison a year ago I had friends whose wives had changed so much they wanted to take a second wife. It took me six months to understand the changes Um Saber had gone through. When I was arrested, I left behind an inexperienced woman. I used to do everything at home. The new situation had made her strong, more masculine. Before 1985 she wouldn't go to the market by herself. We'd go together and we'd shop together and come back home. Now she goes out. She'd been to Egypt and Jordan while I was in jail. Living without me let her think for herself. It strengthened her opinions.

UM SABER: During the *intifada* I had to see to the children's education, make sure they didn't get arrested, make sure they didn't get hurt, that they came home before the curfew, that there was something for them to eat in the house.

ABU SABER: While I was in jail she could do things that would have been considered improper at any other time. She gained a lot of self-confidence, which helped her do things without people finding fault. Now she goes out of the house without even telling me, and I've gotten used to it. If a woman lived alone during that time, then she learned how to manage just by living. If she lived with the *hamula,* the clan, then everything stayed the same.

ABU MAJED: It's bad for a family when one of the daughters-in-law has to go out to work to bring home, food. In our house, my father takes care of everything. But the women are treated with respect. We don't sit in judgment over them. When I was in prison and the children needed their inoculations, my father took them to the clinic. Now that I'm home I let my wife go out with them. My father's not happy with the situation, but he coddled her too much.

UM SABER: Look, character doesn't just come out of nowhere. It comes from experience. In our society a woman who comes home late at night is a bad woman. But her personality develops through her husband if he gives her the opportunity, if he prods her, if he supports her efforts. A woman needs her husband's support to be independent. Consensus at home is very important, but if a woman's not convinced by her husband's opinions then she should cling to her own.

ABU SABER: She always said that I gave her a free hand to do everything, even to discuss things with me.

ABU MAJED: Thank God my wife isn't like that.

On windy days my friend M. likes to drive to the shore early in the morning when the beach is empty and she can find a secluded spot. Far from people, she turns her face to the sea and screams into the wind.

Z., a psychologist
We're not used to crying and yelling, showing our feelings. We can't, because everyone lives so close together. I'm sure the men want to scream too, but they can't let go. Not long ago I started praying. We women have no strength, but I've found that praying gives me strength. It calms me down, like drinking beer does for other people. A woman whose husband beat her asked me where she could go. Who would have her afterward if she went back to her parents' home? I told her to wait until her children grew up and then Allah would solve the problem. If we lived somewhere else I would tell her to leave him. But it's hard

for a woman to get a divorce here and I mustn't make her situation worse, especially with the closures, when we're falling apart economically. This crisis has taken over every part of our lives. It's our major battle now, just struggling to get by. Women and men, are in the same battle, and as long as it controls our lives we can't fight for the other causes. Like that of most other oppressed peoples, our women's thinking has gotten distorted. They'll need time to take up their place in history, not just be driven by it. That was the great achievement of the intifada *that we miss so much: women took part in the struggle. Women made decisions.*

Muslim Women and Fundamentalism

Fatima Mernissi

From *The Middle East Report*, July/August 1998

When analyzing the dynamics of the Muslim world, one has to discriminate between two distinct dimensions: what people actually do, the decisions they make, the aspirations they secretly entertain or display through their patterns of consumption, and the discourses they develop about themselves, more specifically the ones they use to articulate their political claims. The first dimension is about reality and its harsh time-bound laws, and how people adapt to pitilessly rapid change; the second is about self-presentation and identity building. And you know as well as I do that whenever one has to define oneself to others, whenever one has to define one's identity, one is on the shaky ground of self-indulging justifications. For example, the need for Muslims to claim so vehemently that they are traditional, and that their women miraculously escape social change and the erosion of time, has to be understood in terms of their need for self-representation and must be classified not as a statement about daily behavioral practices, but rather as a psychological need to maintain a minimal sense of identity in a confusing and shifting reality.

To familiarize you with the present-day Muslim world and how women fit into the conflicting political forces (including religion), the best way is not to overwhelm you with data. On the contrary, what is most needed is some kind of special illumination of the structural dissymmetry that runs all through and conditions the entire fabric of social and individual life—the split between acting and reflecting on one's actions. The split between what one does and how one speaks about oneself. The first has to do with the realm of reality; the second has to do with the realm of the psychological elaborations that sustain human beings' indispensable sense of identity. Individuals die of physical sickness, but societies die of loss of identity; that is, a disturbance in the guiding system of representations of oneself as fitting into a universe that is specifically ordered so as to make life meaningful.

Why do we need our lives to make sense? Because that's where power is. A sense of identity is a sense that one's life is meaningful, that, as fragile as a person may be, she or he can still have an impact on her or his limited surroundings. The fundamentalist wave in Muslim societies is a statement about identity. And that is why their call for the veil for women has to be looked at in the light of the painful but necessary and prodigious reshuffling of identity that Muslims are going through in these often confusing but always fascinating times.

The split in the Muslim individual between what one does, confronted by rapid, totally uncontrolled changes in daily life, and the discourse about the unchangeable religious tradition that one feels psychologically compelled to elaborate in order to keep a minimal sense of identity—this, as far as I am concerned, is the key point to focus on in order to understand the dynamics of contemporary Muslim life.

If fundamentalists are calling for the return of the veil, it must be because women have been taking off the veil. We are definitely in a situation where fundamentalist men and non-fundamentalist women have conflicts of interest. We have to identify who the fundamentalist men are, and who are the nonfundamentalist women who have opted to discard the veil. Class conflicts do sometimes express themselves in acute sex-focused dissent. Contemporary Islam is a good example of this because, beyond the strong obsession with religion, the violent confrontations going on in the Muslim world are about two eminently materialistic pleasures: exercise of political power and consumerism.

Fundamentalists and unveiled women are the two groups that have merged with concrete, conflicting claims and aspirations in the postcolonial era. Both have the same age range—youth—and the same educational privilege—a recent access to formalized institutions of knowledge. But while the men seeking power through religion and its revivification are mostly from newly urbanized middle- and lower middle-class backgrounds, unveiled women, by contrast, are predominantly of middle-class, urban backgrounds.

As a symptom, the call for the veil tells us one thing. Telling us another thing is the specific conjuncture of the forces calling for it—that is, the conservative forces and movements, their own quest, and how they position themselves within the social movements dominating the national and international scene.

Trespassing

Islam is definitely one of the modern political forces competing for power around the globe. At least that is how many of us experience it. How can a "medieval religion," ask Western students raised in a secular culture, be so alive, so challenging to the effects of time, so renewable in energy? How can it be meaningful to educated youth? One of the characteristics of fundamentalism is the attraction Islam has for high achievers among young people. In Cairo, Lahore, Jakarta, and Casablanca, Islam makes sense because it speaks about power and self-empowerment. As a matter of fact, worldly self-enhancement is so important for Islam that the meaning of spirituality itself has to be seriously reconsidered.

What was not clear for me in the early 1970s was that all the problems faced in recent decades are more or less boundary problems, from colonization (trespassing by a foreign power on Muslim community space and decision-making) to contemporary human rights issues (the political boundaries circumscribing the ruler's space and the freedoms of the government). The issue of technology is a boundary problem: how can we integrate Western technological information, the recent Western scientific memory, without deluging our own Muslim heritage? International economic dependency is, of course, eminently a problem of boundaries: the International Monetary Fund's intervention in fixing the price of our bread does not help us keep a sense of distinct national identity. What are the boundaries of the sovereignty of the Muslim state vis-à-vis voracious, aggressive transnational corporations? These are some of the components of the crisis that is tearing the Muslim world apart, along, of course, definite class lines.

Naive and serious as only a dutiful student can be, I did not know in 1975 that women's claims were disturbing to Muslim societies not because they threatened the past but because they argued and symbolized what the future and its conflicts are about: the inescapability of renegotiating new sexual, political, economic, and cultural boundaries, thresholds, and limits. Invasion of physical territory by alien hostile nations (Afghanistan and Lebanon); invasions of national television by *Dallas* and *Dynasty*; invasion of children's desires by Coca-Cola and special brands of walking shoes—these are some of the political and cultural boundary problems facing the Muslim world today.

However, we have to remember that societies do not reject and resist changes indiscriminately. Muslim societies integrated and digested quite well technological innovations: the engine, electricity, the telephone, the transistor radio, sophisticated machinery, and arms, all without much resistance. But the social fabric seems to have trouble absorbing anything having to do with changing authority thresholds: freely competing unveiled women; freely competing political parties; freely elected parliaments; and, of course, freely elected heads of state who do not necessarily get 99 percent of the votes. Whenever an innovation has to do with free choice of the partners involved, the social fabric seems to suffer some terrible tear. Women's unveiling seems to belong to this realm. For the last one hundred years, whenever women tried or wanted to discard the veil, some men, always holding up the sacred as justification, screamed that it was unbearable, that the society's fabric would dissolve if the mask were dropped. I do not believe that men, Muslim or not, scream unless they are hurt. Those calling for the reimposition of the veil surely have reason. What is it that Muslim society needs to mask so badly?

The idea one hears about fundamentalism is that it is an archaic phenomenon, a desire to return to medieval thinking. It is frequently presented as a revivalist movement: bring back the past. And the call for the veil for women furthers this kind of misleading simplification. If we take the Egyptian city of Asyut as an example, we have to admit that it is a modern town with a totally new cultural feature that Muslim society never knew before: mass access to knowledge. In our history, universities and knowledge were privileges of the elite. The man of knowledge enjoyed a high respect precisely because he was a repository of highly valued and aristocratically gained information. Acquisition of knowledge took years, and often included a period of initiation that compelled the student to roam through Muslim capitals from Asia to Spain for decades. Mass access to universities, therefore, constitutes a total shift in the accumulation, distribution, management, and utilization of knowledge and information. And we know that knowledge is power. One of the reasons the fundamentalist will be preoccupied by women is that state universities are not open just for traditionally marginalized and deprived male rural migrants, but for women as well.

Persons under 15 years of age constitute 39 percent of Egypt's and 45 percent of Iran's total population.[1] The natural annual population increase in Egypt and Iran is 3.1 percent.[2] The time span for doubling the population is 22 years for Egypt and 23 for Iran. Secondary school enrollment in

Iran is 35 percent for women and 54 percent for men. In Egypt, 39 percent of women of secondary school age are in fact there, as compared to 64 percent of men.[3] The same trend is to be found in other Muslim societies.

Centuries of women's exclusion from knowledge have resulted in femininity being confused with illiteracy until a few decades ago. But things have progressed so rapidly in our Muslim countries that we women today take literacy and access to schools and universities for granted. Illiteracy was such a certain fate for women that my grandmother would not believe that women's education was a serious state undertaking. For years she kept waking my sister and me at dawn to get us ready for school. We would explain that school started exactly three hours after her first dawn prayer, and that we needed only five minutes to get there. But she would mumble, while handing us our morning tea: "You better get yourself there and stare at the wonderful gate of that school for hours. Only God knows how long it is going to last." She had an obsessive dream: to see us read the Qur'an and master mathematics. "I want you to read every word of that Qur'an and I want you to answer my questions when I demand an explanation of a verse. That is how the *qadis* [Muslim judges] get all their power. But knowing the Qur'an is not enough to make a woman happy. She has to learn how to do sums. The winners are the ones who master mathematics." The political dimension of education was evident to our grandmothers' generation.

While a few decades ago the majority of women married before the age of 20, today only 22 percent of that age group in Egypt and 38.4 percent in Iran are married.[4] To get an idea of how perturbing it is for Iranian society to deal with an army of unmarried adolescents, one has only to remember that the legal age for marriage of females in Iran is 13 and for males 15.[5] The idea of an adolescent unmarried woman is a completely new idea in the Muslim world, where previously you had only a female child and a menstruating woman who had to be married off immediately so as to prevent dishonorable engagement in premarital sex. The whole concept of patriarchal honor was build around the idea of virginity, which reduced a woman's role to its sexual dimension: to reproduction within early marriage. The concept of an adolescent woman, menstruating and unmarried, is so alien to the entire Muslim family system that it is either unimaginable or necessarily linked to *fitna* (social disorder). The Arab countries are a good example of this demographic revolution in sex roles.

SPACE AND SEX ROLES

Young men faced with job insecurity, or failure of the diploma to guarantee access to the desired job, postpone marriage. Women, faced with the pragmatic necessity to count on themselves instead of relying on the dream of a rich husband, see themselves forced to concentrate on getting an education. The average age at marriage for women and men in most Arab countries has registered a spectacular increase. In Egypt and Tunisia, the average age at marriage for women is 22 and for men 27. In Algeria, the average age at marriage is 18 for women and 24 for men. In Morocco, Libya, and Sudan, women marry at around 19 and men at around 25. The oil countries, known for their conservatism, have witnessed an incredible increase of unmarried youth: age at marriage for women is 20 and for men is 27. And of course nuptiality patterns are influenced by urbanization. The more urbanized youth marry later. In 1980, in metropolitan areas of Egypt the mean age at marriage was 29.7 for males and 23.6 for females. In the urban areas of Upper Egypt, where the fundamentalist movement is strong, the mean age at marriage was 28.3 for men and 22.8 for women.[6]

The conservative wave against women in the Muslim world, far from being a regressive trend, is on the contrary a defense mechanism against profound changes in both sex roles and the touchy subject of sexual identity. The most accurate interpretation of this relapse into "archaic behaviors," such as conservatism on the part of men and resort to magic and superstitious rituals on the part of women, is as anxiety-reducing mechanisms in a world of shifting, volatile sexual identity.

Fundamentalists are right in saying that education for women has destroyed the traditional boundaries and definitions of space and sex roles. Schooling has dissolved traditional arrangements of space segregation, even in oil-rich countries where education is segregated by sex: simply to go to school women have to cross the street! Streets are spaces of sin and temptation because they are both public and sex-mixed. And that is the definition of *fitna*: disorder!

Fundamentalists are right when they talk about the dissolution of women's traditional function as defined by family ethics; postponed age of marriage forces women to turn pragmatically toward education as a means for self-enhancement. If one looks at some of the education statistics, one understands why newly urbanized and educated rural youth single out university women as enemies of Islam, with its tradition of exclusion from knowledge and decision-making. The percentage of women teaching in Egyptian universities was 25 percent in 1981. To get an idea of how fast change is occurring there, one only has to remember that in 1980 the percentage of women teaching in American universities was 24 percent and it was 25 percent in East Germany.[7] Even in conservative Saudi Arabia, women have invaded sexually segregated academic space: they are 22 percent of the university faculty there. Women are 18 percent of the university faculty in Morocco, 16 percent in Iraq, and 12 percent in Qatar.

What dismays the fundamentalists is that the area of independence did not create an all-male new class. Women are taking part in the public feast. And that is a definite revolution in the Islamic concept of both the state's relation to women and women's relation to the institutionalized distribution of knowledge.

Notes

1 *1983 World Population Data Sheet* (Washington, D.C.: Population Reference Bureau).

2 Ibid.

3 "People's Wallchart," *People Magazine* vol. 12 (1985).

4 Ibid.

5 Ibid.

6 *World Fertility Survey* no. 42: "The Egyptian Survey," November 1983.

7 *Annuaire statistique* (Paris: UNESCO, 1980).

A Culture of One's Own:
Learning From Women Living Under Muslim Laws

Madhavi Sunder

Adapted from an article forthcoming in *The Yale Law Journal*

I.

When it comes to religion and women's rights, cultural relativism is more the rule than the exception in current human rights law, notwithstanding law's universalist aspirations. The current status of the Convention on the Elimination of Discrimination Against Women (CEDAW) is a prime example. The only international human rights instrument to exclusively address women's human rights, today 170 countries have either ratified or acceded to CEDAW. On paper, the Convention is a milestone achievement for women's rights, going so far as to call on states to change customary, cultural, and religious laws that are premised upon the inequality of the sexes. But while a few parties have yet to sign CEDAW—most notably the United States and Afghanistan at the time of this writing—many that have signed, particularly Muslim countries, have done so only on the condition that the Convention will not be recognized when it conflicts with religious or customary laws. When other signatory states complained to the UN that the reservations based on religion violated international human rights law, which allows parties to make reservations to treaties only if they do not undermine the "object and purpose" of the treaty, they were cowed into silence by Middle Eastern countries who charged religious intolerance and cultural imperialism. The UN has not followed up on the issue, in effect acquiescing to the reserving countries' cultural relativist claims. The upshot is that while the reservations may be illegal in theory, in practice, the reservations hold.[1]

The traditional approach of human rights law to "conflicts" between women's rights and the freedom of religion and culture is to "balance" a women's right to equality against a group's right to religious autonomy. But in striking this balance, the law frequently takes a cultural relativist view of religion. Presuming that the practice of religion is homogeneous, static, discrete, God-given, and imposed on individuals from the top down, law defers to religious leaders' (often patriarchal) beliefs, reinforcing their claims against the competing claims of dissenters within the religion, who are often women. The irony is that law's view of religion is identical to the view of fundamentalists, who also view religion as having essential, singular meanings that are imposed from above and are unchanging over time. As a result, human rights law has become complicit in the backlash efforts of traditional and fundamentalist leaders to silence internal dissent and change.

This leaves women no possibilities for both equality *and* religion or cultural practices—women must either reject their culture in favor of secular, universal human rights norms or content themselves to remain in a culture that discriminates against them, if the discrimination is linked to religious beliefs. In theory, the cultural relativist approach aims to protect a group's autonomy against the imposition of "Western" values. But, in fact, the challenge to discriminatory norms within Muslim communities is increasingly internal, not external. More and more, advocates of women's rights within Muslim countries and communities are contesting traditional religious and cultural meanings with greater voice and visibility than in the past. And in seeking a right to define culture for themselves, they are implicitly challenging traditional human rights *law*, as well. Many Muslim feminists are pursuing human rights strategies that combine religion and equality claims, advocating that women from Muslim countries and communities reinterpret their culture and religion in nondiscriminatory ways. Where a traditional cultural relativist approach might condone discriminatory practices, such as female genital mutilation, on a theory of tolerant pluralism, what I call a "cultural dissent" approach to women's human rights law recognizes the internal reform efforts of women from Muslim countries and communities and refuses to grant rights to discriminate in the name of culture or religion. This approach treats Muslim religion and culture as publicly circulating meanings to which all Muslims have access, rather than as the privately owned meanings of any one religious faction.

II.

Today, more and more Muslim women are claiming a right to dissent from traditional cultural norms and to make new cultural meanings—that is, to reinterpret cultural norms in ways more favorable to them. Not satisfied to choose between tradition and modernity, women in the modern world want both. They want culture, but on their own terms. The pioneering human rights work of the international network known as Women Living Under Muslim Laws (WLUML) is a case in point. WLUML, also known as the Network, is forging new definitions and constructions of religion and culture that expose the diversity of norms and laws within the Muslim world at a time when fundamentalists increasingly insist on a singular way of being Muslim. WLUML insists on the political nature of so-called "fundamentalist" forces, defining *fundamentalism* as the use of religion (or, often, culture and ethnicity as well) to seek or maintain political power.[2] What's more, WLUML increasingly asserts the affirmative right of women to define cultural and religious community for themselves.

Founded in 1984, WLUML is an international solidarity network for women—whether individuals or those belonging to organizations— around the world fighting against increasingly repressive and fundamentalist regimes that seek to curtail severely women's freedoms in the name of Islam.[3] Over nearly two decades the group has grown into a network linking thousands of women in approximately forty countries,[4] including academics and organizations dedicated to women's human rights.[5]

WLUML's "cultural dissent" approach goes further than merely critiquing the essentialist views of the fundamentalists. While the cultural relativist view accepts culture as imposed from above, the cultural dissent view highlights individuals' *ability and right to contest and shape culture.* [6] As individuals assert a right to autonomy, choice, reason, and plurality within cultural and religious—not just public—spaces, claims to cultural dissent render traditional, rigid conceptions of culture and religion obsolete. The cultural dissent of groups like WLUML heralds a new age of freedom and equality *within* cultural community.

Unlike traditional human rights law, which distances itself from the ostensibly private subject of "identity," WLUML identifies "the imposition of identity by Muslim laws"—and, particularly, a *religious* identity— as the most serious challenge to women's autonomy today in Muslim countries and communities.[7] But WLUML is careful to note that the problem is less religion, per se, than it is a particular conception of religion as static, homogeneous, and imposed from above. In a modern world in which cultural communities are threatened by fears of globalization and Westernization, WLUML observes that nativists and fundamentalists increasingly attempt to define and maintain a distinct Muslim community by limiting the rights of women.[8] WLUML recognizes that the "myth of a homogeneous Muslim world"—a myth fueled by fundamentalists as well as the Western media and well-meaning cultural relativists[9]—empowers fundamentalists in this endeavor. This myth encourages women and men— inside and outside the Muslim world—to believe that the fundamentalist view is the only way imaginable for women who want to maintain their religious or cultural identity.

Fundamentalists attempt to bolster this claim by presenting every rule and custom within Muslim societies as linked to divine religion, or Islam, rather than the daily and diverse practices of people living in Muslim communities. The problem, as Anissa Hélie, office coordinator at WLUML's international coordination office in London describes it, is that laws, despite their great variety throughout the Muslim world, nonetheless "are characterized as Islamic, divinely ordained, and something you therefore can't challenge."[10] Cultural practices such as female genital mutilation, which have never existed in many Muslim communities, elsewhere are considered essential to Islam. "People are led to think that these are religious requirements," says Cassandra Balchin, deputy office coordinator of WLUML's international coordination office in London, and therefore not open to challenge.[11]

WLUML challenges both the "religious" nature of Muslim laws as well as the notion that women cannot question them. To this end, the Network's approach is two-pronged. First, it critiques the *essentialist* view of Muslim laws. Second, WLUML challenges the notion that women *cannot contest or change* Muslim laws.

Let us begin with the antiessentialist critique. Since 1984, one of WLUML's most important aims has been to highlight the real diversity of Muslim laws and customs around the world. In doing this, WLUML exposes women from Muslim countries and communities everywhere to numerous alternative, and more progressive, ways of being "Muslim," and simultaneously undermines the notion that certain practices are essential in a Muslim community. WLUML's research has shown that far from discovering any single way of being Muslim, in fact Muslim women's lives:

> range from being strictly closeted, isolated and voiceless within four walls, subjected to public floggings and condemned to death for presumed adultery (which is considered a crime against the state) and forcibly given in marriage as a child, to situations where women have a far greater degree of freedom of movement and interaction, the right to work, to participate in public affairs and also exercise a far greater control over their own lives.[12]

By sharing the experiences of more liberal options within a Muslim framework WLUML hopes to enable women to imagine better lives for themselves, without the fear of losing their community or culture. Committed to finding and sharing this information, the Network circulates information about progressive laws in Muslim countries and communities; makes available in hardcopy and on the Internet Dossiers, or reproduced academic articles on women and law; produces information kits, a newssheet, and special bulletins; and disseminates Action Alerts on a regular basis that publicize urgent cases requiring immediate solidarity. The Network makes much of this information available in multiple languages.[13] In addition, WLUML fosters "shared lived experiences through exchanges," promoting "face-to-face interactions between women from the Muslim world who would normally not have a chance to travel and meet with women from other, culturally diverse, Muslim societies."[14]

These exchanges help to break women's isolation and undermine the claims of fundamentalists that there is just one way of being Muslim.[15]

"Contacts and links with women from other parts of the Muslim world—whose very existence speaks of the multiplicity of women's realities within the Muslim context—provides an important source of inspiration," explains Farida Shaheed, coordinator of WLUML's regional coordination office for Asia. "Likewise, information on the diversity of existing laws and practices within the Muslim context gives material shape to alternatives. Both encourage women to dream of different realities—the first step in changing the present one."[16] Exposing alternatives also highlights the often hidden forces of politics and power embedded within religious arguments. As one writer observes, seeing the variety of Muslim laws for themselves helps women "to distinguish between patriarchy and religion." [17]

Just as importantly, highlighting the fact that Muslim communities do support women's claims to equality offers a powerful tool against fundamentalist claims that feminism and human rights are Western, and should be rejected as un-Islamic. As Shaheed writes, "the condemnation of any challenges to existing Muslim laws as rejections of Islamic injunctions and the very concept of Muslim womanhood is a very potent formula for maintaining the status quo, as it implicitly threatens challengers with ostracization."[18] Shaheed continues:

> The fear of being pushed beyond the collectivity of one's nation, religion, and ethnic group—of losing one's identity—militates against initiating positive action for change. Under these circumstances, questioning, rejecting, or reformulating "Muslim" laws is indeed a major undertaking. . . .[19]

Balchin agrees. "The threat that you do not belong to the community, that you are Western, is extremely powerful," she says. "It's powerful at the individual level and it's powerful at the collective level."[20] More recently, in preparation for its Feminism in the Muslim World Leadership Institutes,[21] the Network has collected and shared examples of women's rights activism in the Muslim world from the eighth to the twentieth centuries. "It was very important for women participants to discover and reclaim often-forgotten feminist figures from their own culture, and from their personal lives (for example, stories about powerful female relatives, etc.)," Hélie explains.[22] "It's a tool," Balchin says. We are "giving women the tool to be able to say that women's rights are part of our own cultures."[23]

Significantly, WLUML's antiessentialist critique is aimed at both fundamentalists *and* the liberal left. For Mariémé Hélie Lucas, the founder and international coordinator of WLUML, cultural relativism from both sides of the political spectrum is "*the* big threat." "People from the left will say, 'Well, it's their culture. Who are we to interfere in another culture. We are afraid of being accused of racism, hence we can't interfere,'" says Hélie Lucas. The problem, she says, is that "Everything can be tolerated in the name of culture." A better approach, Hélie Lucas urges, is to examine the sources of cultural edicts, and figure out whose interests are being served or disserved by them.[24]

That's where the Network comes in. In one case, a Pakistani woman and a Nigerian man were students in Britain, where they met, married, and had a child. When the couple wanted to divorce, the husband went to a British judge and asked for a divorce under shariah, or Islamic, law. When the judge appeared ready to defer to the man's version of the divorce rules under the shariah, advocates for the wife approached WLUML. The Network sent the judge numerous examples of cases from all over the Muslim world in which marriages were dissolved to the benefit of the woman. "We asked him, the British judge, who are you to decide which is the true shariah?," Hélie Lucas recounts. "It's exposing someone who is a cultural relativist. He was prepared to divorce them in the name of shariah. But what is shariah? And who is he to tell us which one is the right one? We have to expose these people to the variety of state laws."[25]

Hélie Lucas continues, "We have to ask who defines culture. I want to define my own culture. Are you going to deny me this right?" [26] In challenging a traditional, monolithic view of culture, WLUML emphasizes women's rights to forge their own cultural meanings. This is the second prong of WLUML's work: encouraging women's participation in contesting and creating community for themselves. For Hélie Lucas, this is one of the most notable changes she has observed since the Network began in 1984. "It has changed in so far as women feel more and more powerful to change both [religion and culture]," she says. "I think that's what comes out of nearly twenty years of work. They don't swallow what they are told is tradition or is religion. They don't gulp it down anymore."[27]

WLUML's approach challenges not only the fundamentalists' view of religion but the traditional Western view, as well. As Hélie Lucas observes, both, paradoxically, "want a homogeneous view of Muslim laws."[28] But WLUML emphasizes that religion and culture are and *ought to be* plural, contested, and constantly evolving to meet the changing needs and demands of modern individuals.

It is important to note that while WLUML often talks about women's rights within a framework of religion or culture, the group certainly does not limit itself to reading Islamic texts or discovering fundamental truths and essences. Rather, the Network defines religion and community as fundamentally historical—hence, changing with cultural changes—and based on individual autonomy—that is, as emerging from the definitions that individuals themselves forge. To this end, WLUML empowers individual women to define for themselves the ways their religion is practiced, not just based on texts, but also on needs, aspirations, reason, and exchange of information with people inside and outside the Muslim world. While WLUML is convinced that strategies need to be decided upon by the concerned women, since its inception the Network has emphasized the benefits women's rights advocates can gain from networking with allies based outside the Muslim world. Such an approach is beneficial in so far as 1) it helps create the means through which the struggles of women from Muslim countries and communities can be supported by like-minded groups outside the Muslim world; and 2) it provides the space for inspiration from other progressive and emancipatory movements.

WLUML posits that: "It is only when women start assuming the right to define for themselves the parameters of their own identity and stop accepting unconditionally and without question what is presented to them as the 'correct' religion, the 'correct' culture, or the 'correct' national identity that they will be able effectively to challenge the corpus of laws imposed on them."[29] The Network writes:

> The essential issue is who has the power to define what women's identities should be . . . . As the boundaries of identity become increasingly exclusivist, authoritarians are giving people less opportunity to define who they are, what their needs are, and how those needs should be met. It is time to challenge—both politically as well as personally—those who define what the identity of women should be as Muslims . . .[30]

This conception of a "right to identity" is radically new in the context of international human rights. Unlike traditional human rights approaches, which defer to leaders to define a community, WLUML focuses on individual women within a community asserting rights to define their own identities, whether in a religious, cultural, or secular sphere. Working in a collective framework, WLUML calls upon women to "create our own identity" by, among other things:

- asking ourselves and analyzing who is imposing new dress codes on us and why;
- breaking the male monopoly of religious interpretations. . . ;
- and, most importantly, by functioning as alternative legitimising reference points for each other.[31]

This claim goes beyond traditional feminist critiques of the public/private distinction. Where most feminist efforts have concentrated on bringing legal attention to the issue of violence in the private sphere,[32] WLUML demands that women enjoy the right to challenge and to create normative community—that is, the right to make the world.

That said, working purely from within a framework of religion has drawbacks. The most obvious is that religious texts may be limiting. "We can show that what the Prophet said was a step forward" on a particular issue, such as slavery or women's rights, explains Hélie Lucas. "But we cannot limit ourselves to that. If the Prophet says 'Beat your wife lightly,' or 'Be kind to your slave,' a religious approach would limit itself to these" instructions. "Maybe within reinterpretation people can go further than that. But a secular approach would be no slavery" under any circumstances.[33]

In addition, Balchin points out that few Muslim women have the expertise or credentials to challenge traditional Islamic interpretations. "If you are talking about reinterpretations, there the problem is historical—that women have been historically excluded from interpretation, and they therefore lack the capacity in terms of knowledge of Arabic, knowledge of jurisprudence, admission into colleges that teach theology, etc.," says Balchin. "It's very difficult if you don't know classical Arabic. It's difficult if you don't have the legitimacy of education at certain places."[34]

Thus WLUML's work within the framework of religion focuses less on the spiritual than the political. WLUML highlights "the use or misuse of religion," says Balchin. "It's looking at the power relations, it's not talking about faith."[35] But WLUML's work is by no means limited to working within religious contexts. In fact, WLUML supports numerous strategies for pursuing women's rights, "from the exclusively secular to the exclusively theological, with many permutations in between."[36] Staying tuned to what strategies work best in particular contexts, WLUML activists emphasize, "These are choices, not destiny."[37] In fact, many WLUML participants have a secular, universal view of women's rights. Hélie contrasts the Network with the U.S.-based Catholics for a Free Choice, with which WLUML collaborates regularly. "The difference" between the two groups, Hélie says, is that the members of Catholics for a Free Choice "are mostly all believers, which is not the case in the Network. While a number of women linked to WLUML are indeed believers in Islam, in the Network there are many people who choose a secular approach (although they may also be believers), and there are those who are not believers but still, because they were born and raised in a Muslim community, are assumed to be 'Muslim women' to whom Muslim laws are applied to."[38]

Despite WLUML's diverse work—both international and local, secular and within a religious context—the Network is often simply characterized as "Islamic." Hélie Lucas points out that many outside of WLUML try to confine the Network to its "work from within." "Whenever we do a religious interpretation [project] it's really easy to get funding," she says, and "It's usually what we are asked to speak about. There are all sorts of indications that this is what we should be—indigenous." These outsiders incorrectly see all of the group's activities "as reinterpreting the Qur'an," complains Hélie Lucas.[39] "They essentialize us." Of course, there's essentializing from the other side as well. While some view WLUML as primarily religious, "similarly in other countries we are labeled atheists," Hélie Lucas muses.[40]

But unlike some of their Western counterparts, who might be more quick to think of being secular as antireligious, WLUML recognizes the importance of women's being able to influence the content of religion and culture. Indeed, even in a secular state, the private spheres of family, culture, and religion, and not the public sphere alone, profoundly influence women's lives and opportunities. In order to have more freedom in all aspects of their lives, then, women need to be actively involved in critiquing, contesting, and remaking culture. Furthermore, WLUML's approach suggest that, in order to live a full life, women *ought* to have a right to their own culture.

It is in this observation that secular feminists may learn from WLUML. WLUML's approach suggests that current human rights law may be premised upon a thin theory of both liberty and equality. Religious liberty does not mean much if one is continually subject to the version of the religion offered by the patriarchal and the powerful. Similarly, equality does not mean much if it is only available in public, secular spaces. Cultural spaces are equally, if not more, important to our lives. In Muslim countries and communities, women's claims to liberty and equality consist of affirmative rights to interpret culture and religion—that is, they challenge the exclusive authority of religious and cultural leaders to determine religious and cultural meaning. They also challenge hard-line secularists who would give weight to equality but little importance to the role of culture and religion in women's lives.

III.

"We have become politicized about race and class, but not culture," the anthropologist Lila Abu-Lughod writes.[41] The same can be said, if not more forcefully, about religion. How law conceives of religion and culture matters. The presumption that religion and culture are static and hierarchical leads the law to become complicit in the effort to suppress new claims for more reason and rights within religious contexts. Having no way to comprehend women's challenges to traditional religious interpretations, law responds with a myopic choice—equality and choice in the public sphere, or continued discrimination at the hands of traditionalists or fundamentalists, in the private sphere. The "choice" in effect quashes women's critiques and upholds the leaders', or fundamentalists', view of the religion or culture as the *only* valid one. Thus, more often than not, law defers to fundamentalist claims to discriminate in the name of religion or culture, and thwarts the claims of dissenting women and other advocates of change.

But while cultural relativism is premised upon a static, homogeneous view of culture that is antagonistic to change, cultural dissent presents— and promotes—cultural *change*. Cultural dissent both recognizes and facilitates the claims of modern women, who today are demanding more justification from religious authorities than in the past. Armed with new conceptions of religion itself, today more women seek reason, equality, and liberty not just in the public sphere, but also in the private worlds of religion, culture, and family. But, thus far, human rights law has not acknowledged this.

Indeed, the law has made their struggle more difficult. Despite the efforts of individuals to scale religious boundaries and transgress traditional borders, law is reestablishing those boundaries. In some cases, law is making them stronger than ever. This need not be the case. The combined regime of law and religion can either promote individual autonomy or retard it. Just as anthropologists and religion scholars are rethinking their profession, lawyers must also rethink what strategies and goals best promote liberty and equality today.

Notes

1 *Convention on the Elimination of All Forms of Discrimination Against Women,* adopted by G.A. Res. 180, UN GAOR, 34th Sess., Supp. No. 46, at 193, UN Doc. A/34/36 (1979), 9 I.L.M. 33 (1980) (entered into force on Sept. 3,

1981) [hereinafter Women's Convention]. Despite the Women's Convention's bold call for the eradication of discriminatory practices even in the private spheres of culture and tradition, the United Nations has generally accepted many states' ascension to the Women's Convention with official reservations that proclaim that state's acceptance of the treaty only in so far as it does not conflict with their religious traditions. *See* http://www.un.org/womenwatch/daw/; Rebecca Cook, *Reservations to the Convention on the Elimination of All Forms of Discrimination Against Women*, 30 Virginia J. Int'l L. 643 (1990).

While states may make reservations to treaties when signing them, under current international law the reservations should be compatible with the object of the treaty. *See* Henry J. Steiner & Philip Alston, International Human Rights in Context: Law, Politics, Morals 439 (2d ed. 2000) (citing Article 2(1)(d) of the Vienna Convention on the Law of Treaties). In addition, Article 28(2) to the Women's Convention expressly prohibits reservations incompatible with the 'object and purpose' of the Convention.

2 See Cassandra Balchin, *The Network 'Women Living Under Muslim Laws': Strengthening Local Struggles Through Cross-Boundary Networking*, Society for International Development 130 n. 1 (2002).

3 See Farida Shaheed, *Controlled or Autonomous: Identity and the Experience of the Network, Women Living Under Muslim Laws*, 19 Signs 997-98 (1994).

4 *Id.* at 1014.

5 Homa Hoodfar, *Muslim Women on the Threshold of the Twenty-first Century* (Sept. 1998), Dossier 21, Women Living Under Muslim Laws (describing participants including "women lawyers, sociologists, anthropologists, journalists, and other social scientists").

6 *See* Madhavi Sunder, *Cultural Dissent,* 54 Stan. L. Rev. 495 (2001).

7 Shaheed, *supra* note 3, at 1005; Plan of Action — Dhaka 1997, Women Living Under Muslim Laws (identifying concept of one, homogeneous Muslim world as a myth and one of the chief factors undermining "women's ability to control change and re-invent our lives."). *See also* Anissa Hélie, *Feminism in the Muslim World: Leadership Institutes 31* (2000) (observing that "[f]ar from being innocent, this myth limits women's and people's ability to evaluate what pertains to customs, law and religion and therefore undermines their ability to assert their rights.").

8 For good descriptions of this phenomenon see partha Chatterjee, *The Nation and Its Fragments* (1993); Lata Mani, *Contentious Traditions: The Debate on*

Sati in Colonial India, in *Recasting Women: Essays in Colonial History* (Kumkum Sangari & Sudesh Vaid, eds. 1989). See generally *Women, Laws, Initiatives in the Muslim World: Discussions Fom the International Meeting Towards Beijing: Women, Law and Status in the Muslim World,* December 11-15, 1994, Lahore, pakistan 22 (1998) [hereinafter Women, Laws, Initiatives] (observing that women are in a difficult position because "almost all efforts at imposing an Islamic identity focus heavily on restricting women, their rights and mobility, and their very visibility.").

9 See Plan of Action—Dhaka 1997, *Women Living Under Muslim Laws* (criticizing Western media's negative, homogeneous portrayal of Islam and denouncing "well-meaning progressives" in the West who have fallen into the "trap of cultural relativism").

10 Anissa Hélie, Interview with Author, July 11, 2002, London, England.

11 Cassandra Balchin, Interview with Author, July 11, 2002, London, England.

12 Shaheed, *supra* note 3, at 1007 (citations omitted).

13 Ibid. at 1009-1010.

14 Ibid.

15 *About Women Living Under Muslim Laws,* http://www.wluml.org/english/about.htm; Shaheed, *supra* note iii, at 1005.

16 Shaheed, *supra* note 3, at 1007 (describing the Network as "an alternative reference group" that may help Muslim women "redefine the parameters of their current reference group(s)").

17 Ibid.

18 Ibid. at 1005.

19 Ibid.

20 Balchin Interview, *supra* note 11.

21 The Feminism in the Muslim World Leadership Institutes took place in Turkey (1998) and Nigeria (1999) and were organized in collaboration with the Center for Women's Global Leadership.

22 Hélie Interview, *supra* note 10.

23 Balchin Interview, *supra* note 11.

24 Mariémé Hélie Lucas, Interview with Author, June 25, 2002, Montpellier, France.

25 Ibid.

26 Ibid.

27 Ibid.

28 Ibid.

29 Shaheed, *supra* note 3, at 1008.

30 *Women, Laws, Initiatives, supra* note 8, at 24.

31 Ibid. at 46.

32 See, *e.g., Declaration on the Elimination of Violence Against Women,* G.A. Res. 48/104, UN GAOR, 48th Sess., UN Doc. A/RES/48/104 (1994), Art. 4 (asserting that "States should condemn violence against women and should not invoke any custom, tradition or religious consideration to avoid their obligations with respect to its elimination.").

33 Hélie Lucas Interview, *supra* note 24.

34 Balchin Interview, *supra* note 11.

35 Ibid.

36 See Shaheed, supra note 3, at 999. Indeed, many secular feminists hold that "even under the most progressive interpretations of Islam, the danger of reverting to reactionary Islam would be ever present." Shahla Zia, Some Experiences of the Women's Movement: Strategies for Success, in *Shaping Women's Lives: Laws, Practices, and Strategies in Pakistan* 371, 384, 408 (Farida Shaheed et al. eds. 1998) ("The question of secularization continues to divide different strands of the women's movement."). But some secular feminists question whether some of the failures of their movement may in part be due to their reluctance to confront religious issues directly. See id. at 398. For examples of various approaches, see, e.g., Valentine Moghadam, *Modernizing Women: Gender and Social Change in the Middle East* (1993); Fatmima Mernissi, *Beyond the Veil: Male-Female Dynamics in Modern Muslim Society* (1987); Lama Abu Odeh, Post-Colonial Feminism and the Veil: Thinking the Difference, 43 Feminist Rev. 29 (1993) (contrasting her own negative opinion of veiling with arguments in its favor by other Muslim women).

37 Introduction, Dossier 23/24, *Women Living Under Muslim Laws* (July 2001) at 3. See also Farida Shaheed, *Constructing Identities—Culture, Women's Agency and the Muslim World,* in Dossier 23/24, Women Living Under Muslim Laws (July 2001) at 33, 34 (expressing concern that preoccupation with religiously-based reform efforts by Muslim women at the expense of recognizing multiple strategies, including secular, "over-determines the role of Islam in the lives of women," and implies that "Muslims somehow manage to live in a world that is defined solely by a religious identity, is exclusive of all non-Muslims and that is insulated from any other social political or culturally relevant influences such as structures of power, the technological revolution, the culture of consumerism, etc."); M. A. Hélie Lucas, *What Is Your Tribe?: Women's Struggles*

and the Construction of Muslimness, in Dossier 23/24, *Women Living Under Muslim Laws* (July 2001) at 49, 59 ("What is of most interest to me is the fact that amongst [the] different but complementary strategies [of Muslim feminists], only one is artificially isolated, getting most attention, most funding, most recognition. It is seen as the only authentic one, the best for 'Muslims.' Indeed, it is the strategy of religious interpretation."); Shahrzad Mojab, *The Politics of Theorizing 'Islamic Fundamentalism': Implications for International Feminist Movements,* in Dossier 23/24, *Women Living Under Muslim Laws* (July 2001) at 64, 71 (critiquing myth of the "Muslim woman" whose identity is determined singly by religion).

38 Hélie Interview, *supra* note 10.

39 Hélie Lucas Interview, *supra* note 24.

40 Ibid.

41 *See* Lila Abu-Lughod, *Do Muslim Women Really Need Saving?*, American Anthropologist, Sept. 2002, at 5-6.

42 Amartya Sen, *Culture and Identity,* LITTLE INDIA, August 1998.

Understanding the Other Sister: The Case of Arab Feminism

Susan Muaddi Darraj

From *Monthly Review*, March 2002

One evening, shortly after September 11, I was conducting a college English class when one of my students asked a question about the accumulating body of information on women and Islam. It was one of many questions about the Middle East asked of me in the days after the tragedies; this one was about the veil, and why women in the Middle East "had to wear it." I explained that not all women in the Middle East were Muslim (I myself am a Palestinian Christian), but that even many Muslim women did not veil. However, many did, and for myriad reasons: mostly for personal and religious reasons and, for some, upon compulsion.

The student shook her head sadly, her long ponytail swinging in the air, and offered a comment that made it clear she hadn't really digested what I'd said: "I feel so bad for them all. At least Christian women don't have to walk three steps behind their husbands." She added, "That's so insulting."

I understood—and not for the first time—the astounding disconnection between the lives of Arab women, and the lives of Arab women as represented by the American media and entertainment industries, thus as perceived by Americans themselves. Twenty-three years after the publication of Edward Said's seminal book, *Orientalism,* which clarified the historical pattern of misrepresentation and demonization of the Middle East, many Americans continue to purchase wholesale the neatly packaged image of the veiled, meek Arab woman. This pitiful creature follows her husband like a dark shadow, is forced to remain silent and obey her husband at all times, is granted a body only to deliver more children, perhaps even in competition with her husband's other wives.

At some point (like now), the stereotype spins out of control, becoming more wild and ludicrous, like Yeats's ever-widening gyre. The portrayal that persists today, however, is not much of an improvement—if at all—over the portrayal of Arab women in the late 1700s to the early part of the twentieth century.

> Black Hassan from the Haram flies,
> Nor bends on woman's form his eyes;
> The unwonted chase each hour employs,
> Yet shares he not the hunter's joys.
> Not thus was Hassan wont to fly
> When Leila dwelt in his Serai.
> Doth Leila there no longer dwell?
> That tale can only Hassan tell

wrote Byron, in his 1812 poem, "The Giaour." The Giaour is a warrior who avenges the murder of his beloved, Leila, a girl who dwells in the harem of "Black Hassan" and who is put to death by drowning when it is revealed that she has been unfaithful to the sultan with the Giaour. Pierre Loti's 1879 *Aziyadé* and other poems and works of the time featured a similar theme, that of the Western hero breaking the impasse of the harem, to be rewarded with the passion of women who have been sexually isolated and imprisoned.

What this compilation of wildly exaggerated and self-indulgently fantastical images has resulted in is the creation of a stark contrast between modern American women and modern Arab women. The rise of U.S. feminism in the 1970s and 1980s coincided with the rise of Islam as the "new enemy" of the Western world. Images of the Ayatollah Khomeini in Iran, the *mujahedeen* in Afghanistan, Qaddafi in Libya, and Yasser Arafat and the PLO concretized Islam's new role as the author of fear and the enemy of Western democracy, human rights, and, especially, civil law. And those images of Islam were strategically—almost artistically—painted with glimpses of what Islam did to its own women: it turned them into mute shadows, thus flying in the face of the gender equality and democracy that American feminism claimed as its foundation.

The statements made by my ponytailed student smacked of an underlying assumption that I have heard many times before: We American women have finally succeeded in moving the feminist movement to the top of our nation's list of priorities; now it's time to help our less fortunate sisters. Of course, over the years, American feminism has opened its gates (after much pounding) to other versions of feminism, such as black feminism and other non-white, non-upper-middle-class feminisms. Therefore, the focus on Arab women's issues illustrates the good intentions of American feminism; however, my concern is with the "big sister" manner in which those intentions are manifested. Often, Arab women's voices are excluded from discussions concerning their own lives, and they are to be "informed" about feminism, as if it is an ideology exclusive to American women alone.

In fact, many American women would be surprised to learn that the history of Arab feminism (a term often considered oxymoronic) is long, layered, and impressive. That this is not well understood in the West is not surprising. As Dawn Chatty and Annika Rabo write in the introduction to their edited collection, *Organizing Women: Formal and Informal Women's Groups in the Middle East,* "Middle Eastern women's groups are not . . . nearly as well documented as in the rest of the world. . . .There is . . . a great deal of antagonism between the Middle East and the West where the latter sees men from the Middle East as suppressing and secluding their women, and where the Middle Easterner underlines the immorality of women in the West. This conflict is one reason why women in the Middle East do not get international attention when organized in groups."

Not only do the struggles of Arab feminists have a long history, but over the 1980s and 1990s, as Val Moghadam observes in the same book, "Women's Nongovernmental Organizations [in the Middle East and North Africa] have grown exponentially and are taking on increasingly important responsibilities in the context of state withdrawal from the provision of social services and in the context of a global trend in the expansion of civil society." Organizations explicitly devoted to women are growing rapidly in Egypt, Tunisia, and Morocco, while more informal service-oriented organizations led by women play some of the same roles in many other Middle Eastern nations. Some of the leading organizations in Egypt include: the New Woman's Group; Arab Women's Publishing House; the Alliance of Arab Women; the Association for the Development and Enhancement of Women; Together; Progressive Women's Union; the group of women who published *The Legal Rights of the Egyptian Woman in Theory and Practice;* and The Society for the Daughter of the Earth. (See the chapter by Nadje Sadig al-Ali in *Organizing Women.*) Taken as a whole, it is a movement that, if allied with U.S. and other feminisms, could improve the lives of women around the world.

The Beginnings

Shirley Guthrie, author of the recently published *Arab Women in the Middle Ages*, unearths facts about women in the medieval period that challenge the many stereotypes that persist today, such as one that modern Islam reverts to medieval days, thus proof that it is stagnant. However, while it is often thought that medieval Arab women were helplessly bartered off into undesirable marriages, Guthrie informs us that an affluent Arab woman negotiated the details of her marriage contract, and some even included a demand on their husbands to be monogamous, while others demanded the right to initiate divorce proceedings. While lower-class medieval women did not usually have such advantages, they appear to have lived a somewhat egalitarian lifestyle, working side by side with their husbands. Women's issues were not at the fore of social concerns, but medieval Arab culture and the days of early Islam do not seem to have been as uniformly oppressive as they are depicted today.

There is a tradition in Islam of women's equality, and the life of the Prophet Muhammad is often offered as proof of this; it is said that Muhammad washed his own clothes and darned his own socks, and often served meals to his youngest wife Ai'sha, who later led his army into battle and was regarded as an important and respected interpreter of Islamic laws. The *Qur'an* leveled the social balances for women: in Islam, women had the right to inherit property, own and operate businesses, and be educated. It banned several misogynist practices, such as the infanticide of newborn baby girls, who were often unwanted by parents who preferred male children.

The rise of modern Arab feminism, much like everything else in the Middle East, is steeped in controversy. In 1899, Qasim Amin, an Egyptian intellectual and a judge, published his groundbreaking book, *The Liberation of Women*, which caused not ripples, but tsunamis of dissent and discussion across the region. The book, which outlined Amin's claims that the education and liberation of women was essential to strengthen and emancipate the Egyptian nation from British colonial rule, resulted from his travels to and studies in Europe, where he observed the role of women in Western society. He argued that men oppressed and silenced women, which caused society in general to suffer: "Our present situation resembles that of a very wealthy man who locks up his gold in a chest. This man unlocks his chest daily for the mere pleasure of seeing his treasure.

If he knew better, he could invest his gold and double his wealth in a short period of time." He is generally considered the "Father of Arab feminism" (which definitely *is* an oxymoron).

However, recent feminist scholars have effectively and persuasively argued that Amin is not the movement's "founder" in any sense of the word. Margot Badran and Miriam Cooke, the editors of *Opening the Gates: A Century of Arab Feminist Writing*, argue that men's feminism (like Amin's), which developed due to contact with Europe, differs from women's feminism, which arose out of women's reflections on their own lives and problems. Leila Ahmed, an Islamic scholar and professor at the Harvard Divinity School, agrees that Amin bases his arguments on a comparison with the West, in which the West is refined, cultured, and advanced, and the East is not.

"Women's feminism," however, has a champion in Huda Sha'rawi, a contemporary of Qasim Amin's who founded the Egyptian Feminist Union and two important women's periodicals, *l'Egyptienne and al-Misriyya*. By the time she died in 1947, Arab feminism had a figurehead as charismatic and dynamic as American feminism's Gloria Steinem. Sha'rawi advocated pan-Arab feminism, which presented a challenge to Arab nationalist ideologies that championed state identity over a general, unified Arab one. Rather, her model worked closely with the pan-Arabist movements, which was a response to colonialism (i.e., the British colonial presence in Egypt at the beginning of the century). She very much saw the success of the pan-Arabism movement as dependent 50 percent on women, whose rights would enable them to better serve their families and their nation. She also compared Egyptian women with European women, but more positively. She traveled to Europe and energetically networked with European women by attending international women's conferences, trying to make Egyptian feminists part of the expanding global sisterhood.

Arab Feminism Today

One of the most powerful testimonies of Arab feminism today is the recent memoir by Fay Afaf Kanafani, entitled *Nadia, Captive of Hope: Memoir of an Arab Woman*. A Palestinian woman who was married off to her cousin, and then widowed during the Arab-Israeli war, Kanafani describes the gender inequality in Arab society during the 1940s and 1950s; she also highlights the possibility for a woman with determination to live according to feminist principles, as she sought to do. These principles—founded on an insistence of equality—were not learned from Western feminists, but found within Kanafani herself. Her story is a poignant one, and only one of many emerging testimonies of Arab women who develop their own feminist ideals.

However, it is often difficult to abide by those ideals. Today's most noted Arab feminist, Nawal al-Saadawi, recently just managed to keep her marriage intact despite an Egyptian lawsuit designed to separate her from her husband. She had been accused of apostasy—the renunciation of Islam—because of comments she made during an interview; the lawsuit against her claimed that she had abandoned her faith and therefore could not be married to a Muslim. The Egyptian court eventually threw out the case, thus saving her thirty-seven-year marriage, but the case was not the first time that al-Saadawi, a doctor and the most recognized Arab feminist in the West, had been in the spotlight.

Al-Saadawi is the author of several novels, and volumes of her memoirs and autobiography, and the founder of the Arab Women's Solidarity Association (AWSA). Her *Memoirs of a Woman Doctor* recount her difficulties in earning respect in the medical field and achieving her goals under familial and social pressures to conform to the feminine ideal: to marry at an early age, bear children, and be an obedient wife. Her most recent autobiography, *A Daughter of Isis,* details her earliest memories of recognizing gender discrimination in Egyptian society, such as the divorce and inheritance laws regarding women, and the preferential treatment of male children. Her medical experience led her to become an outspoken opponent of female genital mutilation (FGM), an extreme form of female circumcision practiced in some rural parts of Egypt and Africa. Her vocal opposition to this and other issues made her a target of Islamic fundamentalists, who put her name on a death list in 1993, prompting her to immigrate to the United States, where she has been ever since.

One indication of the viability of Arab feminism is that, much like the different branches and offshoots within American feminism, divisions of opinion do exist and thrive within its framework. In fact, some feminists have complained that al-Saadawi's novels are not representative of the higher quality of literature by Arab women, but that her plots, characters, and stories fit neatly into the image the Western feminist movement already has about Arab women. In other words, they believe her work reinforces the stereotype of the universally battered and silenced Arab woman.

Other novelists and writers, such as Hanan al-Shaykh, Fatima Mernissi, Ahdaf Soueif, and Leila Sebbar, tackle this stereotype on different fronts, attempting to render it more accurate. For example, while the lives of some Arab women may fit this stereotype (just as "barefoot and pregnant" rings true for some American women), the experiences of so many cannot be perfectly labeled.

Rejecting the Odalisque

There are other key issues, beside the much-hyped issue of female genital mutilation, around which Arab feminists today organize, including the insurance of fair divorce laws, proper health care for women, family planning education, and others. Two of the most prominent have also received some attention from Western feminists in their quest to encompass all women's voices: recreating a historically accurate picture of Arab women and, of course, the veil.

Historical visions of Arab women have been dominated by the Western-generated frenzy over the odalisque, the favorite subject of many European artists, such as Matisse, Ingres, and Delacroix. In Arabic, *oda* means *room*; thus, the *woman of the room*, or a concubine of the sultan confined to an enclosed space. The odalisque was forbidden to be seen by any other man save the sultan, whose exclusive plaything she was. In Matisse's *Odalisque with Left Knee Bent*, the woman sits in one of the rooms of the harem, lounging idly, forming part of the colorful background but not performing any action. The atmosphere created is one of sensual idleness, a woman keeping herself distracted, perhaps while waiting for the sultan to visit. An epitome of available sexuality, she is a figure who appears in many forms and guises in European artwork and literature (for examples of the latter, one need go no further than George Gordon, Lord Byron, who fancied himself an Eastern hero of adventures, slipping into harems and battling despotic sultans and sheiks). Her image still pervades Western conceptions of the East as lazy, sensual, exotic, and willing to succumb—the same image that Arab women writers like Ahdaf Soueif and Leila Sebbar seek to reconstruct.

In Ahdaf Soueif's first novel, *In the Eye of the Sun*, the main character, Asya, cheats on her husband and has a brief affair with an American student she meets in England, where she is pursuing her Ph.D. She is disturbed by the fact that her lover perceives her as "exotic," because she sees nothing exotic about the simple fact that she is Egyptian. One evening, he dresses her in a necklace (which her husband purchased for her) and spews Orientalist-laden sentiments. She immediately recognizes the odalisque fantasy and refuses to be framed in a stereotype that has no relation to her real life and concerns.

The rejection of the odalisque is masterfully expressed in the fiction of Leila Sebbar, another Arab woman from the East but transplanted to the West (she is an Algerian living in France) and the author of the Shérazade trilogy. Shérazade is a young, Algerian runaway, roaming the underworld of Paris and trying to find herself. Is she French? Is she Algerian? She is often both (and sometimes neither) depending on the situation. Shérazade meets and befriends Julian, a Frenchman with a passion for Orientalist art, who quickly projects his Byronic fantasies onto her. However, Shérazade has been toughened by the Paris streets and the growing awareness of the silencing of Arab women due to a popular image that portrays them as vulnerable and powerless. She leaves Julian, but not before proclaiming, "I'm not an odalisque"—in essence, she has refused to be defined. At the end of the novel, she has hitched a ride to the south of France, from where she intends to find a way to Algeria to seek out her roots.

The examples of these two writers illustrate the effort of Arab women to reclaim their identities and correct a historically maligned portrait.

The Veil

In 1923, Huda Sha'rawi caused a scandal in Egypt when, upon stepping off a boat that had just returned from Europe (where she had been attending an international feminist conference), she seized the media moment and publicly removed her veil, symbolically denouncing its meaning by throwing it into the sea. However, its meaning has never been universally agreed upon in Arab societies, probably because each society and each historical moment has ascribed a different one to it. During a visit a few years ago to the Gaza Strip, I saw five-year-old girls sheathed in black; I also saw teenaged girls in the West Bank wearing *hijabs* that flowed to the waistline of their jeans; in fact, the *hijab* seemed to protect their heads from the hot sun as they played basketball on a full court. What does it all mean? Probably that the veil is not a simple, one-dimensional marker of gender oppression. In *Women and the Middle East and North Africa*, Judith E. Tucker has written of some of the complexity associated with women's choice of dress, which cannot always be attributed directly to patriarchal admonitions:

> "Veiling" has become, certainly in the Western view, a touchstone for women's issues. In the 1980s and 1990s, many women in different parts of the Middle East, particularly in urban areas, have donned a new form of "Islamic" dress that includes a long dress or coat and a head scarf often worn without a turban. Although social pressure cannot always be ruled out, many young women appear to choose this form of dress over the alternatives of Western-style dress or various indigenous styles worn by older women. Several explanations have been offered for this trend. First, sociological reasons include the advantages such dress provides for women who study or work in mixed-sex environments. By wearing Islamic dress, women can proclaim their seriousness and avoid the tensions produced by the rapid erosion of sexual segregation while maintaining access to public space. Second, women, like men, have found that the post-independence promises of progress through Western versions of liberalism or socialism have not borne fruit; they signal a "return" to indigenous culture and authenticity as a guide to a better future. Third, there is a rising tide of religiosity in the region that translates, for women and men, into changing dress styles.

Leila Ahmed, author of *Women and Gender in Islam*, asserts that one of the only elements of Qasim Amin's *The Liberation of Women* (1899) that was considered scandalous was his call for the abolition of the veil. Assim declared that the veil was un-Islamic. (It may surprise some Western feminists to know that they are not the first to criticize the veiling of Middle Eastern women, but rather that it has been a subject of intense debate for over a century.) Ahmed said that dialogue about the veil emerged in a heated political and economic context, one in which some Egyptians sought to advance the nation by adopting the Western ways of the British (who still colonized Egypt at this time) and some who believed the same could be realized only by ousting the British and reviving and preserving Islamic traditions. However, Ahmed illustrated clearly that the British "Victorian male establishment" used the idea that Muslim men oppressed Muslim women as a justifiable pretext for its colonization and "civilizing" of Muslim countries. As one might expect, the veil, interpreted as a symbol of the silencing of women both by Europeans and by some Egyptians, served well as tangible proof of that oppression.

Many women in the Middle East today see the issue of the veil as an important locus of discussion; I personally know of marriages that have broken up because husbands wanted their new brides to be "more conservative" and wear the veil. Many other women see the veil as irrelevant to the central issue of women's rights; arguing over it serves to distract from the real problems of women's access to education and health care, and the increasing poverty in which Arab families find themselves.

After September 11

In the days after September 11, I telephoned friends of mine, women I had known for years to inquire if they were experiencing the backlash against Arab- and Muslim-Americans, and anyone else unfortunate enough to resemble them in the minds of people who don't know better. Several of them—all of whom wore the veil—told me that they had been verbally targeted. "I hated stopping at red lights today," said one of my friends, "because the people in the cars next to me would curse at me and give me the finger." After our conversation, I turned on the news and learned about a Pakistani woman who was almost run over in the parking lot of a grocery store; her attacker then followed her into the store and threatened her life. I did not see a picture of the woman, but wondered whether or not she wore any sort of head scarf that would "mark" her as a target.

And then I thought of how Islam was terribly misunderstood. The few ritual concessions to tolerance uttered by national figureheads such as President Bush and New York Mayor Rudy Guiliani (scarcely consistent with their own actions) did not erase the fact that most Americans remain unaware of the basic facts about the Middle East and Islam, and women were suffering from that ignorance. For example, while Afghan women and their plight had been singled out by the American media as an example of how backwards the Taliban was (even though, to its credit, American feminism had been criticizing and attempting to educate people about the Taliban since 1996), these same women were also forced to herd their families into refugee camps and/or watch their houses be destroyed in the storm of bombing of Afghanistan that followed the September 11 attacks. The media's popular portrayal of Muslim women as universally helpless and dominated by the patriarchy that continues to exist in Arab culture (as if any society is free of it) has reinforced American perceptions that Arabs and Muslims are degenerate and twisted, thus worthy of domination and bombing.

And yet, if Americans, especially American women, understood the long and enduring history of Arab feminism, then perhaps my students would be able to formulate comments on Arab and Muslim women that were more informed and sensitive. Such commentaries would recognize the complexity of historical struggles, rather than making those waging these struggles invisible under a pervasive stereotype. It is not up to Western women to diagnose inequality in Arab society—it has been diagnosed. Rather, American women should recognize that Arab women themselves—and even some Arab men—have grappled with gender inequality for over a century. This is the message that American feminists have largely not heard, although it must be heard and Arab women's voices included in the discussion of building bridges and confronting women's issues on a global scale.

South Asia's Holy Wars

Fascism's Firm Footprint in India

Arundhati Roy

A longer version of this essay is forthcoming as "Democracy: Who Is She When She's at Home?" in a new collection from South End Press.

Gujarat, the only major state in India with a government headed by the Bharatiya Janata Party (BJP), has, for some years, been the petri dish in which Hindu fascism has been fomenting an elaborate political experiment. In spring of 2002, the initial results were put on public display.

It began within hours of the Godhra outrage—in which fifty-eight Hindus were killed when a train returning from the disputed site of Ayodhya, on February 27 was set alight as it pulled out of a station in Godhra, in Gujarat. Even now, months later, nobody knows who was responsible for the crime. The Forensic Department report clearly says that the fire was started inside the coach. This raises a huge question mark over the theory that the fire was set by a Muslim mob that had gathered outside the train. However, the then-Home Minister (now elevated to the post of Deputy Prime Minister) L.K. Advani immediately announced—with no evidence to back his statement—that the attack was a Pakistani plot. On the evening of February 27, Hindu nationalists in the Vishva Hindu Parishad (VHP) and the Bajrang Dal movement put into motion a meticulously planned pogrom against the Muslim community. Press reports put the number of dead at just over 800. Human rights organizations have said it is closer to 2,000. As many as 100,000 people, driven from their homes, now live in refugee camps. Women were stripped, gang-raped, parents were bludgeoned to death in front of their children. In Ahmedabad, the former capital of Gujarat and the second largest industrial city in the state, the tomb of Wali Gujarati, the founder of the modern Urdu poem, was demolished and paved over in the course of a night. The tomb of the musician Ustad Faiyaz Khan was desecrated. Arsonists burned and looted shops, homes, hotels, textile mills, buses, and cars. Hundreds of thousands have lost their jobs.

Across Gujarat, thousands of people made up the mobs. They were armed with petrol bombs, guns, knives, and swords. Apart from the VHP and Bajrang Dal's usual lumpen constituency, there were Dalits (untouchables) and Adivasis (indigenous peoples) who were brought in buses and trucks. Middle-class people participated in the looting. (On one memorable occasion, a family arrived in a Mitsubishi Lancer.) The leaders of the mob had computer-generated lists marking out Muslim homes, shops, and businesses. They used mobile phones to coordinate the action. They had not just police protection and police connivance, but also covering fire. The cooking gas cylinders they used to burn Muslim homes and establishments had been hoarded weeks in advance, causing a severe gas shortage in Ahmedabad.

While Gujarat burned, our prime minister Atal Bihari Vajpayee, was on MTV promoting his new poems. (Reports say cassettes have sold 100,000 copies.) It took him more than a month—and two vacations in the hills—to make it to Gujarat. When he did, he gave a speech at the Shah Alam refugee camp. His mouth moved, he tried to express concern, but no real sound emerged except the mocking of the wind whistling through a burned, bloodied, broken world. Next we knew, he was bobbing around in a golf cart, striking business deals in Singapore.

One hundred and thirty million Muslims live in India. Hindu fascists regard them as legitimate prey. The lynch mob continues to be the arbiter of the routine affairs of daily life: who can live where, who can say what, who can meet whom, and where and when. Its mandate is expanding quickly. From religious affairs, it now extends to property disputes, family altercations, the planning and allocation of water resources. Muslim businesses have been shut down. Muslim people are not served in restaurants. Muslim children are not welcome in schools. Muslim parents live in dread that their infants might forget what they've been told and give themselves away by saying "Ammi!" or "Abba!" in public and invite sudden and violent death.

Notice has been given: this is just the beginning.

No matter who they were, or how they were killed, each person who died in Gujarat deserves to be mourned. There have been hundreds of outraged letters to journals and newspapers asking why the "pseudo-secularists" do not condemn the burning of the Sabarmati Express in Godhra with the same degree of outrage with which they condemn the killings in the rest of Gujarat. What they don't seem to understand is that there is a fundamental difference between a pogrom and the burning of the train in Godhra. We still don't know who exactly was responsible for the carnage in Godhra. But every independent report says the pogrom against the Muslim community in Gujarat has at best been conducted under the benign gaze of the state and, at worst, with active state collusion. Either way the state is criminally culpable.

While the parallels between contemporary India and prewar Germany are chilling, they're not surprising. (The founders of the Rashtriya Swayamsevak Sangh [RSS], the National Volunteer Force that is the moral and cultural guild of the BJP, have in their writings been frank in their admiration for Hitler and his methods.) One difference is that here in India we don't have a Hitler. We have instead the hydra-headed, many-armed Sangh Parivar— the "joint family" of Hindu political and cultural organizations, with the BJP, the RSS, the VHP, and the Bajrang Dal each playing a different instrument. Its utter genius lies in its apparent ability to be all things to all people at all times.

The Sangh Parivar speaks in as many tongues. It can say several contradictory things simultaneously. While one of its heads (the VHP) exhorts millions of its cadres to prepare for the Final Solution, its titular head (the prime minister) assures the nation that all citizens, regardless of their religion, will be treated equally. It can ban books and films and burn paintings for "insulting Indian culture." Simultaneously, it can mortgage the equivalent of 60 percent of the entire country's rural development budget as profit to Enron. But underneath all the clamor and the noise, a single heart beats. And an unforgiving mind with saffron-saturated tunnel vision works overtime.

Whipping up communal hatred is part of the mandate of the Sangh Parivar. It has been planned for years. Hundreds of RSS *shakhas* across the country (*shakha* literally means "branch," and RSS *shakhas* are "educational" cells) have been indoctrinating thousands of children and young people, stunting their minds with religious hatred and falsified history, including unfactual or wildly exaggerated accounts of the rape and pillaging of Hindu women and Hindu temples by Muslim rulers in the precolonial period. In states like Gujarat, the police, the administration, and the political cadres at every level have been systematically penetrated. It has huge popular appeal, which it would be foolish to underestimate or misunderstand. The whole enterprise has a formidable religious, ideological, political, and administrative underpinning. This kind of power, this kind of reach, can only be achieved with state backing.

Under this relentless pressure, what will most likely happen is that the majority of the Muslim community will resign itself to living in ghettos as second-class citizens, in constant fear, with no civil rights and no recourse to justice. What will daily life be like for them? Any little thing, an altercation at a cinema or a fracas at a traffic light, could turn lethal. So they will learn to keep very quiet, to accept their lot, to creep around the edges of the society in which they live. Their fear will transmit itself to other minorities. Many, particularly the young, will probably turn to militancy. They will do terrible things. Civil society will be called upon to condemn them. Then President Bush's canon will come back to us: "You're either with us or with the terrorists."

Those words hang frozen in time like icicles. For years to come, butchers and genocidists will fit their grisly mouths around them ("lip-sync," filmmakers call it) to justify their butchery.

Bal Thackeray, the leader of the Shiv Sena—the right-wing Hindu fundamentalist political party in the state of Maharashtra, responsible for a pogrom in which hundreds of Muslims were massacred in Bombay in 1992-1993—has the lasting solution. He's called for civil war. Isn't that just perfect? Then Pakistan won't need to bomb us, we can bomb ourselves. Let's turn all of India into Kashmir. When all our farm lands are mined, our buildings destroyed, our infrastructure reduced to rubble, our children physically maimed and mentally wrecked, maybe we can appeal to the Americans to help us out. Airdropped airline meals, anyone?

Fascism's firm footprint has appeared in India. Let's mark the date. While we can thank the American president and the "Coalition Against Terror" for creating a congenial international atmosphere for its ghastly debut, we cannot credit them for the years it has been brewing in our public and private lives. The massed energy of bloodthirsty patriotism became openly acceptable political currency after India's nuclear tests in 1998. The "weapons of peace" have trapped India and Pakistan in a spiral of brinkmanship—threat and counterthreat, taunt and countertaunt.

Fascism is about the slow, steady infiltration of all the instruments of state power. It's about the slow erosion of civil liberties, about unspectacular day-to-day injustices. Fighting it does not mean asking for RSS *shakhas* and *madrassas* that are overtly communal to be banned. It means working toward the day when they're voluntarily abandoned as bad ideas. It means keeping an eagle eye on public institutions and demanding accountability. It means putting your ear to the ground and listening to the whispering of the truly powerless. It means giving a forum to the myriad voices from the hundreds of resistance movements across the country who are speaking about real issues—about mining, about bonded labor, marital rape, sexual preferences, women's wages, uranium dumping, weavers' woes, farmers' worries. It means fighting displacement and dispossession and the relentless, everyday violence of abject poverty.

While most people in India have been horrified by what happened in Gujarat, many thousands of the indoctrinated are preparing to journey deeper into the heart of the horror. Look around you and you'll see in little parks, in empty lots, in village commons, the RSS is marching, hoisting its saffron flag. Suddenly they're everywhere, grown men in khaki shorts marching, marching, marching.

Historically, fascist movements have been fueled by feelings of national disillusionment. Fascism has come to India after the dreams that fueled the freedom struggle have been frittered away like so much loose change. Independence itself came to us as what Gandhi famously called a "wooden loaf"— a notional freedom tainted by the blood of the hundreds of thousands who died during Partition. For more than half a century now, that heritage of hatred and mutual distrust has been exacerbated, toyed with and never allowed to heal by politicians. Over the past fifty years, ordinary citizens' modest hopes for lives of dignity, security, and relief from abject poverty have been systematically snuffed out. Every "democratic" institution in this country has shown itself to be unaccountable, inaccessible to the ordinary citizen and either unwilling or incapable of acting in the interests of genuine social justice. And now corporate globalization is being relentlessly and arbitrarily imposed on India, ripping it apart culturally and economically.

There is very real grievance here. The fascists didn't create it. But they have seized upon it, upturned it and forged from it a hideous, bogus sense of pride. They have mobilized human beings using the lowest common denominator—religion. People who have lost control over their lives, people who have been uprooted from their homes and communities, who have lost their culture and their language, are being made to feel proud of something. Not something they have striven for and achieved, but something they just happen to be. Or, more accurately, something they happen not to be.

Unfortunately there's no quick fix. Fascism itself can only be turned away if all those who are outraged by it show a commitment to social justice that equals the intensity of their indignation. Are we ready, many millions of us, to rally not just on the streets, but at work and in schools and in our homes, in every decision we take, and every choice we make?

Or not just yet . . .

If not, then years from now, when the rest of the world has shunned us, as it should, like the ordinary citizens of Hitler's Germany, we too will learn to recognize revulsion in the gaze of our fellow human beings. We too will find ourselves unable to look our own children in the eye, for the shame of what we did and didn't do. For the shame of what we allowed to happen.

Gujarat's Gendered Violence

Ruth Baldwin

"I have never known a riot which has used the sexual subjugation of women so widely as an instrument of violence. There are reports everywhere of [the] gang rape of young girls and women, often in the presence of members of their families, followed by their murder by burning alive."

(*Harsh Mander,* "Cry, the Beloved Country: Reflections on the Gujarat Massacre")

Women's bodies were central battlegrounds in the worst bout of Hindu-Muslim bloodletting to grip India in over ten years, in the western Indian state of Gujarat beginning on February 27, 2002. After an enraged Muslim mob in Godhra allegedly set fire to a train packed with Hindus, killing fifty-eight, a wave of retaliatory violence was unleashed on the minority Muslim population in the region, leaving up to two thousand dead and one-hundred thousand homeless. Under the indulgent gaze of the state government, and against a backdrop of ransacked houses and desecrated temples, at least two-hundred-fifty women and girls were brutally gang-raped and burned alive.

Shabnam Hashmi, founder of SAHMAT (a coalition of artists and intellectuals who work to strengthen secularism within Indian society) believes that although the pogrom was triggered by Godhra, the attacks were premeditated: "These mobs were trained in rape. Why else would the same pattern of brutality be repeated everywhere? Groups of women were stripped naked and then made to run for miles, before being gang-raped and burnt alive. In some cases religious symbols were carved onto their bodies." In the documentary *Evil Stalks The Land* produced by Hashmi's husband, Gauhar Raza, a young boy stares, unblinking, into the camera. "About one hundred to one-hundred-fifty children my age were burnt in a house," he recalls. "The tea stall in which we were hiding was set on fire using gas cylinders. My grandmother's limbs were chopped off and my aunt was brutally raped."

Among all the horrifying testimonies of sexual violence to emerge from

Gujarat, one story has come to symbolize the collective suffering of the Muslim community. It is told and retold in news stories, in NGO reports, and in eye-witness accounts such as that of a young boy on Indian television: "I was running [and] I saw a pregnant woman's belly being cut open," he said. "The fetus was pulled out and thrown up in the air. As it came down it was collected on the tip of the sword."

"[Kausar Bano] was nine months pregnant" recalls Saira Banu at the Shah-e-Alam Camp for refugees. "They cut open her belly, took her fetus with a sword and threw it into a blazing fire. Then they burnt her as well."

"We were to hear this story many times," wrote the Citizen's Initiative fact-finding team of women, who saw photographic evidence of the burned body of a mother with a charred fetus lying on her stomach. Their April 16 report, *The Survivors Speak*, reflects upon the significance of this crime: "Kausar's story has come to embody the numerous experiences of evil that were felt by the Muslims . . . In all instances where extreme violence is experienced collectively, meta-narratives are constructed. Each victim is part of the narrative; their experience subsumed by the collective experience. Kausar is that collective experience—a meta-narrative of bestiality; a meta-narrative of helpless victimhood." The image of Kausar and her unborn child has assumed a dual meaning, for both Hindu aggressors and Muslim victims: The humiliation of the enemy through violation of the female body, and the assault on the future of the Muslim community through the destruction of the next generation.

Why is gender violence such a consistent feature of the communal riots that spasmodically grip India? In an impassioned May 11 editorial in the *Hindu*, India's national daily, Raka Roy, an associate professor of sociology at Berkeley, offered one explanation. Roy asked: "Where does the creation of the inferior Other in India begin?" It begins, she argues, with the divisive caste system that has allowed the principle of inequality to become embedded in Hindu culture. It continues in the belief that "women are not only inferior, but also woman's sexuality has to be patrolled so that it is legitimately accessible to some men and inaccessible to others." If a woman's body belongs not to herself, but to her community, then the violation of that body signifies an attack upon the honor *(izzat)* of the whole community. Hindu nationalists raped and burned minority women to destroy not only their bodies, but also the integrity and identity of Muslim society, the inferior Other. Roy also suggests that the terrible legacy of the partition—with "protected and protectable women on one side and unprotected and rapable women on the other side"—still lingers in both the Hindu and Muslim subconscious.

It was the complicity of the state, however, that made it possible for mass rape to occur in Gujarat. A Human Rights Watch report concluded that the Sangh Parivar—the family of Hindu nationalist organizations including the Baratya Janata Party (BJP), which heads the Gujarat state government—was directly responsible [see Arundhati Roy's essay in this volume]. According to the report, police told terrified groups of fleeing Muslims: "We have no orders to save you."

The thousands of displaced now live in temporary refugee camps, run almost exclusively by Muslim organizations. Harsh Mander writes: "It is as though the monumental pain, loss, betrayal, and injustice suffered by the Muslim people is the concern only of other Muslim people, and the rest of us have no share in the responsibility to assuage, to heal, and rebuild." The Citizen's Initiative report argues that the state's colossal failure to implement "International Human Rights norms and instructions and instruments as they relate to violence per se, especially violence against women," may amount to a crime under international law. The report recommends that a special task force, comprised of people from outside Gujarat, be set up immediately to investigate the cases of sexual violence, and that counseling and rehabilitation programs be established to help the traumatized survivors. Although the government has proposed "Peace Committees," it remains unclear what form these would take. All of this provides little consolation for the Muslim women and their families who must decide where to go when the squalid camps close, which is scheduled to occur before the Assembly elections following the resignation of Narendra Modi, the BJP's Chief Minister of Gujarat. Those who could afford to leave Gujarat have already done so. The rest will return to their villages, to live as second-class citizens in the ruins of their homes amongst the men who raped their sisters, burned their children, and killed their friends.

Hindu Women's Activism in India and the Questions It Raises

Amrita Basu

From *Approaching Gender: Women's Activism and Politicized Religion in South Asia* (Routledge, 1997)

Some of the most powerful images and sounds that live on, since the storm over the Babari Masjid in Ayodhya has abated, are those of Sādhvī Rithambara and Uma Bharati. Their shrill voices filtered through cassette tape recordings goaded Hindu men into violence against Muslims in the course of many riots between 1990 and 1993. On December 6, 1992, these women openly celebrated the destruction of the Babari Masjid. Women's activism has not only found expression among the movement's orators and spokespersons but has also taken hold at the grassroots level. In the early 1990s, thousands of women became skilled in organizing demonstrations, campaigning for elections, and using arms and ammunition.

Perhaps the most startling form of women's activism is their complicity and often direct participation in Hindu violence against Muslim families. In October 1990 in the town of Bijnor in western Uttar Pradesh, Hindu women led a procession through a Muslim neighborhood with trishūls (tridents) in hand, shouting bigoted, inflammatory slogans. In the aftermath of the violence in which several hundred people were killed, these women radiated pride at their actions (Basu, 1995c: 35–78; Jeffery and Jeffery, 1994; Jeffery and Jeffery, 1997). In the riots in Bombay in January 1993, Hindu women often justified violence against Muslims. Following police killings of Muslims in the Pratiksha Nagar Housing Colony in Bombay in January 1993, some Hindu women stood on their balconies looking down at the dead bodies of two Muslim women and insisted that these women had died of natural causes, and in any event, "Muslims deserved to die." Hindu women employees of a state-owned corporation threatened to boycott their jobs until the government

189

destroyed a nearby Muslim slum.[1] In a riot in the outskirts of Bhopal during this same period, a woman who was a member of both a municipal corporation and the Bharatiya Janata Party (BJP) had rushed to the scene of the violence and goaded Hindu men into violence against Muslims.

In the first part of this chapter, I ask whether Hindu women's activism derives its distinctive features from the peculiarities of "communalism," and in particular, traits that distinguish "communalism" from "fundamentalism."[2] Women's activism may be partially explained by the fact that the BJP, which typifies the attributes of "communalism," has supported certain women's rights on the basis of political expediency. However, in the second part of the chapter, I suggest that by overemphasizing the distinctive attributes of "communalism," we risk neglecting its affinities with "fundamentalism." The BJP's "modern" political project resuscitates antimodernist forces, and fundamentalists' claims of authentically representing religious traditions are often shaped by the prevailing political context.

The leadership for Hindu women's activism comes from three women's organizations: the Rashtriya Swayamsevak Sangh (RSS)-affiliated Rashtra Sevika Samiti; the Vishwa Hindu Parishad (VHP)-affiliated Durga Vahini; and the Bharatiya Janata Party (BJP)-affiliated women's organization. While the activities of these organizations are so closely interconnected as to be virtually indistinguishable at the local level, their national personas are quite distinct. The Rashtra Sevika Samiti consists of a small, highly dedicated cadre of women whose lives are guided by RSS principles. It refrains from direct involvement in party politics and concentrates on educating girls and women in the principles of Hindu nationalism and on training them to fight for a Hindu state (Sarkar, 1997). The Durga Vahini's mission is to create Hindu solidarity by helping families during periods of hardship and by providing essential social services. Formed in 1980, the BJP's women's organization remained dormant for many years. Since 1989 it has galvanized women around the Babari Masjid or Rām Janambhūmi issue and the BJP's electoral campaigns.

I observed the events of the tumultuous period 1990–1992 while in India studying the growth of Hindu nationalism. I interviewed numerous women who were associated with the Hindu nationalist campaign from the leadership level to rank-and-file members of the three affiliated women's organizations. I visited several towns that had experienced severe riots and interviewed victims and participants in the violence. I joined processions of women as they marched from door to door, campaigning for the BJP in the

1991 parliamentary elections. This chapter draws upon those observations and experiences.

Women's Activism and "Communal Politics"

Certain distinctive features of Hindu "communalism" appear at first glance to promote women's activism. The movement that has emerged since 1989 is led by the BJP, a political party. It is neither controlled nor even deeply influenced by Hindu priests, scriptures, or doctrines. The BJP's major objectives since it was formed in 1980, but with increasing urgency, have been no more complicated than attaining power in New Delhi and in India's regional capitals. The BJP's independence from religious orthodoxy seems to be a key ingredient of women's activism. It frees the party to assume positions that might conflict with Hindu conservatism and to support women's independence when the BJP finds this politically expedient. Other questions, like female seclusion, that are often a staple of "fundamentalist" movements do not figure on the BJP's agenda.

Several scholars have noted that although "fundamentalist" movements are far from monolithic, they tend to converge in their opposition to women's autonomy (Hélie-Lucas, 1994). Most "fundamentalist" movements share a pre-occupation with regulating women's sexuality and reproduction (Papanek, 1994). By contrast, Hindu "communalism" is not currently obsessed with controlling Hindu women's sexuality and fertility (though see Sarkar, this volume), although as I suggest below, it is obsessed with Muslim women's fertility. It does not oppose abortion and birth control or seek to regulate the number and spacing of children. It has not differentiated itself from other political parties with respect to its positions on premarital sexuality, adultery, and widow remarriage.

An excellent example of how the BJP's expediency may serve women's interests is evident from its attempt to steal the thunder of the Congress Party on a scheme it was considering in 1995 to improve the position of women. The Congress government in the State of Haryana announced that it would invest Rs 2,500 (approximately $78) in the name of a newborn girl in a savings scheme that would yield Rs 25,000 when she turned eighteen, the legal age of marriage. (The scheme is restricted to unmarried girls in families with annual incomes below Rs 11,000 and with no more than two children (*Economist*, 11 March 1995: 40).

Once Congress Party chief Narasimha Rao recognized the electoral potential of this issue and promised to extend the scheme to the whole country, the BJP claimed that it had thought up the idea and implemented it first. The BJP government in Rajasthan had in fact launched a similar scheme in 1993 as a population control measure, not to improve girls' conditions. The Rajasthan government had provided a stipend for girls whose mothers or fathers had undergone sterilization, a condition that the Haryana government does not impose. However, the BJP is sufficiently concerned with electoral success that it was happy to broaden the scheme so that it would be more beneficial to women if this entailed electoral advantage.

Expediency has also meant that the positions the BJP women's organization assumes are often inconsistent. Although its members voice the party line on the Rām Janambhūmi movement, it is difficult to identify a single one of the vital issues before the women's movement—dowry, *satī*, female feticide—on which it holds a unified position. Thus contrary to what one might expect, neither its positions nor its actions on women's issues are all conservative. Kusum Mehdre, an active member of the Madhya Pradesh women's organization and Minister for Social Welfare, felt that women should attain economic self-sufficiency by assuming nontraditional roles. Accordingly, she had provided them employment in the production of generators, electronics, and leather goods.[3] Purnima Sethi, the convener of the BJP women's organization in Delhi, reported that she had created an agency that provided women with free legal counsel on marriage, divorce, and dowry, so that they could extricate themselves from abusive domestic situations.

This lack of consistency is also evident in the BJP itself. Although the BJP brought India to the brink of disaster over the question of where and when Rim was born in Ayodhya, it has not articulated a position on questions that "fundamentalists" consider vital in developing a coherent worldview: how to govern the economy, reform the legal system, and create a religious state. Dipankar Gupta (1991: 579) argues:

> Fundamentalism dictates how criminals should be punished; how business should be conducted; what sartorial ensembles are acceptable; in short all the relevant aspects of secular life are now imbued with religious sanction. . . . Unlike fundamentalism, which represents ethnic identities in a near full blown fashion, communalism picks on one or two important characteristics and emotionally surcharges them.

"Communalism" also offers a striking contrast with "fundamentalism" in its relationship to secularism. Whereas most "fundamentalist" movements reject the separation of religion and state, Hindu "communalism" accepts this separation in principle and rejects a religious alternative to the secular state. Partha Chatterjee (1994: 1768) argues:

> The persuasive power, and even the emotional charge the Hindutva campaign appears to have gained in recent years do not depend on its demanding legislative enforcement of ritual or scriptural injunctions, a role for religious institutions in legislative or judicial processes, compulsory religious instruction, state support for religious bodies, censorship of science, literature and art in order to safeguard religious dogma or any other similar demand undermining the secular character of the existing Indian state.

This point has crucial implications for women because the major alternative to secular law is community-based religious law. In general, safeguards against sexual inequalities are greater in secular than in religious law. By virtue of its supposed commitment to secular principles, the BJP can uphold constitutional protections of sexual equality. The best example of this is the uniform civil code. The BJP has not only emerged as the champion among Indian political parties of a uniform civil code; it has taken over what was historically a major feminist demand. Many feminists now balk at joining hands with the BJP on this issue.

The BJP uses the language of legal and constitutional rights to pit women's rights against minority rights. As Kapur and Cossman (1995: 101) point out, it interprets secularism to mean that Muslims and Hindus should be treated alike, thereby disregarding the vulnerabilities to which Muslims as a minority community are subject. One consequence of juxtaposing the interests of women and minorities is to undermine solidarity among Hindu and Muslim women. "I feel for my Muslim sisters," Uma Bharati commented, "but they do not seem to feel for themselves. Why do they agree to wear the *burqa* (veil)? How can they abide by Muslim law?"[4]

The issue of the uniform civil code provides a lens on some of the most distinctive attributes of Hindu "communalism." Islamic "fundamentalism" in South Asia and the Middle East is inseparable from nationalist opposition to Western domination in its various guises. Women may exemplify what is authentically indigenous and traditional or its antithesis, Westernization and modernity. Deniz Kandiyoti notes that although colonial authorities intervened extensively in the economic and political domains, they provided the colonized greater autonomy in the private sphere. This was the arena that "fundamentalists" claimed as their own (Kandiyoti, 1991b: 8; Devji, 1991). "Fundamentalists' " desire to veil or reveil women in Bangladesh and Pakistan has been a reaction to the supposed Western "unveiling" of women (see Feldman and Rouse, 1997). Similarly, Valentine Moghadam (1994: 13) notes that "fundamentalists" in Iran consider the veil an antidote to the virus of *gharbzadegi*, which is variously translated as "Westoxication," "Westitis," "Euromania," and "Occidentosis."

Hindu nationalists in India, unlike their counterparts in many predominantly Muslim countries, identify their principal enemies as internal rather than external. Even as India has engaged in the process of economic liberalization, and Western economic and cultural influences have grown, Hindu nationalists have not openly expressed anti-Western sentiment.

The issue of the uniform civil code provides the BJP with a means of challenging the legitimacy of the Indian state. Debates about the uniform civil code dating back to the 1950s provide the BJP with an instance of the state's willingness, under Nehru's secular left-leaning leadership, to "appease" religious conservatives. As Zoya Hasan (1993: 7) points out, Nehru passed the Hindu Code Bill, which significantly reformed Hindu law, despite opposition from conservative Hindu groups. By contrast, he acquiesced to pressure from comparable Muslim groups and left Muslim law unreformed. In raising the issue of the uniform civil code, the BJP establishes a parallel between the Congress Party's capitulation to Muslim conservatives in the 1950s and then again in the 1980s around the Shah Bano case (Hasan, this volume).

By decrying the actions of successive Congress regimes on the issue of family law, the BJP seeks to demonstrate its own commitment to secularism and constitutional principles. "Personal law," Uma Bharati argues, "defies the spirit of the constitution."[5] Arun Jaitley, an additional solicitor general and important BJP functionary, argued that the BJP's support for a uniform civil code demonstrated that it alone among political parties respected the Constitution.[6]

More broadly, the BJP often seeks to define itself in relationship to Muslim "fundamentalism" both by asserting its own superiority and by presenting Hindus as beleaguered victims. Hindu women play a key role in both of these constructions. BJP members often express condescension toward Muslims for practicing *purdah* (female seclusion) and extol the greater freedom of Hindu than of Muslim women. Mridula Sinha, the president of the all-India BJP women's organization, described the downfall of Hindu women in the after-math of Muslim rule:

> In the Vedic era, the status of women used to be much higher than it is today. You can see from the statue of *adhinarishvakar*, which is half Shiva and half Parvati, that the roles of men and women were considered interdependent and complementary. And women made important contributions to four domains: employment, religion, procreation, and the economy. After the Muslim invasion all of this changed: Hindus were forced to marry off their daughters at much younger ages, they adopted seclusion, and women's role in public life declined.[7]

Similarly, Atal Behari Vajpayee states, "Historically women were respected in this culture; indeed women wrote verses of the Vedas and Vedantas. . . . Later on because of foreign invasions various evils cropped up in our society."[8] Hindu nationalists claim that Muslim rule contributed to a decline in Hindu women's position both by force an example. Hindu men encouraged their wives to retreat into the domestic sphere to protect them from Muslim invaders.

In claiming that the subjugation of Muslim women reveals the backwardness of the Muslim community, the BJP ironically echoes the colonial view that the downtrodden Indian woman signifies the backwardness of Indians. The nineteenth-century social reform movement sought to "uplift" Hindu women in response to this very charge, to demonstrate Indians' fitness to govern themselves. Similarly for the BJP today, the lowly status of Muslim women signifies the inferiority of Muslims.

Joseph Alter (1994) finds in male celibacy an expression of cultural nationalism among Hindus. He argues that Hindus invest in celibacy notions of the fit body, disciplined according to a rigorous regimen that produces a citizen who embodies national integrity and strength. He further argues that the *brahmacharya*, who renounces sexuality, developed in opposition to colonial characterizations of upper-caste Hindu men as emasculated. In response to feelings of powerlessness amidst sociomoral change, Hindu men responded by demonstrating their capacity for self-discipline and self-restraint through celibacy.

In parallel fashion, Hindu "communalists" depict Muslim male sexuality as unrestrained, undisciplined, and antinational. They advocate rigorous measures to control Muslim family size, prohibit polygyny, and punish rapists. Indeed Hindu communalists' most vicious slogans, speeches, and graffiti allude to Muslims' sexual practices. Take, for example, a cassette recorded by Sādhvī Saraswati, whose hysterical tones mimic Sādhvī Rithambara and Uma Bharati. Saraswati begins by decrying polygyny, which she suggests is sanctioned by Muslim law. It turns Muslim women into sexual objects and breeders and results in large Muslim families. For every five children that Hindus have, Muslims have fifty. She continues:

> And who feeds these fifty children? Hindus do! After Muslims divorce, then the *waqf* (religious charity) boards support the children with taxes that we pay. . . . Within twenty-five years you will be living like a poor minority in this country. . . . Muslims have forty-six countries but Hindus have only one, Nepal! If you become a minority in this country then who will provide refugee status for you? None of the neighboring countries provide the kind of orphanage that India does.

By conjoining the backwardness of Muslims with the weakness of the Indian state, the BJP can extol the superiority of Hindus and the Hindu nation. Women, who figure in "fundamentalist" movements as symbols of tradition and continuity with the past, figure in "communal" movements as symbols of progress and modernity.

Dismantling "Communalism" and "Fundamentalism"

As I have argued elsewhere, one of the BJP's major strengths is its ability to speak in many voices (Basu, 1995b). Thus while in some contexts it may present itself as a champion of women's rights, elsewhere it defends conservative Hindu conceptions of women's place. An excellent example both of the BJP's doublespeak and of its selective conservatism concerns the issue of *sati* (widow immolation). In the aftermath of the Roop Kanwar satī in Rajasthan in 1987, the BJP was closely associated with the pro-satī lobby. In this context, it played the role that I have argued is often associated with "fundamentalist" positions: it sought justification for satī in Hindu scriptures, idealized women's roles as dutiful wives, and accused feminists of being *azād* (promiscuous) Westernized women.

Both the RSS and the Rashtra Sevika Samiti are also characterized by some of the features that are associated with "fundamentalism." In contrast to the BJP women's organization, the Rashtra Sevika Samiti possesses a coherent worldview and rashtra sevikas enjoy a distinctive lifestyle. Like many religious nationalist groups in the Middle East and South Asia, the Rashtra Sevika Samiti offers women the opportunity to remain unmarried and spend their lives in the company of other women.

Although the women's organizations of the RSS, BJP, and Durga Vahini are independent of one another in principle, they are closely affiliated in practice. At the leadership level, some of the most prominent women members of the BJP—Vijayraje Scindia, Uma Bharati, Mridula Sinha—are of Rashtra Sevika background. At the local level, these organizations seem to have overlapping memberships in that the same women participate in the activities that any one of these organizations sponsors.

Perhaps the issue that most reveals the BJP's affinity with "fundamentalist" movements is its anxiety about the moral corruption that modernity entails. For Hindu communalists, political and sexual morality are deeply intertwined. A central theme running through Rithambara's cassettes is the notion that India has lost its moral bearings. "Things have deteriorated to the point that everything is now bought and sold, minds, bodies, religion, and even the honor of our elders, sisters, mothers, and sons," she cries out. "We cannot auction our nation's honor in the market of party politics." In a sweeping gesture, Rithambara ingeniously links the corruption of the political process, capitalist development, and sexual objectification.

Another expression of the women's organization concern for sexual morality is around the issue of pornography. Purnima Sethi reported that the BJP women's organization for Delhi state, over which she presided, had organized a major campaign to ban "obscene" publications.[9] It had organized raids of three hundred establishments that were displaying "obscene" material and had pressured the press commissioner into confiscating this material. In Delhi, Lucknow, Bhopal, and other cities, BJP women organized direct-action campaigns that entailed blackening billboards that displayed women's bodies. The BJP has also demanded that the board of film certification censor vulgarity in Indian cinema. According to Shashi Ranjan, president of the BJP film cell, "Mainstream cinema is being shamelessly imbued with innuendo and vulgarity which is threatening to strike at the very core of our culture so steeped in decency and decorum" (*Indian Express*, February 8, 1994).

The Rām Janambhūmi movement and the events that surround it have given expression to some very conservative ideas that cloak themselves in religious garb. The Gita Press in Gorakhpur published a series of cheap, readable books on the proper roles of Hindu women. They are written in the form of treatises that draw upon the authority of religious scriptures. Portions are in Sanskrit, which are then translated into Hindi. Some chapters are written in question-and-answer format: a disciple poses questions to which he or she receives responses, presumably from religious authorities. The books lay out codes of conduct for women around minutiae of social life: how a woman should behave around her relatives, what she should eat while pregnant, what ornaments she should wear after marriage, and whether she should use birth control.

The series' central message for women is the importance of devotion to their families and the dangers that await those who refuse to conform. One book, *How to Lead a Householder's Life* (Ramsukhdas, 1992a), states that misery awaits the bride who chooses her own husband, and sisters who demand a share in their father's property. It counsels the daughter-in-law to accept the harsh treatment of her mother-in-law and "to pay attention to the comfort of her husband, even at the cost of her own comfort." "What should the wife do if her husband beats her and troubles her?" the disciple asks. The response: "The wife should think that she is paying her debt of her previous life and thus her sins are being destroyed and she is becoming pure" (Ramsukhdas, 1992a: 44–50). Another question raised is whether a widow should remarry. The response: it is "beastliness" for the family to remarry her when she is no longer a virgin and thus cannot be offered "as charity" to anyone else. The main point is that a woman's purity must be safeguarded after marriage, when there is the risk of her acting independently. *Nari Siksha* (Women's Education) (Poddar, 1992) voices the same theme in its open support for satï. In these texts the fear of the widow's attainment of economic independence echoes Muslim "fundamentalists' " worries about Shah Bano gaining maintenance payments from her husband.

Another book, *Disgrace of Mother's Prowess* (Ramsukhdas, 1992b), opposes abortion on grounds that it denies the unborn child the possibility of *mokshā* (liberation through rebirth) and thus constitutes a sin. Ram-sukhdas argues that the sin of abortion is twice as great as the sin of killing a Brahman. Thus a man whose wife has an abortion must disown her. The only acceptable form of birth control, he continues, is celibacy.

These books echo many of the ideas that are associated with "fundamentalism." First, they juxtapose Indian values with Western values and emphasize the links between women's biological and social roles. *Nari Siksha* in particular engages in a diatribe against Western feminism for supposedly destroying the family and with it the moral backbone of society (Poddar,1992). It insists upon the sanctity of motherhood for Hindu women and enjoins them to reject Western notions of liberation. *Nari Siksha* states that for a woman to become *satī* (revered as a devoted wife), she must possess *dharma* (faith) and treat her husband like a god. Among other things this entails cooking well for guests and in-laws, rising early to clean the house, and demonstrating deference to in-laws.

It is difficult to know whether the BJP combine has any direct connection to the authors or publishers of these books. But even if these new voices of Hindu conservatism have no direct link to the family of RSS organizations, the BJP and its affiliates have created a climate that promotes such views.

Although I have used the concepts of "communalism" and "fundamentalism" in hopes of achieving precision, the terms are imprecise and heavily laden with unintended meanings. First, both "fundamentalism" and "communalism" are pejorative terms. It is difficult to understand views that one assumes are irrational. It is also difficult to decouple the concepts of "communalism" and "fundamentalism" from religion, even though the growth of "fundamentalism" and "communalism" have more to do with conflicts over the distribution of power and wealth than with religion per se. Furthermore, the beliefs and practices to which "fundamentalists" and "communalists" refer are selectively filtered from religious doctrines that afford many interpretations.[10]

The connotations of the term "fundamentalism" are especially troublesome (Metcalf, 1997). Through habitual usage, "fundamentalism" has come to be identified almost exclusively with Islam, to the disregard of other religious fundamentalisms, among other places in the United States. A tendency to brand the entire Islamic world "fundamentalist" ignores the experiences of the Muslim countries that are not "fundamentalist." It is also erroneous to assume that "fundamentalists," unlike "communalists," are disinterested in political power. Indeed, they have often compromised their principled commitments to women's seclusion on grounds of political expediency. In Pakistan, for example, although the Jama'at-i-Islami had previously opposed the principle of a woman head of state, by 1965 it had supported a woman presidential candidate because of electoral considerations (Mumtaz, 1994: 232). Similarly, despite the decision of the Islamic state in Iran to remove women from public office in the 1980s, it organized four thousand "*basīj*" women into a militia to guard government ministries and banks (Moghadam, 1991: 278). Moreover it would be wrong to assume the absence of women's activism in "fundamentalist" movements. There are several accounts of women's active support for the Iranian revolution, including its veiling of women. Margot Badran (1994) describes a group of conservative women in Egypt who justify women's political participation on grounds of religious commitment. Khawar Mumtaz (1991) shows that in Pakistan in the 1980s and 1990s, "fundamentalist" women associated with the Jama'at-i-Islami opposed feminism for eroding the barriers between male and female worlds because their own activism was premised upon sexual segregation. We simply do not have the evidence to conclude that women's activism is greater in "communal" than in "fundamentalist" movements.

There is also a danger of implying that "communalism" represents a progressive force that encourages women's activism and empowerment, whereas "fundamentalism" does the opposite. This comparison draws on the assumption that Hinduism compares favorably with Islam in its views on women's place. Several scholars have noted that Hinduism rejects notions of women's inherent weakness and considers them powerful and thus potentially dangerous (Wadley, 1977). The varied personalities of female deities in Hinduism may inspire a range of female personas in political life. Ascetic women have the freedom to remain single, travel extensively, and engage in worldly pursuits (Denton, 1991). But even for "ordinary" Hindu women, religious devotion has always provided a culturally sanctioned escape from domestic drudgery and opportunity for self-realization. However, the qualities of Hinduism cannot explain women's activism in communal politics. The BJP has taken a decentered, pluralist religious tradition and rendered it more centralized. Given its willingness to transform Hinduism in such far-reaching ways, the BJP is hardly bound by religious doctrines on questions concerning women.

Islam too can be interpreted in diverse ways: some Muslim feminists have emphasized its emancipatory features; fundamentalists have found within it justification for sexually repressive practices.

Both "communalism" and "fundamentalism" are responses to the strains of modernity: the erosion of state legitimacy, the integration of postcolonial economies into the global capitalist system, and the influx of Western cultural influences. But at the same time, both "communalism" and "fundamentalism" seek justification from the past. Both employ gendered images of motherhood to romanticize the past and suggest continuity with it. Hindu "communalism" also finds in motherhood imagery a basis in religion because of the ways in which Hinduism worships mother goddesses. But motherhood imagery is not confined to "communalism" or "fundamentalism"; it is a staple of nationalist movements. Both by virtue of its stated commitments and its actions, the BJP can best be described as a religious nationalist party. The BJP asserts a deep affinity between Hindus and the nation-state. This supposed affinity rests upon the notion that Hindus were the original and thus the most legitimate inhabitants of India. Just as the BJP employs an organic conception of citizenship, so too it assumes that the Muslim minority, and the Congress Party, which supposedly appeases it, are implicitly antinational.

In many respects the recent growth of majoritarian nationalism signals a response to the steady growth of minority nationalism in India. Historically, the BJP's predecessor, the Jan Sangh, often mobilized around Hindu issues like cow protection and mandatory use of Hindi following periods of minority linguistic and ethnic mobilization. In the recent past, the backdrop of secessionist movements in the Punjab and Kashmir seem to have played a key role in the BJP's renewed commitment to Hindu nationalism. The growth of minority nationalisms is vital to explaining how the BJP can convincingly present Hindus, who dominate economic and political life in India, as beleaguered victims.

This chapter opened by remarking on the unusual extent and nature of women's activism around the Rām Janambhūmi issue. I argued that women's activism may be partially explained by the BJP's expedient support for certain (Hindu) women's rights. However, expediency is by definition dual-faceted: it encourages the BJP to take up women's rights, and allows the BJP to ignore, disparage, and undermine them.

The BJP is ultimately less committed to women's rights than to the denial of Muslim rights. While it highlights the inequities of Muslim law, it is remark-ably silent about the discriminatory traits of Hindu law.[11] Thus Arun Jaitley defended differences in inheritance rights of sons and daughters on grounds that women's equal rights to inheritance would fragment family landholdings. There are many indications that the BJP's interpretation of a uniform civil code would be modeled on Hindu law. Furthermore, the BJP has championed women's rights in only a narrowly legalistic fashion. Its women's organization has issued statements condemning violence against women but has not campaigned to oppose it. For example, it accepts the dowry system and avoids the issue of dowry deaths.

At this stage it is important to refine the concept of women's activism. Many of the women who took part in processions, campaigns, and riots seemed exhilarated by the opportunity for activism that this provided: leaving their homes, putting aside domestic work, and devoting themselves to a cause. Particularly for lower-middle-class housewives, who form an important part of the BJP's constituency, Hindu nationalist mobilization offered a rare opportunity for self-realization.

But Hindu women's activism has not necessarily challenged patterns of sexual inequality within the home and the world. Nor are women necessarily drawn to the BJP simply because it advocates their rights. Mridula Sinha stated emphatically, "For Indian women, liberation means liberation from atrocities. It doesn't mean that women should be relieved of their duties as wives and mothers. Women should stop demanding their rights all the time and think instead in terms of their responsibilities to the family."[12] Mohini Garg, the all-India secretary of the BJP women's organization, echoed this point: "We want to encourage our members not to think in terms of individual rights but in terms of responsibility to the nation."[13]

Indeed, a striking feature of women's participation in the activities of the BJP's women's organization is women's reenactment of conventional sex-linked roles within the broader public arena. Nirupuma Gour, the organization's secretary in Uttar Pradesh, reported that in preparation for the BJP procession to Ayodhya in October 1990 (the dress rehearsal for 1992), women had developed an elaborate ritual for sending the "*kar sevaks*" (volunteer workers) like warriors to the battlefield.[14] They would congregate at designated spots at the train stations with food, portable stoves, and other paraphernalia. As the men boarded the trains, the women would garland them, place *tilaks* (vermilion marks) on their foreheads, and give them freshly prepared hot food. She said that women were instructed to prepare up to fifty thousand food packets each day. Gour estimates that five to six thousand women arrived in Lucknow from all over the country. Many others could not travel to Ayodhya because transportation was inadequate, but those who reached Lucknow assumed responsibility for protecting men from repression. Thus, for example, when trains approached Ayodhya, the women would sound the alarms to stop them; the men would disembark immediately while the women would confront the train conductors. At Ayodhya, the women would encircle the men to prevent the police from wielding their *lāthīs* (bamboo sticks). When the *kar sevaks* broke through the police cordons and climbed atop the Babari Masjid, however, the women were absent. I asked Mala Rustogi, a member of the Durga Vahini in Lucknow, why the women had not participated in the culmination of their actions. She responded that it would have been undignified for Hindu women to be climbing a mosque in their *sārīs*.[15]

The particular roles that the BJP assigned to women in its very expensive, elaborate electoral campaigns are also significant. Whereas men had primary responsibility for addressing large public gatherings, women engaged in door-to-door campaigning that brought them into contact with housewives who might have been less willing to speak with men.

Women's reenactment of their private roles in the public arena may also play a particularly important place in the context of Hindu nationalism, which has sought to challenge the public/private divide in other ways. The BJP's central platform during the period of its ascendance to power in the late 1980s was its demand that the Congress government demolish the Babari Masjid in Ayodhya and build a Rām temple in its place. Implicit in this demand was the BJP's attempt to accord centrality in political life to questions of religious faith. This proves especially difficult in a democratic context such as India, where the state may intervene to prevent political parties from bringing religious matters into politics. Women are well positioned to further the BJP's project. During the 1991 elections when the election commissioner had prohibited the BJP from shouting religious slogans, I marched with processions of women who appeared to be observing these dictates on the streets. But as soon as they entered the courtyards of people's homes, cries of "*Jāī Shrī Rām!*" (Victory to the Lord Ram!) and "*Mandir vahān banāyenge!*" (We will build a temple there!) filled the air. In this vital phase of Hindu nationalism, women served as emissaries of private-domain religion into the public sphere and of the BJP's supposed religious commitments into the home and family. BJP leaders felt that women's electoral support would affirm the party's religious commitment because, they claimed, women were more devout than men.

What of women themselves? What did they gain from being assigned a role that enabled them to venture out of their homes without challenging norms of sexual subordination? The experiences of Mala Rustogi are instructive. Rustogi said that when she first began working with the Durga Vahini in Lucknow in 1989, she feared the opposition of her husband and in-laws, for her daughter was only three years old at the time. To her surprise, they supported her. She described a newfound sense of pleasure in serving others: "Serving one's husband is expected of women and of course it is important. But serving a third person whom you don't know and aren't expected to serve is much more exciting—for just that reason." Her comment captures some of the traits that were mirrored in women's activism: their experience of self-affirmation through self-sacrifice, and their empowerment through public-sphere activism, which ultimately renewed their commitment to their domestic roles.

Some of the changes under way in Indian society might help explain Hindu women's acceptance of their ambiguous placement between public and private domains. The growth of the BJP coincides with unprecedented economic liberalization, which has truncated the public sphere and redefined the private arena. Women have access to larger markets than ever before, stocked with a range of goods that convey the allure of freedom: ready-made clothes, prepared foods, and gadgets to simplify housework. The Indian women who appear in advertisements for these products have light hair and skin, wear Western or Westernized clothing, and convey a sexy demeanor. Release from domesticity also comes from women's increased employment, particularly among the middle classes in the service sector. Consumerism and employment both lend support to women's growing involvement in the political domain.

The BJP and its women's wing give voice to profound middle-class ambivalence about these social and economic changes. While embracing the modernist project of capitalist expansion, they worry incessantly about the excessive individual freedom that it enables. Indeed, the BJP's changing economic policy is an excellent indicator of this ambivalence. Under the influence of the RSS, it has sought to promote *svadeshī* a nationalist response to globalization that encourages self-sufficiency in certain areas of the economy. But it does so without repudiating economic liberalization altogether.

Many of the forms of women's activism that have been identified with Hindu nationalism are mirrored within anticolonial nationalism in India. Within the anticolonial movement we find very similar patterns of women's entering the public sphere without challenging the norms of sexual segregation and seclusion. Although the most exalted images are Gandhian depictions of women's pacifism, there are many instances of women's complicity in violence: in collaborating with the Punjabi revolutionary Bhagat Singh; in the Chatri Sangh in Calcutta in the late 1920s; and in the Chittagong Armoury Raid in the early 1930s. The nationalist revolutionary Subhash Chander Bose formed a women's militia called the Rani of Jhansi Regiment, which trained women in the use of arms and ammunition. Women were also active in revolutionary violence in the Telengana movement in Andhra Pradesh.

Situating Hindu women's activism within a broader context of nationalist mobilization reveals parallels with a range of political movements that make ascribed identity the basis for political mobilization (Moghadam, 1994). There are striking resemblances between Hindu nationalism and some right-wing and fascist movements that harness women's activism around racist and anti-Semitic campaigns.[16] The extent of women's participation in Islamic movements in the Middle East and North Africa is also striking. Sondra Hale (1994) finds that women have been extremely active in the Islamist party in the Sudan; these women find in the Shari'a justification for their activism and for asserting their rights as women. Similarly the Muslim Sisters in Egypt justify their activism by reference to Islamic principles. Aisha Abd al-Rahman, a well-known *Qur'anic* scholar, argues that the "truly Islamic" and the "truly feminist" option is neither immodest dress nor identical roles for the sexes in the name of Islam. "The right path is the one that combines modesty, responsibility and integration into public life with the *Qur'anic* and naturally enjoined distinctions between the sexes" (Hoffman-Ladd, 1987: 37). Muslim women were active in the "turban movement" in Turkey, which opposed the legal prohibition of the Islamic head scarf for women students; this movement played a vital role in radicalizing the Islamic cause (Toprak, 1994). In all these cases religious idioms provided women with the means of opposing the denigrating forces of Western modernity.

The global dimensions of religious nationalism are striking. The BJP's anti-Muslim propaganda is legitimated by the role of the United States in the Gulf War and the anti-Muslim sentiment that predated and succeeds it, just as Islamic "fundamentalism" finds justification in the U.S. exertion of cultural superiority, political control, and economic dominance in the Middle East. In countries like Iran, leaders can mobilize Muslim sentiment in opposition to Western economic and cultural domination.

In its emphasis on the transnational character of Islamic "fundamentalism," Hindu nationalism finds justification for its own transnational ambitions. The Rām Janambhūmi movement provided the occasion for the development of far-reaching networks among Indians in North America, Africa, Europe, and other regions. These networks can build upon the growth of two groups within the expatriate Indian community: business people who seek ways of demonstrating their nationalist commitments, and self-employed business people for whom Hindu nationalism is a response to racism and discrimination abroad.

Conclusion

Certain features of "communalism," such as its support for a uniform civil code, encourage women's activism, but women do not achieve lasting gains from these spurts of activism. Their intense identification with "communal movements" is likely to be short-lived.

The contrasts between "communalism" and "fundamentalism" diminish when we explore the ways in which both are influence by the economic and political context. Of particular importance are electoral influences. The more committed groups are to exercising power, the more expedient they are likely to be in interpreting religion. This in turn has extremely significant implications for women. The more a group believes itself to be the authentic voice of religion, the more likely it is to treat women as symbols of tradition. Conversely, the more committed a group is to exercising power democratically, the more women count numerically as a means of demonstrating popular support and winning elections. This in turn might entail appealing to women's gender interests.

Furthermore, "communalism" and "fundamentalism" are both essentialist concepts: they infer from religious identities a stable set of values and beliefs. In India, "fundamentalism" is an even more pejorative concept than "communalism." This in turn is partly a reflection of the very influence of

Hindu nationalism. The term "fundamentalism" denotes the beliefs and practices of Muslims; "communalism," those of Hindus. The BJP has strengthened the assumption that Muslims compare particularly unfavorably with Hindus in the treatment of women. Thus the use of the concepts of "fundamentalism" and "communalism" effectively pits Islam against Hinduism. Both terms are so premised on assumptions of primordialism that no amount of creative reinterpretation can sufficiently launder them of it.

In highlighting the modern political ambitions of Hindu "communalism," it is impossible to ignore the complicated ways in which this modernizing project restores, utilizes, and reinterprets traditional forces. Even though the BJP's ambitions are wholly modern—a powerful, expansionist state, integration with the global capitalist system—it also strengthens antimodernist impulses. Thus Vijayraje Scindia at one moment supports a uniform civil code that will accord women legal rights and at another moment suggests that *satī* provides the normative ideal to which Hindu women should aspire.

Hindu nationalists have turned to women as exemplifications of the contradictory qualities they seek to project: a rootedness in the past and a commitment to a modern India in the future. But Hindu women can exemplify these two very different qualities only by taking on another quality: a willingness to render Muslims into dehumanized Others.

Notes

I received valuable comments on an earlier draft of this chapter from participants at the conference Appropriating Gender: Women and Religious Nationalism in South Asia, held at Rockefeller Conference and Study Center in Bellagio, August 1994; the conference Gender, Nation and the Politics of Culture in India, at Cornell University, April 1, 1995; and at the Peace and World Security Studies workshop at Hampshire College on April 3, 1995. I am particularly grateful to Mary Katzenstein for her encouragement and advice, and to Barbara Metcalf for her forceful denunciation of the concept of fundamentalism. I received research and writing support from the Amherst College Research Award and the John D. and Catherine T. MacArthur Foundation.

1 See Bhaktal (1993: 12-13). Kishwar (1993) describes similar forms of women's violence in the Bombay riots in December 1992 and February 1993, and Shah et al. (1993) describe the complicity of Hindu women in the Surat riots in December 1992.

2 As I indicate later in my paper, I find the terms "communalism" and "fundamen-

talism" of limited analytic utility because of their pejorative connotations. I much prefer the terms religious nationalism, or Keddie's "new religious politics" or "religiopolitics" (see Keddie, 1997). However while I use the concept "religious nationalism" whenever possible, I must use the terms communalism and fundamentalism when I seek to compare the two phenomena.

3 Interview with Kusum Mehdre, Bhopal, June 14, 1991.

4 Interview with Uma Bharati, New Delhi, December 17, 1991.

5 Ibid.

6 Interview with Arun Jaitley, New Delhi, April 11, 1991.

7 Interview with Mridula Sinha, New Delhi, February 7, 1991.

8 Speech delivered at the BJP plenary meeting, Jaipur, December 1991.

9 Interview with Purnima Sethi, New Delhi, March 27, 1991.

10 On this question, see Ahmed (1992). On the Pakistani context, see Gardezi (1990); Mumtaz and Shaheed (1987); Rouse (1986); and Shaheed and Mumtaz (1990).

11 Agnes (1995) similarly points to the failures of the Indian women's movement to redress some of the sexist aspects of Hindu law. If two Hindus marry under the Special Marriages Act, according to a 1954 amendment, the secular code that grants equal rights to men and women—the Indian Succession Act of 1925—does not apply. Instead, the couple is governed by the Hindu Succession Act, which grants men coparcenary rights (the rights to the family's ancestral property). Under the Hindu Adoption and Maintenance Act, a Hindu wife can neither adopt nor give a child in adoption. In reformed Hindu law, although marriages are in principle monogamous, in practice they may be polygynous, and co-wives are denied the protection that they are afforded in Hindu customary law.

12 Interview with Mridula Sinha, New Delhi, February 7, 1991.

13 Interview with Mohini Garg, New Delhi, April 11, 1991.

14 Interview with Nirupuma Gour, Lucknow, January 5, 1992.

15 Interview with Mala Rustogi (pseudonym), Lucknow, December 28, 1992. Other references to Rustogi's views are drawn from the same interview.

16 There are many parallels between women's activism in Hindu nationalism and in German fascism; see Koonz (1987); Bridenthal, Grossman, and Kaplan (1984). See Blee (1991) and Klatch (1987) for parallels with women's activism in racist and right-wing organizations in the United States.

An Interview with Taslima Nasrin

Hillary Frey & Ruth Baldwin

Taslima Nasrin is a Bengali physician, writer, and poet who gained prominence in the late 1980s as a secular feminist who decried the oppression of Bangladeshi women and called for the separation of the mosque and state. Her persecution began in 1992, and intensified after the 1993 publication of her novella, Shame (Lajja), *which describes the suffering of one Hindu family under attack from Muslim fundamentalists. She was charged with "blasphemy" by the Bangladeshi government and placed under* fatwah *by Muslim leaders. After months of hiding, Nasrin received asylum from the Swedish Government. She continues to live in exile in Europe.*

Q: As a Muslim girl growing up in Bangladesh, you read the Qur'an in Arabic, which you didn't understand. When you were able to read the Qur'an in Bengali and divined the meanings of the words, what did you discover?

A: Like most of the people who read the Qur'an in Arabic, I did not know the meaning of the verses. But when I was twelve years old, I got a translation of the Qur'an in Bengali, and I was very curious to know the meanings of the verses I had to read almost every day. I was so surprised to learn that Allah said something totally against the science I had been taught. Allah declared that he created the earth, and all the things on the earth, and the sun, the moon, and the sky. He created mountains to support the earth so that it would not fall. Allah ordered the sun to revolve around the earth; He gave light to the sun and moon. He created Adam and Eve as the first man and woman, but because they did not follow the order of Allah and ate an apple, Allah threw them out of heaven, and since then humans have lived on earth. According to this, all humans are from Adam and Eve. But I was a student of science, I knew about the Big Bang theory, our solar system. I knew evolutionary theory, which made sense to me. Allah's six days of creation were like a fairy tale. I also found Allah to be cruel when he declared that only people who praise him and who follow him and the prophet Muhammad's orders will go to heaven and people of different faith will go to hell. I had a strong suspicion that Allah was not sitting in the seventh sky, and the Qur'an was written by Muhammad in his own interest.

Q: How did you interpret what the Qur'an says about women? How did this experience of understanding the Qur'an affect you?

A: Under the Qur'an, men are superior and women are inferior. Women are like fields that men can cultivate as they wish. Women have no equality in marriage, divorce, and child custody. During war, men get orders from Allah to rape their enemy's women. In heaven, Allah will reward faithful men with seventy-two virgins. Women are promised nothing but the same old husband. When I learned the Qur'an's view about women, I started writing against religion. I strongly believe that no woman can be free unless she crosses the barrier of patriarchy and religion. I want to wake women up, so that they can organize themselves and fight for their rights.

Q: What is your response to those who argue that fundamentalists distort the true meaning of Islam, and that a faithful reading of the Qur'an will affirm feminist values?

A: There is no way to find any feminist value in the Qur'an. If people say that it is found, then either they lie, or they try to interpret the verses differently to make it suitable with the present day.

Q: What did you witness as a doctor and citizen in Bangladesh that led you to become an outspoken writer and activist against Islamic fundamentalism? How has Islam been exploited culturally and politically by those in power in Bangladesh and in the greater subcontinental region?

A: As a doctor and a citizen in Bangladesh I witnessed a very backward society where women suffer a lot. Women remain illiterate and jobless; they are often flogged and stoned to death.

I find it difficult to accept fundamentalism as an alternative to secular ideas. My reasons are, first, the insistence of fundamentalists on divine justification for human laws; second, the insistence of fundamentalists upon the superior authority of faith, as opposed to reason; third, the insistence of fundamentalists that the individual does not count, that the individual is immaterial. The idea of group loyalty over individual rights and personal achievements is a peculiar feature of fundamentalism. Fundamentalists believe in a particular way of life; they want to put everybody in their particular straitjacket and dictate what an individual should eat, what an individual should wear, how an individual should live everyday life—everything would be determined by the fundamentalist authority. Fundamentalists do not believe in individualism, liberty of personal choice, or plurality of thought. Moreover, as they are believers in a particular faith, they believe in propagating only their own ideas (as autocrats generally do). They do not encourage or entertain free debate, they deny others the right to express their own views freely and they cannot tolerate anything which they perceive as going against their faith. They do not believe in an open society and, though they proclaim themselves a moral force, their language is about hatred and violence.

The politicians in the subcontinent use religion for their own interest. They feel that because religion is important to the ignorant, illiterate masses, it is a useful tool for control. Even the opposition is hesitant to disturb the fundamentalists for fear of losing political support. Bangladesh is not (yet) governed by mullahs, however; political power is not yet in the hands of any religious fundamentalist party. When the mullahs issue a *fatwah* from time to time, it has no constitutional legitimacy or legal sanction. But seldom is any action taken against those who issue such edicts. I do not think the government or the other democratic parties are really worried about this, though someday they may have to pay a high price for today's small gains. In the meantime, common people will have to suffer because of the activities of the fundamentalists. If there were faster economic growth, less unemployment and better access to education, I think the situation would be different. But until such miracles happen, democrats will have to bear the brunt of fundamentalism in my country. Women will have to suffer not only discrimination but also ignominy and violence, and human rights will remain just a dream for many.

Q: You are against fundamentalism of all kinds, not just Islamic and Hindu. Can you describe what it is about fundamentalism that is so dangerous, especially for women?

A: Fundamentalism is very dangerous for women. Women are burned at the stake, women are thrown on the pyre of their dead husbands. Women, under Hindu law, cannot get property from parents, they are not allowed to divorce their husbands, widows are not allowed to marry again, are not allowed to eat any fish or meat, are not allowed to wear any coloured dresses but white. Of course, women are tortured in the name of traditions and cultures, too, but religious fundamentalism has made women suffer much more than anything else. You can fight cultures and tradition, but it is difficult to fight religion. The fundamentalists are God's soldiers, they are standing everywhere with their so-called holy books, so that women are afraid to live with dignity, because it displeases God.

Q: After *Shame* was published in 1993, Muslim leaders in Bangladesh issued a *fatwah* and put a price on your head. What has your life been like since then, and how have you been able to continue your fight against fundamentalism?

A: *Shame* was banned by the government, but it was not why the Muslim leaders issued the *fatwah*. Fundamentalists were angry at me because of the essays I wrote against religion. They organized demonstrations and processions, they demanded my execution by hanging, and they filed cases against me because of my writings. The government also filed a case against me on the charge of blasphemy, and issued a nonbailable warrant for my arrest. They did this only because I rejected Islam. If any religion allows the persecution of the people of different faith, if any religion keeps people in ignorance, if any religion keeps women in slavery then it is very simple that I can't accept that religion.

In 1994, I was forced to leave my country. Since then, I have been living in exile. I am all the more committed to my cause. I will continue my fight until my death. My pen is my weapon.

Q: How has being in exile changed or reinforced your perspective on fundamentalism's influence in the subcontinental region and elsewhere?

A: I have learned about other persecuted writers and feminists who are in exile. I realize now, more than ever, that fundamentalists are not only in the subcontinent: they are all over the world. But what's happening in Muslim countries is particularly bad. We the secular people from the Muslim countries have to fight Islamic fundamentalism together. Everybody has his or her own way to fight. Writing is my way. I also attend conferences on religion, on human rights, humanism to express my views.

Q: In the subcontinental region, what is the relationship between Hindu and Muslim fundamentalists? Is there tension there? Do you see special dangers for women in that region?

A: If Muslim fundamentalism is on the rise in Bangladesh or Pakistan, Hindu fundamentalism is on the rise in India. But Hindu and Muslim fundamentalists are often very friendly. Actually, in the subcontinent, it is more a conflict between secularism and fundamentalism, it is a conflict between modernity and antimodernity, between rational, logical thinking and irrational blind faith, between innovation and tradition, between the people who value freedom and those who do not. Innocent people are used by the politicians to kill each other. In India, Hindus, Muslims, Jains, Christians, Buddhists, Shikhs, Jews, Parsis, and atheists have lived together for thousands of years; there are a hundred different cultures, a hundred different languages. Fundamentalism is a fairly recent phenomemon. If India, as a secular state, would stop encouraging religious uprisings, then it would be possible to make peace between the communities.

Women are always in danger during riots, during wars. They are often a target to punish the enemies because women are considered their property.

Q: How can secular society be strengthened in the subcontinent? How can others, especially women, fight fundamentalist movements most effectively?

A: Secular society should be strengthened by a strong secular movement. The media is also an important means of spreading secular ideas. Secular education can also help people to grow up antifundamentalist. Women have no choice but to fight fundamentalists to get the right to live as human beings. Women suffer the most from fundamentalism. So women have to move. They have to fight without any compromise. If women remain in a cage, society will remain in the backyard of modern history, so men and women with secular ideas, who believe in human rights, freedom of speech, and democracy should be in the same movement.

Women often become tools of fundamentalism, as they are the tools of patriarchy. There are women in power, too, but I don't think they have any ideological committment to improve the condition of women. They are taught for centuries that they are slaves of men. It is hard to change that mindset. Women who are in power are just used as puppets of male politicians, too.

Q: What is your view of the Bush administration's war on terrorism? What effect has it had on the struggle against fundamentalism in South Asia?

A: There are three kinds of terrorism in this world. Private, group, and state. Among these, state terrorism is the most dangerous terrorism. The

Bush administration is involved in state terrorism; you cannot eradicate terrorists by dropping bombs. In South Asia, religious terrorists have become much more active since the war on terrorism began, and it's because of the inhumane activities of Bush. In the Middle East, the hatred against the United States is increasing, too. More and more people are joining the fundamentalist organizations, and will continue to.

Religion, Culture, and Sex Equality: India and the United States

Martha Nussbaum[1]

Although all religions were initially founded with the aim of purifying men and women and helping them to lead ethical lives through prayer, it was found in some instances that blind traditions, customs and superstition often resulted in—not the cathartic effects of religion—but the spread of communalism, fanaticism, fundamentalism, and discrimination.

—Heera Nawaz, law student,
Bangalore College of Law, 1993[2]

I

Modern constitutional democracies typically hold that the free exercise of religion is an extremely important value, and that its protection is among the most important functions of government. These democracies also typically protect a range of other interests, liberties, and opportunities. Among these are the freedom of movement, the right to seek employment outside the home, the right to assemble, the right to bodily integrity, the right to education, and the right to hold and to inherit property. Among these is also, prominently, and informing all the others, the right to the equal protection of the laws, a legal expression of the fundamental idea that all citizens are entitled to equal respect. Sometimes, however, the religions do not support these other rights on a basis of equality. Sometimes, indeed, they deny important rights to classes of people on grounds that are incompatible with equal respect and equal personhood, grounds such as race or caste or sex. Such denials may not mean much in nations where the religions do not wield much legal power. But in nations such as India, where religions have been given a considerable role in the legal system, they are fundamental determinants of many lives.

In this way, an apparent dilemma is created for the state. On the one

215

hand, to interfere with the freedom of religious expression is to strike a blow against citizens in an area of intimate self-definition and basic liberty. Not to interfere, however, permits other abridgments of self-definition and liberty. It is not surprising that modern democracies should find themselves torn in this area—particularly a democracy like India, which has committed itself to the equality of the sexes and nondiscrimination on the basis of sex in the list of Fundamental Rights enumerated in its Constitution—alongside commitments to religious liberty and nondiscrimination on the basis of religion.[3]

Consider these three cases, all involving conflicts between claims of religious free exercise and women's claims to other important rights under the Indian Constitution:

(1) In 1983, Mary Roy, a Syrian Christian woman, went to court to challenge the Travancore Christian Act, under which daughters inherit only one fourth the share of the son, subject to a minimum of Rs. 5,000 (about $150). (Personal property in India is administered through the various systems of religious personal laws; there is no uniform civil code, and the secular inheritance law, although it exists, is effectively unavailable to those whose ancestral property is in one of the religious systems.) The Indian Supreme Court did not declare the act unconstitutional on the ground that it violated the constitutional guarantee of sex equality; but they held that Christians in Kerala should henceforth be governed by the Indian Succession Act of 1925, which gives equal rights to daughters and sons.[4] Protest greeted the judgment. The Christian Churches of Kerala, which automatically received a portion of the daughter's inheritance under the old law, vociferously protested the court's interference with the free exercise of religion. They argued that the judgment would "open up a floodgate of litigation and destroy the traditional harmony and goodwill that exists in Christian families."[5]

(2) In 1947, at the time of Independence, the Hindu Law Committee submitted a list of recommendations for reform in the system of Hindu personal law. These were presented to Parliament in the form of the Hindu Code bill. Backed by Nehru's law minister, B. R. Ambedkar, the bill granted women a right to divorce, removed the option of polygamous marriage for men, abolished child marriage for young women,[6] and granted women more nearly equal property rights. A storm of protest from

Hindu MPs (led by conservative pandits or Hindu religious authorities) greeted the proposed legislation. Debate focused on the new laws' alleged violations of the free exercise of religion, as guaranteed in the new constitution. Conservative pandits objected to the whole idea of state-initiated reform of the Hindu code: "Hindu law is intimately connected with Hindu religion, and no Hindu can tolerate a non-Hindu being an authority on Hindu law."

Shortly after the new Constitution took effect, in the summer of 1951, a tumultuous session of Parliament formally debated the bill; conservative Pandit Govind Malviya spoke for two hours against the bill, which he called "wrong in principle, atrocious in detail and uncalled for in expediency." Despite Ambedkar's passionate support, the bill seemed bound for defeat, and even Nehru withdrew his support for the time being. In consequence, Dr. Ambedkar resigned his ministerial position, saying, "To leave untouched the inequality between class and class, between sex and sex, and to go on passing legislation relating to economic problems is to make a farce of our Constitution and so build a palace on a dung heap." The bill lapsed. Its provisions were eventually adopted in 1954, 1955, and 1956, but, fifty years later, its provisions continue to arouse controversy, and change in the other direction is a distinct possibility.

(3) In Madhya Pradesh in 1978, an elderly Muslim woman named Shah Bano was thrown out of her home by her husband, a prosperous lawyer, after forty-four years of marriage. (The occasion seems to have been a quarrel over inheritance between the children of Shah Bano and the children of the husband's other wife.) As required by Islamic personal law, he returned to her the *mehr*, or marriage settlement, that she had originally brought into the marriage—Rs. 3000 (less than $100 by today's exchange rates). Like many Muslim women facing divorce without sufficient maintenance, she sued for regular maintenance payments under Section 125 of the uniform Criminal Procedure Code, which forbids a man "of adequate means" to permit various close relatives, including an exwife,[7] to remain in a state of "destitution and vagrancy." This remedy had long been recognized as a solution to the inadequate maintenance granted by Islamic personal law, and many women have won similar cases. What was different about Shah Bano's case was that the Chief Justice of the Supreme Court of India, awarding her maintenance of the equivalent of $180 per month,

remarked in his lengthy opinion that the Islamic system was very unfair to women, and that it was high time that the nation should indeed secure a Uniform Civil Code, as the constitution had long ago directed it to do. Although of Hindu origin, the Chief Justice interpreted various Islamic sacred texts and argued that there was no textual barrier in Islam to providing a much more adequate maintenance for women.

A storm of public protest greeted the opinion. Although some liberal Muslims backed Chief Justice Chandrachud, he had made their task difficult by his zealous incursion into the interpretation of sacred Islamic texts. The Islamic clergy and the Muslim Personal Law Board organized widespread protest against the ruling, claiming that it violated their free exercise of religion. In response to the widespread outcry, the government of Rajiv Gandhi introduced the Muslim Women's (Protection after Divorce) Act of 1986, which deprived all and only Muslim women of the right of maintenance guaranteed under the Criminal Procedure Code. Women's groups tried to get this law declared unconstitutional on grounds of both religious discrimination and sex equality, but the Supreme Court (in rapid retreat from charges of excessive activism) refused to hear their claim. Hindu activists, meanwhile, complained that the 1986 law discriminates against Hindus, giving Muslim men "special privileges."[8]

Here are three examples of the dilemma I have mentioned, no different in kind from dilemmas that arise in the U.S. and Europe, but different in degree, since the religions in India control so much of the legal system. On the one side is the claim of religious free exercise; on the other, women's claims to various fundamental rights—including religious nondiscrimination. In the first case, women won a clear victory—interestingly, in the case involving a small, politically powerless religion. In the second, women made some strides, but the increasing power of Hindu fundamentalism now threatens their situation. In the third, women suffered a painful and prominent defeat. Free exercise and sex equality appear, at least sometimes, to be on a collision course.

The theme of this volume is the relationship between women and fundamentalism. How does this theme bear on an argument that focuses on contemporary India? If by "fundamentalism" we mean a textually literalist strand in a religion, fundamentalism has little pertinence to the Indian debate about religion and its social role. Muslims in India have never been strongly influenced by Islamic fundamentalism, and there is no serious support for a return to the literal use of Islamic legal sources. What is problematic about the Muslim Personal Law Board is not its fundamentalism, but its entrenched conservatism and its nonrepresentative nature. It is a self-perpetuating body of male clerics that nonetheless claims to speak for the entirety of a diverse community. But these properties are also found, in a very similar form, in the Indian Christian community (composed of both Roman Catholics and Protestants), in which a small group of male clerics undertook, until very recently, to make laws for women without consulting them. [9] Similarly, difficulties with Parsi religious law reform, which I shall not be discussing here, stem not from fundamentalism, which has no analogue in the Parsi religion, but from the political power of conservative old men.

Only in Hinduism does anything standardly called "fundamentalism" play a major political role; but the term "fundamentalism" is in many respects misleading as a name for the Hindu right. Hinduism has always been a loosely organized and regionally diverse religion, with different divinities assuming prominence in different regions, rather in the style of ancient Greek religion. Its texts are also plural and diverse: the ancient Vedic poems, highly obscure and susceptible of multiple interpretations; epics (the *Mahabharata* and *Ramayana*); ethical texts (e.g., *Upanishads*); law codes of later date (e.g., the *Laws of Manu*); and other sacred literature (e.g., the *Kama Sutra*). The Hindu right has succeeded in winning popularity for a politically constructed version of Hinduism, in which Rama is the central deity. But the fact that this is a politically constructed version of history rather than ancient tradition is plain from recent attempts to muzzle and discredit serious historians of the history of Hinduism (who, for example, point out that Hindus once ate beef). This version of Hinduism has been able to prevail to the extent that it has in part because of the disregard of the humanities as an essential part of education for citizenship, on the part of Nehru and his generation. Young university-educated people from the Hindu tradition were steered strongly toward science and technology, and rarely gained the detailed knowledge of their own language and tradition that would naturally lead to criticism and the creation of alternative visions of the Hindu past and future. (It is rather as if, in the United States, Southern Baptists were the only people who read, or knew, or cared about the Christian tradition.)

So we may continue to speak of "fundamentalism" as we like, but we should remember that "Hindu fundamentalism" is a mixture of recent inventions with political aims in view. Thus my topic is really "women and the power of religion in law," a topic that intersects at many points with the topic of fundamentalism.

II

Feminists have taken a range of positions on the aforementioned dilemma between religious free exercise and sex equality. Here are two extremes, both prominent in the international debate. The first position, which I shall call the position of *secular humanist feminism*, treats the dilemma as, basically, a nondilemma.[10] The value of women's equality and dignity so outweighs any religious claim with which it might conflict, that the conflict should not be seen as a serious conflict, except in practical political terms. Indeed, the secular feminist tends to view religion itself as irredeemably patriarchal, a powerful ally of women's oppression. She is not unhappy to muzzle it, and does not see it as doing much good in anyone's life. Many secular humanist feminists are Marxists, but some liberal feminists also take a secular humanist line.

The second approach, which I shall call that of *traditionalist feminism*, also sees the dilemma as basically a nondilemma. All moral claims not rooted in a particular community's understanding of the good are suspect from the start; but those that challenge the roots of traditional religious practices are more than usually suspect, since they threaten sources of value that have over the ages been enormously important to women and men, forming the very core of their search for the meaning of existence. In one sense it might seem odd to call this a variety of feminism at all, since it ignores values of sex equality, but there are many women, especially in the U.S., who are traditionalists and who at least like to call themselves feminists, so I shall keep that language for the present.

Secular humanism is deeply appealing for feminists, since there is no doubt that the world's major religions, in their real-life historical form, have been unjust to women both theoretically and practically. It is indeed very tempting to say, fine, let religion exist, but let it clean up its act like anything else. No special privileges will be given to religion. This may ultimately have been the position of Dr. Ambedkar. Before he resigned, Ambedkar, himself from one of the "scheduled castes," stated that Hinduism was too deeply wedded both to the caste system and to the inequality of women to give them up without coercion. "It is for this reason," he concluded, "that law must come to the rescue in order that society may move on."[11] This makes a lot of sense, in a situation where religion is clearly doing wrong; it was the unambiguous position of the Indian Constitution with regard to untouchability.

There are deep pragmatic difficulties with secular humanism, as both Nehru's reform struggle and the Shah Bano case show us. It is rash and usually counterproductive to approach religious people with a set of apparently external moral demands, telling them that you know that these norms are better than the norms of their religion. In the Indian situation it was bad enough when the demands were made by Hindus to Hindus; but when similar demands were made by Hindus to Muslims, they were read, to some extent correctly, as both insulting and threatening, showing a lack of respect for the autonomy of a minority tradition. Moreover, the humanist fails to pursue alliances with liberal forces within each religious tradition. Religions have indeed been sources of oppression; but they have also been sources of protection for human rights, of commitment to justice, and of energy for social change. By announcing that she wants nothing to do with religion, the secular humanist insults potential allies.

But the difficulties with secular humanism are not merely pragmatic. Three arguments cast doubt on it at a deeper level. First is an argument from the *intrinsic value of religious rights and capabilities*.[12] The liberty to pursue religious belief, membership, and activity in one's own way is among the central human capabilities or rights that have been recognized by constitutions the world over. Religion is for many people a major vehicle of cultural expression, of community affiliation, and of the search for the ultimate meaning of life. Modern constitutional democracies typically aim not at establishing religion, giving it a position of privilege in the state, but rather at creating spaces or opportunities for religion, in order to leave to citizens the choice whether to pursue the pertinent human functions through religion or through secular activity. Even states such as Great Britain, Norway, and Finland that do have an established state church are very careful not to impose that religion on all citizens, but to create spaces in which all citizens may pursue the religion of their choice, or a secular conception of life. But the very defense of religious freedom as central involves the recognition that religious functioning often has high value for people: religious conceptions are among the reasonable ones that we want to make room for, as expressions of human powers.

Because religion is so important to people, there is also a strong argument from *respect for autonomy* that supplements these considerations of intrinsic value. When we tell people that they cannot define the ultimate meaning of life in their own way—even if we are sure we are right and that their way is not a very good way—we do not show full respect for them as persons. Obviously no state can allow all citizens to search for the ultimate meaning of life in all ways, especially where these ways involve harm to others. But secular humanism frequently errs in the opposite direction, taking a dismissive and disrespectful stance to religion even when no question of harm has arisen. Even if religious beliefs were only superstition, we would not be respecting the autonomy of citizens if we did not allow them these avenues of inquiry and expression.

Finally, there is a less obvious argument against the secular humanist position that religion shall have no special privileges in a modern state. It is an *argument from minority religion.* In any modern secular society, the so-called secular norms that prevail are typically those that derive from a majority religious tradition. Thus in the United States, where the norm of separation of church and state has been accepted for a long time, secular society has nonetheless been organized largely along Christian lines. Sunday is the day off from work, and people who worship on Saturday are likely to lose their jobs. Wearing a cross around one's neck is regarded as appropriate military apparel; wearing a yarmulke on one's head is not. Drug laws permit the use of alcohol, prominent in Christian ceremonies, but not the use of peyote, prominent in Native American ceremonies. Thus the member of a minority religion has legitimate reason to feel that a so-called secular legal system is really a Christian legal system, and that the only way to guarantee equal respect for members of minority religions will be to attach special privileges to the free exercise of religion, in such a way that people win the right to take Saturday off, to wear a yarmulke in the army, to use peyote in a sacred ceremony. We might thus say that the secular humanism I have described is unthinking and superficial: a more genuine secularism would be more critical of the dominant culture and the burdens it imposes on vulnerable minorities. I shall return to these cases.

If secular humanism has these practical and theoretical problems, how does traditionalism fare? Interestingly, it suffers from very similar problems. On the practical side, it too undermines its own cause by equating religion with its oldest or most reactionary elements: for such identifications have made already tense relations among the religions worse in many nations. And traditionalists, like humanists, have divided where they could fruitfully pursue alliances, since all feminists have common goals in the area of material well-being.

In the theoretical domain, too, traditionalists and humanists have analogous problems. The traditionalist slights the intrinsic value of freedom of religious exercise, when she refuses to acknowledge the many ways people search for religious meanings outside the most conservative element of a tradition. And this error is not only an assault on intrinsic value, it is also an assault on the autonomy of one's fellow citizens, who ought to be allowed to search for the good in their own way, even if this way is unconventional and many people believe that it is incorrect. Finally, traditionalists are likely to be hostile to at least some claims of minority religions and their members. Even if they support a kind of plural traditionalism, with each entrenched form of traditional religion getting certain privileges, this is always unfair to dissident elements within each tradition, and also to small or new religions. Thus American traditionalists do not care much about feminist forms of religious practice, or even about small religions such as those of Native Americans. Traditionalists in Israel are extremely hostile to Reform and Conservative Judaism, and deny it the privileges that they routinely grant to Christianity. And, of course, women are particularly likely to be members of a dissident group within a religion. (In the U.S., for example, more than half of Reform Jewish rabbis are women, and sex equality has long been a major part of the social agenda of that movement, which happens to be my own religion.)

So it seems that we really need to study the dilemma deeply, and to take the claims on both sides seriously. On the one side, then, are claims of religious free exercise and related autonomy claims. On the other side are the rights of all citizens to the whole list of central rights and opportunities that constitutional traditions typically protect, and, let us emphasize, their right to be treated as equals before the law with regard to all of these rights and liberties, and with regard, as well, to all other functions and domains of law.

Before we try to unravel this dilemma, there is one very important thing that we ought to bear in mind. This is that religion and culture are not static but dynamic, and plural not single. It is all too easy to regard a religion, or a cultural tradition, as equivalent to certain statements or interpretations of dominant leaders. But, of course, both religion and culture are far more complex than that. Even text-based religions such as Christianity, Judaism, and Islam contain tremendous heterogeneity of interpretation, and all contain the voices of women striving for full equality, voices that have not always been represented in public characterizations of that religious tradition. With non-text-based religions such as Hinduism, the heterogeneity of belief and practice is even more obvious. Nor should we grant that the religion really is what the dominant male voices say it is, and that any other form is a new rebellion or departure. Often the dissident forms of a religion view themselves with considerable plausibility as more authentic, more true to the religion's genuine spirit, than the patriarchal forms. To use Judaism as my example again, Reform Jews such as I am do not admit that Reform Judaism is new or a breakaway tradition. We say that the core of Judaism is a moral imperative of universal respect for humanity, and, we argue, that all forms of patriarchy, xenophobia, and so on are actually perversions of the core of Judaism. So we should not concede to certain dominant male leaders of religions a monopoly over that tradition. We should understand from the first that traditions are scenes of debate and contestation, and that respect for a tradition means respecting all of its voices, not just those that shout the loudest.

In short, any history of a religious body that portrays uniformity, homogeneity, and an absence of protest and contestation is very likely to be not real history but a modern construct, which may serve various cultural and political purposes, but which should not be accepted as the full story about what a tradition is.

In the following section, I shall suggest some guiding principles that should help us approach the dilemma. I shall then show how the U.S. has tried to approach it without religion-administered "personal laws," and I shall try to understand the case that might be made in favor of such laws. I shall then turn to the Indian situation, and to the three cases I mentioned at the outset.

III

As we approach this difficult dilemma, two principles offer good guidance.

1. *The Principle of Equal Respect.* Any viable approach to the place of religion in a modern constitutional democracy must be guided from the start by the idea of equal respect for persons, or equal respect for human dignity, which is a fundamental value at the heart of all modern constitutional traditions and at the core of international law.

The idea of equal respect is, however, a complex one, and we need to pause to think further about each of its elements: the idea of respect for persons, and the idea of *equal* respect. The idea of respect for persons and their human dignity means that each and every person's dignity shall be respected. Each person is seen as having worth in his or her own right, and none is seen as merely the tool of others. Thus it will not be a sufficient fulfillment of this idea to grant rights to a group as such while allowing systematic subordination of people inside those groups. The equal protection of the laws means equal protection for all citizens, not just for large groups of citizens, which may be internally hierarchical in character. The fundamental holder of a right is the person, and each and every person has the right to equal respect and the equal protection of the laws.

On the other hand, groups play very important roles in people's lives, and it is also obvious that the subordination of persons is very often based on group membership. So the protection of groups as groups may be, and usually is, a necessary means to equal respect for the dignity of the persons who are their members. Antidiscrimination laws and affirmative action policies based on group membership are usually understood to be fully compatible with the principle of equal respect, and indeed, often, to be necessary means to its implementation. Thus carving out special privileges for the "scheduled castes" and the "scheduled tribes" in the Indian Constitution, and more recently for women, was seen as a necessary means to securing full civic and political equality for the members of these traditionally disadvantaged groups as citizens. Giving special prerogatives to religious bodies might also be justified along these lines, especially in a situation where there is grave danger that minority religions and their members will suffer from discrimination. The touchstone should, however, always be the dignity of the person, and so any remedy that gives group rights in a way that ends up subordinating persons is an ill-chosen remedy.

We have mentioned the idea of respect for persons: but what about the "equal" in "equal respect"? How is that equality to be understood? Two legal traditions of interpreting the idea of equality must now be mentioned. The first is the tradition of *formal symmetry*. According to this tradition, two people are treated equally if they are treated the same. On the whole, feminists and people working for the rights of racial minorities have found this understanding of equality insufficient. It does not recognize that different groups in society have different starting points and different obstacles, and that similar treatment may therefore really be treatment that perpetuates group hierarchy and the substantive inequality of persons. Therefore, both Catharine MacKinnon in feminism and leading thinkers about race have by now influenced the U.S. legal system so as to get recognition that equality, and the equal protection of the laws, must be understood in terms of *an end to systematic hierarchy and discrimination.*[13]

In a circumstance of historical subordination and inequality, formal symmetry can, and here did, simply serve as a way of perpetuating the domination of the dominant class. Equal protection means rooting out legal sources of hierarchy, and establishing a legal regime in which no group has supremacy over any other.

The Indian Constitution has on the whole made this antisubordination understanding of equality explicit, in many of its provisions: for example, it is made explicit that provisions of nondiscrimination and equal protection are to be understood as fully compatible with affirmative action programs designed to raise the level of the poor and of women. Of course, the text is one thing, and its interpretation has been, at times, another. Some notable Supreme Court decisions have used a purely formal conception of equality.[14] And yet the dominant trend has been, on the whole, toward a more substantive conception of equality. In this respect, the Indian tradition is ahead of the U.S. tradition, and has understood that symmetrical treatment is often a way of entrenching inequality for traditionally subordinated groups.

2. The Principle of Constraint by Fundamental Entitlements. All nations have an understanding of what the fundamental entitlements of all citizens are, based upon an understanding of social justice. The Indian Constitution is particularly explicit about this, in that the section of Fundamental Rights in the Constitution is set off from other sections in a particularly clear way. My second orienting principle is that these fundamental entitlements shall not be abridged for any citizen, for the sake of giving religion special prerogatives. That leaves a good deal of space for religions to enjoy some special prerogatives, as we shall see. In areas of drug use, military dress, work hours, education—dispensations from existing law may still be granted on grounds of religious free exercise. But whenever a nation has determined that a given entitlement is a fundamental entitlement of all citizens, based upon justice, that entitlement itself cannot be abridged as an exercise of religious prerogative.

Up to a point, all modern nations recognize this principle. For example, none would permit murder just because it is justified by a religious cult. But, of course, there are many fundamental entitlements of citizens that are routinely abridged because of religious dictates, especially in nations where personal laws contain patriarchal norms of property transmission, asymmetrical laws of marriage and divorce, and so forth. In many international documents, for example CEDAW (Convention on the Elimination of All Forms of Discrimination Against Women), it is made clear that religion and culture shall not serve as legitimate grounds for the restriction of a fundamental entitlement. This same principle is to some degree recognized by both the U.S. and the Indian constitutional traditions. In the U.S., the dominant understanding is that the free exercise of religion may not be abridged without a very strong state interest; usually the language of "compelling state interest" has been used. But it has been generally understood that fundamental entitlements of citizens always supply the state with a compelling interest. Unfortunately U.S. constitutional law is rather vague on this question, and there never has been an exhaustive account of what these entitlements are.[15]

The Indian situation is highly complex. The constitution declares that "all laws in force" that are incompatible with the Fundamental Rights are unconstitutional. But the judicial interpretation of that idea, early in the life of the Republic, held that personal laws were not included in the category of "laws in force." Thus the implementation of the principle I have outlined, which seems clearly recognized in the language of the constitution, was derailed by an unfortunate interpretation.

IV

I have argued that religious exercise is a very important right of people, and that it is especially important to protect this right for minority religions, who are all too often at a disadvantage even in a secular society. But other entitlements of citizens are also very important; these prominently include the equal protection of the laws. These other fundamental entitlements are often abridged in the name of religion. To address this problem I have introduced two orienting principles that in some way lie behind constitutional traditions in a wide range of societies. First, the principle of *equal respect for persons*, understood to mean that each and every person is entitled to respect for that person's human dignity, and that equality entails not just symmetry but the absence of subordination and hierarchy. Second, the principle of *constraint by fundamental entitlements*, meaning that, while religions may get some special prerogatives, these prerogatives are always constrained by the non-negotiable place of the fundamental entitlements recognized in a constitutional (or otherwise democratic) tradition, entitlements that have the role of defining a bare minimum of what justice requires.

I shall now advance a proposal that seems a good way, in theory, of resolving the dilemma within the constraint of the two guiding principles. Next, I shall look at two contrasting traditions, the U.S. and the Indian, arguing that they embody opposite errors. The U.S. does not give enough room for dispensations from existing law on the basis of religion, and thereby disadvantages minority religions, who are always in a position of special vulnerability. India protects minority religion, but at the cost of not protecting other fundamental entitlements of citizens on a basis of equal respect.

The theoretical proposal is based on a now-defunct U.S. law, called the Religious Freedom Restoration Act of 1993. It is meant just as a suggestion, not as the best reading of any particular tradition. This law prohibits any agency, department, or official of the United States, or any state, from "substantially burden[ing] a person's exercise of religion even if the burden results from a rule of general applicability," unless the government can demonstrate that this burden "(1) is in furtherance of a compelling government interest; and (2) is the least restrictive means of furthering that compelling governmental interest." What I now add to that law is that the idea of a "compelling governmental interest" is to be understood in terms of the set of fundamental entitlements a nation has recognized as required by basic justice, including the equal protection of the laws and including whatever other fundamental rights are on a nation's central list.

What this law does is to caution the state against arbitrary and unimportant interventions with freedom of religious exercise. What it says is that religion is very important, so if you are going to burden it in a serious way, you need a really strong reason, a reason having to do with something else equally fundamental. In other words, religions and religious people should not be forced to bear a heavy burden just because of people's convenience, as when employers deny employees the right to take a day off on Saturday; or because of some vague fear of public disorder, as when states prohibit the use of peyote in the sacred Native American ceremony. When there is a difficult case, the question to be asked is whether the state law that burdens religion in some way does really deal with a fundamental entitlement that is a matter of basic justice. Thus we protect religious liberty in the widest way that is compatible with basic justice and equal respect.

It is important to understand why such a law seemed necessary. In some recent cases, the U.S. had been riding roughshod over minority religion, denying it adequate protection. For some years there has been an issue, in First Amendment jurisprudence, about how far laws "of general applicability" might be upheld against a religious group or religious individuals, when those individuals claimed that the law imposes a "substantial burden" on their exercise of their religion. For quite a few years, the legal situation was more or less as RFRA later reestablished it: the Supreme Court consistently held that laws of general applicability might impose a substantial burden on an individual's free exercise of religion only if the law furthered a compelling state interest, and in the least burdensome manner possible. The governing case was *Sherbert v. Verner* (1963).[16] A South Carolina woman refused to work on Saturday, because her Seventh-Day Adventist beliefs forbade it. Fired, she was also refused state unemployment benefits on the grounds that she had refused suitable employment. She claimed that the state had violated her religious free exercise; the U.S. Supreme Court agreed. The court held that to attach to a benefit a condition that required violation of a religious duty did impose a substantial burden on her free exercise of her religion; the problem was compounded, the court held, by the discriminatory impact of the benefits laws on workers who celebrate the Sabbath on Saturday.

Under the regime established by *Sherbert*, other laws of general applicability were also found to violate religious free exercise. Notable is the case of compulsory public education of Amish children in *Wisconsin v. Yoder*. There the state argued that the Amish parents could not withdraw their children from the last two years of compulsory public education. The parents argued that their religion would be jeopardized if their children could not learn, at a crucial age, the skills of community-based work that made it possible to continue the tradition. The Supreme Court sided with the parents. Note that there is grave doubt whether this case was correctly decided, according to the approach I am recommending. Here the court may possibly have been too generous to religion. What my approach urges us to ask is precisely what shape a fundamental entitlement to education ought to have. If these last two years are a part of what should be a basic entitlement of all citizens, then the parents should be told that religious values cannot trump these other fundamental entitlements. If, however, the last two years are judged not so crucial, then the religious claim may trump.

Whatever we think of that case, it is clear that by now the court has moved in a direction quite hostile to exemptions for religion—and, as is typically the case where we are dealing with a conflict between established law and religion, the victim is minority religion. In 1990 the Supreme Court changed course with its decision in *Employment Division v. Smith.*[17] The case concerned native American tribes in the state of Oregon, who claimed that it was essential to their religion to use peyote in a particular sacred ceremony, and thus claimed exemption (not generally, but in this one ceremonial instance) from the drug laws of the state of Oregon. The sincerity of their religious claim was not disputed, nor the centrality of the peyote ceremony to their religion. In a lengthy opinion by Justice Scalia, the court held that the free exercise clause did not protect the plaintiffs, since "[w]e have never held that an individual's religious beliefs excuse him from compliance with an otherwise valid law prohibiting conduct that the State is free to regulate." The court explicitly rejected the "compelling government interest" requirement, as making the lawmaker's job far too difficult. Scalia wrote that such a requirement would produce "a private right to ignore generally applicable laws," thus creating "a constitutional anomaly." Three liberal Justices dissented, arguing that no convincing reason had been given to depart from settled First Amendment jurisprudence; joined by O'Connor with respect to their general discussion of principle, they pointed in particular to the danger of disfavoring minority religions, and invoked the Founders' interest in securing "the widest possible toleration of conflicting views."

The Smith decision generated public outrage; Congress stepped in to restore the *status quo ante.* The RFRA law was passed in 1993 by an overwhelming bipartisan majority in both houses, and signed into law by President Clinton. It was declared unconstitutional in June 1997, on grounds relating to the separation of powers.

According to the approach I have recommended, RFRA is right and the current posture of the U.S. Supreme Court is wrong. There is little danger that laws of general applicability will ever "substantially burden" the religion of the majority. There is a grave danger, in this case a reality, that laws of general applicability will burden a small unpopular minority. If Christians used peyote instead of wine in the Mass or communion service, there is little doubt that this ceremonial use of peyote would be generally recognized by law. (One might point in this connection to the legalized use of marijuana during Holi, a Hindu spring holiday, in India.) So when we say that religion may be forced to bear a substantial burden *only when* the state is acting in furtherance of a *compelling interest*, such as is represented by a fundamental right or some other fundamental entitlement, we give minorities the protection that the majority already enjoys *de facto*. There was no such compelling interest in the *Smith* case, and it would not be possible to find one.

India's history provides a most instructive contrast. Before we can approach any particular case, we must first ask whether the whole idea of having systems of religious personal law is incompatible with the principle of equal respect. It obviously poses many difficulties. For the most obvious difference between India and the U.S. is that India has given four religious groups—Hindus, Muslims, Parsis, and Christians—no mere case-by-case exemption from laws of general applicability, but a much larger and more systematic dispensation, namely the right to maintain their own legal systems in areas including not only marriage, divorce, and family law, but also property and inheritance. By "separate legal system" I do not mean separate courts of law or separate legislative bodies. All the relevant laws must be passed by Parliament. But they are drawn up in consultation with the religious communities, and they pertain to the members of those communities.

What are the immediate difficulties such a system poses for equal respect? First of all, it seems to disfavor minority religions not on that list of four, who are not given privileges that the four enjoy. Second, it seems to disfavor minority factions within each religion: for obviously the system of law is highly likely in each case to reflect the wishes of the dominant group, and the minority members of the tradition have not been given the right to set up their own legal system. It is easy to see that, whereas in the U.S. minority and dissident traditions flourish within each religion, this is not the case in India. The systems of personal law ossify the development of each religion, by concentrating power in the hands of conservative leaders.

These problems are compounded by the difficulty of exit from these systems. When family property is tied up in consortia, as is often the case, especially in the Hindu system, it may be impossible for a person to leave the religious legal system if he or she wants to. That is a difficulty not only for equal treatment (people who like the way the majority does things do better than dissidents within the tradition), but also for the free exercise of religion itself. (Similarly in Israel: Jews who want to contract a Reform Jewish marriage cannot do so, and they cannot leave Judaism in favor of any secular system of law.) Since the passage of the Special Marriage Act in 1954, people may elect secular marriage and secular divorce. This was at first taken to mean that they will also be governed by secular inheritance law, but in 1975 the relevant law was amended under pressure from Hindu leaders so that two Hindus who elect a secular marriage will still be governed by the Hindu law of inheritance. Thus exit options are not open.

The primary point and rationale of having religious systems of personal law, at the time of Independence, was to show respect for the Muslim minority, and other minorities, as fully equal citizens. There was, of course, an element of political pragmatism in this decision, and it cannot be regarded as simply a principled choice. Nonetheless, there was at least a plausible rationale for it in terms of respect for a minority. To avoid difficulties such as plague the American system, an extraordinarily generous set of dispensations to religion was worked out. But really, notice, it was a dispensation not to all minority religions, but only to the recognized and dominant forms of four well-populated minority religions. Thus it is not clear that the system solved the problem it was intended to solve.

These difficulties loom large when we look at how women's struggle for equality has fared within these systems. Even if the systems all operated within the constraints that I have proposed, that is, constraints imposed by the list of Fundamental Rights in Section III of the constitution, the difficulties I have just outlined would already be strong reason to disfavor personal systems of law, or at least to construct systems that are much more porous, with carefully guaranteed exit rights for all individuals, either to a secular system or to a different religious system. But, of course, the systems do not operate within these constraints. The early Supreme Court decision that removed them from the constraint of the Fundamental Rights has led to a situation in which sex inequality continues within all of the systems. Women suffer inequalities in the law of marriage and divorce, as well as the law of property and inheritance. Some of these inequalities are staggering. For example, Christian women in India could not win a divorce on grounds of cruelty until 2000; they had to prove both cruelty and adultery, whereas a man could win a divorce on either ground.

Such inequalities run afoul of Article 14 of the Indian Constitution, which guarantees the equal protection of the laws, and Article 15, which prohibits discrimination on grounds of sex. They also run afoul of Article 15's prohibition of discrimination on grounds of religion, since there are many instances in which women do worse by being stuck in one religious system that is doing worse with regard to sex hierarchy than the other systems. Finally, they run afoul of many concrete rights enumerated elsewhere in Section III, especially some of the liberties of association and employment articulated in Article 19, which often suffer abridgment in ways related to inequalities in religious personal law. By now, Article 21, the Indian Constitution's analogue of the due process clause of the U.S. Fourteenth Amendment, has been given an expansive interpretation by the Court, as involving a right to life with human dignity; it has recently been held to include a right against rape as violative of human dignity (*Chairman, Railway Board v. Mrs. Chandrima Das* AIR 2000, SC 988). So we may also say that sex-based inequalities in systems of personal law run afoul of Article 21, directly or indirectly. Directly, because the Hindu system still includes the remedy of forcible restitution of conjugal rights; until very recently, as I have mentioned, a Christian wife who had endured cruelty without adultery could not win a divorce. Indirectly, because the numerous inequalities that affect women's economic position and individual control over land and other resources greatly affect women's ability to exit from an abusive marriage and to protect their bodily integrity in the workplace.

We may now return to the three cases with which this essay began, asking how they were resolved, and how my approach would suggest that they ought to be resolved.

Mary Roy's case is straightforward. The claim made by the Christian Church is simply not a claim about the fundamental religious rights of people. However difficult it is to say what Christianity is and is not, one thing that can be said with confidence is that the ability of the established church to rake in larger amounts of tax revenue, while highly desirable from the point of view of a religious institution, is not itself an instance of the free exercise of religion. No citizen's Christian worship is being burdened by the drop in church revenue that would be occasioned by the new inheritance structure. If the Christian Church were being denied a tax benefit that other churches enjoy, there would indeed be a free exercise issue. But that is not the situation here: Christian inheritance structure was simply being brought into line with the structure that already prevailed in secular law, Hindu law, and Islamic law. In fact, the real free exercise issue is the other way round: before the Supreme Court decision, Christian women were being fined, in effect, for being Christian—just the situation that the U.S. Supreme Court viewed as a paradigm violation of free exercise in *Sherbert v. Verner*. So, there is no "substantial burden" here.

On the other side, the right of women to control property on an equal basis is implicated in the very idea of the equal protection of the laws; as such, it would supply a compelling state interest even were there a *prima facie* legitimate claim on the other side. The fact that the court avoided the question of constitutionality and ruled in Mrs. Roy's favor on a technicality is to be regretted.

The reform of Hindu personal law poses far more difficult problems. Hinduism is a diverse set of traditional practices, with no easily identifiable core. But there is no doubt that here, as with the abolition of caste, some of the proposed reforms touched on very central religious matters. In this case, unlike Mary Roy's, we should grant that a substantial burden is being imposed by the state on the free exercise of religion—at least, the free exercise of some of its more traditional practitioners. (It is helpful here to bear in mind that there had been internal voices of reform for a very long time.) Moreover, the burden affects the functioning of individuals, not just of religious institutions. On the other hand, we can see clearly that central entitlements of women, based on the twin ideas of equal protection and a right to life with dignity, were at issue on the other side. Control over property, the integrity of one's person, rights to mobility, assembly, and political participation, the right to marital consent and to divorce on an equal basis, all these clearly provide the state with a compelling interest in the proposed reforms. As the *Hindustan Times* commented: "The Hindu Code Bill is the [social] counterpart of the new Constitution in which is embodied the political ideal of liberty, equality and fraternity."[18]

My approach suggests that in less central matters the state should allow Hindus broad latitude to act in accordance with their traditions. (I have argued, for example, that marijuana use during Holi is one such matter.) But on these matters of fundamental civic dignity and equality, Ambedkar was correct when he said that the state could not wait for Hinduism to undertake voluntary internal reform: "Law must come to the rescue in order that society may move on."[19] The changes were right. They upheld the intrinsic value of religious exercise, within limits imposed by the protection of the whole range of fundamental entitlements.

The *Shah Bano* case raises difficult issues, since it concerns the rights of a minority religion. While it seemed clear that a recognizable core of Hinduism would surely survive the reorganization of Hindu personal law, there were reasons to fear that Islam in India would suffer greatly were the system of Muslim personal law to be gravely curtailed. While it is not easy to say how legitimate those fears are, it is not surprising that they should surface at a time when Hindu fundamentalism was on the rise, and the whole question of declaring India a Hindu state rather than a secular state had been reopened. Chief Justice Chandrachud was probably correct in his argument that the order of maintenance under the Criminal Procedure Code was consistent with traditional Islamic law, but the very fact that he undertook to say what Islamic law was and was not was alarming, raising the spectre of Hindu domination. The issue of imposing a substantial burden thus becomes particularly sensitive.

In terms of my test, there seems little doubt that the issue of maintenance after divorce is a serious issue, affecting fundamental entitlements. It would appear to implicate several fundamental rights, including the right to nondiscrimination on the grounds of sex, the right to the equal protection of the laws, and the right to life with dignity. This is all the more obvious when we consider the subset of maintenance cases that can be appealed under the Criminal Procedure Code. To win an award of maintenance, the female plaintiff has to show that she would otherwise be without means to support herself, that she has suffered cruelty or neglect that makes it impossible for her to live with her husband, that she did not leave him of her own accord, and that her husband does have adequate means. Subsequent cases in which maintenance has been denied show the burden that the Muslim Woman's Act has put on Muslim women. Maitrayee Mukhopadhyay's study of West Bengal in the post-1986 period shows women facing grave disadvantages and being forced to depend on relatives for even a meager living. (These women are most often illiterate and untrained for any work; frequently they are of advanced age—Shah Bano was 74 when her husband threw her out.) Worse still, these women's destitution has crippled their childrens' education, as children who would otherwise be in school are put to work supporting their mothers.[20]

The issue of discrimination on the basis of religion is equally striking. Only Muslim women are denied maintenance under the Criminal Procedure Code. As Muslim feminist Zoya Hasan argues, there is "little reason to doubt that the denial of rights to Muslim women, which are available to women of other faiths, is a violation of the constitutional provision that the State shall not discriminate against any citizen on grounds of religion."[21] Muslim women's activist Shahjahan put the matter more bluntly in a speech in front of the House of Parliament the day the 1986 law was passed:

> If by making separate laws for Muslim women, you are trying to say that we are not citizens of this country, then why don't you tell us clearly and unequivocally that we should establish another country—not Hindustan or Pakistan but Auratstan (women's land).

Women's groups repeatedly challenged the act by petition in the Supreme Court as violating constitutional provisions of nondiscrimination on the basis of religion.

To summarize: the religious issues themselves do not point in a single direction; indeed, the weightier free exercise claims seem to be on the side of Muslim women. And the issues of equal respect for dignity, and the constraints of other entitlements, lie squarely on their side. The result was therefore a very unfortunate one, both for women and for religion.

What is the remedy for these difficulties in the current situation? On the one hand, support for a Uniform Civil Code to replace the religious personal laws has somewhat declined in recent years, given recognition of the legitimate fears on the part of Muslims and other minority religions that a "uniform code" would be a Hindu code that would turn them, in subtle ways, into second-class citizens. Even the secular women's movement in India has been split on the question of whether to continue to support a Uniform Code in the current political situation. On the other hand, internal reform of all systems, to bring them into line with the constraints of equal protection and other fundamental rights, has proven extremely time-consuming and difficult. The recent success in reforming the Christian Marriage Act suggests that reform is not altogether impossible, and yet serious inequalities remain. It will surely be far more difficult to achieve internal reform within the Muslim community, even with the best will on all sides and even with considerable involvement from Muslim women, whom a recent empirical study by Zoya Hasan and Ritu Menon has shown to be a dynamic, active group eager to promote a wider field of education and action for their daughters.

The famous Shah Bano case now has a sequel, however, that offers some constructive guidance, showing that the Supreme Court may be capable of charting a course both respectful and progressive. In *Danial Latifi v. Union of India*, the court considered a petition[22] alleging that the Muslim Women's Act is unconstitutional. On the one hand, the court holds that if the act is interpreted so as to deprive women like Shah Bano (whose case they revisit) of the type of maintenance guaranteed to all women in India under section 125 of the Criminal Procedure Code, it would clearly be unconstitutional under Articles 14, 15 (because they discriminate on grounds of religion), and 21.

The court then announces three interpretive principles of great interest. First, a statute must be interpreted with reference to the surrounding social context; one of the most prominent facts about the social context of the Muslim Women's Bill is male domination, in particular, economic domination. Second, a statute that implicates matters of "basic human rights, culture, dignity, and decency of life and dictates of necessity in the pursuit of social justice" should "invariably" be decided on "considerations other than religion or religious faith or beliefs or national, sectarian, racial, or communal constraints." Third (a familiar principle of statutory interpretation in both India and the United States), if there is a construction of a statute according to which it is constitutional, that construction should be preferred to one according to which it is unconstitutional, "on the ground that the legislature does not intend to enact unconstitutional laws."

Notice that these three principles correspond very closely to my proposed two principles of *equal respect* and *constraint by fundamental entitlements:* equal respect is attended to in the first principle, which directs interpretation to take account of pervasive social inequalities; both equal respect and constraint by fundamental entitlements are addressed in the second principle, which says in effect that fundamental entitltments constrain how far religion may be used and where it may be used in the interpretation of a statute. The third principle simply urges that instead of invalidating a constitutionally problematic statute, one should prefer an interpretation that abides within these constraints, where one can be found.

The court then engages in a very detailed and somewhat tortuous reading of the statute, arguing that it is possible to interpret it in such a way that the maintenance guaranteed is exactly the same as that guaranteed by the Criminal Procedure Code. Thus, there is no need to invalidate the statute: thus interpreted, it does not violate Articles 14, 15, and 21. But, of course, more or less the same result is achieved as was achieved in Shah Bano's case: Muslim women now get the more generous maintenance that is also guaranteed by the Criminal Procedure Code. This interesting strategy is somewhat preferable to the strategy in the original Shah Bano case, because it goes no further in abrogating the authority of religious law than it needs to do. The special role of the Muslim community is maintained, and respected, but it must henceforth be played out within the constraint of fundamental entitlements. Without commenting on the specific interpretations proposed by the court, one can say that this is an attractive way of cutting through the dilemma, where it can be made to appear convincing.

The Latifi judgment was cautious; it failed to find the statute unconstitutional. And yet it achieved the same result, in a way that was as respectful as possible to the autonomy and authority of a minority religion. The judgment is not a magical panacea, and many severe inequalities remain to be addressed. But in its broad outlines it offers hope that the systems of personal law may, gradually over time, be brought into line with Fundamental Rights, in a way that is respectful of each tradition. Both judicial and legislative processes will need to play a role in this evolution. In the reform of Christian marriage law, the dominant role was played by the legislature; in this judgment about Muslim divorce, the Supreme Court innovated. It may be hoped that over time a cooperative and incremental process will result in establishing sex equality without making any religious group into second-class citizens.

We can see that both the Indian and the U.S. systems contain serious violations of justice. In the U.S. case, unpopular minority religion suffers unnecessary disabilities. In the Indian case, there are, ironically, issues of that sort as well, precisely because not all minorities, and minorities within minorities, are equal. But the greatest problems are those of bringing plural systems of religious law within the constraints of the Fundamental Rights, and thus the basic principle of equal respect for all persons. It is to be hoped that the recent progress on this front will continue.

Let me end with one of the darker episodes in the U.S. constitutional tradition. The principle of slavery had been upheld by the U.S. Supreme Court in the infamous Dred Scott decision, with religious arguments playing a prominent part on both sides of this question. In his Second Inaugural Address, President Abraham Lincoln, speaking near the end of the bitter conflict, commented on the fact that slavery was being defended as a Christian cause:

> Both read the same Bible, and pray to the same God; and each invokes His aid against the other. It may seem strange that any men should dare to ask a just God's assistance in wringing their bread from the sweat of other men's faces. . . .

What Lincoln is saying, with infinite sadness, is basically what Heera Nawaz also said in the quote with which I began this essay: that religion, which is supposed to be about love and humanity, all too often gets hijacked for the purposes of power, fanaticism, and violence against human dignity. When this happens, it is the job of political leaders not to defer to such claims, though they may be made in the name of religion. It is their job to unmask them, by upholding, again and again, the deep value of human dignity which is inherent in all persons, and which is the basis for the idea of law in all decent societies.

Notes

1 This paper was originally prepared for a conference on Sex Equality and Personal Laws sponsored by the Women's Rights Initiative of The Lawyer's Collective, a legal activist organization in New Delhi, India, in December 2001. I am very grateful to Indira Jaising and the other members of this wonderful organization for the invitation, and to Bina Agarwal, Zoya Hasan, Jeff Redding, and other members of the audience for their helpful comments. For a closely related discussion of these issues, see my *Women and Human Development: The Capabilities Approach* (New York: Cambridge University Press, 2000), ch. 3; the present paper, however, offers an analysis that is different in some crucial respects, and adds recent material.

2 From Nawaz, "Towards Uniformity" (a defense of a uniform civil code) in Indira Jaising, ed., *Justice for Women: Personal Laws, Women's Rights and Law Reform* (Mapusa, Goa: The Other India Press, 1996).

3 Article 14 guarantees the equal protection of the laws to all persons; Article 15

prohibits discrimination on the grounds of religion, race, caste, sex, or place of birth; Article 16 guarantees all citizens equality in matters relating to employment, and prohibits employment discrimination on the basis of religion, race, caste, sex, descent, place of birth, and residence; Article 17 abolishes untouchability: "its practice in any form is forbidden." Article 19 guarantees all citizens rights of free speech and expression, assembly, association, free movement, choice of residence, choice of occupation; Article 21 (the basis for privacy jurisprudence in cases involving marital rape and restitution of conjugal rights) says that "no citizen shall be deprived of his life or personal liberty" without due process of law; Article 25 states that all citizens are "equally entitled to freedom of conscience and the right freely to profess, practice and propagate religion," although there is an explicit qualification stating that this does not prevent government from abolishing the caste system and "throwing open . . . Hindu religious institutions of a public nature to all classes and sections of Hindus"; Article 26 gives religious denominations the right to manage their own affairs and to acquire property, "subject to public order, morality, and health"; Article 28 guarantees freedom to attend religious schools, states that no religious instruction shall be provided in institutions wholly funded by the State, and also states that where a school is aided by state funds students may not be compelled to perform religious observances. Finally, Article 13 renders invalid all "laws in force" that conflict with any of these Fundamental Rights and forbids the State to make any new laws that take away or abridge a Fundamental Right. (A subsequent judicial decision, however, declared that "laws in force does not include the religious systems of personal law: see *State of Bombay v. Narasu Appa Mali*, 1952.) For related constitutional discussion, see my "Religion and Women's Human Rights," in *Religion and Contemporary Liberalism*, ed. Paul Weithman (Notre Dame: University of Notre Dame Press, 1997), 93-137, and, in a revised form, forthcoming in Nussbaum, *Sex and Social Justice*, Oxford University Press, 1998.

4 *Mrs. Mary Roy v. State of Kerala and Others*, AIR 1986 SC 1011.

5 P. J. Kurien, author of the Private Members' Bill, in a public statement.

6 This issue had already been dealt with in the Child Marriage Restraint Act of 1929, the first occasion in which the Indian women's movement achieved a big legislative success. It was now included in a more comprehensive package of reforms for the new republic.

7 The recognition of ex-wives as included relations under Section 125 was itself controversial in 1973. When the amendment was discussed in the Lok Sabha,

members of the Muslim League objected, claiming violations of free exercise. Initially the government denied that there was any religious issue: the purpose of the amendment was simply humanitarian. Later, however, the government changed its stand, adding yet a further amendment to exclude divorced Muslim women from the purview of the new amendment. Nonetheless, Muslim women continued to bring petitions to the courts, and the Supreme Court explicitly pronounced, in two prominent judgments, that they were entitled to do so: the purpose of the law was to help destitute women, and the text had to be interpreted in accordance with this social purpose. See *Bai Tahira v. Ali Hussain*, 1979 (2) Supreme Court Reported, 75, and AIR 1980 Supreme Court 1930. Thus the conflict between the Supreme Court and the Muslim leadership was of long standing.

8 This famous case has been discussed in many, many places. The central documents are assembled in Asghar Ali Engineer, ed., *The Shah Bano Controversy* (Delhi: Ajanta Publishers, 1987). See also Veena Das, *Critical Events* (Delhi: Oxford University Press, 1992), chapter 4; Kavita R. Khory, "The Shah Bano Case: Some Political Implications," in Robert Baird, ed., *Religion and Law in Independent India* (Delhi: Manohar, 1993),121-37; Amartya Sen, "Secularism and Its Discontents," in *Unravelling the Nation*, ed. Kaushik Basu and Sanjay Subrahmanyam, 1995; Parashar (above), 173-89 (an unusually comprehensive account of different attitudes within the Islamic community); Zoya Hasan, "Minority Identity, State Policy and the Political Process," in Hasan, ed., *Forging Identities: Gender, Communities and the State in India* (Delhi: Kali for Women, and Boulder: Westview Press, 1994), 59-73.

9 In 2001 Parliament passed a major reform of the Christian law of marriage and divorce, after consultation not only with clerics, but also with Christian women's groups and legal advocates for them.

10 See my *Women and Human Development*, ch. 3, for specific examples of this position.

11 Ambedkar, speech, quoted in *The Statesman*, September 23, 1951.

12 The language of "capabilities" is a key part of my overall approach to political theory: in *Women and Human Development*, and elsewhere, I argue that the right way to think of the fundamental entitlements of citizens in a democracy is as a set of abilities or opportunities to function in certain centrally important ways. The freedom of speech and the free exercise of religion are two of the capabilities that figure on my list.

13 For one famous example, laws against interracial marriage, in the U.S., were

held to violate the equal protection of the laws, on the grounds that, though formally neutral (blacks can't marry whites, whites can't marry blacks), they were in reality but a prop for "white supremacy." In *Loving v. Virginia*, the U.S. Supreme Court stated explicitly the mere fact of a law's equal and neutral application does not mean that it does not constitute "an arbitrary and invidious discrimination."

14 See my "India: Sex Equality and Constitutional Law," in B. Baines and R. Marin, eds., *Engendering Women: the Gender of Constitutional Jurisprudence* (Cambridge: Cambridge University Press, forthcoming 2003).

15 Thus the discussion of a child's entitlement to education in *Wisconsin v. Yoder*, the case in which Amish parents won the right to withdraw their children from the last two years of compulsory public education, proceeded without any clear theory of what a citizen's fundamental entitlements are, and whether education is among them.

16 374 U.S. 398 (1963).

17 110 S. Ct. 1595 (1990).

18 September 22, 1951.

19 *The Statesman*, September 21, 1951.

20 See case studies in Mukhopadhyay, in Hasan.

21 Hasan in Hasan, ed., p. 62.

22 The Indian Constitution allows concerned groups and individuals to approach the Supreme Court by petition without establishing standing. The Court decides which petitions to hear. This opens an avenue of social change that has sometimes proven productive.

Christian Soldiers

Unholy Alliance

Laura Flanders

George W. Bush has spent much of his first term in office declaring war on governments he accuses of supporting terrorism, but that didn't stop his representatives at the United Nations from teaming up with some of those same governments to beat back women's and children's rights.

At the UN Summit on Children in 2002, for example, the U.S. delegation joined forces with Libya, Sudan, Syria, Iran, and Iraq to stonewall a health care initiative. Together with Christian Right nongovernmental organizations, Islamic nations, and the Vatican, Bush's delegates huddled, lobbied, and scampered about the conference corridors in Manhattan pressuring nations to vote against progressive policy that was up for debate. To a staggering degree, it worked. The Bush administration's team stymied and eventually blocked an effort by European and Latin American countries to include a reference in the final conference declaration to "reproductive health care services"—a term the radical right contends could promote abortions.

"It wasn't just pure defense, they are on the offensive here," an observer from the conservative Heritage Foundation told the *Washington Post* at the Summit.

After years of stony opposition to United Nations activities—resistance typified by the rabid antiinternationalism of Jesse Helms, ranking member of the Senate Foreign Relations Committee—Republicans in Washington adopted new tactics. In order to resist the nations of the world that support expanding political protections for women, children, and homosexuals, the Bush team played the game of UN diplomacy to meet its own political goals. It's a "If you can't join 'em, beat 'em" strategy that was pioneered by the Catholic Church.

Unique among religions, the Vatican is represented at the world's premier international body by the world's tiniest state, the Holy See. Despite a spirited campaign by women's groups (the inception of which is described in the piece that follows), the Holy See still enjoys "nonmember state permanent observer status" at the UN, and has been in a political marriage of convenience with rigid Islamic states for years.

In 2001, when George W. Bush came to office, one might say he threw the United Nations as a bone to his supporters on the religious right. To represent the United States at the Children's Summit, along with Health and Human Services Secretary Tommy Thompson, Bush appointed Janice Crouse, a veteran antiabortion advocate at the antifeminist Concerned Women for America; and Paul J. Bonicelli of Patrick Henry College in Virginia, a Christian institution that requires its professors to teach creationism. (Janet Ashcroft, the wife of John, the Pentacostal U.S. Attorney General, is on the college's board.) Also on the delegation: Brother Bob Smith, who runs a Catholic High School in Milwaukee, and John Klink, who's had lots of UN experience—as an advisor to the Holy See.

Klink made a name for himself in UN circles when, as the Pope's emissary there, he lobbied for the UN to deny emergency contraception to raped women in refugee camps. A devout Roman Catholic, Klink is passionately opposed to abortion, the so-called morning-after pill and even using condoms to halt the spread of AIDS. Bush appointed Klink to the United Nations delegation because he couldn't get enough Cabinet support to nominate him to head the State Department's Bureau of Population, Refugees, and Migration. The president's fondness for Klink is one more crack in the administration's "compassionate conservative" facade. In the fall of 2001, First Lady Laura Bush promoted the U.S. war on Afghanistan as a war "to liberate women and girls." At that very same time at the UN, her husband's man Klink was working his own Axis of Evil to keep women and children back. If American voters could see what their government is up to, they might wake up to some surprises. Tragically for much of the world, goings-on at the UN mostly take place beneath the U.S. media's radar.

New York City
July 2002

Giving the Vatican the Boot

From *Ms.* magazine, January 2000

Last June at the United Nations, delegates gathered to draft a document for the General Assembly special session on population and development. The gathering, known as Cairo+5, came five years after the landmark Cairo Conference of 1994, which recognized women's empowerment and reproductive health as key to stemming global population growth. The delegates to Cairo+5 represented 159 nation-states—and Vatican City's Holy See.

It's this last participant that has long irked women's groups, nongovernmental organizations (NGOs), and member states who have struggled for women's equality around the world. The Roman Catholic Church, represented at the UN by the Holy See, is the only religious body to enjoy "nonmember state permanent observer" status. NGOs such as the Women's Environment and Development Organization and UN agencies such as the World Health Organization also observe—but silently, from a raised gallery above the debate floor. The Holy See's "observer" gets to speak, to lobby, and to negotiate on virtually equal footing with any nation. The Holy See may not vote, but it can and does influence the documents the nations vote on. And in the case of Cairo+5, the document contains elements as beneficial to women as they are odious to the Holy See.

Last spring, a coalition of more than one hundred international women's, religious, and reproductive rights groups launched the See Change Campaign to challenge the Vatican's power at the UN—and to downgrade its status from a nonmember state to a traditional NGO. Frances Kissling, president of Catholics for a Free Choice (CFFC), one of the groups spearheading the effort, puts its position clearly: "Why should an entity that is in essence 100 square acres of office space and tourist attractions in the middle of Rome, with a citizenry that excludes women and children, have a place at the table where governments set policies affecting the very survival of women and children? Are we dealing with a religion or a political power here? Or both? Nobody else at the UN claims to represent God." Bene Madunagu, chair of Girls' Power Initiative, in Nigeria, spoke at See Change's launch. "The death toll from HIV and AIDS in Africa," she said, "rises with every Holy See success in intimidating health organizations from broadening prevention and education programs. There is no record of maternal mortality in the male-only Vatican, but Africa sees a massive percentage of pregnancy-related deaths that result from abortion complications because too many poor governments yield to political pressures from the Holy See against providing safe, legal abortion services."

Maria Consuelo Mejia is director of Catholics for the Right to Decide, a Mexico City-based member of the See Change Campaign. "At the end of the twentieth century, the Roman Catholic Church is the most hierarchical and patriarchal institution in the world," she says. "They're entitled to represent themselves and their beliefs," Mejia concedes, but without the status of a nation-state.

The Cairo+5 conference represented the first time since the See Change Campaign's inception that the group could make its presence felt at an event where the Holy See was on hand trying to roll back the gains made by women. In the UN's huge first-floor meeting hall, the Holy See's seven-member delegation, with its laptops and cell phones, sat beside the delegate from Haiti, one of the hemisphere's poorest states. A man and a woman in nonclerical summer suits scanned documents on their computer screens, while a pair of priests in traditional garb hovered like sentinels at their backs. When the discussion got heated, the priests set off to roam the delegates' benches, passing around position papers and clasping hands. While the clerics were cruising, their lay colleagues listened, and every time the conference talk turned to reproductive health or contraception, women's rights, or issues of family and youth, John Klink, a Vatican delegation member and the See's lead talker, raised the sign that delegates use to indicate they want to speak.

Among other things, Klink argued against the use of the so-called morning-after pill for rape victims; opposed any mention of female condoms; and advocated replacing "rights" with "status"—as in "respect for women's status" instead of "respect for women's rights." One busy Monday afternoon, Klink spoke five times in an hour against confidential sex counseling for adolescents and for a reconfirmation of parental rights. "I appeal to delegates of the Holy See to join the consensus," pleaded conference chair Anwarul Chowdhury of Bangladesh. Because UN chairpersons work hard to achieve consensus, the See can delay proceedings with a single dissenting view, as Klink did in this case.

"The Vatican's position in contemporary global debate should be extremely humble," grumbled Amparo Claro, director of the Latin American and Caribbean Women's Health Network, an NGO that, like all NGOs, may watch UN proceedings but may speak to delegates only in the corridors. "The Vatican does not represent the diversity of opinions within the Christian community. It does not even reflect the multiple voices of Catholics."

Delegates from Europe, Canada, and the U.S. fought hard but lost the battle to insert mention of female-controlled methods of contraception and emergency contraception into this year's document. The only other delegates who raised their hands as often as Klink did represented not a tiny entity, but the 300 million people of the U.S. or the thirteen nations of the European Union or the coalition of 133 developing nations, called the G77. Over and over, delegates heard the Holy See's representative declare, "We cannot approve."

When Klink says *we*, he says he's referring to the Catholic Church, which, he asserts, "is comprised of the entire people of God." Clerics have described the See as the "supreme organ of government," not just of Vatican City but of Catholicism. Alone, therefore, among its nation-state colleagues at the UN, the papacy sets its political perimeter not around a country but around the world. And that is how its influence comes to be so widely felt.

The word *see* derives from seat—the official diocese of the Holy Father, or Vatican City, a statelet set up in 1929 to administer the Roman Catholic Church's property and keep it independent from Rome. At less than one square mile, with one thousand citizens—five hundred male cardinals and some five hundred mostly male support staff—Vatican City is no match for your average shopping mall in terms of size, but the place has a post office, a radio station, and a diplomatic corps, and when the UN was being formed a half century ago, that was enough to get it in the door.

It didn't hurt that in the postwar era, the Catholic Church was tied into a network of anticommunist activists and underground priests who reported to the Vatican from every corner of the globe. Throughout the 1950s, Washington and the West supported the Holy See's attendance at the General Assembly and meetings of the World Health Organization, UNESCO, and other key agencies where the Vatican usually came down on their side in the East-West disputes of the cold war. In 1964, when Pope Paul VI named a permanent observer to the UN—like that of neutral Switzerland—U Thant, the UN secretary-general at the time, went along. (Permanent observers are not subjected to the same lengthy approval process as member states.) The Holy See uses this position not only to protect the Vatican's autonomy from outside intervention, but to impose its view on the rest of the world. In 1994, seven months before the population conference in Cairo, Pope John Paul II was busy laying masonry for his antiwoman platform. He got personally involved in the attempt to dissuade participants from adopting a policy that would, in his eyes, legitimize abortion and contraception. As early as February 1994, a full nine pages of *L'Osservatore Romano*, the Holy See's official newspaper, were dedicated to the text of a "Letter to the Family," written by the pope himself. Addressing what he called the protection of the life of the unborn, the pope announced that the doctrine of the church on abortion and contraception would never change. The same day's paper carried an article by a Catholic theologian asserting that even the prevention of conception by artificial means was reason for excommunication, because it's tantamount to abortion, which carries the same punishment.

L'Osservatore's half dozen weekly foreign-language editions distributed the message loud and clear. But that was just the opening salvo. That March, John Paul II escalated tactics with personally signed letters to all heads of state and to UN Secretary-General Boutros Boutros-Ghali, urging them to reject the draft document, which was then being formulated, on the grounds that it was being authored in part by the International Planned Parenthood Federation. The document, which advocated global contraception programs, "leaves the troubling impression of something being imposed," he wrote, "namely, a lifestyle typical of certain fringes within developed societies that are materially rich and secularized. . . . Are countries more sensitive to the values of nature, morality, and religion going to accept such a vision of man and society without protest?"

John Paul II telephoned President Clinton in April 1994 to request his intervention to modify the UN draft, and then pressed his message further in an interview with the president at the Vatican that June. By no coincidence, the U.S. National Conference of Bishops joined the fray, with a declaration urging the administration to support the Vatican position and indicating that voters would not support opponents of the church. "It definitely caused the Clinton administration to consider its position very carefully and look very closely at the language," said Adrienne Germain, president of the International Women's Health Coalition, who was a member of the U.S. delegation at Cairo and again at Cairo+5.

At Cairo, the seventeen-person delegation from the Holy See was eventually able to stall the conference for days over the language in the final document and force concessions. The final Program of Action for the next twenty years did include the dread word *abortion*—saying it should be "safe" where it is "not against the law," but Archbishop Renato Martino, the Vatican's permanent observer to the UN, announced that "Nothing is to be understood to imply that the Holy See endorses abortion or has in any way changed its moral position." Any hopes that the Cairo delegates may have had that the UN might call for countries to liberalize abortion laws were soundly dashed.

But there was forward movement. Overall, the Program of Action agreed on at Cairo was a victory for women because it focused on women's health as the key to population development. As such, it represented a hard-won triumph over the Roman Catholic Church.

At the Cairo+5 gathering, the Vatican's team was determined to regain the ground it had lost at the 1994 conference, but Cairo+5 saw no significant reversal of earlier gains. A delegate from Mexico even chided the See about its claim that confidential sex counseling for teenagers undercuts parental rights. "Does the privacy of the confessional not extend to teens?" the delegate asked, in an unusually direct criticism of the Vatican's rhetoric. Clare Short, the delegate from Great Britain, went even further, issuing a press release that condemned the Vatican's "unholy alliance" with right-wing Catholic groups and fundamentalist Muslim countries seeking to thwart women's reproductive rights around the world.

Part of the reason why the church wields so much power is that in almost every country of the world it has instituted strong antipoverty and refugee programs and is deeply involved in providing health care. And it is this relationship with poor and developing nations regarding resource issues that wins allies for the church's gender fight. It's not for nothing that the Holy See on more than one occasion in the Cairo+5 debates pointed out that the Roman Catholic Church supports more than three hundred thousand health facilities worldwide.

The church has made it very clear that if any government or UN agency attempts to force those facilities to provide abortion services or requires them to offer contraception services, "They'd pull out," said Anika Rahman, director of the international program at the Center for Reproductive Law and Policy.

This creates a hostage situation, especially when it comes to the church's more extreme positions, such as the prohibition on the use of condoms for protection against sexually transmitted diseases, even for married couples in which one partner has HIV.

As governments around the world—such as the U.S.—farm out more health care services to private operators, including the church, the economic realities strengthen the Vatican's hand. Every time a secular hospital merges with a Catholic one, access to safe abortion services and the most modern methods of contraception is reduced. The poorer the country, the greater the Vatican's influence.

In the front row of the UN visitors' gallery during the last week of Cairo+5, a man in a bright-blue suit sat avidly watching the goings-on. Michal Kliment, a citizen of the Slovak Republic, has worked as a gynecologist for almost thirty years and serves as the executive director of the Slovak Family Planning Association. In 1994, he was in Cairo. In 1999, he'd hoped to be part of the effort to consolidate progressive gains made there. Kliment was named one of his country's two official delegates to the Cairo+5. "I've been more involved in this issue than just about anybody in my country," he says.

But halfway into the Cairo+5 meeting, the Slovakian government sent word: Kliment and his colleague (also a reproductive rights advocate) were no longer delegation members. Before business on Friday, "I was told I'd been replaced," says Kliment. Now he perches in the visitors' gallery, looking down on the meeting floor from afar. Asked if he suspects anyone of engineering his ouster, he does not hesitate. He's got no proof, but he points to the delegation from the Vatican.

The replacement delegates are Slovakia's ambassador to Canada—a Christian Democrat and vigorous opponent of the Cairo Plan—and the minister for social affairs. From the assembly floor, the minister has just finished condemning emergency contraception, asserting, as the Vatican does, that the morning-after pill is no different from abortion.

"It's medical nonsense. He's not a gynecologist," says Kliment. "But he is a good Catholic," and now Slovakia is toeing the Vatican line. Although it is a predominantly Catholic state, Slovakia's legal code is currently progressive about abortion, contraception, and divorce. The movement to change the law is growing, with the help of well-endowed European satellites of U.S.-based antiabortion groups. Kliment has started getting death threats. "They've told me they'll kill my children for my killing of Slovak babies," he says. Then Kliment pauses. "The people of the Vatican don't see women after illegal abortions; they don't have to take responsibility for an unwanted child. What right have they to tell the world what to do on such issues?"

The same question has now been raised by women's groups from every region of the world.

"This is not a campaign likely to achieve its goal in the short term," acknowledges See Change's Kissling. "What the campaign does is keep the Vatican on its toes in terms of being excessive, and it encourages people to speak out on the issues."

Christian Wahhabists

Barbara Ehrenreich

From the *Progressive*, January 2002

There has been a lot of loose talk, since September 11, about a "clash of civilizations" between musty, backward-looking, repressive old Islam and the innovative and freedom-loving West. "It is a clash between positivism and a reactionary, negative world view," columnist H.D.S. Greenway writes in the *Boston Globe*.

Or, as we learn in the *Washington Post*: While the West used the last two centuries to advance the cause of human freedom, "The Islamic world, by contrast, was content to remain in its torpor, locked in rigid orthodoxy, fearful of freedom."

So it is a surprise to find, on turning to the original text—Samuel P. Huntington's 1996 *The Clash of Civilizations and the Remaking of World Order* (Simon & Schuster)—a paragraph-long analogy between the Islamic fundamentalist movement and the Protestant Reformation: "Both are reactions to the stagnation and corruption of existing institutions; advocate a return to a purer and more demanding form of their religion; preach work, order, and discipline."

Whoa, there! Weren't the Protestants supposed to be the up-and-coming, progressive force vis-à-vis the musty old Catholics? And if we were supposed to root for the Protestants in our high-school history texts, shouldn't we be applauding the Islamic "extremists" now?

Huntington doesn't entertain the analogy between Islamic fundamentalism and reforming Protestantism for very long. But let's extend the analogy, if only because it implicitly challenges the notion that we are dealing with two radically different, mutually opposed "civilizations."

Like the Protestants of the sixteenth century, the Islamic fundamentalists are a relatively new and innovative force on the scene. Wahhabism—the dour and repressive creed espoused by Saudi Arabia, Osama bin Laden, and other Islamic fundamentalists throughout the world—dates from only the mid-eighteenth century. Deobandism, the strain of Islam that informed the Taliban (and which has, in recent decades, become almost indistinguishable from Wahhabism), arose in India just a little over a century ago. So when we talk about Islamic fundamentalism, we are not talking about some ancient and venerable "essence of Islam"; we are talking about something new and even "modern." As Huntington observes, the appeal of fundamentalism is to "mobile and modern-oriented younger people."

Islamic fundamentalism is a response—not to the West or to the "modern"—but to earlier strands of Islam, just as Protestantism was a response to Catholicism. Wahhabism arose in opposition to both the (thoroughly Muslim) Ottoman Empire and to the indigenous Sufism of eighteenth-century Arabia.

Sufism is part of Islam, too—much admired in the West for its relative tolerance, its mysticism and poetry, its danced, ecstatic rituals. But it is also, especially in its rural forms, a religion that bears more than a casual resemblance to late-medieval Catholicism: Sufism encourages the veneration of saint-like figures at special shrines and their celebration at festivities—sometimes rather raucous ones, like the carnivals and saints' days of medieval Catholicism—throughout the year.

Just as the Protestants smashed icons, prohibited carnivals, and defaced cathedrals, the Wahhabists insisted on a "reformed" style of Islam, purged of all the saints, festivities, and music. Theirs is what has been described as a "stripped-down" version of Islam, centered on short prayers recited in undecorated mosques to the one god and only to him.

The Taliban imposed Wahhabism in Afghanistan as soon as they came to power in 1996 and took on, as their first task, the stamping out of Sufism.

The closest Reformation counterpart to today's Islamic fundamentalists were the Calvinists, whose movement arose a few decades after Lutheranism. Pundits often exclaim over the Islamic fundamentalists' refusal to recognize a church-state division—as if that were a uniquely odious feature of "Islamic civilization"—but John Calvin was a militant theocrat himself, and his followers carved out Calvinist ministates wherever they could.

In sixteenth-century Swiss cantons and seventeenth-century Massachusetts, Calvinists and Calvinist-leaning Protestants banned dancing, gambling, drinking, colorful clothing, and sports of all kinds. They outlawed idleness and vigorously suppressed sexual activity in all but its married, reproductively oriented, form.

Should he have been transported back into a Calvinist-run Zurich or Salem, a member of the Taliban or a Wahhabist might have found only one thing that was objectionable: the presence of unveiled women. But he would have been reassured on this point by the Calvinists' insistence on women's subjugation. As a man is to Jesus, asserted the new Christian doctrine, so is his wife to him.

Calvinism—or "Puritanism" as it is known in America—was, of course, immensely successful. Max Weber credited it with laying the psychological groundwork for capitalism: work hard, defer gratification, etc. Within the West, the Calvinist legacy carries on most robustly in America, with its demented war on drugs, its tortured ambivalence about pornography and sex, its refusal to accord homosexuals equal protection under the law. It even persists in organized form as the Christian right, which continues to nurture the dream of a theocratic state. Recall the statement by one of our leading warriors against Islamic fundamentalist terrorism—John Ashcroft—that "we have no king but Jesus."

In a world that contains Christian Wahhabists like Ashcroft and Islamic Calvinists like bin Laden, what sense does it make to talk about culturally monolithic "civilizations" like "Islam" and "the West"? Any civilization worthy of the title is, at almost any moment of its history, fraught with antagonistic worldviews and balanced on the finely poised dialectics of class, race, gender, and ideology. We talk of "Roman civilization," for example, forgetting that the Roman elite spent the last decades before Jesus's birth bloodily suppressing its own ecstatic, unruly, Dionysian religious sects.

There is no "clash of civilizations" because there are no clear-cut, and certainly no temperamentally homogeneous, civilizations to do the clashing. What there is, and has been again and again throughout history, is a clash of alternative cultures. One, represented by the Islamic and Christian fundamentalists—as well as by fascists and Soviet-style communists—is crabbed and punitive in outlook, committed to collectivist discipline, and dogmatically opposed to spontaneity and pleasure. Another, represented both in folk traditions and by elite "enlightenment" thought, is more open, liberatory, and trusting of human impulses.

Civilizations can tilt in either direction. And individuals—whether they are Christian, Muslim, or neither—have a choice to make between freedom, on the one hand, and religious totalitarianism on the other.

Fundamentalism and the Family:
Gender, Culture, and the American Pro-family Movement

Margaret Lamberts Bendroth

From the *Journal of Women's History*, Winter 1999

It would be hard to imagine modern "culture wars" without the disputed and beleaguered traditional family playing a central role. Among the religious and political groups that scholars have labeled "fundamentalist," the rhetoric of family decline has served to focus a range of objections to modernity. In many Islamic movements, for example, the defense of the traditional family is a way of airing related anxieties about gender roles and female sexuality, as well as long-standing grievances against imperialism and Western secularism. In the United States over the past twenty years, the family has become a key issue in the moral and political agenda of the broad conservative coalition known as the "religious right."[1]

But in the American case, the link between the family and conservative religious politics is neither obvious nor simple. True, the rhetoric of anxiety and protest has become a staple of the self-described profamily movement, and antiabortion politics in particular. Cast within its historical perspective, however, this alienated language is far from accurate. Indeed, since the mid-1970s, the "family values" debate has brought millions of politically uninvolved, conservative Protestants into the voting booth. Over the past two decades, the profamily agenda has expanded to include abortion, homosexuality, and the Equal Rights Amendment (ERA), as well as school board politics and parental rights legislation. These issues first pushed conservative Protestants into the national political arena, and have proved a lucrative fund-raising and vote-getting tool ever since.[2]

This article traces the process by which the family became the moral terrain of religious conservatives. It covers a lengthy time span—from the turn of the century to the present; however, my gallop across this century is not necessarily superficial. The analysis in this article relies on a great deal of work on the history of fundamentalism and gender and the recent rise of the religious right in American politics. One of my goals is to bridge the two areas of study. Relatively little of the historical literature on American fundamentalism, which tends to focus on theology and denominational politics, explains why sexuality and family issues have become such an overriding concern among present-day evangelicals. Alternatively, few observers of the contemporary religious right have taken seriously enough its historical and theological origins to explore them in depth. Any examination of the evangelical profamily movement must consider its religious origins; behind the political organizing, which has met with much media attention, specific theological convictions consistently have motivated its leadership as well as the rank and file. Observers who look only at the political issues from a Washington, D.C., perspective are hard-pressed to understand the movement fully.[3]

The historical origins of the modern profamily movement also serve as a barometer of change in the cultural role of religion and family life. American Protestant fundamentalism was around for a long time before it took up the family as a theological, much less political, concern. In the late-nineteenth and early-twentieth centuries, gender issues were central to the movement's identity and progress; however, this did not result in a full-fledged agenda to shore up the traditional family.[4] That change came fairly recently, beginning in the years following World War II and accelerating in the late 1970s. The timing and content of this transition are important, having as much to do with the evolving nature of the modern family as with the developing shape of religion in American society. More specifically, the shift reflects the transformation of erstwhile "fundamentalists" into a new group calling themselves "neo-evangelicals."

In American religious history, these two conservative Protestant types—fundamentalist and neoevangelical (or, simply, evangelical)—are significantly different in theology and social attitudes, and it is worth the trouble to track the discontinuities, especially in regard to women and the family. Early-twentieth-century fundamentalists, as precursors of the modern evangelical movement, said little about the family and, for practical and theological reasons, valued it less. But with the emergence of a neoevangelical movement out of fundamentalism in the 1940s and 1950s, the family became a central metaphor. The difference in rhetoric about the family before and after World War II is a response to contradictory tugs toward separatism and cultural compromise. The need to be left alone and the fear of being ignored has been a tension within the conservative wing of American Protestantism for the past hundred years. Rather than an example of rising militancy among American religious conservatives, the profamily movement (and perhaps its political agenda) illustrates its losing battle against modernity; the military metaphors are more an index of secularization than of true religious radicalism.

Fundamentalism and American Culture

In the American religious marketplace, achieving outsider status is difficult and costly. The pluralistic array of denominations and sects, which has characterized American religion since the seventeenth century, has proven remarkably tolerant of strangers.[5] Yet, fundamentalists became outsiders through a complex historical process. The movement arose in the late-nineteenth century among Protestants who found themselves intellectually and spiritually—but not economically or politically—disenfranchised from white, middle-class culture. Their discontent centered around the increasingly this-worldly cast of religion in the Gilded Age, and with the rising skepticism in universities and theological seminaries concerning the staples of the faith, including the infallibility of the Bible.[6]

Fundamentalism began as a faith designed to stir lethargic churchgoers into action. It sought to keep all that was best about the "old-time religion"— a commitment to revivalism, personal conversion, and veneration of the Bible as a source of spiritual inspiration and propositional truth—but, in other ways, fundamentalism drew in the boundaries of Protestant orthodoxy more tightly than ever before. This was especially true around matters of biblical interpretation, where fundamentalists insisted on an inerrant scripture (without factual or scientific error). Fundamentalist eschatology, or study of the "last days," was apocalyptic and premillennial, and focused on biblical passages that predicted a sudden, cataclysmic Second Coming of Christ. These were doctrines calculated to serve as a spiritual antidote to lukewarm piety and theological compromise—although also fated to expose fundamentalist belief to ridicule and caricature by a skeptical American public.[7]

But fundamentalists were never as disenfranchised as their angry rhetoric often claimed. Almost from its inception, the movement took an ambivalent stance toward American culture as both "Babylon" and "Zion," a place of wickedness and land uniquely blessed by God. After fundamentalists lost their hold in the Protestant denominations during the 1920s, the movement flourished in less public venues, but retained its complex sense of mission. Throughout the 1930s and 1940s, fundamentalists never gave up hoping to redeem the nation from corruption, even as they waited impatiently for its downfall.[8] In the American context, therefore, fundamentalism emerged as a mass of contradictions that over the years have proved vexing to outsiders. It was at once antiauthoritarian and obsessed with order; it was fervently apocalyptic, sometimes to the point of otherworldliness, and at the same time enmeshed in American middle-class culture. It was critical of American society, especially its rampant consumerism and pursuit of individual pleasure, yet temperamentally conservative and suspicious of radical change.

Fundamentalism's influence on modern, conservative evangelical Protestantism is hard to gauge precisely. After World War II, old-style separatist fundamentalism had in many ways run its course, giving way to the neoevangelical movement of the late 1940s and 1950s. This new form was not separatist, or as alienated from American intellectual culture as classic fundamentalism, but it did maintain strong resemblances, holding to an inerrant Bible and belief in a premillennial Second Coming as the standard.[9] During the 1970s, even this neoevangelical version of fundamentalism was supplanted rapidly by the "born again" phenomenon, a diverse religiosity that tapped into different regional and theological sources in popular religious culture.[10] Still, the modern evangelical movement exhibits many of the contradictory tendencies toward cultural embrace and rejection that emerged so powerfully in fundamentalism half a century earlier, although with far less internal tension. Modern evangelicalism—that catchall term which includes the heirs of old-line fundamentalism as well as a variety of conservative Protestant cobelligerents—is in some ways dismissive of middle-class American culture and at the same time almost indistinguishable from it.

New Victorians?

Fundamentalist ambivalence about the family owes much to the movement's origins. It emerged in the late-nineteenth and early-twentieth centuries as a reaction against Victorian social and religious conventions, and the domestic ideal in particular. As defined in popular literature, sermons, and music, and by household furnishings, the domestic ideal raised the respectable middle-class family as a civilizing, Christianizing force above all others.[11] Proponents of Victorian domesticity, a central metaphor of white, middle-class Protestantism, elevated the home to near sacramental status and enshrined woman as its saintly protector.

Early fundamentalists despised such sentimentality, especially when it all but absolved women of original sin. In the opening decades of the twentieth century, the masculine rhetoric of American politics filtered across American Protestantism, and served as a rallying cry in churches where women had long held numerical majorities.[12] Fundamentalists participated enthusiastically in the trend; by the 1920s, they employed aggressive discourse, and identified the cause of orthodoxy as primarily a masculine endeavor. The leading fundamentalist periodical *Bible Champion*, for example, declared it "manly" to follow Christ, upheld the Bible as "virile literature" and praised Christ himself as "the most manly of men." Indeed, in 1946, Baptist preacher and evangelist John R. Rice condemned the alleged religious superiority of women as a "lie out of hell" and the alleged religious inferiority of men as a "wicked, hellish, ungodly, satanic teaching."[13]

The Victorian domestic ideal did not suit the intense piety that characterized fundamentalism. Emphasis on self-denial and duty demanded a vigorous "emptying of self" to allow for divine infusion. Any competing loyalty, including a human relationship, that stood in the way of complete consecration to God could block the Holy Spirit's power in the believer's life. Fundamentalists saw the Victorian veneration of home and family as a subtle form of idolatry.[14]

Fundamentalism's yearning for religious revival also fed ambivalence about family obligations. Popular fundamentalist revivalists usually offered standard talk about the "old-fashioned family" and the need for Christian homes. Yet their own lives were an ironic counterpoint, since their careers necessitated constant travel away from their wives and children. In a letter written shortly after his wife had suffered what was to be a fatal heart attack, evangelist Harry A. Ironside confessed to a friend that "I do wish I did not have to be away so much while she is ill, but that is one of the trials of the path which one must enter while seeking to minister Christ to others. I often feel," Ironside admitted, "'like saying with the bride in the Song of Solomon, 'They made me the keeper of the vineyards, but my own vineyard I have not kept.'"[15] People who believed they were living in the shadow of the Second Coming could not let the ties of sentiment overtake religious duty.

Fundamentalists were not the only American Protestants who were ambivalent about Victorian domesticity, but they were among the few with systematic theological reasons for doing so. Leading premillennialist James H. Brookes, for example, declared that the true believer should "take no part in the trifles and contentions that are going on around him . . . [for he] is no longer at home in the world and he will never be at home until he is with the Lord." Contemporary premillennialist Elizabeth Needham described the world as a "leprous house," advising Christians to keep themselves "unspotted from its contagion" and to live in "wholesome loathing" of its diseased and poisoned air.[16]

By the end of the nineteenth century, male fundamentalist leaders were careful to distinguish their vigorous piety from the sentimentalized conventions of "feminized" religion. This was hardly simple, given that fundamentalist institutions were, like the rest of American religion, predominantly female. But few male leaders acknowledged that touting masculine religion to largely female congregations was at best contradictory, and few women within fundamentalist ranks openly objected to such rhetoric. In the late-nineteenth century, fundamentalism defined itself within the conventions of masculine individualism. Like previous generations of Christian zealots, martyrs, and monastics, many early fundamentalist male leaders adopted Christ's lonely example as a model of holiness. Individualists all, they rejected the conflation of godliness with the middle-class family, and along with it the pious notion that the outside world was an extension of the home, waiting to be "domesticated" by middle-class, white women. The world was a source of temptation and compromise to the Christian seeking to choose the hardest, and truest, path.

Fundamentalist Families

Not surprisingly, fundamentalists in the 1930s and 1940s produced little constructive literature on family life. They viewed the family's role as didactic and defensive, a fortress to be guarded or a sanctuary from "the burden of the battle."[17] From time to time, fundamentalists joined the chorus of worry in Protestant circles and the culture at large, predicting the family's imminent demise. But given that such diatribes have been a standard element of religious publishing in America since its inception, their pessimism about the family was hardly a defining characteristic.

Fundamentalist unease with the family fed into conflicting attitudes about sex. Although often caricatured as terrified of their libidos, fundamentalists

in the 1930s and 1940s discussed them far more often than did other mid-twentieth-century Protestants. Advice columns in fundamentalist periodicals frequently warned against the widely believed dangers of sex and obliquely counseled forms of sublimation for healthy, young, single people. But not all fundamentalist leaders were models of restraint. Revivalists from Aimee Semple McPherson to Billy Sunday traded upon a certain amount of sex appeal to gather crowds, and from the platform discussed with startling frankness the specifics of birth control and sex education.[18]

Fundamentalists also said little about religious nurture in the home. Rejecting popular child-rearing advice manuals, they held the line on principles of order and discipline, displaying an almost visceral dislike of psychological experts and their nurturant, relational language. Rice, author of one of the few acceptable fundamentalist manuals on child rearing, dismissed "that foolish theory that love can rule adequately without any punishment for sin." Such sentiment, he scoffed, "denies every fundamental doctrine of the Bible."[19] In the 1940s, fundamentalist writers stood at considerable cultural distance from most middle-class, white Americans, at least on family matters. Most viewed the disparity as a point of pride, a measure of their righteous separation from immorality and disorder. Not only did fundamentalist writers decry the absence of moral authority in "modernist" homes, they doubted the possibility of love and joy. "How empty and cheerless a home without Christ must be!" one writer observed in 1945, guessing that "what happiness there is rests only upon a physical and material basis."[20]

Another measure of separatism for fundamentalists by the end of World War II concerned women's role in the family. To this point, most discussions about women had been in terms of their role in the church and what duties the scriptures warranted. However, this dialogue gave way to one where fundamentalists attempted to codify women's familial role along submissive lines. In strict, hierarchical language—terminology generally missing from fundamentalist discussions of women's roles before the 1940s—writers insisted that the "scriptural home" placed men at the top of a ladder of command.[21] The consistently embattled tone of this writing suggests that fundamentalists adopted this ethic with difficulty, and that its standards of feminine submission had never been normative for the movement as a whole. Still, the growing emphasis on hierarchy and obedience was not minor doctrine, despite its late emergence; by the 1960s and 1970s, many

religious conservatives wrote about wifely submission as if it was, and always had been, a central article of Christian faith.

Fundamentalist rhetoric stood in contrast to upbeat discussions about the family among mainline and liberal Protestants. For these culturally dominant Christians, the family was a major concern throughout the first half of the twentieth century. They had their own theological warrant for such an emphasis, beginning with the theology of Christian nurture in the writings of Horace Bushnell in the mid-nineteenth century. Bushnell, a Congregational theologian, emphasized the unfolding of religion in the children of Christian families as a corrective to the stress on dramatic adult conversions that were a feature of religious revivals. His views, scientifically amplified by educational philosopher John Dewey, became institutionalized among religious educators and parents in the early-twentieth century. Writings on the family within the large, white, Protestant denominations—primarily Methodist, Northern Baptist, Presbyterian, and Congregationalist—also tracked the rise of an expressive ideal of family life, then gaining currency in American middle-class culture. The modem family, whether described by pediatrician Dr. Benjamin Spock or a Presbyterian education curriculum, was idealized as a nurturing haven for individuals beset by the impersonal push and shove of the outside world.[22]

From Fundamentalist to Neoevangelical

By the postwar era, the American middle-class family ideal was vastly different from its early-twentieth-century form. Now the emphasis was on the quality of relationships among parents and children, replacing Victorian language of order and duty with a new ethic of individual self-expression. The home became a site for leisure pursuits and interpersonal companionship, rather than a place of economic production. Even the terminology changed, as the postwar generation of psychological care givers spoke less of "the home"—a social institution with an overarching moral reality of its own— and more about "the family"—meeting the emotional and psychological needs of human beings within an ever-changing set of interpersonal relationships. This shift, which had been under way since the turn of the century, locked in place with the postwar explosion of economic prosperity and suburban living of the baby boom generation.[23]

By the 1950s, the home no longer served as a citadel of defense against worldliness, even for the most determined fundamentalist. For over two

decades, the world had been coming into the home on a regular basis, first through radio and then television. In the 1930s, fundamentalists embraced radio with initial reluctance and then enthusiasm as they recognized its potential for evangelistic outreach. In the late 1940s and early 1950s, the same conversation went on about television, but with an air of inevitability. "The boast of one network," a fundamentalist pastor wrote in 1955, "is that it 'brings the world right into your home.' Who wants the world as we know it in our homes?" Yet, like most American families, the majority of fundamentalists could not resist the television invasion, despite its dubious moral effects on home and family life.[24]

However, by the late 1950s, mainline Protestants, much more than fundamentalists, were losing faith in the Christian family. Members of these predominantly white, middle-class churches typified the new relational family, with its emphases on cooperation, togetherness, and democratic relationships. Church leaders struggled to adapt religious education curriculum to meet the set of needs these cultural changes demanded. "Religious illiteracy" among parents was so widespread even in the churchgoing 1950s, denominational officials reported, that the home no longer could be counted on to provide religious nurture. The rising specter of middle-class divorce, as well as charges of excessive "familism" among churches in "suburban captivity," discouraged promises that by praying together Christian families would stay together. In the late 1950s and early 1960s, conversations about the home began to shift from matters around child rearing and religious nurture into a series of debates about family—related issues, beginning with divorce and then spiraling on to birth control, abortion, and homosexuality.[25]

Neoevangelicals quickly advanced into the unoccupied territory, momentarily casting aside skepticism their fundamentalist forebears might have demanded. Since World War II, some fundamentalists have moved toward the centers of social power. Weary of their cultural marginalization, such neoevangelical leaders as Harold John Ockenga and Carl F. H. Henry urged a return to biblical scholarship and intellectual engagement. Their call to action spurred the hopes of those who believed that only a religious revival would save the nation from calamity, and met with increasing success in the postwar years. Billy Graham, who had been raised a fundamentalist, mounted televised evangelistic crusades that reached a cross section of Americans and brought him into the corridors of the White House.[26]

The neoevangelical postwar revival joined mainstream American culture at its new center, a return to the traditional family. By the 1960s and 1970s, "evangelicals talked about the family with about the same regularity and with nearly the same passion with which the fundamentalists had discussed the Second Advent."[27] For the first time in a long time, religious conservatives—including erstwhile fundamentalists as well as such other conservative groups as Southern Baptists, Mormons, Orthodox Jews, and many Catholics—and secular, middle-class Americans were in hailing distances on matters concerning women and the family.[28] Neoevangelicals spoke an inherited fundamentalist language of crisis and doom, emphasizing the need for order and obedience. But in discussing the family, they clearly had uncovered a topic which all but guaranteed them an appreciative audience and a spot closer in from the margins of American society.

Before the ERA became a polarizing symbol for conservatives, evangelicals' enthusiasm for the cultural mainstream allowed a certain amount of openness toward feminism, at least for a time. In the early 1960s, *Eternity* magazine published pro-ERA editorials, and, by the early 1970s, its more conservative counterpart, *Christianity Today*, cautiously followed. To be sure, both magazines regularly received a flood of angry letters against feminism, but the editorial bent remained constant in favor of equal rights as a minimum standard, until the mid-1970s.[29]

Disputes over women's roles continued for decades, as the winds of feminism clashed head-on with biblical texts on female submission. American Protestants had long debated the meaning and implication of these texts, and, failing to arrive at a consensus, generally agreed to disagree. In the 1970s, however, evangelical scholars and activists took up the debate with renewed passion for both sides of the issue. In the early 1970s, a small, left-wing, evangelical movement organized the Daughters of Sarah to uphold a generous interpretation of the texts. Other evangelicals, troubled by any attempt to "explain away" the words of scripture, sought to apply the command for submission in a nuanced, egalitarian manner. As the controversy continued, it became more than an arcane discussion of biblical literature; a liberal or conservative perspective on the role of women was a powerful means of marking one's stance toward secular culture, and the feminist movement in particular.[30]

As evangelicals geared up for cultural conquest, they slowly but inexorably surrendered territory. By the 1960s, it was impossible, even for erstwhile fundamentalists, to talk about "the family" without falling into the relational language they once had despised. In 1961, even S. Maxwell Coder, dean of the fundamentalist enclave, the Moody Bible Institute, agreed that reading the Bible in the home could help alleviate the "mental stress" of modern living.[31] Overlooking the disdain of their fundamentalist forebears for secular child-rearing professionals, neoevangelicals began to produce their own parental advice experts, each one better than the last at speaking the nurturant language of middle-class parenting.[32]

The authoritarian advice in some manuals masked their gradual appropriation of a more relational approach. In the 1970s, Bill Gothard's popular Youth Conflicts seminars taught a rigid model of "chain of command," beginning with God and moving downward through fathers, mothers, and children. Despite his use of military metaphors, Gothard's insistence on divine authority did not negate the importance of personality development and relationship skills. Families who used Gothard's methods reported they found personal peace in its moral certainties, and a measure of "relief" from dealing with life's ambiguities.[33]

Gothard's heir, and undisputed leader of the new evangelical family movement, was James C. Dobson, a Nazarene minister's son with a Ph.D. in child development from the University of Southern California. In the late 1970s, Dobson's folksy wisdom and no-nonsense approach to discipline won him almost instantaneous success. By the early 1980s, his first book, *Dare to Discipline*, had sold over 1.2 million copies and his seven-part film series entitled "Focus on the Family" had reached over 10 million viewers. Dobson's weekly radio broadcast, which began in 1977 with forty-three radio stations, grew to over four hundred by 1982.[34]

As successors of fundamentalist John Rice during the 1960s and 1970s, Bill Gothard and James Dobson proved remarkably adept at negotiating between the old fundamentalist-style authoritarianism and the increasingly relational ethos of child rearing. Dobson in particular attracted a middle-class audience of evangelical parents who for religious reasons were not comfortable with the "child-centered" philosophies of such secular authorities as Haim Ginott (Parent Effectiveness Training) and Dr. Spock. Dobson's emphasis on discipline and parental authority led some observers to misread him as an advocate of corporal punishment; in fact, Dobson rarely advocated spanking (although he did not rule it out), preferring to emphasize responsibility and mutual respect among parents and children.[35]

Dobson's success is not surprising. By the late 1970s, evangelicals were hardly a sectarian group out to punish their children into conformity. Although at one time, self-defined evangelicals and fundamentalists were lower on the economic and educational ladder than more liberal Protestants, the gap closed quickly in the 1970s. The evangelicals whom sociologist James Davidson Hunter studied in the mid-1980s were in some instances almost impossible to distinguish by income or education—and in many cases by social attitudes—from their secular, white, middle-class neighbors.[36]

Pressed to locate differences between believer and nonbeliever, the evangelical family literature of the 1960s and 1970s made much of the disparities between a "Christian" family and its secular counterparts. They picked up the older fundamentalist discussions of the home as a hierarchically ordered religious fortress, and reworked it into the secular optimistic language of human potential and psychological "adjustment." Few noticed the contradictions. Husbands and wives who followed God's directions for their life together could expect happiness; those who chose otherwise risked everything. As popular author Larry Christiansen warned, "If we accept a prescription for marriage completely dependent upon the belief structure of secular humanism, then we must be prepared that the result will be something other than Christian family life." Non-Christians had no stake in the family at all.[37]

Such confidence is a bit breathtaking, given the moral complexity of family life in the 1980s and 1990s. The definition of the "family" was becoming a matter of dispute in American culture, in view of rising numbers of divorced, single-parent, blended and reblended, and same-sex households scattered across the population. Perhaps, in some cases, the single-minded simplicity of advice manuals like Christiansen's found readers weary of complexity. But, one need not delve into their motives, when the fundamentalist roots of neoevangelical literature on the family are obvious. Hidden within the relational language of the 1960s and 1970s are the truths—respect for authority and necessity of obedience—that have framed fundamentalist discussions of the family since the 1930s and 1940s.

Profamily Politics

As political and religious analysts have told the story over the past decade, evangelical, profamily politics galvanized around key issues. The list usually includes the 1962 and 1963 Supreme Court decisions banning prayer and

Bible reading in public schools; the 1973 *Roe v. Wade* abortion decision; the rise of the Moral Majority in the late 1970s; the raucous 1980 White House Conference on Families; and Ronald Reagan's election as an antiabortion, profamily presidential candidate later that fall. By the early 1980s, as conservative think tanks and political action lobbies met on Capitol Hill in Washington, D.C., the agenda for the religious right seemed clear: Behind all the talk and activity about abortion, homosexuality, public schools, and sex education was a single-minded crusade to protect the moral future of the traditional family through fund-raising and electoral campaigning.[38] Small wonder that in 1991, Hunter tagged the family as the "most conspicuous field of battle" and "most decisive battleground" in the ongoing "culture wars" in American society.[39]

Journalists, academics, and politicians struggled to find an explanation for it all, their opinions forming as quickly as lobbyists descended on Capitol Hill. Some saw the religious right as resurgent traditionalism—an antifeminist backlash or a neo-Victorian morality movement—while others argued it was dangerously new—a stalking horse for secular right-wingers in old-line conservative Republican lobbies, or part of a larger "fundamentalist" uprising against modern culture. The analyses contained elements of truth, but proved difficult to apply to the rapidly diversifying mix of evangelical Protestants and conservative Catholics on Capitol Hill. By the mid-1980s, the "religious right" label included such large numbers and so many types of evangelicals, as well as Catholics, that it obscured more than it promised to elucidate. Although often dubbed "fundamentalist" by the media, the new profamily movement was far more, incorporating an array of newly politicized conservatives, everyone from Sun Belt Southern Baptists to "megachurch" Californians, pre-Vatican II Catholics, and the charismatic, Pentecostal followers of television evangelists Jim Bakker and Pat Robertson.

Charting the present and future of the religious right will be a longterm project for journalists and academics, although at this point little has been written about the movement's past. Historians have only begun to sort through the narrative of twentieth-century religious history, and much of the literature on American Protestant fundamentalism disassociates the movement from the more recent religious right, or is bogged down in disputes about the theological ancestry of present-day evangelicals. It is not surprising that so much of the talk about the religious right is framed in psychological and political terms rather than historical, theological ones. But even a brief historical survey yields relevant conclusions about the meaning of religious right politics today. First is the ongoing difficulty in politicizing American fundamentalism, a movement devoted to spiritual, evangelistic ends for much of its twentieth-century history. Political lobbying on behalf of a social gospel has been the province of liberal and mainline Protestants—people with a long-standing theological stake in redeeming American culture.[40] Indeed, television evangelist Jerry Falwell's much-publicized Moral Majority was almost as controversial in doctrinaire fundamentalist circles as it was in the secular media. Fundamentalist educator Bob Jones III dubbed Falwell "the most dangerous man in America" for trading in his separatist credentials for a seat at the table of Washington, D.C., insiders.[41]

A second historical oddity about the religious right is the centrality of the family in its moral and political agenda. As I have argued, the family was the province of more theologically liberal Protestants for most of the twentieth century; even sexuality issues associated with the family—abortion, homosexuality, and premarital and extramarital sex—alarmed mainline Protestants far earlier than they did fundamentalists and conservative evangelicals. Indeed, until the 1960s, "left-wing" Protestants were most likely to mount a political, profamily movement, if the times called for such—not fundamentalists or evangelicals.

Why a politically and theologically conservative evangelical profamily movement? One reason for the politicization of family issues in the 1970s and 1980s is the religious realignment occurring during this time. After the 1960s, membership in mainline and liberal denominations declined precipitously, while conservative evangelical churches boomed. By the late 1980s, the trends were so obvious that the term mainline was an embarrassing misnomer.[42]

The profamily movement emerged when religious conservatives were beginning to feel a sense of cultural power in the wake of Southern Baptist Jimmy Carter's presidential election; *Time* dubbed 1976 the "year of the evangelical." One sign of success was their new role as leading advocates for the American middle-class family. By the early 1970s, evangelicals had constructed a media empire around the family and related issues of gender roles, child discipline, and the moral hazards of adultery and divorce.

The efficacy of the pro-family movement is testimony to the emotions that its moral agenda provoked among grassroots religious conservatives. Well before the Christian Coalition emerged in the national media, a dedi-

cated group of neoevangelical leaders discovered that family matters resonated with churchgoers, providing clear lines between the godly and the
unrighteous. Such issues allowed preachers to invoke personal and social
morality; and they laid down moral boundaries that differentiated believers
from nonbelievers, without rendering religion socially irrelevant. Opposing
abortion, divorce, homosexuality, or teenage pregnancy permitted evangelical leaders to evoke a separatist, fundamentalist past and speak a prophetic
word to present-day American culture. They could be distinctively "Christian" individuals and modern, late-twentieth-century people.

The politicization of abortion among conservative evangelicals provides
an example of this ongoing tension. Before the late 1970s, few evangelicals
worried about abortion, perceiving it primarily as a "Catholic issue."
Indeed, in 1973, the Southern Baptist Convention endorsed *Roe v. Wade*
because it facilitated greater separation between church and state, a long-
standing Baptist emphasis.[43] In 1979, however, two respected evangelical
leaders, Francis A. Schaeffer and C. Everett Koop, published a book and
produced a film series (both with the same title) aimed at stirring conservative Protestants to action. As the 1980 presidential election approached,
Whatever Happened to the Human Race made its way through the evangelical subculture, arguing that the new acceptance for abortion, as well as
euthanasia and infanticide, placed Christians in direct opposition to the secular world. The polarities of the argument, and its sense of moral emergency,
made abortion a center of conflict with secular American society. It also
opened an imperative for political action. The topic of abortion became a
touchstone for a list of moral ills, including homosexuality, pornography,
and extramarital sex—all of which evangelicals traced to the spread of what
they termed "secular humanism." Evangelicals came to understand that
"legal abortion must be stopped not only because it was wrong, morally and
biblically wrong, but also because it was part of a hostile campaign to impose
liberal ideas upon an unwilling Christian populace." Political organization
was the logical recourse, a step vindicated by Reagan's victory in 1980.[44]

Despite the gathering success of the prolife movement among evangelicals, their leaders continued to scout for signs of moral compromise. In
1984, Schaeffer, a staunch fundamentalist Presbyterian during the 1930s
and one of the most respected moral leaders of the neoevangelical revival in
the 1960s and 1970s, published a follow-up book entitled *The Great Evangelical Disaster*. His son Franky Schaeffer, a filmmaker, produced the

accompanying documentary. Together they presented a popular jeremiad against the "post-Christian" spirit of the age—signified most deeply in the feminist movement—and against all evangelicals who embraced it. "Sixty years ago could we have imagined that unborn children would be killed by the millions here in our own country?" the elder Schaeffer demanded. "Or that we would have no freedom of speech when it comes to speaking of God and biblical truth in our public schools? Or that every form of sexual perversion would be promoted by the entertainment media? Or that marriage, raising children, and family life would be objects of attack? Sadly," Schaeffer concluded, "we must say that very few Christians have understood the battle we are in," one of "cosmic proportions." Significantly, *The Great Evangelical Disaster* closed with a passionate diatribe against liberal feminism and a defense of the "biblical pattern" for male and female relationships, spurring a new round of controversy within the evangelical camp about feminism and gender roles.[45]

Events of the past two decades suggest that abortion has served a largely effective "boundary issue," separating the ranks of American evangelicals from the secular world. Opposition to abortion has become a fairly accurate measure of one's separation from "worldliness" and loyalty to evangelical institutions. It has operated as a shorthand protest against a range of moral ills that threatened the sanctity of family life, including undisciplined sexuality, loss of parental control, and (except in the case of a Human Life Amendment to the U.S. Constitution) unwarranted government intrusion.

Conclusion

Although there are many reasons why conservative, evangelical Protestants should be concerned about the family, nostalgia is not one of them. For fundamentalists in the early part of the twentieth century, the family was a worldly metaphor of personal compromise and secular burdens. And while they often joined the chorus of worry about middle-class morality, they were content to let other Protestants, more entangled with secular obligations, lead in its defense. All this changed rapidly after World War II, but many of the basics of fundamentalist piety about the family—the defensive imagery and emphasis on authority—emerged as the scaffold for the new family movement among evangelicals in the 1960s and 1970s. The more recent phase of the profamily movement has lacked the intellectual and cultural resources necessary for broad social leadership—especially through such a moral and political tangle as the family has become in the late-twentieth century. Some of the moral absolutism comes down to cultural inexperience, reflecting the intellectual and moral shallowness of fundamentalist and evangelical engagement with American society.[46]

The persistent mixture of cultural triumphalism and despair in evangelical profamily politics has proven a durable combination. Having recaptured territory that fundamentalists largely had abandoned, modern-day evangelicals are not likely to renounce it without a struggle, as the movement's militant rhetoric continually testifies. At the same time, however, the overall trajectory of the evangelical profamily movement has been toward a broader cultural acceptance and leadership. Evangelicals are "modern" people, quick to adopt technologies or modes of expression they judge useful. While they may see themselves as Babylonian exiles, lost in a culture headed for ruin, they are not likely to abandon it to destruction. In American culture, the family has been a symbol of morality, respectability, and social power. It is a conservative symbol, though as the past few years have made abundantly clear, one with radical implications for the future shape of American society.

Notes

The author wishes to thank the Pew Charitable Trusts for support of the research and writing of this article, and the editors of this issue of the *Journal of Women's History*, Nikki R. Keddie and Jasamin Rostam-Kolayi, and Virginia Brereton, Michael Hamilton, and David Watt for helpful criticisms.

1 Martin Riesebrodt, *Pious Passion: The Emergence of Modern Fundamentalism in the United States and Iran*, trans. Don Reneau (Berkeley: University of California Press, 1993); and Helen Hardacre, "The Impact of Fundamentalism on Women, the Family, and Interpersonal Relationships," in *Fundamentalisms and Society*, ed. Martin E. Marty and R. Scott Appleby (Chicago: University of Chicago Press, 1993), 129-50.

2 William Martin, *With God on Our Side: The Rise of the Religious Right in America* (New York: Broadway Books, 1996); and James Davidson Hunter, *Culture Wars: The Struggle to Define America* (New York: Basic Books, 1991).

3 John C. Green, James L. Guth, Corwin E. Smidt, and Lyman Kellstedt, eds., *Religion and the Culture Wars: Dispatches from the Front* (Lanham, Md.: Rowman and Littlefield, 1996).

4 Betty DeBerg, *Ungodly Women: Gender and the First Wave of American Fundamentalism* (Minneapolis: Fortress Press, 1990); and Margaret Lamberts

Bendroth, *Fundamentalism and Gender, 1875 to the Present* (New Haven, Conn.: Yale University Press, 1993).

5 On pluralism, see R. Stephen Warner, "Work in Progress toward a New Paradigm for the Sociological Study of Religion in the United States," *American Journal of Sociology* 98 (March 1993): 1044-93; and R. Lawrence Moore, *Religious Outsiders and the Making of Americans* (New York: Oxford University Press, 1986).

6 The best source is George Marsden, *Fundamentalism and American Culture: The Shaping of Twentieth-Century Evangelicalism, 1870-1925* (New York: Oxford University Press, 1980).

7 Timothy Weber, *Living in the Shadow of the Second Coming: American Premillennialism, 1875-1982* (Chicago: University of Chicago Press, 1987).

8 The story of the latter stage is told in Joel Carpenter's *Revive Us Again: The Reawakening of American Fundamentalism* (New York: Oxford University Press, 1997).

9 See George Marsden, *Reforming Fundamentalism: Fuller Seminary and the New Evangelicalism* (Grand Rapids, Mich.: Eerdmans, 1987); and Jon R. Stone, *The Boundaries of American Evangelicalism: The Postwar Evangelical Coalition* (New York: St. Martin's Press, 1997).

10 Thus, the term *evangelical* has become exceedingly difficult to define precisely and its lineage is the subject of considerable debate by religious historians and sociologists. See, for example, Donald Dayton and Robert Johnston, eds., *The Variety of American Evangelicalism* (Downers Grove, Ill.: InterVarsity Press, 1991); and Mark Shibley, *Resurgent Evangelicalism in the United States: Mapping Cultural Change since 1970* (Columbia: University of South Carolina Press, 1996).

11 Colleen McDannell, *The Christian Home in Victorian America, 1840-1900* (Bloomington: Indiana University Press, 1986).

12 Gail Bederman, "'The Women Have Had Charge of the Church Work Long Enough': The Men and Religion Forward Movement of 1911-1912 and the Masculinization of Middle-Class Protestantism," *American Quarterly* 41 (September 1989): 43265.

13 Margaret Lamberts Bendroth, *Fundamentalism and Gender*, quotations on 3, 65.

14 See, for example, Charles Trumbull, "Have You Surrendered All?" in *The Victorious Christ* (Philadelphia: Sunday School Times Company, 1923), 106. Christine Heyrman describes a similar reaction among evangelicals within the

antebellum South in *Southern Cross: The Beginnings of the Bible Belt* (New York: Knopf, 1997).

15 Harry A. Ironside's letter quoted in E. Schuyler English, *H. A. Ironside: Ordained of the Lord* (New York: Loizeaux Bros., 1946), 192.

16 James H. Brookes, "At Home with the Lord," *Truth, or Testimony for Christ* 5, (December 1876): and Elizabeth Needham, "Leprosy in Houses," *Truth, or Testimony for Christ* 8 (August 1882): 418. See also Margaret Lamberts Bendroth, *Fundamentalism and Gender*, chap. 2.

17 L. W. S., "The Christian Home," *Presbyterian Guardian* 7 (January 1940): 73.

18 Edith L. Blumhofer, *Aimee Semple McPherson: Everybody's Sister* (Grand Rapids, Mich.: Eerdmans, 1993); and William McLoughlin, *Billy Sunday Was His Real Name* (Chicago: University of Chicago Press, 1995). "I would rather have my children taught sex hygiene than Greek and Latin," Billy Sunday told an audience of women in 1917. See Billy Sunday, "Sunday's Sermon 'For Women Only,'" *Boston Globe*, 12 January 1917, 9.

19 John R. Rice, "Whipping Children," *Sword of the Lord*, 11 May 1945, 3. See also John R. Rice, *The Home, Courtship, Marriage, and Children* (Wheaton, Ill.: Sword of the Lord Publishing, 1945).

20 "Making the Home Christian," *Northwestern Pilot* 25 (October 1945): 26.

21 Charles C. Ryrie, "Is Your Home Scriptural?" *Bibliotheca Sacra* 109 (October-December 1952): 346-52.

22 See Horace Bushnell, *Christian Nurture* (1861; reprint, Cleveland, Ohio: Pilgrim Press, 1994); Stephen A. Schmidt, *History of the Religious Education Association* (Birmingham, Ala.: Religious Education Press, 1983); and Elaine Tyler May, "Myths and Realities of the American Family," *A History of Private Life: Riddles of Identity in Modern Times*, ed. Antoine Prost and Gerard Vincent (Cambridge, Mass.: Harvard University Press, 1991), 539-92.

23 Elaine Tyler May, *Homeward Bound: American Families in the Cold War Era* (New York: HarperCollins, 1988).

24 Robert W. Battles, "What about Television?" *Sunday School Times*, November 26, 1955, 941-42. See also Margaret Lamberts Bendroth, "Fundamentalism and the Media, 1930-1990," *Religion and Mass Media: Audiences and Adaptations*, ed. Daniel Stout and Judith Buddenbaum (Thousand Oaks, Calif.: Sage Publications, 1996), 74-84.

25 Dennison Nash and Peter Berger, "The Child, the Family, and the 'Religious Revival' in Suburbia," *Journal for the Scientific Study of Religion* 1-2 (October-April 1961-1963): 85-93. For the story of one particular denomination, see

William B. Kennedy, "Neo-Orthodoxy Goes to Sunday School," *Journal of Presbyterian History* 58 (winter 1990): 326-71.

26 Marsden, *Reforming Fundamentalism*; and William Martin, *A Prophet with Honor: The Billy Graham Story* (New York: William Morrow, 1991).

27 David Harrington Watt, *A Transforming Faith: Explorations of Twentieth-Century American Evangelicalism* (New Brunswick, N.J.: Rutgers University Press, 1991), 85.

28 See Phyllis Airhart and Margaret Lamberts Bendroth, eds., *Faith Traditions and the Family* (Louisville, Ky.: Westminster/John Knox Press, 1996).

29 See, for example, JoAnn Menkus, "Women: How Far Will They Go?" *Eternity* 21 (June 1970): 34; "Antifeminism: Are You Guilty?" *Eternity* 21 (September 1970): 7; "That Women's Rights Amendment," *Christianity Today* 14 (6 November 1970): 134; and Ruth Schmidt, "Second-Class Citizenship in the Kingdom of God," *Christianity Today* 14 (1 January 1971): 321-22.

30 Literature on this subject abounds. See, for example, Watt, *Transforming Faith*, 93-136; Judith Stacey, *Brave New Families: Stories of Domestic Upheaval in Late Twentieth Century America* (New York: Basic Books, 1991), 41-174; and Mark Chaves, *Ordaining Women: Culture and Conflict in Religious Organizations* (Cambridge, Mass.: Harvard University Press, 1997).

31 S. Maxwell Coder, "The Christian Family and the Word of God," *Moody Monthly* 61 (August 1961): 15-16.

32 See Diane Chico Kessler, *Parents and the Experts: Can Christian Parents Accept the Experts' Advice?* (Valley Forge, Penn.: Judson Press, 1974).

33 Wilfred Bockelman, *Bill Gothard: The Man and His Ministry: An Evaluation* (Santa Barbara, Calif.: Quill Publications, 1976). See also Bill Gothard, Jr., "The Chain of Command," *Faith for the Family* 3 (March/April 1975): 11-12. For a similar testimony, see Nancy Ammerman, *Bible Believers: Fundamentalists in the Modern World* (New Brunswick, N.J.: Rutgers University Press, 1987).

34 Rodney Clapp, "Meet James Dobson, His Father's Son," *Christianity Today* 22 (7 May 1982): 14; and "Focus at Fifteen," *Focus on the Family Magazine* 16 (March 1992): 10.

35 See, for example, Philip Greven, *Spare the Child: The Religious Roots of Punishment and the Psychological Impact of Physical Abuse* (New York: Vintage Books, 1990); and Donald E. Sloat, *Growing Up Holy and Wholly: Understanding and Hope for Adult Children of Evangelicals* (Brentwood, Tenn.: Wolgemuth and Hyatt, 1990).

36 James Davidson Hunter, *Evangelicalism: The Coming Generation* (Chicago: University of Chicago Press, 1987).

37 Larry Christiansen and Nordis Christiansen, *The Christian Couple* (Minneapolis: Bethany Fellowship, 1977), 21-22.

38 Martin, *With God on Our Side*; and Michael Lienesch, *Redeeming America: Piety and Politics in the New Christian Right* (Chapel Hill: University of North Carolina Press, 1993).

39 Hunter, *Culture Wars* (New York: Basic Books, 1999), 176.

40 William McGuire King, "The Reform Establishment and the Ambiguities of Influence," *Between the Times: The Travail of the Protestant Establishment in America, 1900-1960*, ed. William R. Hutchison (Cambridge, Mass.: Harvard University Press, 1989),122-40.

41 James Guth, "The Politics of the Christian Right," *Religion and the Culture Wars*, 9-29.

42 Robert Wuthnow, *The Restructuring of American Religion: Society and Faith since World War II* (Princeton, N.J.: Princeton University Press, 1988).

43 Cynthia Gorney, *Articles of Faith: A Frontline History of the Abortion Wars* (New York: Simon and Schuster, 1998), 340-42.

44 Ibid, 343. See also Elizabeth Mensch and Alan Freeman, *The Politics of Virtue: Is Abortion Debatable?* (Durham, N.C.: Duke University Press, 1993); and Kristin Luker, *Abortion and the Politics of Motherhood* (Berkeley: University of California Press, 1984).

45 Francis A. Schaeffer, *The Great Evangelical Disaster* (Westchester, Ill.: Crossway Books, 1984), 23. See, for example, "The Danvers Statement" (paid advertisement, sponsored by the Council on Biblical Manhood and Womanhood) *Christianity Today* 32.

46 See, for example, Mark Noll, *The Scandal of the Evangelical Mind* (Grand Rapids, Mich.: Eerdmans, 1994).

The Pro-Life Gospel

Susan Friend Harding

From *The Book of Jerry Falwell* (Princeton University Press 2002)

> *Someone else's words introduced into our own speech inevitably assume a new (our own) interpretation and become subject to our evaluation of them; that is, they become double-voiced. All that can vary is the interrelationship between these two voices. Our practical everyday speech is full of other people's words; with some of them we completely merge our own voice, forgetting whose they are; others, which we take as authoritative, we use to reinforce our own words; still others, finally, we populate with our own aspirations, alien or hostile to them.*
>
> —M. M. Bakhtin, 1984

The bedroom scene on the dust cover of *If I Should Die before I Wake . . .* evokes a sense of innocent remembrance, a wistfulness, a moment you will never forget, a moment laced with haunting, foreboding feelings.[1] The room is bare. The bassinet is empty. Something's missing. The ellipsis in the book's title bespeaks incompleteness as well. More literally, the title alludes to the nearness of death, appropriating an old, familiar Protestant Prayer (Now I lay me down to sleep/ I pray the Lord my soul to keep/ If I should die before I wake/ I Pray the Lord my soul to take), and converting it into an eerie allusion to abortion. Not any abortion—it could have been me, it could have been you. The empty cradle flashes back and forth between womb and coffin, a spooky place that mingles sleep and terror, birth and death, safety and danger, innocence and error.

Jesus Christ, the Lord of the prayer, silently brackets the title. He is imaged in the light, accompanied by the Holy Spirit in the gentle wind, coming through the window, bringing hope and the possibility of overcoming evil. He merges with the visible sense that "something is missing," a phrase that appears frequently in conversion stories. Christ is the "something" that is missing. Christ and the missing baby coalesce. The bassinet

281

intimates the manger and the empty tomb. Abortion echoes crucifixion, the slaughter of innocents. Saving babies partakes of Bethlehem, the resurrection, salvation, and the Blesséd Hope.

In the words of the dust jacket blurb: "If I Should Die before I Wake . . . is *the story of Falwell's dedication to creating an alternative to abortion—but with an unusual twist. Jennifer Simpson, one of the first young women to join the Liberty Godparent Homes program (providing homes for pregnant teenagers) tells the story of the decision she made. With chapters alternating between Falwell and Jennifer,* If I Should Die before I Wake . . . *breaks down the barriers of misunderstanding by offering a hopeful alternative to this overwhelming issue."*

The two voices, Jerry's and Jennifer's, and their stories unfold and intertwine across twelve chapters. Their narrative moves are interdependent. She must choose, twice, whether to sacrifice her unborn child. He is called, twice, and must choose how to sacrifice himself on behalf of the unborn. The fetal person is passed back and forth between them, first aborted, then newborn. Her stories prepare the ground for his action; she participates, speaks upon, jointly produces, becomes the landscape for his heroic response, his sacrificial action, which then opens the way for her narrative to move on, indeed, changes the world around her so that her story may have, through her reciprocal sacrificial action, a new ending, a new beginning. She bears her baby; he bears the world in which her baby may be born.

If I Should Die before I Wake . . . is a masterfully seductive and intimate missive of almost love-letter intensity from its preacher-author to his people-readers. Jerry Falwell's born-again readers know they are handling a gospel text—a life-changing text of love, death, and redemption—if not from his name alone, then from the dust cover intimations of something missing. If they read *If I Should Die* as they read the Bible, its juxtaposed and laminated stories will pile up, talk to each other, and narrate a multidimensional world that speaks to readers, pulls them into its inner spaces, and becomes truth. The text will prepare a place for its readers, a kind of gospel passage, through a series of sacrifice stories that are perpetually incomplete, marking a loss, an absence, something given and not returned—an empty cradle—and engendering a desire, a longing, for wholeness, completion, return—rebirth. Readers may fill in what is missing by contributing substantially to the gospel at hand and, more meaningfully, they may be themselves infilled by the Holy Spirit, that is, they may undergo subtle and much sought-after changes of habit and of heart.

These born-again cries and whispers would likely be lost on unborn-again readers, especially unborn-again feminist readers, who might be more inclined to read through the name Jerry Falwell, the book's title, the dust jacket, and all the stories to a polemical subtext about abortion, sexuality, gender, family, feminism, and patriarchy. The sentimental language of *If I Should Die* would become translucent—like a veil thinly disguising what the book is "really" about—reaffirming gender differences, vilifying abortion and feminism, revitalizing patriarchy, and raising money. Jerry and Jennifer's enticing labyrinth of stories of sacrifice, redemption, and unearthly love would give way to something more sinister, monolithic, authoritarian, conspiratorial, and profitable. This and other hypothetical unborn-again readings are not necessarily wrong, but they tell us more about feminist than fundamentalist subjectivity.[2]

Falwell's book is an instance of born-again Christian language whose principal interlocutor is feminism. The text—and Falwell's pro-life gospel more generally—appropriates a central feminist narrative ("women are sexual victims of men and patriarchy, and abortion liberates them"), renarrates it from a born-again point of view, and thus produces and reproduces that point of view in willing readers. The language of *If I Should Die* does not express or reflect, say, male domination as if it were a code underlying the text. Rather, the text is more like a workshop producing born-again Christian subjectivity out of raw materials provided by the feminist, and particularly the pro-choice, movement. That is, the book, and the pro-life campaign generally, performs an act of cultural domination, one in which born-again language appropriates and converts feminist language to its terms.

The fact that *If I Should Die* is written as a collection of vignettes, rather than, say, a polemic, is what makes it productive, subjectively speaking, for born-again readers. Bible-based story-telling transfers access to born-again Christian discourse, as a whole and in its parts. Being born-again means figuring oneself and one's world in biblically framed stories, on a narrative landscape which simultaneously speaks biblical and contemporaneous dialects, submitting the latter to the terms of the former. *If I Should Die*'s biblically framed stories of transformation fashion a narrative rite of passage, which, as readers undergo it, as they infill its strategic gaps, transfers narrative authority to them: the right, the ability, and the desire to speak the pro-life gospel and to bring about the world it speaks.

The transfer of born-again narrative authority from speaker to listener depends on gender, on a difference between "male" and "female," in two ways: it is a movement across the gender boundary from a "male" (saved, speaker, author) to a "female" (lost, listener, reader) position; and it is a moment of rebirth, a second (spiritual, Fathered) birth that overtakes the first (fleshly, mothered) birth, converting the lost into the saved, "female" into "male."

Modern feminism challenges fundamental gender asymmetries, hence the very mechanism by which born-again Christian subjectivity is reproduced. The narrative rituals of *If I Should Die* contest the feminist challenge in a number of ways: first, through its reiterated enactments of gendered asymmetries, both in and across male and female bodies; second, by inventing a born-again, that is, biblically framed, tradition of opposition to abortion; and third, by reconfiguring and occupying the cultural turf claimed by feminism, the space of women's reproduction, before and after birth.

If the dust cover scene intimated that the languages of gender and born-again Christianity would intersect in *If I Should Die*, its prologue ("Who Will Answer the Challenge?") carries the whole project in embryonic form. The opening scene, an encounter between Falwell and a presumably secular female reporter, transforms, or converts, Falwell and launches him on his journey across the landscape of women's bodies, authorizing both his book and his mission. Cornered by reporters in a nameless airport, flashbulbs popping, microphones thrust into his face, Jerry Falwell endures another impromptu press conference. Just as he breaks away, a young newswoman, also nameless, tags him with one last question, as Falwell reports: *"You say you are against abortion . . . but what practical alternative do pregnant girls have when they are facing an unwanted pregnancy?" "They can have the baby,"* Falwell replies. The reporter persists: *"Do you really think it's that simple?"* Falwell is taken aback. *I looked at her for a moment in silence. This was not just a reporter's question, asked to fill space in a paper or on the evening news. The look in the eyes of that reporter made me feel that her question came from deep and private places down inside her. . . .*

"Most of the girls in this country facing an unwanted pregnancy are young and poor and helpless," she said, taking advantage of my silence. . . . *"Is it enough to take a stand against abortion,"* the woman concluded, *"when you aren't doing anything to help the pregnant girls who have no other way?. . . . Out of that confrontation a dream was born. I decided that the reporter was*

right. It wasn't enough to be against abortion. Millions of babies were being killed, and I would go on fighting to save their lives, but what about the other victims of abortion, the mothers of those babies who desperately need help to save their babies? [3]

The encounter appears mundane but it is charged with born-again Christian allusions and biblical pretexts. Echoing of Paul's encounter on the road to Damascus, Falwell's appropriation of women's reproductive issues is an oblique replay of Christian conversion in which a spiritual birth mediated by the Father subverts, overcomes, natural female birth. As a story of Falwell's election to answer the challenge, the encounter recalls biblical tales of God's calling prophets and apostles in which unwitting moral inferiors figure as messengers, momentarily occupying the "male" position of superior speech as they deliver God's word to a man of God. *Out of that confrontation a dream was born* implies an annunciation of sorts and reinforces the figuring of Falwell in the "female," or listening, position.

Born-again readers come to a gospel text prepared to place themselves in its stories in the "female" position and to undergo its transformations. Falwell makes this understanding between himself and his readers explicit at the end of the prologue, where he begins to fashion the sacrificial passage and to prepare a reciprocal place for his readers, both men and women. He makes plain that his sacrifice will soon enough call forth theirs: *This book is my answer to that reporter's question. I've asked Jennifer Simpson . . . to tell her dramatic true story in chapters that alternate with mine. You may know a young lady like her. Or you may be facing this problem now, just as she did. Or you may be simply watching the abortion battle from the sidelines, as I once did, trying to decide what you believe and whether or not to become involved. "Is there no other way but abortion?" I believe we have found an answer to that reporter's question. Read on and see if you agree.*[4]

What's missing in the airport encounter? The lack, the incompleteness, in the scene is opened up by the reporter's question: the space of reproduction, women's bodies, will become the ground for redemptive speech and action. As Falwell ("man") publicly acknowledges the right of the reporter ("woman") to speak for herself and other women, he acquires the right to appropriate her concern, in effect, her power, and with it strikes out to fashion a new pro-family rhetoric. The reporter is a working woman, assertive and articulate, representing women's point of view. She stands for feminism, though a feminism domesticated before it is even spoken—she hails him as

"Dr. Falwell." Her words do not close off but rather open up the subject—women, their reproductive power and problems—to him, his gaze, his speech. It is she who portrays women who need abortions as young, helpless, poor victims. It is she, not he, who places them under him and, like the babies they carry, in need of his help.

She, in effect, delivers him the feminist story line, which he then reimagines. The feminist image of a woman gaining control over her body and her life through abortion rights becomes *the other victim of abortion,* a helpless girl who is driven to abortion because she has no other way. With a few more strokes of a pen, *If I Should Die* converts another feminist image, that of men opposing abortion rights to deprive women of elemental, bodily equality and liberty, into an image of a born-again male hero rising up in the country of reproducing women, a man-father-Father figure who will save girl-mothers, as well as babies, from the maw of abortion.

We are forewarned that this occupation of the rhetorical territory claimed by feminism with born-again narrative figures and frames will be a complex one by the unusual gender arrangements in the encounter: a female reporter asks Jerry Falwell a question he cannot answer, and Falwell, silenced, opens up, listens to this brassy young woman who throws him off guard in public. Their exchange is intimate—she holds him with her speech at some length, and he looks into her eyes, into *deep and private places down inside her.* As her words enter him, his gaze enters her, and he is infilled with a dream. Together they become, in a way, the first Liberty Godparents. What is unusual, of course, is the role reversal in the reproductive metaphor: she takes on a "male" privilege, public speech, and he is feminized in the encounter by submitting, by listening, to a woman and giving birth to a dream—the Liberty Godparent gospel and ministry.

Men may occupy the "female" position and women the "male" position in Christian dialogues; but the point is not that men and women are equal, any more than the fact that the "male" speaking position is marked "superior" means that men necessarily dominate women. The gender reversals in the encounter between Falwell and the female reporter are not "really" about bodily men and women; instead, the reversals engender, and reengender, the essential subject positions in born-again discourse. The point is that gender differences produce born-again Christian subjectivity, not the reverse. Gender differences are, of course, created in the process of being deployed, but as a side effect or, rather, an a priori supplement of born-again discourse. Gender is both the rib and the "without which not" of born-again Christian identity formation.

To the extent that feminism made gender a public issue and declared war on its asymmetries, the movement was liable to provoke a reaction from born-again Christians, who speak themselves through a submerged display of asymmetrical gender meanings. How abortion rights came to be such an incandescent issue for born-again Christians is somewhat less straightforward.

Catholics drew on a long tradition of speech and action to protest promptly the 1973 Supreme Court decision *Roe v. Wade* repealing state bans on abortion. Evangelical Protestants did not respond immediately, but by the early 1980s they had become formidable abortion foes, contributing much materially, organizationally, and rhetorically to what had become known as the pro-life movement. Social movements often seem to arise abruptly, but a little historical inquiry usually reveals precedents and roots, a network of premovement organizations and ideas that anticipated and gave form and content to the movement. No such prior history exists in the case of the born-again movement against abortion.

The mid-nineteenth-century campaigns which banned abortion in many states were led by physicians, not Protestant preachers. There is little record of organized public opposition to abortion by conservative Protestants in the twentieth century until the late 1970s.[5] Debate over abortion in the late 1960s and early 1970s was largely limited to evangelical scholars and physicians who disagreed about the conditions under which therapeutic abortion was advised—and they generally agreed that therapeutic abortions were permissible under some circumstances. In 1968, an institute run by *Christianity Today*, the leading evangelical magazine, organized a symposium on the subject of birth control and abortion. A variety of positions were aired but the official publication of the symposium affirmed the principle that "the Christian physician will advise induced abortion only to safeguard greater values sanctioned by Scripture. These values should include individual health, family welfare, and social responsibility."[6] A special issue of *Eternity* magazine on abortion in 1971 still presented a range of opinions on the circumstances under which abortion might be advised.[7]

A more extreme position that opposed abortion under any circumstances first emerged around the same time in the course of internal debates among conservative Protestants. The forums organized by *Christianity Today* and

Eternity marginalized that position, but the tables turned in the middle and late 1970s. After the 1973 *Roe v. Wade* decision, which rendered legally moot the whole category of "therapeutic abortion" by defining abortion as a woman's right, a half dozen conservative evangelical scholars intensified the critique of the moderate evangelical position, "laying the deeper scriptural and social reasons for opposing abortion."[8] A consensus against any notion of "abortion-on-demand," which is how conservative evangelicals generally defined a woman's right to abortion, crystallized very quickly, and gradually prominent supporters of therapeutic abortion either publicly changed their minds or stopped speaking out.[9] By the mid-1980s, most conservative Protestants were convinced that a strict pro-life position was both God's word and the traditional Christian position.

Occasionally, there appeared public evidence that a number of theologically conservative Protestants continued to support a less strict position on abortion rights. In 1984, when pro-life campaigns were reaching their peak, an attempt by the student government of Wheaton College, the nation's premier evangelical liberal arts college, to adopt a strong anti-abortion resolution produced such a heated public debate among the faculty and the college-at-large that no public resolution was possible. And according to 1992 figures, 50 percent of the white evangelical Protestant voters surveyed said they were pro-life, but the rest did not, including 25 percent of regular church attendees who said they were pro-choice.[10] The point, therefore, is not that conservative Protestants all agree about abortion rights—they do not—but that during the course of the 1980s a "pro-life gospel" was invented, traditionalized, and became so dominant among them that dissenters seemed to disappear. Moreover, the formation of this consensus was a major, perhaps the major, linchpin of both born-again Christianity as a cultural hybrid and the New Christian Right as a political movement.

The born-again pro-life tradition came together in three overlapping stages and venues. The first was the above-mentioned internal debate among evangelical scholars and intellectual leaders that heated up after the 1973 *Roe v. Wade* decision. Much of the debate was published in *Christianity Today*, which became markedly more conservative after Harold Lindsell took over the editorship from Carl Henry in September 1968, a month after the *Christianity Today* symposium on birth control and abortion. The second stage, the effort to convert conservative Protestant leaders more generally to a stricter antiabortion position, was launched in 1975 when Billy Graham convened a two-day leadership meeting to "determine a proper Biblical response to abortion-on-demand."[11] That meeting produced the Christian Action Council dedicated to challenging existing abortion policies as well as to internal education.

Perhaps the most important event in this second stage was the production and distribution in 1978 of the five-part film series *Whatever Happened to the Human Race?*. The film and an accompanying book with the same title were written by Francis Schaeffer IV and C. Everett Koop, then surgeon-in-chief at the Children's Hospital in Philadelphia and later to become Ronald Reagan's surgeon general.

Schaeffer and Koop starred in *Whatever Happened to the Human Race?*, which was scripted and directed by Francis Schaeffer's son Franky, and it is widely credited with turning the tide of popular evangelical opinion against abortion. Schaeffer and Koop were disappointed by the turnout for the seminars they conducted after the film was released, but the film itself, which was distributed to churches all over the country, took on a life of its own.[12] It probably did directly, or indirectly through hearsay, convert many conservative Protestants to an antiabortion position. More importantly, it created and popularized a good many of the subsequently staple pro-life rhetorical stances, including highly compelling ethical, historical, and biblical rationales for born-again Christian activism more generally.

The film series, first of all, never tried to proof-text opposition to abortion or to certify its position in narrow biblical literal terms. Instead, the film grounded its opposition in a version of biblical inerrancy that had become Schaeffer's signature. He argued for the truth of the whole Bible, for the presuppositional truths regarding the existence and character of God upon which the Bible's truth rests.[13] The personhood of the fetus, according to Schaeffer, logically follows from the facts of God's existence and his nature, and because all persons are made in God's image, abortion, like the killing of any other innocent person, violates God directly. The film also exploited scientific disagreements and the changing legal definitions of fetal viability, arguing that such uncertainty could only lead to a constant erosion of constraints. Koop may or may not have invented the practice of reciting in graphic detail how every available abortion technique actually terminates the life of a fetus, but his recitation, as the camera panned slowly over a thousand naked baby dolls scattered on the dimly lit salt flats of the Dead Sea, was perhaps the film's most disquieting episode.

The film also featured the faces, voices, and lives of ordinary men, women, and children who had been saved by heroic medical measures as infants under Koop's care, but whom other doctors, Koop said, would have let languish and die. Koop argued passionately that passive infanticide and euthanasia were already occurring in many hospitals and nursing homes. He and Schaeffer asserted over and over that, if tolerated, these practices would inevitably result, first, in active, and then in state-managed, mandatory infanticide and euthanasia of unwanted individuals and groups.

All this was coming about because of the *Roe v. Wade* decision and the deeper social change it signaled, the eclipse of the Judeo-Christian consensus as the moral and legal basis of Western society. *Roe v. Wade* was possible because the Judeo-Christian consensus and its "high view of human life" had been displaced by humanism (materialism, naturalism) and its "low view of human life." This is another one of Schaeffer's signature arguments, as was the slippery slope-ism that saturated *Whatever Happened to the Human Race?*. Because abortion is permitted, passive infanticide and euthanasia are increasingly tolerated, and later all three will be mandated, and then we will be living in a state exactly like Nazi Germany. Eerie, dark images of shackled blacks, old-world Jews, elderly men and women, handicapped children, and babies in cages combine with the film's voice-over to fashion a rhetoric of equivalence between slavery, the holocaust, abortion, infanticide, euthanasia, and state control.[14]

In the immediate context of the debates among conservative Protestants during the 1970s over the validity of therapeutic or partial abortion rights, the film's coup de grâce was its failure even to acknowledge any internal conflict. There was one not-Christian, humanistic, position, which would permit abortion under some or all circumstances, and there was one Christian position, which would not.

Whatever Happened to the Human Race? did not create overnight legions of pro-life born-again cadres as Schaeffer and Koop had hoped it would, but it produced and disseminated the grounds for that mobilization. Through the starkness of its terms, its powerful, memorable visual and verbal rhetorics, and its national grassroots distribution to conservative Protestant churches of all stripes, the film established the framework within which opposition to abortion rights came to be understood as the modal, "traditional" Christian position. During the early 1980s, in the third stage in the formation of the tradition of born-again opposition to abortion, this framework was customized and filled in by hundreds of local and national ministries. And it was this process that created pro-life cadres, men and women who would sacrifice themselves financially and otherwise in New Christian Right campaigns against abortion.

This final stage of born-again cultural mobilization against abortion was similar to what happened among American evangelical Protestants in the North in the 1830s, when rhetoric against slavery rather suddenly intensified, shifting from a commitment to gradual abolition to a call for immediate abolition. Preachers, each in their own idiom, reinscribed slavery as the ultimate expression of sinful self-gratification, and the commitment to immediate abolition became a kind of rebirth, hence a sign of whether or not someone was truly saved. Abolition accordingly became, like faith in Christ itself, a form of evangelism and preaching the gospel of abolition, a sacred vocation.[15]

In the early 1980s, preachers and lay leaders around the country "biblicalized" total opposition to abortion each in their own idioms, piling up varied ways of figuring and framing the abortion issue in both theological and vernacular terms that resonated with their communities. Overall, they pulled opposition to abortion into the very heart of what it meant to be a born-again Christian, made it a sign of faith and a gospel that must be preached far and wide. For Jerry Falwell, the Liberty Godparent Home campaign also presented the opportunity for him to combine two major dialects, his natal fundamental Baptist tongue and the more mainstream conservative evangelical tongue he was in the course of acquiring.

Early in the evolution of his pro-life rhetoric, Jerry Falwell, in his sermons and in the literature produced by his ministry, demonstrated God's opposition to abortion in the conventional fundamentalist manner. He and his collaborators cited dozens of biblical verses that "prove" God opposes abortion; he also embedded the "sin of abortion" in the premillennial vision of the end-times, a period of rampant immorality and social decay that precedes the rapture, the Great Tribulation, the Battle of Armageddon and the Second Coming of Christ.[16] Although resistance to more liberal sexual practices and gender relations is audible here, Falwell and his copastors did not directly elaborate the sin of abortion as an attack on the family or family values. Rather, from the beginning, they figured it as an ultimate violation of the relationship between person and God. Probably borrowing from

Schaeffer and Koop, they put abortion, on a par—a slippery slope—with murder, the holocaust, the slaughter of innocents, and, they added, the crucifixion of Christ.

Falwell's Liberty Godparent campaign intensified and expanded this process of biblicalizing opposition to abortion. In terms of imagery, the campaign's major innovation was to place the womb and the fetus in the background and instead to foreground pregnant girls—the female bodies, lives, and experiences that surround endangered fetuses. In *If I Should Die,* this ground, the embodied landscape upon which Falwell acts, is most fully fashioned by Jennifer, in other words, by a woman-in-need-of-abortion elaborated as helpless victim.

Falwell's own early chapters, on the other hand, narrate the birth of the hero who would save her as they describe Falwell's gradual conversion to pro-life activism. Thus we are given to understand that even before he met the reporter in the airport or formed the Moral Majority, he was at least on the road to Damascus. Given the agreement of born-again readers to undergo the transformations of anointed authors, Falwell's story becomes his readers', and his prehistory becomes their experience. Falwell's story, though only lightly marked by biblical cues, also manages to nest abortion and antiabortion activism fully in the central narrative frames that transfer—reproduce—authority in born-again culture, that is, within the frames of the gospel of Christ's death, burial, and resurrection. Later on in her chapters, Jennifer takes on and embodies this rhetorical innovation.

One of the "credentials" of hard-core pro-life activists is that they can remember where they were and what they were doing the day the *Roe v. Wade* decision came down.[17] In his first chapter in *If I Should Die,* Falwell describes reading about the decision in the newspaper as his eggs, bacon, raisin toast, and coffee grew cold—and, behold, antiabortion rhetoric came fully formed into his head. Indeed, it had been there a long time:

I will never forget the morning of January 23, 1973. . . . The Supreme Court had just made a seven to two decision that would legalize the killing of a generation of unborn children. I couldn't believe that seven justices on that Court could be so callous about the dignity of human life. Were they misinformed? Had they been misled? Were they plunging the nation into a time of darkness and shame without even knowing what they were doing? . . . I had preached on abortion and its meaning to my people and had used abortion as an example in several sermons over the past ten years.[18] But, as I read the paper that day, I knew something more had to be done, and I felt a growing conviction that I would have to take my stand among the people who were doing it.[19]

There were other signs, small moments of *growing conviction*—for example, when Jerry *saw a full-color picture of an unborn child . . . a tiny, trusting child whom God had created*—but he *still hesitated to take a public stand.*[20] It was his children who officially mediated his actual conversion to political action. During family devotions, when Falwell laments *the legal murder of millions of America's unborn children,* his children call him to task: *"Why don't you do something about it, Dad?" my spunky red-headed son finally interrupted, rising up on one elbow and looking me in the eye. "Yeah," chimed in my daughter. "Do something for the babies."* [21] His children hounded him for weeks. He prayed and argued, his *convictions began to grow,* and he finally overcame his fundamentalist scruples about activism and *jumped into the political arena feet first.* If God later would use a woman, the reporter, to deliver Falwell access to women's reproductive issues, he first used children to give him access to the plight of the unborn.

Still, according to the official record, years passed between this moment and Falwell's public debut as a political leader, when he formed the Moral Majority. Falwell occupied the time, it turns out, educating himself, reading everything he could get his hands on concerning the issues, voraciously consuming all manner of texts, academic and popular, legal, medical, scientific, and political. When, in his second chapter, Falwell takes us through what he learned, we find ourselves caught up in a welter of stories of fetal life and death.

Jerry tells us about the dumpster in Los Angeles stuffed with the remains of 1,700 human babies, mutilated, tiny fetal bodies all torn to pieces, hands chopped off, and the incinerator of burning bags of dead babies from a hospital in Wichita. He lifts the terror briefly to envision how Jennifer's first baby would have developed had she (yes, "she") lived, only to recount, in graphic detail, how she was torn from her *liquid nursery,* her *secret sanctuary,* and disposed of by medical personnel. *There would be no monument for the courageous struggle for life the baby mounted until she died.* [22] Lengthy, detailed, vivid descriptions of abortion methods follow. *Picture it.* Cutting the body into pieces, crushing the head, extracting, sucking the pieces into a container.

Falwell's recounting here is, for him, notably free of biblical citations which would prove that the fetus is "life" and abortion "murder." He refrains from overtly sacralizing the first birth, and, instead, renders it in secular terms and deploys "scientific facts" to construct abortion as murder. The account's relentless, detailed facticity squares with the tradition of "common sense empiricism" in fundamentalism, and also with Falwell's personal narrative, by generating the worldly ground upon which he will take his public stand—and enjoin his readers to take theirs.[23]

Still, there is a way in which Falwell's figuring of fetal life and death in *If I Should Die* worms its way into the core of born-again discourse. Any narrative reiteration of life versus death would, but the fetal struggle also has the potential of meta-commentary, of commenting on Christian discourse itself, which Falwell's account fully realizes. In effect, he figures abortion as the death of the first ("female") birth, a death which precludes the second ("male") birth and thus disrupts the narrative transfer of spiritual authority.

All that chopping and cutting, the excessively vivid, repeated dismembering of little unborn babies resonates, not automatically, but as an outcome of preacherly rhetoric, as sinful sacrifice, as ritual action that defiles and destroys the relationship between person and God, as abolishing the very context in which the relationship might be restored. Among fundamental Baptists, as we have seen, the first birth prefigures the second birth in the same way that Abraham's willingness to sacrifice Isaac prefigured Christ's death and resurrection. The first story frames, enables, anticipates the second story. It marks an incompleteness which the second story fills, fulfills. The second story depends on, cannot happen without, the first story. What if Abraham had disobeyed God in the end and actually killed his son? No Isaac, no Christ. That, Falwell's rhetoric implies, is what abortion does. It destroys the first story/birth ("female," flesh) which prefigures the second story/birth ("male," spirit), thus cutting, chopping the narrative channel which transfers born-again authority. Constituted in these terms, the right to abortion puts the very heart of born-again Christianity— the central narrative frames and figures by which it produces, and reproduces, subjectivity—at stake.

Jennifer's chapters weave in and out of Falwell's, unfolding the intimate, vulnerable, embodied landscape upon which Falwell, and other born-again preachers and believers, must act. He invites his readers to look at abortion from "the woman's point of view," first implicitly in his long review of the physical and psychological damage (ranging from uterine perforations to drug addiction, from bad marriages to suicide) inflicted on women who have abortions, and then explicitly just before Jennifer begins her abortion story. *Try to feel how she felt that awful day her baby died.*[24] But it is she who takes up where the reporter left off and constitutes the born-again version of the woman's point of view, filling the feminist space of "adult women exercising control over their bodies" with the image of "a teenage girl who needs help."

Whereas Falwell was inventing born-again tradition in fashioning a prehistory and new biblically based narrative grounds for anti-abortion activism, Jennifer works against the grain of a born-again interpretive legacy regarding teenage unwed mothers. That legacy would cast girls like Jennifer in a war against sin, vilifying them as sexual transgressors, framing the maternity homes, the homes for unwed mothers, as places to hide in shame, and posing childbirth and child rearing as the price that must be paid for sin. With Falwell's help, Jennifer reinscribes the girls as innocent, in the sense of naive or abused, victims. The home for unwed mothers becomes a place where teenage lives are restored, and out-of-wedlock childbirth, God's will. It turns out that the better way which Falwell conceives in his prophet-making scene with the reporter includes giving up for adoption the babies saved from abortion, and, accordingly, the Liberty Godparent Home is at once a pleasant maternity home for teenage girls and an adoption agency for married, born-again Christian couples.

It seems that Falwell and his collaborators were not simply responding to feminism but also adjusting their language and practice to certain facts of born-again life in the 1980s. Even in their communities, more teenagers were having sex, girls were getting pregnant and having abortions, and (white) couples who wished to adopt were finding (white) babies scarce.[25] The adjustment was not an easy one, however. By what narrative logic may girls be led to give their babies up for adoption after so much ink has been spilled convincing them to save them from abortion? Several chapters of *If I Should Die* are devoted directly to making this "difficult decision," and Jennifer's and the other Liberty Godparent Home girls' stories seem to work overtime on behalf of "adopting out." Their stories lean toward adoption most notably in their portrayal of the girls as innocent and dependent victims whose lives need to be restored, in the ongoing sacralization of the fetus-child, and in the radical marginalization of the biological father. Ultimately, and rather miraculously in the sense of being utterly unprecedented, adopting out is constituted as the second birth anticipated by the first birth, at least in the lives of unwed teenage girls.

While Falwell's story is one of steady if slow progress toward the pro-life light, Jennifer, as we shall shortly see, goes way down before she goes up. As she moves through her moment of maximum descent, the abortion, through the turning point when she decides to save her second baby, to her triumphant arrival at the Liberty Godparent Home in Lynchburg, Jennifer's story accumulates biblical tropes which exculpate her, demonize abortion, and sanctify giving birth—all without naturalizing the relationship between biological mother and child.

Details of time and space frame Jennifer's abortion as an anti-worship service, as sacrilegious sacrifice: Jennifer and her parents drive past their church on their way to the abortion appointment at 11:00 one Sunday morning. *Nobody noticed us drive by.* The sky is overcast, storm clouds are piling up, the wind is blowing dirty paper plates and empty beer cans across the highway, and by the time they arrive at the Planned Parenthood clinic (anti-church), they are irritable and grumpy—and scared. The waiting room is full of naive girls, frightened and listless, many of whom had been there before. The nurse (anti-Sunday School teacher) lectures them on abortion procedures. *I suppose we didn't really listen to the nurse for the same reason passengers on an airplane don't really listen to the warnings of the stewardess. Who wants to hear the bad news* [anti-good news]?[26]

I'll always remember how embarrassed I felt that day when the young male doctor [anti-pastor] *entered the room to find my two bare legs sticking almost straight up into the air and my hands gripping the table* [anti-altar] *for dear life.*[27] Jennifer glimpses the suction tube in the doc-tor's hand just before he injects the anesthesia: *I don't know what he did to me after that. I woke up on a bed. A nurse was removing a bloody pad from between my legs. It was gross. . . . I lay there thinking I was going to die when the receptionist entered the room and placed a glass of milk and a plate of Oreo cookies beside me. . . . I felt ter-ribly foolish. It didn't look anything like a last supper* [anti-bread and wine]. *The abortion was over. The little intruder was gone forever. I felt weak and dizzy and high.*[28]

The "last supper" spins an explicit thread between the abortion and Christ's sacrifice that clinches the web of allusions implicit in the situating details. It also evokes the last meal of a convicted murderer and intimates "the wages of sin is death," at the same time as Jennifer's naive narrative voice and the image of milk and cookies deflect those connotations from her and suggest that she is innocent.

Abortion is evil—it carries the full weight of sin—and Jennifer emerges scathed but untainted. She is the girl next door, a sixteen-year-old middle-class Baptist Georgia city girl whose father is a deacon, her mother the church secretary. Neither she nor those who counseled her to get an abortion—her parents, the Health teacher, a Baptist pastor—denies the personhood of the fetus. They are oblivious to it. *Nobody thought about the baby. Not even me,* Jennifer laments in retrospect.[29] Ignorance, not sin, was the culprit as far as these otherwise good Christians are concerned.

If Jennifer's abortion is an anti-worship service, the moment she decides to save her second baby is a cross between an annunciation and a salvation experience. Her parents had *just seen a special on TV about a place in Virginia* and thus knew about a better way when Jennifer told them she was pregnant again. She balks at the idea of going there to have her baby, but then, while driving alone about midnight on a highway, she runs out of gas, pulls into a filling station that was closed for the night (a liminal time, place, and circumstance with connotations of sexual danger and a sign of spiritual hope—the filling station) and has a revelation. Having called a friend to come get her, she curls up in the back seat of her car to wait and watches a moth fly into a hot light and sizzle to death.

I pictured myself fluttering and dancing about the light. I determined that this time I would be smart enough to fly away to safety. That awful night was one of the best things that ever happened to me. There beside the filling station in the middle of nowhere, something changed within me. I grew up. "Dear Lord, please help me." I hadn't prayed for a long time, not a real prayer, not like this one. "I'm in real trouble again, Lord, and I don't know what to do about it." I stared out into the darkness trying to find God out there.[30]

Jennifer's moment of decision echoes of Mary's annunciation—an unmarried girl visited by a messenger, a male birth foreshadowed. Those echoes are mixed with allusions to Christ's death—a meaningful death: he died so that we might live. And something changed within Jennifer. That night she submits to God (*Dear Lord, please help me*), and the next day she tells her parents she wants to go to that place in Virginia. Jennifer chooses life over death, joins God's plan, and the hidden meaning of things and events will begin now to infill her.

The biblical connotations and allusions break the textual surface when Jennifer arrives at the Liberty Godparent Home. As the director, Jim Savley, ushers Jennifer and her parents into his office, she notices the pictures of his wife and family, a framed telegram from President Reagan, certificates and diplomas, and *an impressive painting of Mary riding on a donkey carrying the baby Jesus in her arms. Joseph walked close by.* Jennifer tries to remember the story, *but all I could see was the look in Mary's eyes as she stared lovingly into her baby's face.* Mr. Savley, answering her unasked question, tells her that Mary and Joseph were fleeing to Egypt *to save the life of their baby.*[31] *I understood why the painting was chosen for his office. My family and I had traveled to Lynchburg for a similar reason—to save my baby. There was an unborn child growing inside me and this time the baby would not die.*[32] Jennifer becomes Mary; Liberty Godparent Home, Egypt; and, by narrative implication, the abortionists are King Herod bent on slaughtering the innocents. Falwell, the absent author of it all, casts a decidedly supermundane shadow. This time, the baby—Christ—will be spared.[33]

Jennifer's arrival scene at Liberty Godparent Home foreshadows, as did the filling station scene, a male birth and clinches the equation, first intimated on the dust cover, between Christ and the baby-saved-from-abortion. It also cleanses Jennifer, wrapping her in Mary's mantle, symbolically restoring virginity to the unwed, pregnant teenage girl threatened by the specter of abortion-Herod, at the same time as it locates her reproductive issue squarely in God's plan, not in her hands, much less in the hands of the biological father. These threads are spun out in the rest of Jennifer's story and in Jerry's, which begins to merge with Jennifer's once she enters Liberty Godparent Home.

When her parents first told Jennifer about the Liberty Godparent Home, she imagined a *haunted house with army nurses and big needles behind locked doors and barred windows,* in effect, a place where she would be punished, drilled, and terrorized.[34] Before Jennifer got there, Falwell, in an intervening chapter, assures his readers that nothing could be further from the truth, rewriting the maternity home from darkness to light, from shame to self-confidence: *We now know that an unwanted pregnancy makes a teenage girl feel ugly, embarrassed, and unwanted.... The young woman feels like hiding her shame from the world.... That's why it becomes so easy to kill the baby, to end the nightmare, and to try to begin again. That's why Liberty Godparent maternity homes provide a sense of permanence, safety and beauty to restore the self-confidence and self-worth in the pregnant girls it exists to serve.*[35] And, of course, Jennifer is greeted by the warm, intuitive Mr. Savley, not an army nurse, and the place is surrounded by oak trees and blue jays, green lawns and bright yellow flowers, and inside there were bay windows overlooking the garden, Early American maple tables and chairs, and a chef, her arms brimming with grocery bags.

Jennifer and Jerry collaborate in reconfiguring the maternity home, converting a nineteenth- and early-twentieth-century figment of antisex rhetoric into a 1980s antiabortion sanctuary. Accordingly, the stories of how Jennifer and the other girls at Liberty Godparent Home became pregnant portray them as passively, not actively, sexually transgressive, not as sinners but as victims. When she was sixteen, surrounded by the tempting music, visual images, and banter of teen culture, Jennifer feels her body changing and stirring (*just brushing past a boy going through a classroom doorway made me feel excited and curious and a little afraid*) and vulnerable to any boy's attention (*I felt ugly and rejected and alone most of the time*).[36] She spends a weekend unchaperoned at a summer cottage with some other girls; boys arrive one night; she finds herself alone on the dunes with a strange boy and *. . . the romantic dream became a nightmare.*[37] After her abortion, she is *miserable and angry most of the time and desperately needed someone or something* [to make her] *feel good again.*[38] That someone is Jeff, that something is sex, and she gets in trouble again.

The other Liberty Godparent Home girls fall into two camps, sexually speaking. There are girls like Jennifer, victims of physical urges, low self-esteem, teen culture, and lack of supervision, who "made mistakes," implying that "these things happen even in (middle-class) Christian families." And there are other girls to whom unthinkable things happen, (lower-class, not Christian) victims of incest, rape, pornography, poverty, negligence. Missy, age thirteen, was abused by her father and impregnated by a stranger. JoAnn's alcoholic father beat his four daughters, sexually abused three of them, and got JoAnn pregnant at fourteen. An unnamed fourteen-year-old girl called the Liberty Godparent Home hotline operator from Baltimore and said her father sexually abused her, made pornographic movies with her and her two-year-old brother, and had just killed their mother. Either way, whether they are victims of bad boys or evil men, the girls are let off sin's hook lightly as the causes of their pregnancies are narratively dispersed in circumstances rather than lodged in the girls, in their sinfulness or their "sin nature."

The victimizers lurk on the margins of the girls' stories, misguided boyfriends who mislead girls who make mistakes and cruel fathers/strangers who rape defenseless girls. Just once, in a few lines, Falwell casts a light on the boys, pointing out that some of them try to change, some try to help the girls they have hurt, not all of them are irresponsible and uncaring, though, by implication, the rest, and all the adult men who impregnate teenage girls, are.[39] Their narrative banishment—the erasure of the natural father—combines with the mariological insinuations surrounding the girls to intensify the sense of fetal divinity and denaturalize the relationship of fetus-child to both its parents. Biological fathers are given no say in the fate of the babies, before or after birth, and, while the girls must make the difficult decisions, it is absolutely clear, given that fetuses belong to, are essentially of, God, that the first birth ought not be aborted.[40] It is not so clear—or rather it must be clarified with much storied attention—what the girls ought to do with God's issue after birth.

Alongside tales of personal and spiritual growth, that is, restoration, at Liberty Godparent Home, Jennifer narrates her painful search for the right thing to do for the baby as she listens to other girls make up their minds and talks over her qualms with the women who work at Liberty Godparent Home. Falwell, in his parallel chapters, is likewise much preoccupied by the choice the girls must make between keeping their babies and giving them up for adoption. Its importance, delicacy, and complexity is forcefully indicated by the narrative space it occupies—Jennifer and Jerry slow down the pace of their storytelling, expand the details, and fill the margins of their thoughts with inset tales that explore other options and outcomes. Although other choices are permitted fairly good endings, the girls are under unequivocal narrative pressure to "adopt out," rightfully to sacrifice their children for their own good to Christian couples.

Andrea kept her son and started a new life in Lynchburg, but working full time meant long hours in daycare for little Brian and the abrupt end of her own adolescence; the failure to make a timely sacrifice called for other sacrifices with uncertain, open-ended consequences. Tammy kept her baby even though she, at age fourteen, had been counseled that adoption was the preferred option, but later we find her happily married to a tall, blond seminary student from Chicago who told Falwell, "I don't agree with all your politics . . . but you saved my son and I'll always love you for that." [41]

JoAnn did not, as did Tammy, have a middle-class home to return to, and her story, drawn out over several pages, accentuates the costs of keeping the baby. A fourteen-year-old victim of incest, poverty, and neglect, JoAnn took her baby back home to the perils of her father's house. Falwell said, *I selected JoAnn's story because struggling with her kind of complex and confounding reality is the responsibility of any person who takes a serious stand against abortion. . . . JoAnn's story isn't over yet. We don't know what God has in mind for her little girl. Whatever it is, we are glad and grateful that God will have His chance in her life. It is risky business reaching out to people in despair. It is risky business helping babies be born into our world.*[42]

The echoes of a second birth deferred are strong in this passage. *JoAnn's story isn't over yet. . . . We don't know what God has in mind. . . . It is risky business reaching out to people in despair*—these are phrases out of in-house meta-gospel talk, forms of speech used among soul winners consoling themselves over lost souls who said "no" when they heard the message of Christ's saving grace. Though the timing is always ultimately given back to God, no born-again Christian has any doubt that the better way, if not necessarily the only route to narrative completion, is to choose Christ (adopt out to a born-again couple) now.

Jennifer decides to give her child up for adoption shortly after witnessing a conversation between thirteen-year-old Missy and Rosemary, a Liberty Godparent Home volunteer who herself had given her baby up for adoption a few years before. Rosemary tells Missy, *You love your baby too much to keep her. You don't have a home or a family or a husband to offer your baby. You can't provide anything you want her to have. . . . There is a young couple right this minute who cannot have a baby of their own. They have a good income. They have a beautiful home with a nursery and toys and baby clothes and an empty cradle. They are praying for a baby, Missy. They can take care of the baby. They can give the baby what you want to give her.* [43]

There is that empty cradle again, that sense of something missing, no longer the consequence of abortion, now the space of awaiting adoption. Jennifer, like Missy and several other girls, decides to fill, to fulfill, that other empty cradle, but their decisions are labored, even belabored.

Jennifer agonizes over adopting out for months, worrying if she will have the courage to stick to it, dwelling on the moment when she will have to give up the baby. The sense that she is engaged in making a rightful sacrifice is clinched when she receives word of her baby's sex and name by way of Falwell: *I had chosen Stephen for my baby's name. I was convinced I was going to have a boy after Dr. Falwell had preached on Stephen, the first Christian martyr.*[44] Just before he *is* born, Jennifer writes Stephen a letter he will never receive: *"You were not unwanted. . . . I want the very best for you, and if I could give it to you, don't think for a moment that I wouldn't. God has a very special plan for you and right now it's for you to have both a mother and a father. . . . I love you."* [45] Some thoughts are being precluded through all this self-denial, most especially any suggestion that giving Stephen up for adoption was the "convenient" thing for Jennifer to do.

Jennifer, the other girls, and Falwell—their pro-life gospel—must sanction adoption for teenage girls without resorting to language which born-again Christians impute to feminism. They must suppress any implications that babies are "unwanted" or "inconvenient," that they get in the way with girls resuming their adolescence, going to college, having a career, or getting properly married. Hence, the sacrificial excess: *"Do you know that I love you, son?" I whispered into his tiny ear. "Will you remember? We have to trust God now. He'll take care of you. Will you forgive me? Will you love me anyway?" Words poured out of me. Stephen looked as if he was trying to understand. . . . When they took him back to the nursery, I pulled the thin yellow blanket up so that the nylon edge was touching my face. The heavy drapes covered the huge windows. It was twilight outside. The room was almost dark. I was alone again.*[46]

This bedroom scene completes, fulfills, the one on the dust cover. Jennifer has sacrificed herself so that Stephen might live. Although we are given to understand it is a blessing of God, a free gift, not a motive, Jennifer's death-unto-self also marks her own rebirth as she walks boldly back into a middle-class adolescence restored and brimming with possibilities. By the time she reappears in Falwell's final chapter, which jumps ahead a few years and narrates a Memorial Day celebration on the grounds of Liberty Godparent Home in memory of "the unborn children who have died from abortion," Jennifer has become a communications major at his Liberty University and is emerging as a national spokesperson for Liberty Godparent Homes. Clearly, God blesses those who seek and follow his will.

When Falwell finally makes his appeal, in the penultimate chapter, for readers to assume their place in the sacrificial landscape unfolded for them, it is relatively soft and pro forma, concluding with a vague entreaty, *Will you seriously consider joining us in helping save the unborn babies of our nation?*[47] Although the book rehearses all the moves of gospel speech, marking out a multitude of "lacknesses" for readers to complete, *If I Should Die* is a gospel text not so much for the unconverted as for the converted. It is a training manual, comparable to a collection of sermons, for the elaboration and refinement of gospel speech. Instead of building toward a moment of salvation in which pro-life rhetoric is acquired, the stories assume saved readers and effect a continuous transfer of advanced Christian narrative authority.[48]

The stories of Jerry Falwell's pro-life campaign appropriated and displaced feminist rhetorics in ways that were crude and simple. Much was blotted out: feminism and the feminist movement were never named in *If I Should Die,* and adult women and married teenage girls who choose abortion made no appearances. Feminist positions, images, and story lines were caricatured. All of the women who need abortions were unmarried teenage girls, all of them were sexual victims, and all of them needed help. Jennifer, by dint of dependency, age, name (Falwell's children's names begin with "J") resonated as a daughter to Falwell's father/Father. Such choices and devices plainly tilted the narrative campaign in favor of Falwell's authority.

Yet in other ways the campaign was nuanced and complex. It deployed the most powerful and sophisticated narrative resources of born-again Christian culture, resources which have countless times proven themselves capable of reconfiguring the subjective springs of action. The campaign, in figuring abortion as the death of the first birth, saving babies as the first birth, and adopting out as the second birth, lodged the pro-life movement in the discursive heart of born-again culture, in the irresistible play of reciprocal sacrificial action across stories, written, spoken, and lived.

The stories of *If I Should Die* did not represent preexisting asymmetries as fixed eternal truths that must be swallowed whole. They generated the asymmetries anew and transferred them from author to reader with tremendous force and tenderness through the narrative logic of prefiguration and fulfillment. Repeatedly, "superior" persons, terms, stories, and rhetorics appropriated and transcended their "inferior" counterparts. The logic binding "inferior" and "superior" is neither literary nor causal, but divine, foreordained, indelibly written by God. If Isaac, then Christ. If first birth, then second birth. If "female," then "male." If Jennifer, then Falwell-as-maternity-homemaker.

Born-again preachers and pro-life leaders were able to engage their communities in an escalating movement against abortion by embedding it in the greatest story ever told. What they, in collaboration with their followers, achieved as they traced out alterations of character, motif, motive, action, and circumstance across sequences of stories and events was nothing less than the further working out of God's will in history.

If I Should Die ends with Jennifer Simpson making her debut as a public speaker at the Memorial Day celebration. As Jerry Falwell sits on the platform and listens to her, he ponders what would have happened *if people hadn't cared enough to save* the babies of the girls at Liberty Godparent Home. *I imagined their children sliced into pieces and suctioned from their mother's womb or burned and blackened by salt poisoning and born dead.... "You are alive, little Brian," I said quietly to myself. "Thank God, Stephen, you are alive."* [49]

In the book's opening scene, the female reporter handed Jerry Falwell the feminist story line and the woman's point of view, and Jennifer and Jerry renarrated them in born-again terms across their intertwining chapters. Together they converted the cradle emptied through abortion into the cradle filled, and fulfilled, through adoption. In the book's closing scene, once again, a woman speaks in public while Falwell listens, but this time it is he who created the grounds upon which she speaks, even as she embodied the landscape upon which he acted. Although Jennifer has a public voice, she acquired it through Falwell's sacrificial action. The hint of feminism carried by the female reporter has finally been erased.

Notes

1 Falwell, 1986.

2 *If I Should Die* also presents certain conundrums of authorship which might elude unborn-again readers but not believers. Although Falwell appears on the book's dust cover and in the credits as sole author, the chapters are clearly co-authored with Jennifer Simpson, a subsuming which neatly implies that he is her author. Nor did Falwell make a secret of the fact that Mel White ghostwrote the book for both of them.

Such authorial ambiguities, rather than casting doubt on the text's veracity, enhance it by recalling debates over the authorship of biblical books and thus nesting *If I Should Die* in a corpus whose authority (authorship) is accepted as a testament of faith. As we have seen, it is the responsibility of faithful readers to "unify" the authorial and narrative voices in their interpretation and to "harmonize" the text with other texts, spoken and written, so that it comes "true." Falwell's words, like the words of all men of God, are always already double-voiced in any case, in the sense that it is never entirely clear whether he or God is the author.

3 Falwell, 1986, 10–11.

4 Falwell, 1986, 11.

5 Many conservative Protestant ministers spoke out against feminism in the late nineteenth and early twentieth centuries, and they sometimes included abortion when listing sins associated with feminism and modern society. John R. Rice, for example, condemned abortion (as well as birth control) in his 1945 manual on the Christian family. But Protestant preachers were not active participants in the campaign to criminalize abortion. See Bendroth 1993, DeBerg 1990, and Luker 1984.

Regarding Falwell's position on abortion, see, for example, Falwell 1973: *Some come* [to Falwell's church] *seeking forgiveness, as a young father who was guilty of pressuting his wife to get an abortion; he wondered if God would* forgive *him* for *murdering an unborn child* (53). (Elmer Towns ghostwrote this early text.)

In 1976, abortion appeared on Falwell's list of "America's sins" in his bicentennial "I Love America" crusade sermons and tracts, but it was just one among many other sins, not the cause célèbre it was to become. Elmer Towns told me in an interview that it was he who finally convinced Falwell, in spring 1978, to speak out at length against abortion—and that he, Towns, wrote Falwell's first pro-life sermon. Still, it was a while before the issue took off; *How You Can Help Clean Up America* (Falwell 1978) reprints the sermon "Abortion: Is It Murder?" (probably the one Towns was talking about), but *America Can Be Saved* (Falwell 1979) does not mention abortion.

The chapter on abortion in *Listen America!* (1981) is Falwell's first extended treatment in print; it relies heavily on right-to-life rhetoric, on the work of Bernard Nathanson, an "abortionist" who converted to the pro-life movement, and on Francis Schaeffer and Dr. C. Everett Koop's *Whatever Happened to the Human Race?* (1979), the first highly successful born-again polemic against abortion.

6 Spitzer and Saylor, 1969, xxvi.

7 *Eternity*, February 1968.

8 Paul Fowler, 1987, 72. Fowler mentions Harold O. J. Brown, John Warwick Montgomery, Clifford Bosgra, and Richard Ganz.

9 See Fowler, 1987, 72–77.

10 Regarding Wheaton, see Fowler 1987, 83; for 1992 figures, see Green et al. 1996, 251, 283. This evidence of internal conflict argues against the notion that pro-life mobilization emerged, as if inevitably, out of a preexisting "worldview," a position most fully developed by Luker (1984).

11 Fowler, 1987, 73.

12 Fowler, 1987, 73.

13 See Schaeffer and Koop, 1979, 117.

14 See Burke (1989). Burke describes Hitler's use of a similar rhetorical technique, which Burke calls "associative merger," in *Mein Kampf*. It is common in much political rhetoric and enables the formation of larger, conglomerate, political identity groups.

15 See Scott 1959.

16 A list of proof-texts called "Scriptures for Life" invariably accompanied pro-life literature put out by the LGH campaign. It listed twenty-three Bible passages (there are others) as "proof-texts" against abortion; that is, they prove that God opposes it. For example, and oft-cited, is Jeremiah 1:5: "Before I formed thee in the belly I knew thee; and before thou camest forth out of the womb I sanctified thee." Inscribed on the Monument to the Unborn, a huge gravestone placed on Falwell's Liberty University campus, is Matthew 18:6: "But whoso shall offend one of these little ones which believe in me, it were better for him that a millstone were hung around his neck and to be drowned in the sea."

17 Ginsburg, 1989. *If I Should Die* presents itself as "true stories" and, we may ask, "true" in what sense? As we have seen, "truth" in born-again culture is authenticated by its author; everything in the Bible is "true" because God wrote it, and everything Jerry Falwell (a man anointed by God) says is "true" because he said it. Discrepancies in parallel stories are not unsettling (because stories do not represent a fixed natural reality) but, rather, revealing (because the alterations constitute the working out of God's will).

18 As noted above in 5, I found no evidence that Falwell had preached on abortion before 1973; what evidence there is suggests that he realized the potential and importance of the abortion issue gradually during the late 1970s and early 1980s.

19 Falwell, 1986, 31–32.

20 Falwell, 1986, 36.

21 Falwell, 1986, 37.

22 Falwell, 1986, 67.

23 See Marsden, 1980, 16–19. Note here Falwell's discursive interlocutors on the matter of abortion as such; those whose authority he would appropriate seem to be scientists, doctors, lawyers, justices, politicians, as well as feminists.

24 Falwell, 1986, 47.

25 Teenage sexuality (once an unthinkable juxtaposition of terms for born-again Christians, especially fundamentalists) became in the mid-1980s a frequent topic of sermons, books, and seminars. Josh McDowell, a widely read writer on the subject, reported that "between 55 percent and 60 percent of evangelical Christian youth are involved in sexual activity" (1987, 15).

I was told in Lynchburg that the waiting list of Christian couples who wish to adopt LGH babies was a long one and that they pay substantial "fees" for the privilege, conditions which suggest that the success of Falwell's Liberty Godparent campaign may be as much due to its adoption as its antiabortion aspect.

26 Falwell, 1986, 55.

27 Falwell, 1986, 56.

28 Falwell, 1986, 57.

29 Falwell, 1986, 29.

30 Falwell, 1986, 95.

31 Falwell, 1986, 125.

32 Falwell, 1986, 126.

33 Note here that Jennifer's discursive interlocutors, whose authority she is displacing, include Catholics and Jews as well as feminists.

34 Falwell, 1986, 91.

35 Falwell, 1986, 110.

36 Falwell, 1986, 14, 15.

37 Falwell, 1986, 23.

38 Falwell, 1986, 85.

39 Falwell, 1986, 191–92.

40 If *I Should Die* establishes the primacy of the fetal-God relationship (and the independence of the fetus from the mother) through largely narrative means, but its readers bring other arguments to that effect to the text. Perhaps the strongest among them is the argument that the fetus is a "person," which

lodges opposition to abortion in the founding premise of Protestantism, "the priesthood of the believer"—that the relationship between person and God is mediated by no man, or woman. ("The personhood of the fetus" is, of course, originally a Catholic doctrine, yet in the mouths of these Protestants it acquires a slight anti-Catholic spin.)

41 Falwell, 1986, 211.

42 Falwell, 1986, 158–59.

43 Falwell, 1986, 139.

44 Falwell, 1986, 194–95.

45 Falwell, 1986, 202.

46 Falwell, 1986, 202–3.

47 Falwell, 1986, 191.

48 Pointed demands for money, "a sacrificial gift of $400 to save the life of a baby," come in televised and direct-mail fundraising pitches. *If I Should Die* figured in these pitches as a persuasive force after the fact, that is, as a "free gift" given in return to those who sacrificed themselves by sending in $400 to become "Liberty Godparents."

49 Falwell, 1986, 216.

The Church's Tug of War

Angela Bonavoglia

From *The Nation*, August 19, 2002

It is a harrowing time for the U.S. Catholic Church. While the American bishops at their Dallas meeting in June agreed nearly unanimously to remove from active ministry any priest guilty of sexually abusing a minor, they didn't render that decision with enthusiasm. For many, anger and resentment roiled just below the surface.

Take the closing remarks of Chicago's Francis Cardinal George. In an elliptical rant, he held the church's opponents responsible for the hierarchy's diminishing power. George's targets included the campaign of Catholics for a Free Choice (CFFC) to downgrade the church's status at the UN to a nongovernmental organization; feminists working for laws requiring Catholic institutions that serve and employ the general public to provide reproductive health services, including contraceptive insurance; anyone suing the church; Catholics with a shaky faith; Protestants; and American culture in general.

"There's been an erosion of episcopal authority and a loss of Catholic faith for a generation," George scolded. American culture, he said, is "a form of secularized Protestantism . . . self-righteous and decadent at the same time. . . . There's external opposition . . . to the Holy See's being in the United Nations...the attack on our healthcare institutes, the attack on our social services through various insurance policies . . . the attack upon our institutional presence that is only beginning . . . as plaintiffs begin to go forward in order to bankrupt the Church. All of these . . . are not coincidental. I believe personally—without looking at it as some kind of cabal—that we have to be very serious about how we're going to go forward."

"Going forward" to George means a smaller, more orthodox Church. It would be free of all those "dissidents" who, as the Catholic League's William Donahue has said, "enabled the behavioral deviance." Reflecting similar sentiments, America's cardinals, upon their return from a visit to the pope in April, issued a statement instructing pastors "clearly to promote the correct moral teaching" and "publicly to reprimand individuals who spread dissent."

One thing is clear from the unprecedented gatherings in Rome and Dallas: If fundamental change is to come to the American Catholic Church, the bishops will not be leading the way. Nor will the pope, who in Canada recently for World Youth Day finally acknowledged publicly the shame of the sex abuse scandals, but not the hierarchy's culpability. That makes the work of the church's progressive reform movement more important than ever.

Anne Barrett Doyle is a recent recruit. She says she "literally woke up" in January when she read the *Boston Globe*'s stories of clergy sex abuse and diocesan cover-up. The same spirit that had moved her as a tenth grader in a packed Roman Catholic Church to protest her priest's refusal to baptize the baby of prochoice parents inspired her again. Instead of going to their usual parish, she and her family drove to the Cathedral of the Holy Cross, where Bernard Cardinal Law would be serving mass. Carrying her scrawled It's My Church sign, Doyle joined a picket line of seven.

"I was so overcome with the sinfulness of the Church and also of myself, as a layperson who had enjoyed being part of this little club and had not fought against [my] subservient role," says Doyle. Her wake-up call resulted in the birth of one of Boston's most spirited church-reform organizations, the Coalition of Catholics and Survivors. As a leader of that group, Doyle joins the ranks of a largely invisible but driving force behind the church's progressive change movement: women.

Arguably, the best known is Sister Joan Chittister. A fiery orator and prolific author, this 66-year-old Benedictine nun made international news last year when she refused to obey a Vatican order forbidding her to speak at an international conference in Dublin on the ordination of women. Chittister made her decision in the face of Vatican threats of "grave penalties," which could have ranged from excommunication to expulsion from her monastery in Erie, Pennsylvania. "The Church that preaches the equality of women but does nothing to demonstrate it within its own structures . . . is . . . dangerously close to repeating the theological errors that underlay centuries of Church-sanctioned slavery," she told the emboldened crowd at the gathering.

Though Chittister would have defied the pope alone, in the end, she didn't have to. The Vatican had demanded that the prioress of Chittister's monastery, Christine Vladimiroff, issue the "precept of obedience" forbidding Chittister to speak, or face grave penalties herself. Vladimiroff refused to be the Vatican's henchman. "I could not order something I was in total disagreement with, and that is silencing," says Vladimiroff. Despite advanced age and infirmity, all but one of 128 active members of the Erie Benedictines cosigned Vladimiroff's letter to Rome. An additional letter of support came from nuns in twenty-two other Benedictine communities. The Vatican backed down.

For some, the courage of the Erie Benedictines has been an inspiration. Father Walter Cuenin is a Newton, Massachusetts, parish priest who helped to found another reform group, Priests' Forum. The forum gives Boston priests a private, independent venue to discuss the previously undiscussable—from "whether mandatory celibacy should remain" to Church teachings like the birth-control ban. Cuenin remembers the Benedictines' action well. "It had an impact on me personally," he says. "A lot of us have lived in fear—I can't speak because something will happen. If enough people speak, there's nothing that anyone can do."

There is no question that the pedophilia scandal has torn the mantle of sanctity off the Catholic Church. Long subject to a litany of illogical and unconscionable sexual prohibitions—which the church labors worldwide to have written into secular law—Catholics now see that the hierarchy has failed to live up to even the most basic moral standards. That, explains Catholic University sociologist William D'Antonio, has exacerbated their outrage. His research revealed that only 20 percent of American Catholics look to church leaders as a source of moral authority, and that was before the scandals broke. Most also believe that the church should be more democratic. "What our data show," D'Antonio says, "is that people are ready for the reform movement."

And the reform movement is ready for them. The welcome surge of interest, however, has created some internal challenges for the movement, as the influx of new activists has radically changed its composition. Catholics never active before in Church affairs are demanding a voice. Some have joined the progressive movement, while others are mapping out a new middle ground. What's different, says Tom Fox, publisher of the independent *National Catholic Reporter,* is that "there is a large cross-section of Catholics calling for change. From left to right, Catholics are calling upon the bishops [for] greater accountability. They're saying the church that we have, the governance we have, is not working."

In the spirit of the Second Vatican Council (1962-65), the progressive reform groups embrace a broad agenda. They want women at all levels of ministry and decision-making; married clergy; optional celibacy; acceptance of homosexuals, the divorced, and the remarried; an end to Vatican silencings; lay involvement in church governance and in teachings on human sexuality (though abortion support varies, even among reformers); new forms of liturgy and nonsexist language; academic freedom at Catholic universities; and an affirmation of conscience as the final arbiter in moral matters.

This agenda is embraced by such groups as Call to Action—the nation's oldest and largest, with twenty-five thousand members and forty chapters; the gay rights group Dignity/USA; the Women's Ordination Conference; the reproductive rights groups CFFC and Catholics Speak Out; Corpus, which supports married and female priests; Women-Church Convergence, a coalition committed to feminist spirituality; and FutureChurch, which raises awareness of the priest shortage and of women's ministerial roles in the early and the contemporary Church. All are led or coled by women.

By contrast, the new "center" is occupied by reformers with a narrower agenda. Like the progressive groups, they support the long-neglected victims of clergy sexual abuse—represented by the Survivors Network of Those Abused by Priests (SNAP) and Linkup. But they call for change in only one area: church governance. They want the hierarchy to share power, giving lay Catholics a real voice in administrative affairs such as financial decision-making and the hiring and firing of priests and bishops. Another new group, Voice of the Faithful in Boston, is working swiftly and systematically to move the agenda of church accountability forward. With 22,500 members in forty states and twenty-two countries, VOTF is building an exploding network of independent, parish-based groups. In addition, VOTF has set up a charitable fund through which Catholics can redirect their donations from Boston's archdiocesan coffers to Catholic agencies—the only real power Catholics currently have.

While VOTF has members who also participate in progressive reform groups, the organization does not consider itself part of the progressive community. Founder Jim Muller, a cardiologist who also founded International Physicians for the Prevention of Nuclear War, describes VOTF as a centrist organization. "We are building a representative structure for the laity that will be more like Congress than the Democratic or Republican Party," he says. According to one insider, however, VOTF has gone to great lengths to make conservatives feel welcome while distancing itself from progressive groups. It has also, observes Call to Action spokeswoman Claire Noonan, "been very careful not to take positions on issues of big controversy, like women's ordination and optional celibacy." Depending on how large VOTF becomes and how its members vote on contentious issues, it could have the effect of either strengthening or marginalizing the larger progressive reform agenda.

As for the progressive reformers, they see in the current crisis dramatic evidence of the need for change. They are incensed by the hierarchy's scapegoating of homosexual priests as the cause of the scandals. In fact, they point out, that contention cannot be separated from the church's denial of the rampant sexual abuse of girls and women by Catholic priests, which some contend far outstrips the abuse of male children in its incidence. Half the members of both SNAP and Linkup are women. Last year internal church documents revealed a pattern of sexual abuse and exploitation of nuns—and other girls and women—by priests in some twenty-three countries, on five continents. What's more, according to the research of psychotherapist and former Catholic monk Richard Sipe, at any one time, at least a third of priests, regardless of sexual orientation, are sexually active with adults. Whether those relationships are exploitative or consensual, they indicate the depth of the hypocrisy inherent in the claim of a celibate priesthood.

Progressive reformers see women's overall subordinate role in the Church—including the ban on ordination—as contributing to this crisis. Another Call to Action spokeswoman, Linda Pieczynski, suggests that if women—particularly mothers—had been at the table, "We wouldn't have tried to save Father Bob's reputation. We would have protected the children." Indeed, we have seen how women in male-dominated institutions—Sherron Watkins at Enron, Coleen Rowley at the FBI—have blown the lid off secret shenanigans. But integrating women into positions of power in the church means taking on an issue absent from the public dialogue: misogyny. As Chittister has observed, the Roman Church "built a bad theology of male superiority on a bad biology that defined women as passive incubators of male sperm . . . inferior by nature and deficient of soul, the servants of men and the seducers of civilization."

While reformers in the new middle are trying to force the hierarchy to share power, plenty of progressive reformers have chosen to go their own way, while continuing obstinately to call themselves Catholic. Last

November Mary Ramerman lay prostrate on a stage before three thousand jubilant supporters in Rochester, New York's Eastman Theatre, where she was ordained a Catholic priest. While Ramerman was ordained in the Old Catholic rather than the Roman Catholic Church (the Old Catholics broke with Rome when it declared the doctrine of papal infallibility in 1870), she took that action against the orders of Rochester Bishop Matthew Clark, who directed her "to abandon your leadership role" at Spiritus Christi. A vigorous congregation of fifteen hundred, Spiritus grew out of the smoldering ashes of another Catholic parish, Corpus Christi. That was after Clark dismissed both its pastor, in part for allowing Ramerman on the altar during mass, and Ramerman for refusing to step off.

"They are a real problem [for the Catholic Church] because that's the most alive faith community in that whole area," says Sister Maureen Fiedler, advisory board member of Catholics Speak Out and host of the radio show "Interfaith Voices." CFFC president Frances Kissling agrees. "What is the best example of Church reform in the United States right now? Spiritus Christi. They have a vital, lively church that is not connected to the institution, but that views itself as Catholic."

Revving up the rebellion, on June 29 seven women—four Germans, two Austrians and one with dual Austrian–American citizenship—were ordained Roman Catholic priests on a cruise ship, the MS *Passau*, on the Danube River, just outside of Passau, Germany. Romulo Braschi of Argentina was the presiding bishop. While Braschi was ordained a Catholic priest and, later, a bishop, he leads a splinter sect and has no standing with the Vatican. As a result, some reformers distanced themselves from the ordination. Others, like Fiedler, who attended, saw it as an important step forward. "I think what Rome worries about is that this could start breaking out all over," she says.

While much smaller than Spiritus Christi—some have only a handful of members—hundreds of Catholic intentional eucharistic communities exist around the country. In the tradition of the early Christian church and Latin America's small-base communities, these worship communities—some decades old—meet regularly, often in people's homes; celebrate the eucharist, with their own liturgies; and choose their own worship leaders, including married Catholic priests, openly gay Catholic priests and Catholic women.

Reformers also labor outside the church to curb its power in the world. No group has worked longer to challenge the institutional church's attempts to restrict access to reproductive healthcare than Catholics for a Free Choice (I served for a time on CFFC's board). More recently, secular women's groups have joined in this work.

After toiling in near-obscurity, progressive church reform groups have been hurled by the current crisis into the spotlight. They report increased hits on their websites, more calls and letters, jumps in membership, more donations. Though their membership rosters remain very low, considering that the country has 63 million Catholics, there is a lot of talk about the demand for Church reform finally having reached critical mass.

Intent on keeping the heat on, VOTF organized its first national conference, which drew more than four thousand people to Boston on July 20. Call to Action is planning its annual national conference for November in Milwaukee. The Women's Ordination Conference has endorsed the ordination of the new women priests in Germany and is considering a similar event in the United States. On the narrower issue of clergy sex abuse, the groups will be monitoring to see that priests are removed and lobbying for penalties for complicit bishops. Governor Frank Keating of Oklahoma, head of the national lay committee established by the bishops' conference, has pledged that he will appeal to the pope for sanctions against offending bishops, but is already tempering his tough talk.

Even if the reformers do nothing more, many believe the church hierarchy has already forfeited its moral authority—potentially a loss to advocates for the poor, but a boon for reproductive rights. Certainly the Church has lost its protected status with the media and, now, with law enforcement. A grand jury convened by Westchester County, New York, District Attorney Jeanine Pirro recommended criminal penalties for those who recklessly allow an employee with a record of child sexual abuse access to minors—which could provide a way to prosecute offending bishops.

For its part, the church is not taking these incursions into its power lying down. During the American cardinals' visit to Rome earlier this year, Cardinal Law had his top aide, Bishop Walter Edyvean, send a letter to parish priests in the Boston Archdiocese instructing them "not to join, foster or promote" the efforts of a lay group to combine existing diocesan-run lay councils into an association. In a meeting with VOTF representatives, Edyvean invited them several times, according to VOTF spokesman Paul Baier, "to shut your group down." VOTF reports pressure on parish priests to prohibit VOTF chapters from meeting on church property—a prohibition long imposed on Call to

Action chapters. Such obstacles, VOTF's Muller told the *New York Times*, could lead the group to "become more radical."

And, in a dramatic contrast to its coddling of sex abusers, the Vatican threatened to excommunicate the women ordained on the Danube if they didn't renounce their ordinations by July 22. The women refused, and have since sent a letter challenging their excommunication to the Vatican. Ironically, July 22 was also the Feast Day of St. Mary of Magdala (*a k a* Mary Magdalene), on which several thousand people attended more than two-hundred woman-led celebrations. Those celebrations were developed by reform groups to mend the reputation of the most famous prostitute in church history, who was actually not a prostitute at all but the first of Jesus' disciples to witness his resurrection.

The power of the institutional church to intimidate stands. Some reformers remain protective of the identities of priests who allow women to preach at mass and of independent eucharistic communities. Vladimiroff never got official word that the pope was finished with the Erie Benedictines, and she's waiting for the other shoe to drop. Organizers of the ordinations on the Danube restricted press access to protect guests from church reprisals.

The progress to be made, in the end, depends on the will of the laity. "Catholics need to get much more vocal with the diocesan leadership about what kinds of things they're going to tolerate and what kinds of things they're not," says FutureChurch executive director Sister Chris Schenk. "And they're going to have to link it to the pocketbook." That's a special challenge for devout Catholics used to obeying, and for so-called cafeteria Catholics, who may feel little responsibility for the institutional church.

As to how quickly change will come, Chittister offers a perspective. "I'm talking about the movement of tectonic plates," she says, reflecting on the magnitude of the challenges ahead. "I am not talking about tiny, little organizational cosmetics, a new set of rules for how we report on something. I'm talking about a whole institutional church, about the conversion of this clerical institution into a real Church society."

The Agony of Afghanistan

What Women Want

Sharon Lerner

From the *Village Voice*, October 31–November 6, 2001

A year ago, when women's rights and peace advocate Hibaaq Osman was giving a speech at the United Nations, she cited only one cause for which the use of military force might be justified: to oust the oppressive Taliban regime from Afghanistan. Now that the bloody effort is underway, however, Osman, who heads the Center for Strategic Initiatives in Washington, feels differently.

"I said it, but I was just making a point," a distraught Osman recalls. "This predicament is a test for feminists. We have seen our worst nightmare—women being dehumanized and shot in public—and it makes us more radical. It makes us angry enough to entertain the idea of war. But do I support war?" Osman pauses to consider her own country, Somalia, with its brutal history, before bursting out with an emotional "No. No. No. War is not OK under any circumstances," and then concluding, "The whole thing simply breaks my heart."

The four-week-old military attack on Afghanistan is proving to be an excruciating dilemma for feminists. In heart-wrenching conversations and e-mail exchanges across the city and the globe, feminists find themselves split over how to handle possibly the most misogynistic regime in history. Many are deeply uncomfortable with the specter of a wealthy nation bombing a poor and already ravaged one—a discomfort that is only deepened by the knowledge that more women than men die as a result of most wars. And as national loyalties are stoked by current events, feminists are further strained to reconcile their patriotism with the desire to reach out to women throughout the globe.

Perhaps most frustrating has been the world's failure to heed feminists' urgent warnings about the Taliban, which they've been decrying since it took power in 1996. Under the fundamentalist militia's rule, women have been publicly executed for such "crimes" as traveling with men who are not their relatives and being suspected of adultery. The government has banned women from work, education, and examination by male doctors. Women have even been forbidden from making noise when they walk (the sound draws men's attention, according to Taliban rulers).

Back in 1997, the Feminist Majority's Eleanor Smeal was among the first to sound alarms about the ghastly treatment of Afghan women, urging the U.S. against diplomatic recognition of the Taliban and to halt construction of a pipeline through Afghanistan that would have supplied millions in profits to the regime. The pipeline project was eventually stopped, but others of the group's suggestions, including a U.S. designation of the Taliban as an international terrorist organization, have yet to be carried out.

Perhaps it's no surprise that some feminists, including Smeal, now feel the backward and violent regime deserves whatever it gets. The rare overlap between feminist and military interests made for particularly warm relations in the greenroom at an NBC station in Los Angeles when Smeal met up with three generals who were about to appear on Chris Matthews's "Hardball." "They went off about the role of women in this effort and how imperative it was that women were now in every level of the air force and navy," says Smeal, who found herself cheered by the idea of women flying F-16s. "It's a different kind of war," she says, echoing the president's assessment of Operation Enduring Freedom.

Indeed, the gender gap in support for this U.S. military effort is unusually small. Historically, female support for war has lagged between 10 and 15 percent behind men's, according to Joshua Goldstein, author of *War and Gender: How Gender Shapes the War System and Vice Versa*. But in a recent survey released by the Pew Research Center for the People and the Press, 79 percent of women, compared to 86 percent of men, said they support the ongoing military intervention, a near parity Goldstein believes may be explained by the fact that the Taliban is anathema to women.

Still, many women are unwilling to translate their opposition to the Taliban into support for war. The U.S. air strikes against the country and the recent addition of ground troops—which, depending on the estimate, have together resulted in anywhere from a few dozen to almost a thousand civilian casualties—clash with long-held feminist sensibilities. Some worry that bombing will further endanger Afghanistan's already brutalized women, who account for 70 percent of Afghanistan's refugees.

Feminists also have a pragmatic argument: Missiles and soldiers won't topple the Taliban. "I continue to wish with all my heart for the regime to be overthrown; I just don't think the U.S. military can do it," says author Susan Sontag, whose September 18 article in the *New Yorker* set the tone for criticism of U.S. military policy. The choice "isn't bombs or nothing," says Sontag, who doesn't consider herself a pacifist. "The world is a complicated place. We can put pressure on our allies and offer bribes and rewards."

The peace position was also taken by the Worldwide Sisterhood Against Terrorism and War, an organization of about eighty feminists that includes women from Central Asia as well as such U.S. notables as Gloria Steinem, Alice Walker, and Susan Sarandon. In a petition headlined "Not in Our Name," the group declared, "We will not support the bombing or U.S. invasion of Afghanistan, for it would only punish suffering people and increase the hatred on which terrorists feed."

While the wording leaves open the possibility of support for UN-sponsored military intervention—an option many find more palatable than U.S. and British forces acting independently—reaching consensus even on that phrasing took days of rapid-fire e-mails and skillful negotiation. Questions about the future of Afghanistan have been even thornier.

Sunita Mehta and Fahima Danishgar, who recently cofounded Women for Afghan Women—the first grassroots group for women from Afghanistan and its neighbors living in New York—were among the dozens of feminists who gathered for a post-September 11 meeting at the Manhattan apartment of Eve Ensler. But, coming from the region—Mehta is Indian and Danishgar, twenty-three, left Afghanistan at age nine—they found they had less of an us-versus-them perspective than many Americans reacting to the recent terrorist attacks.

"We are us *and* we are them," says Mehta. "We came in feeling very close to the land that was going to be bombed." That closeness—and a superior knowledge of history and politics that comes with it—allowed her to temper the more utopian dreams of Western feminists. While some at the meeting seriously suggested that the Revolutionary Association of the Women of Afghanistan should rule the country, for instance, Mehta pointed out that the two-thousand-member RAWA is "a small, Maoist organization." It would be nice if women could be in charge, she says, "but we don't have the luxury of dreaming big dreams right now."

Indeed, the women of Afghanistan—for whom makeup, forbidden by the Taliban, is a symbol of liberation—have different priorities from their

Western counterparts. RAWA, whose members have documented Taliban atrocities through slits in their Taliban-mandated robes, has thrown its own political support behind the exiled Afghan king. And although many Westerners have focused on that robe, the *burqa*, as an emblem of women's oppression, Afghan women don't always see it that way. "Some women choose to wear it. It can be a symbol of respect" for tradition, says Danishgar, whose own mother sometimes wore a burqa.

The burqa has been a touchy subject before, particularly when Oprah Winfrey lifted one off an Afghan woman in a performance of Ensler's *Vagina Monologues*, instead of letting the woman perform the symbolic liberation herself. For some, the gesture reeked of Western arrogance, even though the talk-show star has been credited with raising awareness of the Taliban in the TV-watching core of our country by having RAWA members on her show. (RAWA's Web site, www.rawa.org—a fascinating crosscultural women's effort that features digital video of Afghan women being executed— welcomes Oprah viewers specifically.)

Osman, who wears a head scarf and robes, sees the East-West tension as rooted in religion. "I love my Western feminists," she says, "but I'm just finding out how ignorant they are." Osman, a Muslim, offers a definition of feminist many Western women might share: "a woman who is very comfortable with who she is and believes the sky is the limit." Still, she says, "Every now and then I hear 'What is it with Islam that makes your men this way?' And I think to myself, 'What is it with Christianity that makes *your* men this way?' "

No doubt, many Americans are feeling somewhat smug about our heroic, enlightened men just now. Ironically, though, the crisis seems to be inspiring a reversion to traditional gender roles. While the press dubbed First Lady Laura Bush the "comforter-in-chief," Peggy Noonan giddily declared that "Men are back." "I'm speaking of masculine men," the former Reagan aide wrote in the *Wall Street Journal*, "men who push things and pull things and haul things and build things."

Of course, men have never really gone away. The power structure remains overwhelmingly male—a fact that was highlighted by the never-ending emergency press conferences featuring wall-to-wall men. Indeed, National Security Adviser Condoleezza Rice is one of only four women among nineteen cabinet-level officials. Roughly one in seven members of Congress is female. All of the twenty-three committee chairs in the House of Representatives are male, as are all of the Senate's twenty-two chairs. And a mere 6 out of 189 ambassadors to the UN are female.

The numbers are, not surprisingly, more skewed when it comes to conflict. "After childbirth, war making has possibly been the most segregated of activities along gender lines," says Felicity Hill, director of the UN office of the Women's International League for Peace and Freedom. Perhaps that doesn't have to be true. Last year, the UN passed a resolution calling for women's participation in decision making about war and peace. Nevertheless, "war remains the domain of men," says Hill. "Women's voices are missing from decisions on priorities in peace processes."

These days, it's hard for anyone to stray from the political mainstream, and harder still for women. Like many others on the left, Canadian activist Sunera Thobani accused the U.S. of "unleashing prolific levels of violence all over the world," but unlike many other lefties, Thobani was subject to the Canadian equivalent of citizen's arrest and, intriguingly, sent porn by her critics. The Canadian secretary of state for the status of women, Hedy Fry, almost lost her job for just listening to Thobani's speech.

The response to Susan Sontag's *New Yorker* piece neared witch-hunt pitch. The *New York Post* suggested that Sontag be drawn and quartered. A scrawled sign recently posted in Manhattan's Old Town bar referred to the author as "an old battle-axe." And a piece in the *New Republic* began, "What do Osama bin Laden, Saddam Hussein, and Susan Sontag have in common?" (The desire to dismantle America, it turns out.)

While Sontag sees the reaction mostly in political terms, she also sees a gender-related biliousness she likened to that aimed at Hillary Clinton. "It has to do with the very deep anxiety and fear and dislike of a woman who seems to be very smart and powerful," Sontag said of the Hillary hatred. Smart women "arouse huge feelings of resentment and dislike on the part of a lot of people," added Sontag. "Why should I think I'm exempt?"

The public clobbering is yet another reminder that despite having a common enemy, the U.S. government and feminists are not necessarily friends. "Everything is being manipulated to get what the U.S. wants, which isn't primarily women's rights," says Jessica Neuwirth, president of Equality Now, a New York-based women's group. "The U.S. military did not intervene to remove the Taliban because of anything to do with women."

That divergence of interests is becoming clearer as the U.S. considers including "moderate Taliban forces" in a future coalition government and joins forces with countries where female genital mutilation is widespread (Egypt) and women are forbidden from driving cars (Saudi Arabia). Our rising political partners, the Northern Alliance, are particularly horrendous to women. The group's No. 2 political leader, Abdul Rasul Sayyaf, reportedly believes so strongly in the inferiority of women he doesn't even speak to them. And Ahmed Shah Massood, the recently assassinated Northern Alliance leader, partook in campaigns of systematic rape that predated Taliban rule.

"The only difference between the crimes they committed and the Taliban is that the Taliban officially announced the restrictions on women," says a RAWA member who does not reveal her name. "The Northern Alliance committed many, many crimes against women—rapes, forced marriages. Women were afraid of going outside when they were in control," she continues, referring to the period between 1992 and 1996, before the Taliban seized power.

Back then, RAWA, which was founded in 1977, had already been trying to call attention to women's plight for years, though few were listening. The RAWA representative worries that her country's next government might be as woman hating as its predecessors. Perhaps it's a cultural difference, but the Feminist Majority's Smeal is optimistic that this calamity will finally change things for women. "Next time women speak about international issues, they'll listen," she says hopefully. "Our credibility will have gone up."

Behind the Burqa

Polly Toynbee

From the *Guardian* (London), September 28, 2001

Something horrible flits across the background in scenes from Afghanistan, scuttling out of sight. There it is, a brief blue or black flash, a grotesque *Scream 1, 2,* and *3* personified—a woman. The top-to-toe *burqa*, with its sinister, airless little grille, is more than an instrument of persecution, it is a public tarring and feathering of female sexuality. It transforms any woman into an object of defilement too untouchably disgusting to be seen. It is a garment of lurid sexual suggestiveness: what rampant desire and desirability lurks and leers beneath its dark mysteries? In its objectifying of women, it turns them into cowering creatures demanding and expecting violence and victimization. Forget cultural sensibilities.

More moderate versions of the garb—the dull, uniform coat to the ground and the plain headscarf—have much the same effect, inspiring the lascivious thoughts they are designed to stifle. What is it about a woman that is so repellently sexual that she must diminish herself into drab uniformity while strolling down Oxford Street one step behind a husband who is kitted out in razor-sharp Armani and gold, pomaded hair and tight bum exposed to lustful eyes? (No letters please from British women who have taken the veil and claim it's liberating. It is their right in a tolerant society to wear anything including rubber fetishes—but that has nothing to do with the systematic cultural oppression of women with no choice.)

The pens sharpen—Islamophobia! No such thing. Primitive Middle Eastern religions (and most others) are much the same—Islam, Christianity and Judaism all define themselves through disgust for women's bodies. There are ritual baths, churching, shaving heads, denying abortion and contraception, arranged marriage, purdah, barring unclean women access to the altar, let alone the priesthood, letting men divorce but not women—all this perverted abhorrence of half the human race lies at the maggotty heart of religion, the defining creed in all the holy of holies.

Moderate, modernized believers may claim the true Bible/Qur'an does not demand such things. But it hardly matters how close these savage manifestations are to the words of the Prophet or Christ. All extreme fundamentalism plunges back into the dark ages by using the oppression of women (sometimes called "family values") as its talisman. Religions that thrive are pliable, morphing to suit changing needs: most Christianity has had to moderate to modernize. Islamic fundamentalism flourishes because it, too, suits modern needs very well in a developing world seeking an identity to defy the all-engulfing West. And the *burqa* and *chador* are its battle flags.

The war leaders are coy about this mighty cultural war of the worlds that is fought out over women's bodies. Other considerations always did come first. When the *mujahedeen* were Western heroes against Russia and Western TV reporters pranced about hilltops in teatowels extolling them, the *Guardian* women's page had just about the only non-Russian inspired writers pointing to the plight of hidden mujahedeen women. Now again there is a danger. Western leaders seek to blur the issue, to mollify semi-friendly Arab countries. Already our new allies, the "Northern Alliance" or the "United Front" sneak into the language now as our brethren, the good guys. Already their name emits a warm glow of security as we imagine our boys going in behind their lines to support them to victory for democracy, freedom, human rights and equality for women. But wait, what's that in the background of all those nightly pictures of our gallant allies? Flitting burqas, just like the Taliban women. Talking to those in the UN, aid agencies, and others who have lived there, they all say there is little difference between the two sides beyond old ethnic and tribal allegiances. The Taliban are Pashtuns, the Alliance is an unstable mix of minority ethnic groups. Turn to the Amnesty or Human Rights Watch websites and there are atrocities aplenty on both sides. As for women, a UN official I spoke to was sitting in his office in Kabul back in 1992 when our friends the Alliance barged in to demand all women staff be sent home at once: they banned women from jobs long before the Taliban. Far from a "united" front, this makeshift Alliance is just tribal warlords each with their own supporters abroad, some selling heroin, many with a history of ratting and reratting across the battlelines. Their assassinated leader, Ahmad Shah Masood, had a pleasing, French-speaking Westernized, educated aspect, but his past was hardly savory. He cannily wooed Western support with promises that women can work and girls attend school, with a few women engineers in evidence, but life for women in burqas on both sides of the divide is virtually identical servitude.

Does it mean the war is not worth fighting? No, but it requires extreme circumspection about our allies and no illusions about how difficult it will be to build a stable or half-civilized government. Given the Northern Alliance's past, we should draw up a human rights contract now and make Alliance leaders sign the UN's International Covenant on Civil and Political Rights, binding them personally against atrocities before fighting begins. Raping, burning, slaughtering, and ethnic revenge killings marked their last victorious entry to Kabul. Present eagerness to chase out bin Laden must not make human rights an afterthought in our intervention in this black hole of humanity. Global moral authority on universal rights and women's equality will matter more in the long run than appeasing the Islamic sensibilities of coalition members now.

This is a rationalist *jihad*. This war against terrorism is not a war against moderate Thought-for-the-Day Islam but against the fundamentalism that breeds murderous martyrs. But the war leaders are fudging even this, on anxious visits to Iran where BBC women correspondents are forced into *chadors*. Women are missing from the story so far when they should be up at the front—literally and metaphorically: This war between reason and unreason is ultimately about them. With such a dearth of satisfactory allies, the coalition should turn to one Afghan group completely ignored so far— the Revolutionary Association of the Women of Afghanistan. Their leader was a poet called Meena, who was assassinated by the KGB with fundamentalist help, in exile, in Quetta in 1987. They are secular, sane, and working hard in the camps of Pakistan, running schools and clinics. They get no help from any government because rationalist feminists naturally have no sway with any tribal warlords. With all the money now flooding in, pushing these women forward and backing their progressive work would be an act of good faith in a democratic equal rights future. Or will realpolitik come before real women?

After the Taliban

Katha Pollitt

From *The Nation*, December 17, 2001

What if Hillary Clinton, not Laura Bush, had taken to the airwaves during her husband's first year in office and become the first First Lady to deliver the entire weekly presidential radio address—about women's rights, no less? Dragon lady! Castrating feminist man-hating bitch! All together now: Who Elected *Her*? The Republicans would have started impeachment proceedings that very day. In fact, the down-to-earth and nonthreatening Laura Bush spoke so eloquently in support of Afghan women's rights I actually found myself not wanting to believe the Democratic Party accusation that this was a cynical attempt to appeal to women and narrow the eleven-point gender gap that bedeviled Bush in the 2000 election—not that a shortage of votes turned out to matter, but that's another story. Perhaps Mrs. Bush—and Cherie Blair, who gave a similar speech on November 19—was sending a message to the sorry collection of warlords and criminals, power-grabbers and back-stabbers vying for power in the new Afghanistan: This time around, women must have a seat at the table. As I write, Afghan women are swinging into action, with a major conference planned for early December in Brussels to insist on equality and political power in their post-Taliban nation.

Wouldn't it be wonderful if the defeat of the Taliban also marked the end of the cultural-relativist pooh-poohing of women's rights? Only a few weeks ago, a Bush administration spokesperson was refusing to promise that women would play a role in a new Afghan government: "We have to be careful not to look like we are imposing our values on them." A week before it began, no women had been mentioned as participants in the UN-sponsored Bonn conference to plan for a postwar Afghanistan. As it turned out, there are three among the twenty-eight delegates: two in the delegation of the former king and one in that of the Northern Alliance, plus at least two more attending as advisers. Whether it means anything, who knows—of the four factions gathered in Bonn, only the Northern Alliance controls any actual territory, and its record with regard to women's rights and dignity is nothing to cheer about. While some alliance leaders speak encouragingly of girls' education and women's right to work, early signs are mixed: In Kabul, women can once more freely walk the streets, but the newly reopened movie theater is off-limits, and a women's rights march was halted by authorities; in late November, according to the *Los Angeles Times*, women were banned from voting for mayor in Herat, whose de facto ruler, Ismail Khan, has presented himself as sympathetic to women's rights.

Still, whatever government takes shape in Afghanistan will probably be better for women than the Taliban—how could it be worse?—as long as the country does not degenerate into civil war, as happened the last time the Northern Alliance was in power. But let's not kid ourselves: This war is not about freeing women from government-mandated *burqas*, or teaching girls to read, or improving Afghan women's ghastly maternal mortality rate of seventeen in one thousand births—the second highest in the world. Those things may happen as a byproduct of realpolitik, or they may not. But if women's rights and well-being were aims of U.S. Afghan policy, the Carter, Reagan, and Bush administrations would never have financed the *mujahedeen*, whose Neanderthal treatment of women, including throwing acid at unveiled women, was well-documented from the start; the Clinton administration would not have initially accepted the Taliban even after they closed the girls' schools in Herat; and the current Bush administration would have inundated the millions of Afghan women and girls in Pakistan's refugee camps with teachers, nurses, doctors, and food.

As other commentators have pointed out, if Laura Bush wants to make women's rights a U.S. foreign policy goal, she's got her work cut out for her. Saudi Arabia, our best friend, is positively Talibanesque: Women are rigidly segregated by law, cannot drive, cannot travel without written permission from a male relative; top-to-toe veiling is mandated by law and enforced by a brutal religious police force. In a particularly insulting twist, U.S. women soldiers stationed there are compelled to wear the veil and refrain from driving when off base; so far the Bush administration has refused to act on soldiers' objections to these conditions.

One can go on and on about the situation of women in Muslim countries—unable to vote in Kuwait; genitally mutilated in Egypt and Sudan; flogged, jailed, murdered with impunity and even stoned to death for sexual infractions in a number of countries—and Muslim women everywhere are fighting back (for a serious, nonsensationalist approach, check out the website of Women Living Under Muslim Laws, www.wluml.org). But the Islamic world is hardly the only place where women are denied their human rights: How would you like to have to get a divorce in an Israeli rabbinical court or need an abortion in Chile, where it's illegal even to save your life? The United States makes no bones about using its economic and political might against illegal drugs—in fact, the administration rewarded the Taliban for banning opium production by making a $43 million donation to the World Food Program and humanitarian NGOs (not, as is usually reported, to the Taliban proper). If it cared to do so, the United States could back the global women's movement with the same zeal.

Instead, it does the opposite. In order to curry favor with conservative Catholics at home, Laura Bush's husband has shown callous disregard for women's rights and health abroad: He reinstated the Mexico City policy, which bars family-planning groups receiving U.S. funds from discussing abortion; he sent antichoice delegations to wreck the consensus at international conferences on children's rights and public health; he tried to nominate John Klink, former adviser to the Holy See, to head the State Department's Bureau of Population, Refugees, and Migration, which would have thrown the United States behind the pope's call to deny emergency contraception to raped women in refugee camps.

That the Taliban are gone is cause for joy. A world that cared about women's rights would never have let them come to power in the first place.

An Uneasy Peace

Jan Goodwin

From *The Nation*, April 29, 2002

In January, Hamid Karzai, chairman of the Afghan interim administration, quietly signed the "Declaration of Essential Rights of Afghan Women," which guarantees equality between men and women, equal protection under the law, equal right to education in all disciplines, freedom of movement, freedom of speech and political participation, and freedom to wear or not wear the *burqa* or any form of head covering. After five years of Taliban oppression, the worst in the world for women, such freedoms are heartening indeed. Their exercise, however, depends on certain conditions—not least of which is basic security—that do not currently exist in Afghanistan.

Equal protection under the law is meaningless when the courts are not functioning and there is no reliable national police force or army. The exiled King Zahir Shah has twice delayed his return to Afghanistan because of assassination threats. At the beginning of April, a coup d'état in the making by alleged associates of former Prime Minister Gulbuddin Hekmatyar was foiled when hundreds were arrested for planning "terrorism, abductions, and sabotage." It's a misnomer to call the forty-five-hundred-strong British-led International Security Assistance Force (ISAF) "peacekeepers" since they are confined to the capital and have a mandate to defend only the UN and the government, which precludes any protection for ordinary Afghans. UN Secretary General Kofi Annan and Karzai himself have said that the ISAF needs to be increased to thirty thousand and deployed throughout the country, but President Bush continues to reject such expansion.

"How can we win the war, and lose the keeping of the peace?" asks Eleanor Smeal, whose organization, the Feminist Majority Foundation, led the U.S. campaign against the Taliban's oppression of women. "President Bush said he would not turn his back on Afghanistan, but not having more security forces is a disaster. It doesn't make sense." The situation on the ground belies the Bush administration's claims that it has won the war on terrorism in Afghanistan, averted a famine, and liberated women. As the U.S. military struggles to stamp out persistent pockets of now-you-see-them, now-you-don't Al Qaeda and Taliban, death from hunger is common, lawlessness rampant, and little has changed for the vast majority of Afghan women.

Under such circumstances, it is not surprising that very few women have discarded the burqa—a garment best described as a body bag for the living—because they fear for their safety. Recent reports of gang rapes by armed Afghan factions echo the indiscriminate sexual violence of the four-year civil war of 1992-96, which paved the way for the Taliban, with their promises of restoring law and order. Human Rights Watch now reports a "wave of killing, rape and widespread ethnic persecution" in northern Afghanistan, where an anti-Pashtun pogrom is raging. "We have found case after case of gang-raping of women, and even children," says senior researcher Peter Bouckaert. Adds Jessica Neuwirth, president of Equality Now, a New York-based international women's human rights organization: "Rape is being tolerated and condoned by regional Afghan authorities. They are complicit in the assaults. The people running these parts of the country have a history of such abuse themselves."

Hafiza Rasouli, forty-six, a UNICEF project officer, spoke for many women when she told me during a recent visit to Kabul: "We felt safer under the Taliban. We could sleep with our doors open at night, but no longer. When it comes to our security, we have not forgotten Nahida."

Thirteen-year-old Nahida Hassan became a symbol for Afghan women and girls who were raped during the two decades of war. When a commander and twenty of his troops broke into her Kabul apartment, killing her twelve-year-old brother and gunning down her other male relatives, Nahida understood she was the target. To avoid being sexually savaged, she leapt from the sixth-floor window to her death. Today, there is a shrine on the spot where she fell. "Everyone knew who the commander was. But no one dared touch him," said the girl's sixty-four-year-old grandfather, Muhammad Hassan. The commander enjoyed the protection of his party, whose fundamentalist cleric leader, Burhanuddin Rabbani, headed the government at the time and, more recently, the Northern Alliance, which holds key positions in the new interim administration. And with Hekmatyar back in the picture—a notorious warlord and rabid extremist who during the anti-Soviet war in the 1980s was a major recipient of U.S. military aid funneled through Pakistan's intelligence service—security for women could become much worse. In his brief sojourn at Kabul University in the 1960s, Hekmatyar was infamous for throwing acid in the faces of unveiled female students. Since then, he has been responsible for a vast list of atrocities and assassinations.

A growing schism between a few apparent progressives and the conservative hard-liners in the interim administration was highlighted when, days before Karzai signed the emancipation document, his justice minister announced that the new government would still impose a strict form of shariah law. In an interview with the French news agency Agence France-Presse, his chief justice explained that public executions and amputations would no longer be held at Kabul's sports stadium, but that they would continue. "The stadium is for sports. We will find a new place for public executions," he said, adding that adulterers, too, will still be publicly stoned to death. The new interior ministry, meanwhile, requires women to have the permission of their male relatives before traveling or applying for passports, just as the Taliban did.

For the first time in its history, Afghanistan has a ministry of women's affairs, but Minister Sima Samar, three months into her six-month tenure, already feels she is being marginalized, even by Karzai.[1] She has also received a number of death threats, and not long ago, one of her private clinics in Bamiyan was targeted and the staff massacred. Samar, a forty-five-year-old physician, is now talking about resigning, possibly before her term ends. "She's not being taken seriously by her own government. Very few of the men in the interim administration believe there should be a women's ministry," says a senior UN official. "These are not for the most part liberal, progressive men; many of them have similar attitudes to the Taliban."

In conversations with visitors, Samar frequently relates how, toward the end of a wide-ranging meeting with U.S. Secretary of State Colin Powell, she passed a note to Karzai reminding him that he hadn't once mentioned women's issues. "I wanted Powell to know we are serious about women's issues. But we are not," she said. On International Women's Day, March 8, she was asked to write Karzai's speech for him. Samar was decidedly unhappy when he eviscerated it, cutting it by 50 percent.

Samar, who is given to wearing jeans or pants and leaving her head uncovered, has other problems, too. Despite crowds of women who daily clog the entrance to the ministry looking for assistance, thus far she has received no operating funds. The ministry building is still under renovation;

it was full of bomb rubble when it was assigned to her and lacked a roof, windows, and many doors. Afghanistan's land-line phone system is as devastated as the rest of the country's infrastructure. Samar has no Internet access and can't afford to use her satellite phone. At the end of March the ministry had received only $64,000 for building repairs and renovation, and $30,000 from a foundation for a school uniform project.

The Afghan Interim Authority Fund, set up after the Bonn Agreement established the interim administration, channels funding from twenty-five donor countries, including the United States, and is intended to meet urgent needs. The UN Development Program, which manages the fund, says $50 million is required; $37 million has been pledged, but only $26 million has been received, and much of that still sits in New York. "The running cost of the government was not included in this amount," says Julia Taft, who heads the fund. With the Afghan economy in tatters and the treasury all but empty, omitting day-to-day operating expenses would appear to be a colossal oversight.

In addition to the shortfall in donor funding, one of the biggest difficulties, says Taft, is getting the money into Afghanistan. "We've had to resort to flying in plane loads of cash because the banks aren't functioning, and we couldn't wire it. This, of course, is a major security issue."

"When we have no money, how can we work, or pay staff?" asks Samar's deputy minister, Shafiqa Yargin, a former magazine editor. "There is much we want to do, but all we hear is that the countries who have promised us money have not given it."

Slamming the international aid bureaucracy for being "way too slow" for the needs of the country, Eve Ensler, the *Vagina Monologues* playwright, brought in bundles of banknotes and satellite phones for the women's ministry on a recent trip to Kabul. "Since Sima Samar has no money to pay her phone bill, V-Day will do it," says Ensler, the founder of V-Day, an organization aimed at stopping violence against women and girls.

Some of the responsibility rests with the finance ministry in Kabul, through which all incoming funds are distributed. "If the ministry doesn't like you, they can be very slow, or simply not give it," said one insider. Sohaila Sidiq, the minister of health and the other woman in the Cabinet, is having an easier time than Samar, according to Shafiqa Habibi, a prominent journalist in Kabul and former director of the Afghan Women's Journalists Association, because the ministry of health is more established and has the support of the World Health Organization and other international bodies. And whereas health care is universally accepted in Afghanistan, women's rights are not.

Samar's battle to be accepted has been compounded by other factors: Because she is Hazara, a minority ethnic group reviled by many Afghans, her support within the country is largely limited to other Hazaras.

There is a growing school of thought in Kabul among the expat aid community and the UN that Samar was appointed to fail. The minister's biggest problem, she herself says, is that Afghans don't think she is a real Muslim, that she is too Westernized, too secular, too radical for the country's orthodox leaders and opinion-makers. It hasn't helped that she once espoused Maoist politics. Samar's first husband, who shared her party philosophy, was arrested in 1979 and never seen again, and she was forced to flee to Pakistan. Samar was also one of the founders, in 1977, of RAWA, the Revolutionary Association of the Women of Afghanistan, a group that has garnered considerably more publicity in the United States than it has credibility in its own country. RAWA's leader and two colleagues were assassinated in the 1980s, and it continues to be marginalized within the culture.

Ensler recognizes that Samar walks a thin line in her position. "I don't envy her. She's trying to appease a Western agenda, and a feminist approach doesn't help her in Afghanistan, since women's rights there need to be incrementally introduced."

A major challenge will be undoing five years of Taliban indoctrination on gender roles. "Small boys as young as six or seven are treating women like dogs," says Rachel Wareham, a women's rights lobbyist in Kabul for Medica Mondiale, a German humanitarian agency, and a newly appointed planning, strategy, and policy adviser to Samar. "There's incredible arrogance and lack of respect in boys so young. They refuse to let their mothers speak, and speak for them."

The return-to-school program, which is sending 1.5 million children (nearly half of them girls) back to school this month, will still leave more than two out of three without access to education, the vast majority female. Currently, only four percent of women and girls are literate. There's an estimated shortage of 100,000 teachers, and thousands of schools were destroyed during the fighting. Even before the Taliban ban on girls' education, enrollment was rarely higher than 5 percent. Also, since schools were frequently used as military bases, many have been heavily landmined. "And how do you educate children when they are hungry? People are in dire need of food," says Ensler.

Security issues have hampered food aid distribution. UN aid convoys are regularly attacked and robbed. Compounding the problem, the World Food Program has only received five percent of the nearly $300 million it needs for emergency food aid this year. And because the bulk of the food aid sent to Afghanistan is confined to wheat flour, the daily diet for too many families is limited to flat nan bread and sugarless green tea, if they can afford the latter, or nonpotable water if they can't. Death from hunger has become tragically commonplace. I spoke to many women who related how they had lost as many as five, six, seven children to starvation and exposure in the past two years. According to UN statistics, 12 million Afghans—seventy percent of the population—are severely malnourished, and one in two children is stunted. Children's health is so fragile that a quarter don't survive to the age of five, and thirty-five thousand a year succumb to measles.

Since only twelve percent of women have access to even basic health care, it is perhaps not surprising that every thirty minutes an Afghan woman dies from pregnancy-related causes, according to UNICEF. The British medical journal *Lancet* also reports that the maternal death rate among Afghan refugees in Pakistani camps is among the highest ever recorded. Two decades of war, poverty, and the recent drought have given Afghanistan one of the worst health profiles in the world, says Dr. Sidiq.

In this desperate situation, the U.S. pledge of $296 million at the donors' conference in Tokyo this past January for the first year's reconstruction demonstrates a lukewarm commitment at best (especially compared with the $1 billion a month the United States says it has spent on the war effort). And the Tokyo pledge is even smaller than it seems: Only $50 million of the $296 million is new funding; the remainder had been previously committed for existing programs. Worse, with the delays in money transfer to Afghanistan, any funding not transmitted expires at the end of the year, and cannot be carried over.

The interim administration will run only to June, when a traditional *Loya Jirga*, or grand council of elders of some 1,450, headed by the 87-year-old king, if it is safe for him to return, will help select a subsequent transitional government. This is expected to lead to democratic elections eighteen months later. Since proof of citizenship is usually a prerequisite for voting and ninety-eight percent of Afghan women do not possess identity cards, their voting rights could be threatened unless they are registered in the next two years, according to Noeleen Heyzer, head of UNIFEM, the UN women's affairs agency.

In the meantime, Afghan women activists are working hard to make sure they are fairly represented at the June *Loya Jirga*. "We sincerely hope it will be better than what we had in Bonn, when it was three out of thirty," says Sima Wali, president of Refugee Women in Development in Washington, D.C., and a delegate at both Bonn and the Afghan Women's Summit in Brussels that followed. While 160 seats are guaranteed for women, early indications are that their numbers are unlikely to exceed 200, making the ratio considerably lower than the fifteen percent they had in the last meaningful *Loya Jirga*, in the mid-1970s.

The twenty-one members of the UN-appointed loya jirga commission, charged with convening the larger body, are of key importance—especially amid reports of large amounts of money changing hands in factionalized horse-trading as warlords jockey for position. Interested states are also involved. "We know the Russians gave a lot of money to Rabbani before Bonn; they printed the Afghanis for them," says Barnett Rubin, a leading Afghan analyst and director of studies at the Center on International Cooperation at New York University. "The U.S. is paying their people, and the Iranians are supporting their own [Afghanistan's Shi'ites, a fifteen percent minority]."

Many Afghans are outraged that a number of those on the *Loya Jirga* commission were ranking Communists during the Soviet occupation, including Soraya Parlika, one of the commission's three women. Parlika was head of the Democratic Afghan Women's Association, a government-affiliated organization, during the Najibullah regime. "Afghanistan's tragic legacy of total destruction began with the Communists. The Marxist-Leninists killed more than a million Afghans trying to force their ideology on us," complains Zieba Shorish-Shamley, an anthropologist and executive director of the Women's Alliance for Peace and Human Rights in Afghanistan, based in Washington, D.C., who was a delegate at Brussels.

Even as Karzai calls for a Truth and Reconciliation Commission for Afghanistan, the sad fact is that his interim administration includes a number of known war criminals, such as Abdul Rashid Dostum, a barely literate, brutal and self-appointed general. Dostum was named deputy defense minister, a classic case of the wolf guarding the chickens, in an attempt to stop him from being a bloody spoiler. The transitional government is unlikely to escape such associations, as feudal warlords, many of them big-time drug traffickers, and war criminals from the 1980s Communist regime are certain to make the final cut. Despite *Loya Jirga* restrictions meant to exclude such people, the commission's chairman, Ismail Qasimyr, has already stated that all members of Karzai's administration have an automatic right to attend.

A number of insiders believe that the UN—including Lakhdar Brahimi, the UN Secretary General's special representative for Afghanistan—is willing to turn a blind eye to such problems. "The truth is, Brahimi's priority in Afghanistan is not human rights," says the senior UN official. "This has been a major concern of Mary Robinson [the UN human rights chief, who recently said she was stepping down]. Brahimi's imperative is to make sure the political process in Afghanistan works. Karzai could be a donkey with a red rosette pinned to his back. The UN's entire credibility is behind him and the political process. But if nothing is done about the human rights violations, there will be major problems down the road."

Afghanistan's challenges appear almost insurmountable. But now, says Shorish-Shamley, is the best time to fight for women's rights. "Patriarchy has existed for thousands of years in Afghanistan," she says. "As we reconstruct the country, we are also restructuring the society. If we don't push now, we will not get anywhere." Many women in Kabul would agree with her.

"Young women especially are raring to go and want to have opportunities. They have such spirit," says Wareham of Medica Mondiale. "Girl students and women teachers who are back in school are thrilled to be there. There's a *tae kwon do* class for women starting in Kabul, even a driving course. These are things they couldn't have dreamed of before." But right now, funding and security are the biggest obstacles.

Afghan women activists see a parallel between their lives and the condition of the once much-loved women's garden, Barg-i-Zenana, in the capital. The flowers and lawns are gone, and so, too, are the almond trees, their trunks blown up, their branches taken for kindling by the Taliban. All that remains today is a barren, walled-in plot. "It was a magical place before the fighting, a huge, beautiful garden, where women and girls loved to come and relax," says Fatima Gailani, who was an adviser at Bonn. "The garden, when it is restored, will be a symbol for Afghan women. If it can come back, so can we and the country. It will be a microcosm for the nation."

Notes

1 Under pressure from Islamists in the interim government, Sima Samar resigned as minister of women's affairs in July 2002. She is now a member of Afghanistan's human rights commission.

Returning From Kabul

Eve Ensler

I see my stomach in the barely-standing full-length mirror in my room at the Intercontinental Hotel in Kabul. I am surprised that my stomach is not huge. It is lean, but lean the way an older body looks lean. It is not clean-lean. I am surprised that it is not full—pouring out. Full of the broken dust that has fallen and continues to fall over everything, full of the cold, shivering impoverishment that creeps deep into one's skin, full of the loss— there is nothing green, nothing whole, nothing working, nothing depend- able here. Full of the stupidity that has leveled concrete, shattered glass, smashed wood. There are very few roofs. There is nothing to eat. Full of the stories. Stories like thoughtless episodes that often came out of nowhere and undid everything forever.

Stories—like the orphan girl who tells of the Taliban breaking into her family's house in Mazar-I-Sharif—they were eating dinner. The Taliban, as they often did, insisted that her father build a fire to make them warm and her mother go quickly and cook for them. Her brother was sent to get petrol for the gas stove. The mother anxiously set about cooking. Nothing was moving fast enough. Her brother rushed with the gas and accidentally dropped it on the floor, which started a fire. The Taliban, now convinced the family was mocking them, trying to set them on fire, argued with the father outside who was desperate to convince them it was an accident and return to his screaming son, now on fire in the living room. The son was completely burned in the fire. The father rushed back in too late, burning most of his upper body trying to save what is left of his son, which makes him unable to work ever again. The mother lost her mind.

Or the story of the bomb that accidentally got lost from the car over a river—the car door opened, and the bomb fell out into the water. Several weeks later, an orphan girl's brother, who was her twin and her best friend, came upon the bomb while playing in the river with his friends. They wres- tled with it and rode it and brought it out of the river. It exploded in their hands, blowing them each in half, in pieces.

343

Stories. Full of stories, full of the emptiness that comes when the infra-structure of hope, the reason for tomorrow, is blown away. Full of the smells that remain after everything is charred. Full of the body, the female body that goes on anyway, despite madness, despite losing one's husband, despite the dust. Full of misery.

I look at my stomach in the full-length mirror that could crumble as every-thing else has. My stomach that usually has instincts or at the very least hunches, is now mute, not knowing anything, so stunned by the massive acts of cruelty—the twenty-three years of cruelty—stunned into utter submission.

I am starving and there is nothing to eat. Nothing that would make this better, unless we started over again as a species, were able to admit that we've spun off in the wrong direction. Were able to just stop. But I wonder if even that would make things better, would remove the mark of cruelty, the stain of violence in the cellular structure—this stain that now directs and redirects everything. We are products of violence, each and every one of us. We are its outcome and its creation.

Here in Kabul, the dust has gathered. It gets so deeply and quickly into your lungs that it has created something called the Kabul cough. What is left after the buildings and mosques and people are gone gets into your lungs, making you cough and gag. Here where the history of invasion, usurpation, domination, obliteration, interrogation, here the dust is the new weather. When it rains, the dust becomes mud; when there is heat, a thermal lining.

We walk through an old women's garden, thick in mud. The soldiers who stand outside to guard it take us through. It's as if they are now guarding a memory, a knowledge of another time in Kabul that was luscious and green, where the almond groves and apple trees and flowers were alive in the sun, and the dancing rooms and the theater thrived. The soldiers guarding this story walk us around, pointing out what was once there. You can smell the greenness and even though most of the trees are skeletons and stumped, you can remember their blooming. The soldiers become tender, proud when they describe the dancing, when they tell of the days of joy. But these days are not days they remember. They were born into dust. It is the memory of their parents, or their parents' parents, which they need to trust. These soldiers, no more than twenty-one, have never lived without the Kabul cough. It is like an allergy. You get used to it.

They walk us around until we come upon what was once the most beau-tiful tree in the park. We stand around its charred remains. An open wounded blackened trunk in the ground. It was once the grandest tree of all. When the Taliban took the garden, they chopped down most of the ancient trees for kindling to keep themselves warm. They tried to chop this tree but it would not come down. So, one night, they put a bomb in the trunk and blew it up—blew it up—the most beautiful, the grandest and greenest, the most luscious, the holder-of-hope tree. They blew her up. Now there is a blackened-out hole in the ground. I remember this tree. Or maybe it's my mother's memory or her mother's memory. Someone must remember all this before there were landmines and guns and bombs. Someone must remember before this dust seemed so familiar, before this dust seemed like the future. The soldiers blew her up because they could not cut her down.

I hold fast to the memory of greenness as I cough. I see the garden alive. I hold fast to my belief that we will one day survive the beauty. That we will surrender to it rather than blowing it up.

Women for Afghan Women:
Building Community Across Difference

Sunita Mehta and Homaira Mamoor

From *Women for Afghan Women: Shattering Myths and Claiming the Future* (Palgrave/St. Martin's Press, 2002)

Women for Afghan Women, a New York-based organization dedicated to Afghan women's liberation that was founded a full five months before the Twin Towers were razed, cosponsored the earliest Muslim peace rallies and teach-ins in New York after the September terrorist attack. While we were tormented by the jingoism and warmongering pervading the media, we could not adopt the unrealistic pacifism of the American peace movement. We knew the urgency of Afghanistan's liberation from terrorist rule, and we asked *how* peace might come about without forceful intervention. If invasion proved necessary, we advocated against a unilateral U.S. force and in favor of a global coalition under UN auspices, a coalition that would remain in Afghanistan until peace and economic stability returned.

It was an ironic moment of personal identity politics for us. We had never been more acutely conscious of being immigrants; and yet we had never felt more like New Yorkers, like Americans. Terrorists thought they were attacking America, and indeed they were—except that the victims of 9/11 hailed from all corners of the world. Something terrible had happened to our home, our beloved New York, and at the same time a bloody retaliation was inevitable against Afghanistan because Osama bin Laden was being harbored there. We were "us" and we were "them" at the same time. And of course, as it turned out, the United States did retaliate: "We" dropped food and bombs on "us," the innocent men, women, and children of Afghanistan.

Cautious Optimism for a New Afghanistan

On November 29 and 30, 2001, WAW held a conference at the Graduate Center of the City University of New York, entitled "Women for Afghan Women: Securing Our Future." It was the first Afghan women's conference ever held in

New York. The panels traced the history of women's rights in Afghanistan, addressed the human rights abuses under the Taliban regime and the resulting humanitarian crisis, and charted specific steps to be taken to ensure a just rebuilding of the country, respectful of the human rights of all its people.

Our conference coincided with the historic meetings in Bonn, Germany (November 27–December 6, 2001) that led to the formation of the interim government of Afghanistan. Sima Wali, who was originally scheduled to be our keynote speaker, was the first of only three Afghan women invited to participate as delegates in these UN-sponsored meetings. Women hold only two key positions in the new government: Sima Samar is the minister of women's affairs and deputy prime minister, and Suhaila Seddiqi heads the interim Department of Public Health.[1] As in Bonn, women are certainly underrepresented. After all, women make up more than half of the population of Afghanistan.

On January 28, 2002, members of WAW attended an event introducing interim prime minister Hamid Karzai to the local Afghan community at the Grand Hyatt Hotel in New York. We sat behind a group of young Afghan children, who were dressed in ethnic clothes and were ready to welcome the prime minister. The children streamed to the stage and honored Mr. Karzai. As they returned, one of them, a girl, found that her front-row seat had been taken by a boy originally in the second row. She looked at him and said forcefully, "No." We asked the boy to return to his original seat, but he simply grinned, knowing even at his early age the privileges of his gender. The little girl sat down near us, annoyed beneath her green shimmering head covering.

But the prime minister's heartfelt and optimistic message, inviting the Afghan diaspora "back home" to be a part of reconstruction, uplifted us. We shared the community's optimism, though it was laced with a chilling realization that the odds were steeply stacked against him. When the audience was invited to write down questions, we addressed ours to Deputy Prime Minister Samar, who was seated on the stage but had not spoken. We also asked the little girl if she had a question for the prime minister. She asked us to write, "My name is Hosni Noorzi, and I am nine years old. When I grow up, I want to be a doctor. When can I return and cure everybody?"

Neither our question nor Hosni's was answered. The prime minister and his colleagues left abruptly. We had experienced the hope of the entire community, and yet we were saddened that so few women had come; that Sima

Samar hadn't spoken, indeed hadn't even looked over as we spontaneously chanted "Sima Jan, welcome"; and especially that little Hosni's question was left unanswered.

In Afghanistan itself, girls are beginning to attend school and women's magazines are starting up, but brothels are proliferating, poverty has led some families to sell their children, and widows continue to beg on the streets in order to provide for their children. And there is pervasive warlordism and rape.

It seems clear that women's issues are not at the forefront of the new government's priorities and that women are only receiving token representation—possibly to placate the Western world. Perhaps some members of the government mistakenly believe that women's issues are less important than other objectives, such as national security and humanitarian aid. This would not be the first time that such a set of priorities has been invoked. In 1994 Fatima Gailani—the only woman in the guerrilla army of the Afghan Resistance against the Soviets—disagreed with her father's perspectives regarding women. Her father, Pir Sayed Ahmad Gailani, was the founder of the National Islamic Front of Afghanistan and religious leader of many Sunni Muslims in the country. Though a modern and liberal leader, he believed that women's suffrage should be addressed only after national stability was attained. Fatima disagreed, saying, "I know this will not happen because if you take a first step that is wrong, the rest of the way will be crooked."[2]

These words remain true today and are the core principle of WAW. While we are cognizant of the aspirations of the entire country of Afghanistan for basic goals such as national stability, we maintain that women must be part of every aspect of that stability. Women must play a role in rebuilding every facet of that society. The huge struggle over an entire nation's priorities and its destiny was reflected in our experience of a single boy's disregard for his sister's rights. We know that in the large and the miniature realms, in the public and the private domains, the struggle of Afghan women continues.

The Cornerstones of WAW

It has been nine tumultuous months since WAW was founded, and we have established the cornerstones of our work: diversity, community, commitment to a just reconstruction, and, of course, to peace and justice for women.

Diversity

WAW is a nonpolitical organization. The ethics that guide and unify us are those of human rights for all and equal and full participation of all women. Our platform can include all Afghans, all people. We have a single faith—a deep faith in the human capacity for justice and human rights.

Our luxury, our privilege, is that we are free, and, despite our concern that Afghan women are still not receiving priority treatment, we are optimistic. The solution to the problem of Afghanistan lies in the banding together of its different ethnic and political factions for the sake of their nation and their people. WAW is a diverse group, with women of many faiths, nationalities, and ideologies; the Afghan members themselves are diverse in ethnicity and background. If *we* can work together, addressing and overcoming our differences, united in our efforts to empower Afghan women, perhaps we can serve as a model for the way forward.

Community

The constituency that we serve and empower is Afghan women in Afghanistan and New York City, who live in communities and families and work within and outside the home. Ninety-nine percent of Afghans are Muslim.[3] The most effective way of reaching them is to speak from the standpoint of their own religious and national history, which accords them rights and equality. In fact, "The emancipation of women was a project dear to the Prophet's heart. The Qur'an gave women rights of inheritance and divorce long before Western women were accorded such status."[4] As early as 1921, King Amanollah Shah abolished the mandatory donning of the burqa, and his wife, Queen Soraya, appeared in public unveiled and wearing skirts that revealed her legs. Afghanistan's 1964 constitution guaranteed equality and the vote for women; in fact, women participated in the drafting of that constitution. Immediately before the Taliban took power, women in Kabul did not wear burqas. Seventy percent of schoolteachers, 50 percent of civilian government workers, and 40 percent of health care workers were female. At Kabul University, more than 50 percent of students and 60 percent of teachers were women.[5]

WAW members who hail from Afghanistan but not from Kabul remind us that not all of Afghanistan was a part of the liberalization process that took place in the last century. Rural Afghanistan—especially Pashtun Afghanistan—is, and has been, tremendously patriarchal. WAW hopes to prioritize reconstruction projects in the most conservative parts of the country.

Tamim Ansary, an Afghan writer and poet who is concerned that the world's attention on Afghan women's status is too narrowly focused on the elite, cautions that:

> The Taliban did not spring directly from hell. They sprang from Afghan culture strained through hell. . . . Wherever Afghans choose their traditional way of life . . . the international community should work with rather than against the grain of the culture. Empowering women through their traditional roles may lead to the deepest changes. To me, right now, a historic opportunity exists to support the real empowerment of Afghan women without engaging in a cultural tug of war with traditional Afghanistan.[6]

We agree with Mr. Ansary, but only up to a point. Our tug-of-war is with extremism rather than with tradition. The empowerment of Afghan women will be possible through their traditions, provided that the traditions themselves are just. Our commitment to community does not forgive injustice within community. It is high time that Muslims reclaim their religion from the hands of extremists, who know only war and hatred and who have no respect for people's dignity and fundamental human rights. It has been said that "the position of women in Muslim society mirrors the destiny of Islam: when Islam is secure and confident so are its women; when Islam is threatened and under pressure, so, too, are they."[7]

A Just Reconstruction

WAW is eager to support the reconstruction efforts, but we realize that the situation in Afghanistan is fragile and uncertain. We therefore hold the world accountable to its promise to help the Afghan people attain peace and stability. We implore the world to:

- Help Afghanistan attain a basic level of security, which is essential for any reconstruction to take place.
- Give aid and monitor all aid to ensure that the money is spent on projects that foster and promote the empowerment of women.
- Support traditional Afghan democratic processes such as the *Loya Jirga* (representative council of leaders), through which the Afghan people can choose their own leaders.

Women

American feminist Eleanor Smeal of the Feminist Majority Foundation, activist Mavis Leno, and Senator Hillary Rodham Clinton were pioneers in bringing to global attention the plight of Afghan women under the Taliban as early as 1997. Their efforts succeeded in changing U.S policy "from unconditionally accepting the Taliban to unconditionally rejecting them."[8] Now it is time for Afghan women to take action, confident in the support of the world. WAW's greatest aspiration is to enable this to happen. Afghan women will never again be alone, because their cause is just. We will not cease our efforts until the day that Afghan women reclaim their right to dignity, self-determination, a life without violence, and full participation in society.

Addendum

It is almost September 11, 2002. Women for Afghan Women (WAW) has been in existence for a year and a half. The organization is hard at work on our second annual conference, which will be held at Barnard College, Columbia University, on October 19. On September 11, 2002, our members will take part in two interfaith peace vigils, one at Washington Square Park in lower Manhattan and one at the Brooklyn Heights Promenade, looking out over where the Twin Towers no longer stand.

Since September 11th, Women for Afghan Women has been engaged in human rights advocacy at the national and international levels, community outreach at the very local level, and direct support of women's projects on the ground in Afghanistan. We have published a book of essays, *Women for Afghan Women: Shattering Myths and Claiming the Future* (Palgrave/St. Martin's Press, September 2002). Our book contains essays by religious and secular Afghan women involved in the reconstruction of Afghanistan, non-Afghan Muslim women who speak to women's rights within Islam, and American feminists and United Nations representatives whose work addresses the Afghan women's struggle in key ways. Through speaking engagements, celebrations, fundraisers and other venues in New York and around the country, we have sought not only to bring a discourse on women's rights into the local Afghan community, but also to bring Afghan women's concerns and voices into mainstream and progressive circles. We continue to speak out about the need to keep women at the fore of reconstruction in Afghanistan, and we have reiterated in both mainstream and progressive gatherings that the struggle for the rights of Afghan women must respect the Muslim faith of most Afghan women. We have been particularly saddened by the many civilians in Afghanistan who have lost their lives to American "friendly" bombs, and have agitated and advocated for the creation of an Afghan Victims Fund.

We are raising funds for projects in Afghanistan that focus on the education of girls and young women and vocational training for women who cannot return to school for their formal education but who need to acquire skills to become self-sufficient. And we are in the process of facilitating a commitment on the part of a Long Island school district to adopt a high school in Kabul, a program we hope will become a model for school districts around the country.

That the interim women's affairs minister lost her post because of an accusation of blasphemy is an indication that we are a long way from democracy and women's self-determination in Afghanistan. Foreign aid and peacekeeping efforts have focused on Kabul, and we urge the United States and the world to help Afghanistan bring security to all its regions.

The world has not learned the true lesson of 9/11, which is really very simple. We are one—if we drop a bomb, it falls on us. But in our small organization, we have understood this deeply. Diverse individuals—Afghan women of different ethnicities, a core group of Jewish American women, Hindu women from India, Muslim women from Pakistan, European women—transcend our enormous differences to work for women's rights in Afghanistan. Every one of us is strengthened by this work, and our understanding of each other and ourselves is deepened.

While the world's attention has shifted from Afghanistan and its women, our *dharma* is to insist that the world never again abandon the women, men and children of Afghanistan.

—Homaira Mamoor and Sunita Mehta, August 2002.

Notes

1 The interim government was replaced by a new transitional government after the 1,500-delegate *Loya Jirga*, which took place in Kabul in June 2002. This new government will remain in place until the general elections planned for 2004. Hamid Karzai was reelected as President of Afghanistan although for the first time in that country's history, a woman, Masooda Jalal, also ran for that office. During the *Loya Jirga*, reminding feminists around the world that vigilance is of

the essence, Sima Samar was accused of blasphemy by conservatives in the Northern Alliance, and her life was threatened. Dr. Samar lost her post as deputy prime minister and minister for women's affairs, and instead holds the lesser, non-governmental post of human rights commissioner. There are three women in Afghanistan's new transitional government. Habiba Sarabi, a pharmacist by profession, a women's rights activist, and a leader in the organization Humanitarian Assistance for the Women and Children of Afghanistan (HAWCA), is the new minister for women's affairs. Mahbooba Hoqooqmal is minister of state for women's affairs, and Dr. Suhaila Seddiqi retains her position of public health minister.

2 Quoted in Jan Goodwin, *Price of Honor: Muslim Women Lift the Veil of Silence on the Islamic World* (New York: Dutton/Plume, 1995), p. 84.

3 Jim Garamone, "Afghanistan: A Battleground through the Ages," American Forces Press Service, September 19, 2001.

4 Karen Armstrong, *Islam* (New York: Modern Library, Random House, 2000), p. 16.

5 Foreign Policy in Focus, www.fpif.org/faq/0111afghwomen_body.html.

6 Tamim Ansary, "Leaping to Conclusions," *Salon.com*, December 17, 2000.

7 Ahmed Akbar, quoted in Goodwin, *Price of Honor*, p. 47.

8 Ahmed Rashid, *Taliban: Militant Islam, Oil and Fundamentalism in Central Asia* (New Haven, Conn.: Yale University Press, 2000), p. 182.

Responding To Terror

Phantom Towers:
Feminist Reflections on the Battle between Global Capitalism and Fundamentalist Terrorism

Rosalind P. Petchesky

Adapted from a speech delivered at a Hunter College Political Science Department teach-in on September 25, 2001

The attack on the World Trade Center has left many kinds of damage in its wake, not the least of which is a gaping ethical and political confusion in the minds of many Americans who identify in some way as "progressive"—meaning antiracist, feminist, democratic (small d), antiwar. While we have a responsibility to those who died in the disaster and their loved ones, and to ourselves, to mourn, it is urgent that we also begin the work of thinking through what kind of world we are now living in and what it demands of us. And we have to do this, even while we know our understanding at this time can only be very tentative and may well be invalidated a year or even a month or a week from now by events we can't foresee or information now hidden from us.

So I want to try to draw a picture of the global power dynamics as I see them at this moment, including their gendered and racialized dimensions. I want to ask whether there is some alternative, more humane and peaceable way out of the two unacceptable polarities now being presented to us: the permanent war machine (or permanent security state) and the regime of holy terror.

When I suggest that we are currently facing a confrontation between global capitalism and an Islamist-fundamentalist brand of fascism, I do not mean to imply their equivalence. If, in fact, the attacks of September 11 were the work of Osama bin Laden's al Qaeda network or something related and even larger—and for the moment I think we can assume this as a real possibility—then most of us in this room are structurally positioned in a way that gives us little choice about our identities. (For the Muslim-Americans and Arab-Americans among us, who are both opposed to terrorism and terrified to walk in our streets, the moral dilemma must be, I imagine, much more agonizing.) As an American, a woman, a feminist, and a Jew, I have to recognize that the bin Ladens of the world hate me and would like me dead; or, if they had power over me, would make my life a living hell. I have to wish them apprehended, annulled, so I can breathe in some kind of peace. This is quite different from living at the very center of global capitalism—which is more like living in a very dysfunctional family that fills you with shame and anger for its arrogance, greed, and insensitivity but is, like it or not, your home and gives you both immense privileges and immense responsibilities.

Nor, however, do I believe we should succumb to the temptation of casting our current dilemma in the simplistic, Manichean terms of cosmic Good vs. Evil. Currently this comes in two opposed but mirror-image versions: the narrative, advanced not only by the terrorists and their sympathizers but also by many on the left in the U.S. and around the globe, that blames U.S. imperialism and economic hegemony for the "chickens coming home to roost"; versus the patriotic, right-wing version that casts U.S. democracy and freedom as the innocent target of Islamist madness. Both these stories erase all the complexities that we must try to factor into a different, more inclusive ethical and political vision. The Manichean, apocalyptic rhetorics that echoed back and forth between Bush and Bin Laden in the aftermath of the attacks—the pseudo Islamic and the pseudo Christian, the *jihad* and the crusade—both lie.

So, while I do not see terrorist networks and global capitalism as equivalent, I do see some striking and disturbing parallels between them. I picture them as the phantom Twin Towers arising in the smoke clouds of the old—fraternal twins, not identical, locked in a battle over wealth, imperial aggrandizement and the meanings of masculinity. Feminist analysts and activists from many countries—whose voices have been inaudible thus far in the present crisis—have a lot of experience to draw from in making this double critique. Whether in the United Nations or national settings, we have been challenging the gender-biased and racialized dimensions of *both* neoliberal capitalism and various fundamentalisms for years, trying to steer a path between their double menace. The difference now is that they parade onto the world stage in their most extreme and violent forms. I see six areas where their posturing overlaps:

1. Wealth—Little needs to be said about the U.S. as the world's wealthiest country, nor the way in which wealth accumulation is the Holy Grail, not only of our political system (think of the difficulty we have even in reforming campaign finance laws), but of our national ethos. We are the headquarters of the corporate and financial megaempires that dominate global capitalism and influence the policies of the international financial institutions (IMF, World Bank, WTO) that are its main governing bodies. This reality resonates around the globe in the symbolic pantheon of what the U.S. stands for—from the McDonald's and Kentucky Fried Chicken ads sported by protestors in Genoa and Rawalpindi to the WTC towers themselves. Acquisitiveness, whether individual or corporate, also lurks very closely behind the values that Bush and Rumsfeld mean when they say our "freedoms" and our "way of life" are being attacked and must be defended fiercely.

Wealth is also a driving force behind the al Qaeda network, whose principals are mainly the beneficiaries of upper-middle-class or elite financing and education. Bin Laden himself derives much of his power and influence from his family's vast fortune, and the cells of Arab-Afghan fighters in the 1980s war of the *mujahedeen* against the Soviets were bankrolled not only by the Pakistani secret police and the CIA—to the tune of $3 billion—but also by Saudi oil money. Moreover, the values animating the terrorist organizations include—as bin Laden made clear in his famous 1998 interview—defending the "honor" and "property" of Muslims everywhere and "[fighting] the governments that are bent on attacking our religion and on stealing our wealth. . . ." Political scientist Paul Amar, in a recent talk at Hunter College, rightly urges us not to confuse these wealthy networks—whose nepotism and ties to oil interests eerily resemble those of the Bush family—with impoverished and resistant social movements throughout the Middle East and Asia. There is no evidence that economic justice or equality figure anywhere in the terrorist program.

2. Imperialist nationalism—The Bush administration's initial reaction to the attacks exhibited the mindset of a superpower that knows no limits, that issues ultimatums under the cover of "seeking cooperation." "Every nation in every region has a decision to make," pronounced Bush in his speech to the nation that was really a speech to the world. "Either you are with us or you are with the terrorists." He went on, "This is the world's fight, this is civilization's fight"—the U.S., then, becoming the leader and spokesman of "civilization," relegating not only the terrorists but also those who refuse to join the fight to the ranks of the uncivilized. To the Taliban and to every other regime that "harbors terrorists," he was the sheriff stonewalling the cattle rustlers: "Hand over all the terrorists or you will share in their fate." As the war campaign progresses, its aims seem more openly imperialist: "Washington wants to offer the groups [the small, also fundamentalist, drug-dealing *mujahedeen* mostly routed by the Taliban] a role in governing Afghanistan after the conflict," according to the *New York Times* of September 24, as if this were "Washington's" official role. Further, it and its allies are courting the octogenarian, long-forgotten Afghan king (now exiled in Italy) to join in a military operation to oust the Taliban and set up—what? a kind of puppet government? Nothing here about internationally monitored elections, nothing about the UN, or any concept of the millions of Afghan people—within the country or in exile—as anything but voiceless, down-trodden victims and refugees.

Clearly, this offensive involves far more than rooting out and punishing terrorists. Though I don't want to reduce the situation to a crude Marxist scenario, one can't help wondering how it relates to the longstanding determination of the U.S. to keep a dominant foothold in the Gulf region and to maintain control over oil supplies. At least one faction of the Bush team, clamoring to go after Saddam Hussein as well, is clearly in this frame of mind. And let's not forget Pakistan and its concessions to U.S. demands for cooperation in return for lifting of U.S. economic sanctions—and now, the assurance of a sizable IMF loan. In the tradition of neoimperial power, the U.S. does not need to dominate countries politically or militarily to get the concessions it wants; its economic influence backed up by the capacity for military annihilation is sufficient.

Though lacking the actual imperial power of the U.S., the bin Laden forces mimic its imperial aspirations. We need to recognize their world-view as an extreme and vicious form of nationalism—a kind of fascism, I would argue, because of its reliance on terror to achieve its ends. In this respect, their goals, like those of the U.S., go beyond mere punishment. Amar says the whole history of Arab and Islamic nationalism has been one that transcended the colonially imposed boundaries of the nation-state, one that was always transnational and pan-Arabic, or pan-Muslim, in form. Although the terrorists have no social base or legitimacy in laying claim to this tradition, they clearly seek to usurp it. This seems evident in bin Laden's language invoking "the Arab nation," "the Arab peninsula," and a "brotherhood" reaching from Eastern Europe to Turkey and Albania, to the entire Middle East, South Asia and Kashmir. Their mission is to drive out "the infidels" and their Muslim supporters from something that looks like a third of the globe. Provoking the U.S. to bomb Afghanistan and/or attempt to oust the Taliban would likely destabilize Pakistan and possibly catapult it into the hands of Taliban-like extremists, who would then control nuclear weapons—a big step toward their perverted and hijacked version of the pan-Muslim dream.

3. Pseudoreligion—As many others have commented, the "clash of religions" or "clash of cultures" interpretation of the current scenario is utterly specious. What we have instead is an appropriation of religious symbolism and discourse for predominantly political purposes, and to justify permanent war and violence. So bin Laden declares a jihad, or holy war, against the U.S., its civilians as well as its soldiers; and Bush declares a crusade against the terrorists and all who harbor or support them. Bin Laden declares himself the "servant of Allah fighting for the sake of the religion of Allah" and to protect Islam's holy mosques, while Bush declares Washington the promoter of "infinite justice" and predicts certain victory, because "God is not neutral." (The Pentagon changed the "Operation Infinite Justice" label to "Operation Enduring Freedom" after Muslim-Americans objected and three Christian clergymen warned that "infinite" presumed divinity, the "sin of pride.") But we have to question the authenticity of this religious discourse on both sides, however sincere its proponents. A "Statement from Scholars of the Islamic Religion," circulated after the attacks, firmly denounces terrorism—the wanton killing of innocent civilians—as contrary to *shariah* law. And Bush's adoption of this apocalyptic discourse can only be seen as substituting a conservative, right-wing form of justification for the neoliberal internationalist discourse that conservatives reject. In either case, it is worth quoting the always wise Eduardo Galeano, writing in Mexico's la *Jornada*: "In the struggle of Good against Evil, it's always the people who get killed."

4. Militarism—Both the Bush administration and the bin Laden forces adopt the methods of war and violence to achieve their ends, but in very different ways. U.S. militarism is of the ultra-high-tech variety that seeks to terrorize by the sheer might, volume, and technological virtuosity of our armaments. Of course, as the history of Vietnam and the survival of Saddam Hussein attest, this is an illusion of the highest order. (Remember the "smart bombs" in the Gulf War that headed for soda machines?) But our military technology is also a vast and insatiable industry for which profit, not strategy, is the driving rationale. As Jack Blum, a critic of U.S. foreign policy, pointed out in the *Sacramento Bee*, "The national defense game is a systems and money operation" that has little, if any, relevance to terrorism. Missiles were designed to counter hostile states with their own fixed territories and weapons arsenals, not terrorists who sneak around the globe and whose "weapons of mass destruction" are human bodies and hijacked planes; nor the famously impervious terrain and piles of rubble that constitute Afghanistan. Even George W., in one of his most sensible comments to date, remarked that we'd know better than to aim "a $2 billion cruise missile at a $10 empty tent." And yet four days after the attack, Congress piled madness atop madness and approved Bush's costly and destructive "missile shield," voting to restore $1.3 billion in spending authority for this misconceived and dangerous project. And the armaments companies quickly started lining up to receive their big orders for the impending next war—the war, we are told, that will last a long time, maybe the rest of our lives.

And yet the war-mania and rallying around the flag exhibited by the American people express desire, not for military profits, but for something else, something harder for feminist and antiwar dissidents to understand. Maybe it's just the need to vent anger and feel avenged, or the more deep-rooted need to experience some sense of community and higher purpose in a society where we are so atomized and isolated from one another and the world. On September 25, Barbara Kingsolver wrote in the *San Francisco Chronicle* that she and her husband reluctantly sent their five-year-old daughter to school dressed in red, white, and blue like the other kids because they didn't want to let jingoists and censors "steal the flag from us." Their little girl probably echoed the longings of many less reflective grownups when she said that wearing the colors of the flag "means we're a country; just people all together."

The militarism of the terrorists is of a very different nature—based on the mythic figure of the Bedouin warrior, or the Ikhwan fighters of the early-twentieth century who enabled Ibn Saud to consolidate his dynastic state. Their hallmarks are individual courage and ferocity in battle; Malise Ruthven's *Islam in the World* quotes one Arab witness who described them, foreshadowing reports of Soviet veterans from the 1980s Afghan war, as "utterly fearless of death, not caring how many fall, advancing rank upon rank with only one desire—the defeat and annihilation of the enemy." Of course, this image too, like every hypernationalist ideology, is rooted in a mythic golden past and has little to do with how real terrorists in the twenty-first century are recruited, trained, and paid off. And, like high-tech militarism, terrorist low-tech militarism is also based on an illusion—that millions of believers will rise up, obey the *fatwah*, and defeat the infidel. It's an illusion because it grossly underestimates the most powerful weapon in global capitalism's arsenal—not "infinite justice" or even nukes but infinite Nikes and CDs. And it also underestimates the local power of feminism, which the fundamentalists mistakenly confuse with the West. Iran today, in all its internal contradictions, shows the resilience and variety of both youth cultures and women's movements.

5. Masculinism—Militarism, nationalism, and colonialism as terrains of power have always been in large part contests over the meanings of manhood. Feminist political scientist Cynthia Enloe remarks that "Men's sense of their own masculinity, often tenuous, is as much a factor in international politics as is the flow of oil, cables, and military hardware." In the case of bin Laden's Taliban patrons, the form and excessiveness of the misogyny that goes hand in hand with state terrorism and extreme fundamentalism— which the U.S. ignored for years—have been graphically documented. Just go to the website of the Revolutionary Association of the Women of Afghanistan (RAWA), at www.rawa.org, to view more photos of atrocities against women (and men) for sexual offenses, dress code offenses, and other forms of deviance than you'll be able to stomach. And it's not just the Taliban. Gulbuddin Hekmatyar, the "rebel" leader in the Soviet-Afghan war who received the most generous U.S. support—and who later fought against the Taliban—was notorious for throwing acid in the faces of unveiled women at Kabul University before the war.

In the case of transnational terrorists and bin Laden himself, their model of manliness is that of the Islamic "brotherhood," the band of brothers bonded together in an agonistic commitment to fighting the enemy to the death. The CIA-Pakistani-Saudi-backed camps and training schools set up to support the "freedom fighters" (who later became "terrorists") in the anti-Soviet war were breeding grounds not only of a worldwide terrorist network but also of its masculinist, misogynist culture. Bin Laden clearly sees himself as a patriarchal tribal chief whose duty is to provide for and protect not only his own retinue, wives, and many children, but also his whole network of lieutenants and recruits and their families. He is the legendary Arabic counterpart of the Godfather.

In contrast to this, can we say that the U.S. as standard bearer of global capitalism is "gender-neutral"? Don't we have a woman—indeed an African-American woman—at the helm of our National Security Council, the president's right hand in designing the permanent war machine? Despite reported "gender gaps" in polls about war, we know that women are not inherently more peace-loving than men. Remember all those suburban housewives with their yellow ribbons in Midwestern airports and shopping malls during the Gulf War? Global capitalist masculinism is alive and well but concealed in its Eurocentric, racist guise of "rescuing" downtrodden Afghan women. Feminists around the world, who have tried for so long to call attention to the plight of women and girls in Afghanistan, cannot feel consoled by the prospect of U.S. warplanes and U.S.-backed guerrilla chiefs coming to "save our Afghan sisters." Meanwhile, the U.S. will send single mothers who signed up for the National Guard when welfare ended to fight and die in its holy war; U.S. media overlook the activism and self-determination of groups like RAWA, Refugee Women in Development and NEGAR; and the U.S. military establishment refuses accountability before an International Criminal Court for the acts of rape and sexual assault committed by its soldiers stationed across the globe. Masculinism and misogyny take many forms, not always the most visible.

6. Racism—Of course, what I have named fascist fundamentalism, or transnational terrorism, is also saturated in racism, but of a very specific, focused kind—which is anti-Semitism. The WTC towers symbolized not only American capitalism, not only finance capitalism, but, for the terrorists, *Jewish* finance capitalism. We can see this in the misreporting of the September 11 attacks in some Arabic-language newspapers in the Middle East as probably the work of the Israelis; their erroneous allegation that not a single person among the dead and missing was Jewish, so Jews must have had advance warning, etc. In his 1998 interview, bin Laden constantly refers to "Jews," not Israelis, in his accusations about plans to take over the whole Arab peninsula. He asserts that "the Americans and the Jews . . . represent the spearhead with which the members of our religion have been slaughtered. Any effort directed against America and the Jews yields positive and direct results." And, finally, he rewrites history and collapses the diversity of Muslims in a warning to "Western governments" to sever their ties to Jews: "The enmity between us and the Jews goes far back in time and is deep rooted. There is no question that war between the two of us is inevitable. For this reason it is not in the interest of Western governments to expose the interests of their people to all kinds of retaliation for almost nothing." (I cringe to realize I am part of the "nothing.")

U.S. racism is much more diffuse but just as insidious; the pervasive racism and ethnocentrism that fester under the American skin always boil to the surface at times of national crisis. As Sumitha Reddy put it in a recent teach-in, the targeting of Sikhs and other Indians, Arabs, and even tan-skinned Latinos and African-Americans in the wave of violent and abusive acts throughout the country since the disaster signals an enlargement of the "zone of distrust" in American racism beyond the usual black-white focus. Women who wear headscarves or saris are particularly vulnerable to harassment, but Arab and Indian men of all ages are the ones being murdered. The state pretends to abhor such incidents and threatens their full prosecution. But this is the same state that made the so-called Anti-Terrorism Act, passed in 1995 after the Oklahoma City bombing (an act committed by native white Christian terrorists), a pretext for rounding up and deporting immigrants of all kinds; and that is now once again waiving the civil liberties of immigrants in its zealous antiterrorist manhunt.

If we look only at terrorist tactics and the world's revulsion against them, then we might conclude rather optimistically that thuggery will never win out in the end. But we ignore the context in which terrorism operates at our peril, and that context includes not only racism and Eurocentrism but many forms of social injustice. In thinking through a moral position on this crisis, we have to distinguish between *immediate causes and necessary conditions.*

Neither the United States (as a state) nor the corporate and financial power structure that the World Trade Center symbolized *caused* the horrors of September 11. Without question, the outrageous, heinous murder, maiming and orphaning of so many innocent people—who were every race, ethnicity, color, class, age, gender, and some 60-odd nationalities—deserve some kind of just redress. On the other hand, the *conditions* in which transnational terrorism thrives, gains recruits, and lays claim to moral legitimacy include many for which the U.S. and its corporate/financial interests are directly responsible, even if they don't for a minute excuse the attacks. It is often asked lately, why does the third world hate us so much? Put another way, why do so many people including my own friends in Asia, Africa, Latin America, and the Middle East express so much ambivalence about what happened, both lamenting an unforgivable criminal act and at the same time taking some satisfaction that Americans are finally suffering, too? We make a fatal mistake if we attribute these mixed feelings only to envy or resentment of our wealth and freedoms and ignore a historical context of aggression, injustice, and inequality. Consider these facts:

1. The United States is still the only country in the world to have actually *used* the most infamous weapons of mass destruction in the nuclear bombing of innocent civilians—in Hiroshima and Nagasaki.

2. The U.S. persists to this day in bombing Iraq, destroying the lives and food supplies of hundreds of thousands of civilian adults and children there. We bombed Belgrade—a dense capital city— for eighty straight days during the war in Kosovo and supported bombing that killed untold civilians in El Salvador in the 1980s. In the name of fighting Communism, our CIA and military training apparatus sponsored paramilitary massacres, assassinations, tortures and disappearances in many Latin American and Central American countries in Operation Condor and the like in the 1970s and has supported corrupt, authoritarian regimes in the Middle East, Southeast Asia, and elsewhere—the Shah of Iran, Suharto in Indonesia, the Saudi dynasty, and let's not forget the *mujahedeen* of Afghanistan. September 11 is also the date of the coup against the democratically elected Allende government in

Chile and the beginning of the twenty-five-year Pinochet dictatorship, again thanks to U.S. support. Yes, a long history of state
terrorism.

3. In the Middle East, which is the microcosm of the current
conflagration, billions in annual U.S. military aid and the Bush
administration's refusal to pressure the Sharon government are
the sine qua non of continued Israeli government policies of
attacks on Palestinian villages, demolition of homes, destruction
of olive orchards, restrictions on travel, continual human rights
abuses of Palestinians and even Arab citizens, assassination of
political leaders, building of roads and enlarging of settlements—
all of which exacerbate Palestinian despair and create the conditions that breed suicide bombers. The U.S. thereby contributes
to deepening the illegal occupation and the "bantustanizing" of
the Palestinian territories, thus perpetuating hostilities.

4. Despite its pretense to uphold women's rights, the U.S. is one
of only around two dozen countries that have failed to ratify the
UN Convention on the Elimination of All Forms of Discrimination Against Women, and the only country in the world [as of
April 2002, when Somalia finally agreed to sign] that refuses to
sign the UN Convention on the Rights of the Child. It is the
most vocal opponent of the statute establishing an International
Criminal Court as well as the treaties banning land mines and
germ warfare; a principal subverter of a new multilateral treaty to
combat illegal small arms trafficking; and the sole country in the
world to threaten an unprecedented space-based defense system
and imminent violation of the ABM treaty. So who is the
"outlaw, " the "rogue state"?

5. The U.S. is the only major industrialized country to refuse
signing the final Kyoto Protocol on Global Climate Change,
despite compromises in that document designed to meet U.S.
objections. Meanwhile, a new global scientific study shows that
the countries whose productivity will benefit most from climate
change are Canada, Russia and the U.S., while the biggest losers

will be the countries that have contributed least to global climate change—i.e., most of Africa.

6. As even the World Bank and the United Nations Development Programme attest, two decades of globalization have resulted in larger rather than smaller gaps between rich and poor, both within countries and among countries. The benefits of global market liberalization and integration have accrued disproportionately to wealthy Americans and Europeans (as well as small elites in the third world). Despite the presumed democratizing effects of the Internet, a middle-class American "needs to save a month's salary to buy a computer; a Bangladeshi must save all his wages for eight years to do so." And despite its constant trumpeting of "free-trade" rhetoric, the U.S. remains a persistent defender of protectionist policies for its farmers and steel and textile manufacturers. Meanwhile small producers throughout Asia, Africa, and the Caribbean—a great many of whom are women—are squeezed out by U.S. imports and relegated to the informal economy, while others toil in sweatshops producing goods for multinational corporations.

7. The G-8 countries, of which the U.S. is the senior partner, dominate decision-making in the IMF and the World Bank, whose structural adjustments and conditionalities for loans and debt relief help to keep many poor countries and their citizens locked in poverty.

8. In the aftermath of the September 11 attacks, the U.S. Congress was able to come up with an immediate $40 billion for "anti-terrorism" activities, another $40 billion to bail out the airlines, and a twenty-year contract with Lockheed to produce military aircraft for $200 billion—enough to eliminate contagious diseases from the face of the earth. Yet our foreign assistance appropriations (except for military aid) have shrunk; we, the world's richest country, contribute only one-seventh of 1 percent of our GNP to foreign aid—the least of any industrialized country. A recent WHO report tells us the total cost of providing

safe water and sanitation to all of sub-Saharan Africa would be only $11 billion, only no one can figure out where the money will come from; and the UN is still a long way off from raising a similar amount for its proclaimed Global Fund to combat AIDS, malaria, and TB. What kind of meanness is this? And what does it say about forms of racism, or "global apartheid," that value some lives—those in the U.S. and Europe—far more than others in other parts of the globe?

And the list goes on, with McDonald's, Coca-Cola, CNN, and MTV and all the uninvited commercial detritus that proliferates everywhere on the face of the earth and offends the cultural and spiritual sensibilities of so many—including transnational feminist travelers like me, when we find pieces of our local shopping mall transplanted to central Manila, Kampala, or Bangalore. But worse than the triviality and bad taste of these cultural and commercial barrages is the arrogant presumption that our "way of life" is the best on earth and ought to be welcome everywhere; or that our power and supposed advancement entitle us to dictate policies and strategies to the rest of the world. This is the face of imperialism in the twenty-first century.

None of this reckoning can comfort those who lost loved ones on September 11, or the thousands of attack victims who lost their jobs, homes and livelihoods; nor can it excuse the hideous crimes. As the Palestinian poet Mahmoud Darwish writes, "Nothing, nothing justifies terrorism." Still, in attempting to understand what has happened and think how to prevent it happening again (which is probably a vain wish), we Americans have to take all these painful facts into account. The United States as the command center of global capitalism will remain ill equipped to "stop terrorism" until it begins to recognize its own past and present responsibility for many of the conditions I've listed and to address them in a responsible way. But this would mean the United States becoming something different from itself, transforming itself, including abandoning the presumption that it should unilaterally police the world. This problem of transformation is at the heart of the vexing question of finding solutions different from all-out war. So let me turn to how we might think differently about power. Here is what I propose, tentatively, for now:

1. The slogan "War Is Not the Answer" is a practical as well as an

ontological truth. Bombing or other military attacks on Afghanistan are not likely to root out networks of terrorists, who could be hiding deep in the mountains or in Pakistan or Germany or Florida or New Jersey. But they are likely to destroy an already decimated country, killing civilians as well as combatants and creating hundreds of thousands more refugees. And they are likely to arouse so much anger among Islamist sympathizers as to destabilize the region and perpetuate the cycle of retaliation and terrorist attacks. All the horror of the twentieth century should teach us that war feeds on itself and that armed violence reflects, not an extension of politics by other means, but the failure of politics; not the defense of civilization, but the breakdown of civilization.

2. Tracking down and bringing the perpetrators of terrorism to justice, in some kind of international police action, is a reasonable aim but one fraught with danger. Because the U.S. is the world's only "superpower," its declaration of war against terrorism and its supporters everywhere says to other countries that we are once again taking over as global policeman. Here at home a "national emergency" or "state of war"—*especially* when defined as different from any other war—means the curtailment of civil liberties, harassment of immigrants, racial profiling, and withholding of information (censorship) or feeding of disinformation to the media, all without any time limits or accountability under the dubious Office of Homeland Security and the "U.S.A Patriot Act." We should oppose both U.S. unilateralism and the permanent security state. We should urge our representatives in Congress to diligently defend the civil liberties of all.

3. I agree with the Afro Asian Peoples Solidarity Organization (AAPSO) in Cairo that "This punishment should be inflicted according to the law and only upon those who were responsible for these events," and that it should be organized within the framework of the United Nations and international law, not unilaterally by the United States. This is not the same as the U.S. getting unanimous approval from the Security Council to commandeer global security, which is a first step at best.

Numerous treaties against terrorism and money-laundering already exist in international law. The International Criminal Court, whose establishment the U.S. government has so stubbornly opposed, would be the logical body to try terrorist cases, with the cooperation of national police and surveillance systems. *We should demand that the U.S. ratify the ICC statute.* In the meantime, a special tribunal under international auspices, like the ones for the former Yugoslavia and Rwanda, could be set up as well as an international agency to coordinate national police and intelligence efforts, with the U.S. as one participating member.

4. No amount of police action, however cooperative, can stop terrorism without addressing the conditions of misery and injustice that nourish and aggravate terrorism. The U.S. has to undertake a serious reexamination of its values and its policies with regard not only to the Middle East but also to the larger world. It has to take responsibility for its impact on the world, finding ways of sharing its wealth, resources and technology; democratizing decisions about global trade, finance, and security; and assuring that access to "global public goods" like health care, housing, food, education, sanitation, water, and freedom from racial and gender discrimination is given priority in international relations. What we even mean by "security" has to encompass all these aspects of well-being, of "human security," and has to be universal in its reach.

Let me again quote from the poet Mahmoud Darwish's statement, which was published in the Palestinian daily *al Ayyam* on September 17 and signed by many Palestinian writers and intellectuals.

We know that the American wound is deep and we know that this tragic moment is a time for solidarity and the sharing of pain. But we also know that the horizons of the intellect can traverse landscapes of devastation. Terrorism has no location or boundaries, it does not reside in a geography of its own; its homeland is disillusionment and despair.

The best weapon to eradicate terrorism from the soul lies in the solidarity of the international world, in respecting the rights of all peoples of this globe to live in harmony and by reducing the ever increasing gap between north and south. And the most effective way to defend freedom is through fully realizing the meaning of justice.

What gives me hope is that this statement's sentiments are being voiced by growing numbers of groups here in the U.S., including the National Council of Churches, the Green Party, a coalition of one hundred entertainers and civil rights leaders, coalitions of peace groups and student organizations, New Yorkers Say No to War, black and white women celebrities featured on Oprah Winfrey's show, parents and spouses of attack victims, as well as some five hundred petitioners from women's peace groups here and across the globe calling on the UN Security Council to "Stop the War, Rebuild a Just Society in Afghanistan, and Support Women's Human Rights." Maybe out of the ashes we will recover a new kind of solidarity; maybe the terrorists will force us, not to mirror them, but to see the world and humanity as a whole.

Bringing the Holy War Home

Ellen Willis

From *The Nation*, December 17, 2001

It often happens that the lunatic right, in its feckless way, gets closer to the heart of the matter than the political mainstream, and so it was with Jerry Falwell's notorious response to September 11. In suggesting that the World Trade Center massacre was God's judgment on an America that tolerates abortion, homosexuality, and feminism, Falwell—along with Pat Robertson, who concurred—exposed himself to the public's averted eye. For most Americans, from George W. Bush on down, resist the idea that the attack was an act of cultural war, and fewer still are willing to admit its intimate connection with the culture war at home.

Opponents of the "clash of civilizations" thesis are half right. There is such a clash, but it is not between East and West. The struggle of democratic secularism, religious tolerance, individual freedom, and feminism against authoritarian patriarchal religion, culture, and morality is going on all over the world—including the Islamic world, where dissidents are regularly jailed, killed, exiled, or merely intimidated and silenced. In Iran the mullahs still have police power, but reformist President Khatami has overwhelming popular support, and young people are in open revolt against the Islamic regime. In Pakistan the urban middle classes worry that their society may be Talibanized. Even in the belly of the fundamentalist beast, the clandestine Revolutionary Association of the Women of Afghanistan (RAWA) has opposed both the Taliban regime and the scarcely less thuggish Northern Alliance.

At the same time, religious and cultural reactionaries have mobilized to attack secular modernity in liberal democracies from Israel to the post-Communist countries of Eastern Europe to the United States. Indeed, the culture war has been a centerpiece of American politics for thirty years or more, shaping our debates and our policies on everything from abortion, censorship, and crime to race, education, and social welfare. Nor, at this moment, does the government know whether foreign or domestic terrorists are responsible for the anthrax offensive. Yet we shrink from seeing the relationship between our own cultural conflicts and the logic of *jihad*. We are especially eager to absolve religion of any responsibility for the violence committed in its name: For that ubiquitous current cliché, "This has nothing to do with Islam," read "Antiabortion terrorism has nothing to do with Christianity."

But why then do the great world religions all have brutal fundamentalist fringes that traduce their professed moral principles for the sake of power? The contradiction mirrors the conditions of the patriarchal culture with which these religions are intertwined—a culture that mandates the repression of desire and the control of women in the name of law and order, but which is nonetheless permeated with violence, from rape to war. Is this simply proof of innate evil, original sin, or is it rather that repression gives rise to hidden rage, which constantly seeks an outlet in sanctioned violence—the punishment of wayward children, women, enemies of the state? And of course there can be no violence more sanctioned than holy war.

This dynamic might explain why an undercurrent of sadism is always available to be tapped by demagogues seeking to exploit mass economic misery, the dislocation of war or other social crises. As with fascism, the rise of Islamic totalitarianism has partly to do with its populist appeal to the class resentments of an economically oppressed population and to anger at political subordination and humiliation. But, again like fascism, it is at bottom a violent defensive reaction against the liberal values of the Enlightenment. By its very intensity, moreover, that reaction suggests a defense against not only an external threat but an inner temptation. If exposure to forbidden freedoms aroused in Osama bin Laden and his confrères unconscious rage at their own repression, what better way to ward off the devil than to redirect that rage against it? And if the World Trade Center represented global capitalism—the engine of American might and economic inequality, but also of modernity itself, of all that is solid melting into air—wasn't there yet another, more primal brand of symbolism embodied in those twin phalluses? With one spectacular act, the hijackers could annihilate both the symbol of temptation and its real source—themselves.

Only a small minority of extremists will ever go that far. But throughout the Islamic world many more will admire, sympathize, tolerate, and obstruct opposition. For along with the economic suffering and political complaints that terrorists exploit, most of the population shares a cultural formation grounded in the patriarchal conservatism that pervades everyday life in Islamic countries—including those with secular governments like Iraq and Turkey—especially outside the cities and the educated classes. Post-Enlightenment, post-Reformation, postfeminist, postsexual revolution, liberal democratic America offers a far smaller pool of people in which abortion-clinic bombers and their ilk can hope to swim. Yet the legacy of patriarchalism still weighs on us: Our institutions resist change, and our psyches remain more conservative than the actual conditions of our lives. As a result we are deeply anxious and ambivalent about cultural issues, and one way we deal with this is to deny their importance, even sometimes their existence.

For the most part Americans speak of culture and politics as if they were two separate realms. Conservatives accuse the left of politicizing culture and see their own cultural-political offensive against the social movements of the 1960s as an effort to restore to culture its rightful autonomy. Centrists deplore the culture war as an artifact of "extremists on both sides" and continually pronounce it dead. The economic-justice left regards cultural politics as a distraction from its efforts to win support for a populist economic program. Multiculturalists pursue the political goal of equality and respect for minority and non-Western cultures, but are reluctant to make political judgments about cultural practices: Feminist universalists like Martha Nussbaum have been regularly attacked for "imposing Western values" by criticizing genital mutilation and other forms of female subjection in the third world.

The artificial separation of politics and culture is nowhere more pronounced than in the discourse of foreign policy and international affairs. For the U.S. government, economic, geopolitical, and military considerations determine our allies and our enemies. Democracy (almost always defined narrowly as a freely elected government, rather than as a way of life) and human rights (only recently construed as including even the most elementary of women's rights) are invoked by policy-makers mainly to justify alliances or antagonisms that already exist. While the cold war inspired much genuine passion on behalf of freedom and the open society, there's no denying that its fundamental motive was the specter of an alternative to capitalism spreading across the globe and encouraging egalitarian heresies at home. The one cultural issue that seems genuinely to affect our relationship with foreign states is our mania for restricting the international drug supply (except when we ourselves are arming drug cartels for some strategic purpose). The left, meanwhile, criticizes the aims of American foreign policy;

yet despite intensified concern with human rights in recent years, many left-ists still share the government's assumptions about what kinds of issues are important: the neoliberal economic agenda and struggles over resources like oil; the maintenance of friendly client states versus national self-determination; and so on. And like the United States, leftists have displayed their own double standard on human rights, tending to gloss over the abuses of populist or antiimperialist regimes.

Given these tropisms, it's unsurprising that the absence of religious and personal freedom, brutal suppression of dissent and extreme oppression of women in Islamic theocracies have never been a serious subject of foreign policy debates. Long before the Taliban, many feminists were upset by the singleminded cold war agenda that led the United States to support, even foment, Islamic fundamentalism in Afghanistan; yet this never became a public issue. Even now our enthusiasm for the Northern Alliance, which is to the Taliban what Trotsky was to Stalin, is restrained only—irony of ironies!—by the ethnic objections of our new ally, that champion of religious freedom, Pakistan. While the Bush administration makes self-congratulatory noises about Afghan women's liberation, it is in no hurry to stop fundamentalist warlords from reclaiming power.

Back in the 1950s, in pursuit of our cold war aims in Iran, we overthrew an elected secular government and installed the tyrannical and deeply unpopular Shah, then dumped him in the face of Khomeini's 1979 revolution. Except for feminists, the American left, with few exceptions, enthusiastically supported the revolution and brushed off worries about the Ayatollah, though he had made no secret of his theocratic aims: The important thing was to get rid of the Shah—other issues could be dealt with afterward. Ten years later, on the occasion of the *fatwah* against Salman Rushdie, the Bush I Administration appeared far more interested in appeasing Islamic governments and demonstrators offended by Rushdie's heretical book than in condemning Khomeini's death sentence, while an unnerving number of liberals and leftists accused Rushdie and his defenders of cultural imperialism and insensitivity to Muslim sensibilities. Throughout, both defenders and detractors of our alliance with "moderate" Saudi Arabia have ignored Saudi women's slavelike situation, regarding it as "their culture" and none of our business, except when it raises questions about how Americans stationed in the Gulf are expected to behave. It's as if, in discussing South Africa, apartheid had never been mentioned.

There are many things to be learned from the shock of September 11; surely one of the more important is that culture is not only a political matter, but a matter of life and death. It follows that a serious, long-range strategy against Islamic fundamentalist terrorism must entail open and emphatic opposition to theocracy and to the subjugation of women, backed up by support for the efforts of secular and religious liberals, modernizers, democrats, and feminists to press for reforms in Middle Eastern and South Asian societies. We might start by including RAWA and other secular elements as players in the discussion of Afghanistan's future; and by giving active aid and comfort to the Iranian reformers and their increasingly rebellious constituents. So far, no Afghans associated with the secular leftist government that predated the 1978 Soviet-backed coup have been party to the political negotiations—indeed, they are the great unmentionable. (While the United States has no problem supporting warlords with gory histories of rape and pillage, evidently any whiff of association with Communism is still beyond the pale.) As for Iran, recent antigovernment, anticlerical, pro-American mass demonstrations in the wake of the World Cup soccer matches have been virtually ignored by the Bush administration and, remarkably, have gotten almost no attention in the American press. This must change.

Yet to recognize that the enemy is fundamentalism itself—not "evil" anti-American fundamentalists, as opposed to the allegedly friendly kind—is also to make a statement about American cultural politics. Obviously nothing of the sort can be expected from Bush and Ashcroft. But our problem is not just leaders who are in bed with the Christian right. There is also the tendency of the left and the center to appease the right and downplay the culture war rather than make an uncompromising defense of freedom, feminism, and the separation of church and state. It remains to be seen whether fear of terrorism will trump the fear of facing our own cultural contradictions.

Why Gender Matters in Understanding September 11: Women, Militarism, and Violence

Amy Caiazza

From a briefing paper published by the Institute for Women's Policy Research, November 2001

Ever since the Taliban claimed victory and sovereignty over Afghanistan in 1997, it has waged war against Afghan women. The Taliban's radical fundamentalist form of *shariah*, Islamic rule, banned women's education, activism, and even physical presence in Afghan society. Women have been beaten and put to death for violating these rules. Under a system of legalized hatred for women, women are subject to increasing, so-called "private" forms of violence, including rape and domestic violence, with little recourse (Human Rights Watch 2001). Arab and other Muslim feminists in Pakistan, Bangladesh, Malaysia, India, and Turkey have publically criticized and taken organized action against the Taliban's and others' use of religion and state power to repress women (Afkhami 1995; see websites for the Revolutionary Association of Women in Afghanistan's and Women Living Under Muslim Law). In the United States, the Feminist Majority and other women's advocates have repeatedly called attention to the Taliban's antiwomen activities.

Until recently, few Americans paid attention to the Taliban's actions. Men and women on the left and the right dismissed Taliban policies as culturally specific, or as an internal political situation in which the United States or the United Nations had no stake (in contrast, there was global uproar over the destruction of Buddhist statues by the Taliban; Pollitt 2001). In our ignorance of Islam, the Arab world, other Muslim societies, and Afghan society in particular, most Americans assumed that Afghan women never enjoyed independence or autonomy. In fact, there was an Afghan women's movement as early as the 1920s. By the 1970s, two decades before the Taliban, Afghan women benefited from relatively high levels of education and leadership in Afghanistan.

Perhaps our collective neglect of the treatment of women in Afghanistan was a missed opportunity to foresee or even prevent the events of September 11, 2001. Societies that condone and even promote violence against women have shown over and over again that they tend to be violent in other ways as well. Even if we dismiss the claim that women's rights are central to human rights, there are centuries of evidence that physical, political, and economic violence against women is a harbinger of other forms of violence. Few societies that are plagued by it are otherwise peaceful.

The United States should pay particular attention to women when attempting to counteract terrorism and encourage more peaceful and democratic political systems in Afghanistan and throughout the world. In our foreign and domestic policies, we should look at both the victims and perpetrators of violence and terrorism. We should pay particularly close attention to the work of those who are effective opponents of violence against women. By doing so, we are more likely to address the root causes of terrorism and violence at home and in the wider world.

This paper analyzes women's roles as victims, supporters, and opponents of violence, terrorism, and militarism and proposes policy recommendations from its findings. It outlines important links between economic development, violence, women's activism, and peace-building efforts. Economic instability, combined with patriarchal views of women's roles, breeds conditions that lead to violence against women and undermine their capacity to build peaceful societies. In turn, violence against women heightens economic instability—as a result it sows the seeds of other forms of violence committed worldwide by men. In reaction, women sometimes resort to violence themselves, although more often they become activists for peace. Understanding why and when women fight for peace—and including them in peace building efforts—is crucial to guaranteeing higher levels of peace and security throughout the world.

Women as Victims of Militarism and Violence

"What has happened to us—our properties have been damaged, our bodies have been damaged. Everything—our life has absolutely changed . . . The spirit has been damaged."

—Mozambican woman and victim of civil war
(quoted in Turshen 2001, 60)

Where institutionalized violence and terrorism exist, women are often singled out as targets. Like men, they are victims, innocent bystanders, loved ones of victims, or refugees displaced by war. Because men are more likely to be involved in violence as soldiers and militants, women are more often displaced by their absence. The UN Human Rights Commission reports that two thirds of all people who have been turned into refugees in recent years have been women and their dependent children. Women are also targeted directly through deliberate murder, rape, and injury. In Christian, Muslim, and Buddhist societies, especially in modern ethnic and religious conflicts, male fighters have used rape to impregnate "enemy" women as a form of genocide. Terrorists' sperm "dirties" an ethnic line, and raped women may be rejected by their own societies. Such rape tactics are also designed to demoralize enemy men (Stiglmayer 1994; Turshen 2001). The recent genocidal movements in the former Yugoslavia and Rwanda saw rape used as a method of terror on a grand scale (Human Rights Watch 1996; Stiglmayer 1994).

Even in relatively peaceful societies like the United States, women are targets of violent acts such as rape and domestic violence. Elected officials, judges, and public policies in many states ignore or dismiss the right to freedom from violence as impractically complicated to enforce. Such acts of violence are often treated as private matters with little public consequence. But this purportedly "private" form of violence has important political ramifications. It stops women from being involved in their communities, and it reinforces the notion that they are second-class citizens (Caiazza 2001; Caiazza and Hartmann 2001; Enloe 1993; Sapiro 1993). This kind of violence is a form of daily terrorism against women as a class of citizens (Fineman and Mykitiuk 1994).

Whenever women are the victims of violence that goes unaddressed socially or politically, their victimization indicates that violence is an official, popular, and acceptable strategy for achieving political, social, or economic power. Violence is self-perpetuating: sons watch and do; daughters watch and submit and often do. In the United States, neglected and abused children are nearly twice as likely to commit crimes and be arrested as are other children (Harvard School of Public Health, Division of Public Health Practice, Violence Prevention Programs 2001). Similarly, men who beat, rape, or kill women are likely to be violent in other areas of their lives. They are likely to abuse children and to use violence to achieve a variety of goals in addition to subordinating women, such as achieving political power (Friedman 1994). Simply stated, violence against women and other forms of violence are inextricably linked.

In addition, where violence against women is particularly endemic or ignored, women are often less able to care for their families, thanks to their increased physical and, often, economic insecurity. This, in turn, contributes to insecurity and instability in society as a whole (Friedman 1994). Where violence of any sort is an acceptable strategy for achieving power, societal instability only encourages its further use.

Finally, even without considering violence per se, "non-violent" forms of repressing women's rights also contribute to a country's economic and political instability. Across the globe, when women have more rights and equality, national standards of living also rise life expectancy is higher, incomes and education levels are higher, and birthrates are lower. As countries more fully include women in political, economic, and social rights, standards of living improve as well (Crossette 2001). A country with little violence, but relatively few opportunities for gender equality, is unlikely to achieve high levels of economic and political development.

Women as Terrorists and Supporters of Militarism

"Violence is the only way to answer violence!"
–Gudrun Ensslin,
female leader of Germany's 1970s Baader-Meinhof Gang
(quoted in Huffman 1999)

Women are not only passive victims of terrorism and violence. Some women, although a relatively small number, participate in or encourage terrorism. Women have committed acts of terrorism, including suicide bombings, in India, Palestine, and other countries. In one of the few cases when a world leader was killed during an act of terrorism, a woman assassinated India's Rajiv Gandhi in 1991. In Norway, a right-wing group has a "women's wing" of terrorists (Fangen 1997). In the United States, there has been a deliberate policy by the KKK's male leadership to recruit women as racist activists (Blee 1992).

But it is men who comprise the overwhelming majority of individuals who practice terrorism. In part, this is because of sexist and patriarchal norms that preclude women from militaristic action and limit their public or activist roles. Since many terrorist groups are rooted in diverse religious fundamentalist or right-wing ideologies, their male leaders often refuse to let women assume men's traditional roles as soldiers, terrorists, martyrs, or so-called freedom fighters. Their terrorist actions are often justified as defending a social order that is dependent on women's "purity" and requires the exclusion of women from many facets of public life.

Some women take part in terrorism when there are few perceived outlets for gender equality. Frustrated with a lack of outlets for their public activism, women turn to the kinds of strategies that many alienated groups have adopted: to fight against mainstream political institutions using extreme tactics (Fangen 1997).

When not playing the role of terrorists directly, some women support men's militancy in their traditional roles as mothers by nurturing families committed to militarist or terrorist causes (Ibanez 2001). In many societies, women have been traditionally charged with passing on the cultural norms and expectations of their communities to sons and daughters. When those norms include the use of violence for political ends, women encourage the radicalism and militaristic self-sacrifice that lead to terrorist acts. Notably, women's roles perpetuating these values are not unique to non-governmental terrorist groups: the values of "feminine sacrifice," in which mothers give their sons to militarist causes, are promoted by many military policymakers who would loathe being compared with terrorists (Enloe 2000a).

Women's support for militarism has been a resource that sustains both terrorist and formal military conflict. Such support can bring moral weight to militarist movements and encourage involvement in them. In some cases, women are moved to provide active logistical support for militarism and terrorism (i.e., by feeding and clothing militants, delivering messages, and providing other resources). Women have played all these roles prominently in recent decades in areas as diverse as El Salvador, Nicaragua, Northern Ireland, Palestine, and Israel (see Hammami 1997; Sharoni 1997 and 2001).

For many women, participating in and supporting (though rarely planning) acts of terrorism are ways to "protect" their families, homes, and communities. As mothers and wives, many women accept their traditional roles as protectors of their husbands' and children's well-being. In times and places of violent conflict, political disjuncture, and economic insecurity, women may feel unable to do so. When women live in oppressed or alienated communities, they may also have few formal ways to work for political change. Being allowed inside small, elected, secret terrorist organizations may allow some women to see themselves as fighting for the promise of a more just and stable way of life (Hammami 1997; Ibanez 2001).

Men's support of and participation in terrorist or militarist activities can also stem from a desire to bring about justice in the face of economic or political insecurity. However, their goals and aspirations are justified more often by the rhetoric of building a society based on religious or political ideals than in explicitly protecting or bettering the lives of their children and families. These "private" concerns are considered women's realm. And, because of traditional gender roles, women approach these concerns through different activities than men.

Women as Peacemakers

"[We should] cease to be silent . . . protest against those who bear the responsibility for this cursed war . . . [and not] relinquish the struggle until our sons come home."
–Shoshana Shmueli, founder of the Israeli Parents against Silence
(quoted in *Sharoni* 1997, 152)

Not all women who react to terrorism or militarism support it. In many cases, women respond by becoming activists for peace. Again, they often do so because they accept their traditional responsibilities for guaranteeing their families' private social, economic, and physical well-being, but feel unable to fulfill them. They are moved to fight the circumstances, including conditions of violence, causing their uncertainty. They hope to build a society that will allow them to ensure their families' safety. In the Middle East, Latin America, and Northern Ireland, for example, women have fought state-sponsored and non-state-sponsored terrorism through their activism (Aretxaga 1997; Fisher 1989; Sharoni 1997). Their efforts are not based on an inherently "feminine" predisposition toward peace but result from their desire to fulfill their traditional responsibilities as mothers and wives.

In many cases, women act on behalf of peace because they moved from wanting to protect only their own families to protecting all children. At some point, they recognize that to address their own political and economic insecurity, they need to address a larger set of conditions facing their communities (Fisher 1989). In Russia, Israel, Serbia, Italy, and Spain, mothers have come together to protest militarism precisely because they first felt a need to protect their children. They have resorted to protests and other highly visible and disruptive tactics in the absence of democratic mechanisms for change. In part, because they have the moral weight of motherhood behind them, they have, at times, been very effective (Caiazza forthcoming).

Many women's peace movements demand greater accountability and more responsiveness from their governments and other institutions. They become activists for democracy. Because their activism is often rooted in their family roles, when women activists are included in building a country's democratic systems and civil society, they are also more likely to prioritize policies that focus on building the well-being of families and overall systems of social welfare. This, in turn, can lead to more economic stability and political security.

Policy Recommendations: Counteracting Terrorism by Addressing Women's Concerns

Throughout the world, violence and radicalism are associated with political and economic disjuncture, alienation, and dysfunction. Men and women who become terrorists do so because they see few alternatives for pursuing political change. They are frustrated by their economic and political insecurity. They have little trust in government or other institutions. As a result, they turn to movements that promise them justice, power, and access to resources. These movements are often rooted in a desire to return to a more conservative culture and win greater independence from Western hegemony. In many cases, they are based on extremist right- or left-wing ideas. The men and women involved in them see violence as a justified, or even the only, way to achieve their goals. These conditions politicize both men and women—both in support of and against militarism.

For women, radicalism often stems from a desire to protect their homes and communities in times of economic and political insecurity. They turn to political movements that promise safety, better living conditions, and broader economic opportunities, as well as political or religious justice.

These conclusions point to a set of policy implications that the United States and other industrialized democracies should heed if they hope to encourage democracy throughout the world. These recommendations encompass a long-term strategy for developing women's rights as a tool for building global peace and security.

- U.S. international policy should unequivocally oppose violence against women and regimes that condone it. Efforts to combat it should be as central to our evaluations of democracy as competitive elections and universal suffrage.

While direct and indirect violence against women exists in virtually every country, we should not ignore it as incidental to other forms of violence. In most countries marked by political violence, violence against women is particularly rampant. Often, political institutions in those countries treat women as second-class citizens by denying them the right to participate fully in all aspects of society. They officially or unofficially encourage violence against them. U.S. policy should use every available economic and diplomatic means to vigorously oppose these regimes.

As part of its program to fight violence against women, U.S. policy should provide women with the resources that allow them to escape violent situations and achieve individual autonomy. Such efforts can include providing educational and health care assistance to women, through legislation and policies like the Afghan Women and Children Relief Act of 2001, introduced in the U.S. Congress in November of 2001. This legislation would provide such assistance through local institutions and nongovernmental organizations, particularly women's organizations, as much as possible (Feminist Majority 2001).

Turning a blind eye to violence against women—at home and abroad— also needs to be publicly recognized as a sign that violence is an acceptable part of a society that undermines a country's stability. The seeds of terrorism are sown in violence against women and the repression of women's rights.

- Women need to be included as equal partners in implementing political and economic development. U.S. foreign policy should make women's involvement in democratization central to its international aid programs.

Women's concerns need to be taken seriously and incorporated into development policies. As the United States and other countries pursue policies encouraging development, they should make including indigenous women's voices a top priority, not an afterthought.

Incorporating women into development efforts offers many positive outcomes in addition to improving women's status. Because of women's central roles in caring for their families, and women activists' resulting focus on social welfare, including women's perspectives can also encourage more stability, growth, and well-being. Empowering women to take part in political processes can be a successful way to encourage democracy and stability (Enloe 2000b).

Policies requiring women's participation in nation- and peace-building would mandate that any government established in Afghanistan with U.S. assistance respect and guarantee women's rights; design reconstruction programs to give women and girls access to health care, education, and other social welfare resources; and distribute humanitarian assistance equitably. These policies should be central to U.S. development programs worldwide.

- As countermovements to terrorism, women's peace movements should be especially encouraged and targeted for financial aid under U.S. foreign policies. They should also be specifically incorporated into reconstruction efforts supported by the United States.

Women's peace movements have been effective agents of change in many settings where terrorism and military conflict are rampant. They draw attention to the consequences of militarism on a community's families, and they bring moral weight to arguments for peace. In many settings, they could provide the basis for large-scale efforts to counter terrorist organizations. But, as currently constituted, these movements are usually small and have few resources to mobilize women and demand attention from terrorist organizations or governments. More investment in these movements by U.S. international aid efforts would encourage peace around the world.

Because women's peace movements have been so effective, and because of women's clear stake in peacemaking processes, in October of 2001 the UN Security Council adopted a resolution (#1325) formally calling on peace officials in the United Nations, NATO, and other official organizations to explicitly include women in negotiations for ceasefires and postwar reconstruction. The United States should wholeheartedly support this recommendation in the implementation of both international and U.S. peace and development programs. In some of its programs—including its grants to grassroots women's and refugees organizations in Afghanistan and Pakistan starting in 1997—it has already done so. These efforts should be widened and continued.

- In the long term, U.S. foreign policy and international organizations should place a higher priority on programs to encourage economic and political development, especially in the most authoritarian and impoverished countries. These programs are among the most likely to increase levels of security among men and women and address the conditions that encourage terrorism.

Economic and political development efforts can diminish many of the national and international hatreds that currently plague the world. They can create more obvious opportunities for men and women to promote change through less violent means and to achieve economic success. Perhaps most importantly, they can also make it easier for women and men to protect their families—economically, politically, and physically. As a result, they can alleviate some of the pressures that inspire men and women to take up arms and/or engage in terrorist activity.

In combating terrorism, the United States and other governments should rely on more than traditional intelligence and counterterrorism strategies. Overall, total spending on U.S. foreign economic aid is currently about three times spending on military aid. But in the tense and highly militarized countries of the Middle East, U.S. military aid outstrips economic aid by about 50 percent (U.S. Department of Commerce, Bureau of the Census 2000). We should spend at least equal effort and resources encouraging effective economic development around the world, especially in this region. Investing more in economic aid, especially in the Middle East, could partially counterbalance our image as a country that funds violence by supplying military arm; it would also address some of the root causes of terrorism.

References

Afkhami, Mahnaz. 1995. *Faith and Freedom: Women's Human Rights in the Muslim*

World (Gender, Culture, and Politics in the Middle East). Syracuse: Syracuse University Press.

Aretxaga, B. 1997. *Shattering Silence: Women, Nationalism, and Political Subjectivity in Northern Ireland.* Princeton: Princeton University Press.

Blee, Kathleen. 1992. *Women of the Klan: Racism and Gender in the 1920s.* Berkeley: University of California Press.

Caiazza, Amy. 2001. "Women's Community Involvement: The Effects of Money, Safety, Parenthood, and Friends." Research-in-Brief. Washington, DC: Institute for Women's Policy Research.

Caiazza, Amy. Forthcoming. *Mothers and Soldiers: Men's and Women's Organizing in 1990s Russia.* New York: Routledge.

Caiazza, Amy, and Heidi Hartmann. 2001. "Gender and Civic Engagement." Paper presented to the working group on Work, Family, Democracy, organized by the Johnson Foundation and the Harvard School of Public Health, June (Milwaukee, WI).

Crossette, Barbara. 2001. "Living in a World without Women." *The New York Times,* November 4. Available at website: www.nytimes.com. Accessed November 2001.

Enloe, Cynthia. 1993. *The Morning after: Sexual Politics at the End of the Cold War.* Berkeley: University of California Press.

Enloe, Cynthia. 2000a. *Maneuvers: The International Politics of Militarizing Women's Lives.* Berkeley: University of California Press.

Enloe, Cynthia. 2000b. "Masculinity as Foreign Policy Issue." *Foreign Policy in Focus,* vol. 5, issue 36. Washington, DC: Institute for Policy Studies.

Fangen, Katrine. 1997. "Separate or Equal? The Emergence of an All-Female Group in Norway's Rightist Underground." *Terrorism and Political Violence* 9 (3): 122-64.

Feminist Majority. 2001. "Senate to Consider Bill for Afghan Women." *Feminist Daily News Wire, November 2, 2001.*

Fineman, Martha Albertson, and Roxanne Nlykiduk. 1994. *The Public Nature of Private Violence: The Discovery of Domestic Abuse.* New York: Routledge.

Fisher, Jo. 1989. *Mothers of the Disappeared.* London: Zed Books.

Friedman, Sara Ann. 1994. *Creating Violence-Free Families: A Symposium Summary Report, New York, May 23-25, 1994.* New York: Baha'i International Community, United Nations Development Fund for Women, and United Nations Children Fund.

Hammami, Rema. 1997. "Palestinian Motherhood on the West Bank and Gaza

Strip." In Alexis Jetter, Annelise Orleck, and Diana Taylor, eds., *The Politics of Motherhood Activist Voices from Left to Right,* 161–8. Hanover: University Press of New England.

Harvard School of Public Health, Division of Public Health Practice, Violence Prevention Programs. 2001. "Violence Statistics."Webpage available at www.hsph.harvard.edu/php/VPP/peace.html.

Huffman, Richard. 1999. "Gudrun Ensslin." Available at website www.baader-meinhof.com/who/terrorists/bmgang/ensslingudrun.html. Accessed October 2001.

Human Rights Watch. 1996. *Shattered Lives: Sexual Violence during the Rwandan Genocide and Its Aftermath.* New York: Human Rights Watch.

Human Rights Watch. 2001. *Afghanistan: Humanity Denied, Systematic Violations of Women's Rights in Afghanistan.* New York: Human Rights Watch.

Ibanez, Ana Cristina. 2001. "El Salvador: War and Untold Stories—Women Guerrillas." In Caroline O.N. Moser and Fiona C. Clark, eds., *Victims, Perpetrators, or Actors? Gender, Armed Conflict, and Political Violence,* 117–39. London: Zed Books.

Politt, Katha. 2001. "Where are the Women?: Subject to Debate." *The Nation,* October 22. Available at website www.thenation.com. Accessed November 2001.

Sapiro, Virginia. 1993. " 'Private' Coercion and Democratic Theory: The Case of Gender-Based Violence." In George E. Marcus and Russell L. Hanson, eds., *Reconsidering the Democratic Public,* 427–50. University Park, PA: Pennsylvania State University Press.

Sharoni, Simona. 1997. "Israeli Women Organizing for Peace." In *The Politics of Motherhood—Activist Voices from Left to Right,* ed. Alexis Jetter, Annelise Orleck, and Diana Taylor, 144–60. Hanover, NH: University Press of New England.

Sharoni. 2001. "Rethinking Women's Struggles in Israel-Palestine and in the North of Ireland." In Caroline O.N. Moser and Fiona C. Clark, eds., *Victims, Perpetrators, or Actors? Gender, Armed Conflict, and Political Violence,* 85–98. London: Zed Books.

Stiglmayer, Alexandra, ed. 1994. *Mass Rape: The War against Women in Bosnia-Herzegovina.* Lincoln: University of Nebraska Press.

Turshen, Meredith. 2001. "The Political Economy of Rape: An Analysis of Systematic Rape and Sexual Abuse of Women during Armed Conflict in

Africa." In Caroline O.N. Moser and Fiona C. Clark, eds., *Victims, Per-petrators, or Actors? Gender, Armed Conflict, and Political Violence*, 55-68. London: Zed Books.

U.S. Department of Commerce, Bureau of the Census. 2000. *Statistical Abstract ofthe United States: 2000*. Washington, DC: Government Printing Office.

Whose Fundamentalism?

Minoo Moallem

From *Meridians*, volume 2, No. 2, 2002

September 26, 2001

In the wake of the horrific events of September 11th, "Islamic fundamentalism," a discourse which has been decades in the making, has finally come into its own. Islamic fundamentalism is taken to connote something that lies outside the West, a reversion to an archaic and barbaric age. It is seen as Islam's essence and the ultimate source of otherness. The barbaric other is/belongs outside civilization; he is in a permanent war with civilization but with no possibility of entering history. He penetrates civilization with the intention of destroying it; he is a man of destruction. His freedom is the taking away of others' freedom. The barbaric other is there to legitimize and give meaning to the masculinist militarism of the "civilized" and his constant need to "protect." Protection enables an alliance between protector and protected against a common foe. This alliance effaces the protector's will to power.

The representation of Islamic fundamentalism in the West is deeply influenced by the general racialization of Muslims in a neoracist idiom, which has its roots in cultural essentialism and a conventional Eurocentric notion of "people without history." Islamic fundamentalism has become a generic signifier used constantly to single out the Muslim other, in its irrational, morally inferior, and barbaric masculinity and its passive, victimized, and submissive femininity. New forms of Orientalist discourse not only legitimize Western intervention and the protection of Western economic and political interests in the "Middle East," but also justify discrimination and the exclusion of Middle Eastern and Muslim immigrants in diaspora. It reduces all Muslims to fundamentalists, and all fundamentalists to fanatical antimodern traditionalists and terrorists, even as it attributes a culturally aggressive and oppressive nature to all fundamentalist men, and a passive, ignorant, and submissive nature to all fundamentalist women. Such totalizing discourses not only deny the presence of dissenting social movements in the region, but also dissimulate the existence of various forms of negotiation over the meaning and interpretation of Islam in many different Muslim countries, perpetuating what Edward Said identified as Orientalism. The depiction of Islam as a static system transcending cultures and peoples is the condition, in the context of modernity and postmodernity, of what is being called "the Islamic revival" or "the Islamic resurgence." This process accords with the expansionist logic of the West, the quest for oil and political control of strategically located "Middle Eastern" countries. It also accords with Western measures to ensure the preservation or establishment of friendly local regimes, and with the steady deterioration of culture and social values of the people in this area. That means that it has no relation to history and no connection to any other forms of fundamentalism, either in the U.S. or elsewhere in the world. The collapse of the Soviet Union, and with it the bipolar logic of the cold war, left a vacuum in American cultural and political life; Islamic fundamentalism was on hand to shore up a dualistic moral framework of good and evil.

Islamic fundamentalism functions both as a transnational movement and a system of representation. It moves by way of global networks of communication, trade, and travel; its vectors are money, ideas, bodies, and consumer goods. It has brought to the surface deep fears of "difference"; it disavows by projection what is intolerable in the "enlightened" West. The question therefore arises: Can it be that Islamic fundamentalism is the noxious reservoir of an unresolved past and an unexamined present in the West? Can it be that, in the mirror of what we call Islamic fundamentalism, we (are afraid to) see the problems of modernity carried over to the complex conditions of postmodernity? Is it easier for us to consign Islamic fundamentalism to a mythic, barbaric past, whereby we moderns are assured of the superiority of our civilization? Where, after all, are we to put the history of colonialism, genocide, and slavery?

The presence in the West of masses of immigrants and refugees from Muslim cultures has added new anxieties about hosting the Muslim "other" from the postcolonial territories. The new cosmopolitan centers of the contemporary world, far from being a paradise of hybridity, are marked by what Abdulrazak Gurnah calls "the twin traditions of asylum and xenophobia." The discourse of asylum coexists with xenophobia narratives to construct the foreigner as forever alien and tragic. Refugees and immigrants from postcolonial territories and Muslim cultures in the U.S., Canada, and Europe are under constant pressure to identify—or disidentify—with—with their cultural and religious traditions, which are considered to be a threatening source of contamination and barbarism.

Etienne Balibar has said that the "sharpest edge of racist discourse and mentalities tends to press on the populations of 'Arab-Islamic' origin who have permanently settled in Europe and North America; this is because a condensation or superimposition of the colonial and anti-Semitic schemes has occurred in this case, so that imagery of racial superiority and imagery of cultural and religious rivalry reinforce each other."

In the aftermath of September 11th, all Muslims—of whatever national and ethnic origin—have been branded as somehow on the side of "evil" and therefore in need of punishment, deportation, even extermination. While the liberal-corporate media have displayed some finesse in making Muslims into the demonic other and in excluding feminist and antiracist voices, fundamentalist America—Jerry Falwell and his ilk—added feminists, pagans, gays, and lesbians to the list. Despite later disclaimers, Falwell's anathemas found their true echo in the presidential invocation of a "crusade" against the Muslim enemy, and an explicit Manichean logic whereby "those who are not with us are against us."

Those who lead a crusade of good against evil and divide the world between two camps have no tolerance for ambiguity, displacement, or fragmentation. Any transaction between one pole and the other is disavowed, even though most of the men now represented as belonging to the forces of evil were at some point, even very recently, on the side of "good." It is not difficult for me, as a Middle Easterner and someone who survived bombardment by the Iraqi air force, to give instances. Saddam Hussein and the Taliban were our allies, and therefore necessarily on the side of good, as long as they were in a war against Iran and the former Soviet Union.

So this seems an appropriate moment to raise a number of obvious questions. Who determines who is good and who is evil, and on what basis? What happens when the agents of good are reassigned, and vice versa? What if good and evil are entangled in a relation of mutual construction, are bound up in a single history? Am I mistaken in thinking that to deny this is in fact a fundamentalist position, since it allows no space for any position "in between"—that is to say, a position that refuses the erasure of actual history in favor of the mythos of good and evil? What if the dichotomous categories of good/evil, West/Islam, us/them were arifacts of a history of racism, segregation, colonialism, and displacement? What if all these categories were linguistic traps that conceal the workings of power? Don't we need to investigate this anyway, no matter if the good is "us" and the evil is "them," because of the very possibility of reversal? As a woman displaced from Iran, I am long familiar with patriarchal formulations of "us" versus "them," to be found no less in Europe or North America than the Middle East. And I cannot help but question the consequent binaries and borderings, protean in nature—sometimes spatial (West/Islam), sometime temporal (modern/archaic), sometimes moral (good/evil). It certainly has not served me as a gendered and racialized subject. Indeed, as an Iranian, I have leaned the hard way: The cost was displacement, since we were the first to be "othered" as soon as the need for unity at the moment of revolution was over.

It is important to remember that every single life is precious, including those lived in the third world where death from poverty, war, and oppression is represented as an everyday banality. Geopolitical location is a matter of privilege, a fact that brings us to the limits of humanism. It is crucial to keep in mind that every loss of life demands that the living entertain a certain failure, even our silent complicity with the conditions in which death becomes desirable. I say this in the face of the masculinist vulgarity, if not cruelty, of those, above all in the U.S. media, who, even in the shadow of horror, take pleasure in fantasizing with the familiar heterosexist and Orientalist tropes of a "Muslim paradise."

What concerns me, in the end, is the convergence of various forms of fundamentalism, both secular and religious, both here and elsewhere. I see that they share a gendered militarism whose terms of unity are made possible through "killing the 'other.'" In the world of words, where those in power make such unity out of fragmentation, dualism out of moral ambiguity, good out of evil, I find wisdom in the questioning of fundamentalism, which in my own theoretical work I have come to define as a regime of truth based on discourses identified with, or ordained either by a God (taken literally or metaphorically) or by a medico-military-scientific constitution, which establishes, and binds its observants, to a fundamental opposition between good and evil, normal and abnormal, civilization and barbarism.

Unholy Wars

Seyla Benhabib

From *Contellations,* volume 9, No. 1, 2002

It has become clear since September 11 that we are faced with a new form of struggle that threatens to dissolve the boundaries of the political in liberal democracies. The terror network of Osama bin Laden, and its various branches in Egypt, Pakistan, Malaysia, Indonesia, the Philippines, Algeria, and among Islamist groups in western Europe, is wider, more entrenched, and more sophisticated than it was believed to be. The attacks unleashed by these groups (and their potential sympathizers in the U.S. and Europe among the neo-Nazis and white supremacists), especially the use of the biological weapon anthrax to contaminate the cilivian population via the mail, indicate a new political and military phenomenon which challenges the framework of state-centric politics.

Historians always warn us that the unprecedented will turn out to have some forerunners somewhere and that what seems new today will appear old when considered against the background of some longer time span. Nevertheless to "think the new" in politics is the vocation of the intellectual. This is a task at which Susan Sontag, Fred Jameson, and Slavoj Zizek have failed us by interpreting these events along the tired paradigm of an antiimperalist struggle by the "wretched of the earth." [1] Neglecting the internal dynamics and struggles within the Islamic world and the history of regional conflicts in Afghanistan, Pakistan, India, and Kashmir, these analyses assure us that we can continue to grasp the world through our usual categories, and that by blaming the policies and actions of western governments one can puge onself of the enmity and hatred which is directed toward one as a member of such western societies. These analyses help us neither to grasp the unprecedented nature of the events unfolding since September 11, 2001 nor to appreciate the internal dynamics within the Arab-Muslim world which have given rise to them.

The line between *military and civilian targets*, between military and civilian populations, had already been erased during the aerial bombings of World War II. This is not what is new since Sepbember 11. Faced with the total mobilization of society, initiated by fascism and National Socialism, it was the democracies of the world, and not some marginal terrorist group hiding in the mountains of Afghanistan, that first crossed that line and initiated "total war." The civilian population at large became the hostage of the enemy, as during the bombing of London by the Nazis and then of Dresden, Hiroshima, and Nagasaki by the Allies.

In the 1950s, the Algerian War marked a new variation in this process of the erasure of the line between the front and the home, the soldier and the civilian. The Algerian Resistance against the French aimed at destroying the *normalcy of everyday life* for the civilians of the occupying population. By blowing up the French residents of Algeria in cafes, markets, and stations, the Resistance not only reminded them that they were the enemy but that there could be no "normal life" under conditions of colonial occupation. Since that time, this kind of terror—which fights against the superior military and technical weapons of a mightier enemy by tearing apart the fabric of everyday life through interrupting normal routines, and by rendering every bus or railroad station, each street corner or gathering place, a potential target—has become one of the favorite "weapons of the weak." The strategy of this kind of struggle is to make life so unlivable for the enemy cilvilans that they concede defeat even if they enjoy superior military power. The Palestinian Intifada at least in part follows the Algerian model: by creating conditions of continuous fear, insecurity, and violence in the land of Palestine, it aims at destroying the resolve of the Israeli civilian population to continue a normal life.[2] In recent years, however, infiltrators from Islamist groups like the Hamas and the Hizbollah into the ranks of the Palestinians, and the widespread practice of "suicide bombings," are changing the nature of the Intifada as well.

The bombing of the World Trade Center and the Pentagon is unlike both the total war waged in the struggle against fascism and the terrorism against the occupier initiated by the Algerians. These new attacks, perpetrated against a civilian population in its own land and against a country in no state of declared hostility with the attackers, not only defy all categories of international law but reduce politics to apocalyptic symbols. Until Osama bin Laden released his terse video celebrating September 11, his deed had *no* political name: In whose name or for whom was his group acting? What political demands was it voicing? The brief references to the stationing of U.S. troops in Saudi Arabia, to U.S. sanctions against Iraq, and to U.S. support of Israel were shrouded in the language of *jihad* (holy war) and obfuscated by allusions to the lost glory of Islam in the thirteenth century through the loss of "al Andalus" (Spain) to the Christians. While is it conceivable that Palestinian terror could end one day if Isreal withdrew from the occupied West Bank, released Palestinian prisoners of war, found a settlement for the refugees, and somehow resolved the question of Jerusalem, it is unclear, what, if anything, could end the *jihad* of the Osama bin Laden network against the U.S. and its allies. Theirs is a war of "holy" vengeance, a war designed to humiliate the mighty "Satan" in New York and Washington by turning the weapons of the most developed technology against the society which created them.

The result is a sublime combination of high tech wizardry and moral and political atavism, which some have named "jihad online." But this unholy politics threatens to undo the moral and political distinctions that ought to govern our lives, distinctions between enemy, friend, and bystander; guilt, complicity, and responsibiltiy; conflict, combat, and war. We have to live by them even if others do not.

One of the most commonly heard contentions in the aftermath of September 11 was that even if the terrorist attacks upon the World Trade Center and Washington equaled war in the civilian and property damage they inflicted, the deliberateness and precision with which they were executed, and the brazenness with which they violated customary moral, legal, and international norms, the U.S. Congress could not actually declare "war," not because the enemy was as yet unknown, but because a state can declare war only against another state. The idea that a democratic nation-state would declare war upon a global network of loosely organized sympathizers of a religious-cum-civilizational cause strained all categories of international law with which the world has lived since 1945 and in which nation-states are the principal recognized actors. For this reason, the current military action in Afghanistan has not been preceded by a declaration of war; rather the Congress has authorized the president to do whatever is necessary to fight the global terror network and to bring the perpetrators to justice, but declared war neither on the Taliban (whom most nations do not recognize as a legitimate regime) nor on the Afghani people. It is as if the territory, the terrain of Afghanistan, is our enemy, in that this terrain offers a sanctuary and an operational base for one of the great fugitives of our time—Osama bin Laden. Ironically, the people of Afghanistan have themselves fallen "captive" or "prisoner" to one who operates on their territory, and to whom the Taliban had granted refuge. Afghanistan is a decaying or failed nation-state, and this very condition of decay permits us to understand all the more vividly the principles of national sovereignty which have governed international relations since the Second World War.

Recall here Max Weber's classically modernist definition of the state as "the legitimate monopoly over the use of violence within a recognized and bounded territory.[3] Modern statehood is based upon the coupling together of the principles of *territoriality, administrative and military monopoly*, including the use of violence, and the *legitimacy* to do so. When states decay, dissolve, or secede, these three principles fall asunder. Their territory can become a staging ground for operations not only of guerilla warfare, but of drug smuggling, weapons production, contraband, and other illegal activities; administrative and military competence is overtaken by units at the substate level such as warlords, commandos, traditional chieftains, or religious leaders; and legitimacy loses its representational quality in that there is no longer a unified people to whose will it either refers or defers—legitimacy either flows from the barrel of a gun or from other sources of supra- and subnational ideological worldviews, be these race-, religion-, or civilization-based.

The decaying and weak nation-states of the contemporary world bear similarities as well as differences with the totalitarian regimes of the mid-twentieth century. The breakdown of the rule of law, the destruction of representative and democratic institutions, the pervasiveness of violence, and the universalization of fear are features of both state-forms. Although at times they mobilized "the movement" against the state bureaucracy, the totalitarian regimes of the mid-twentieth century by and large strengthened and rebuilt the state by rendering it subservient to their ideologies. But the postmodern/quasi-feudal states of the present, like Afghanistan, Chechnya, Bosnia, and Rwanda, emerge as a result not of the strengthening but of the destruction of the territorial and administrative unity of the state in the name of subunities, which are then globally networked. As Hannah Arendt has shown us, totalitarian movements also had globalizing ambitions in that they touted supranational ideologies like pan-Germanism and pan-Slavism.[4] Yet the global ideologies of today's terror movements are both larger and smaller in range: instead of the ideology of linguistic or cultural unity among the Slavic or Germanic nations, for example, today we are dealing with ideologies aimed at tribes, ethnicities, or a vision of a community of believers that transcends them all—namely the Islamic *umma* of the faithful. The new unit of totalitarianism is the terrorist cell, not the party or the movement; the goal of this new form of war is not just the destruction of the enemy but the extinction of a way of life. *The emergence of nonstate agents capable of waging destruction at a level hitherto thought to be only the province of states and the emergence of a supranational ideological vision with an undefinable moral and political content, which can hardly be satisfied by ordinary political tactics and negotiations, are the unprecedented aspects of our current condition.*

This remark should not be taken to suggest that I attribute an overarching rationality or normativity to the state use of violence. State terrorism can also be brutal, unjust, and merciless—recall the war of the Yugoslav state against the Bosnians and the Kosovar Albanians! The point I am emphasizing, however, is that in liberal democracies the monopoly which the state claims over the use of the means of violence is always in principle, if not in fact, subject to the rule of law and to democratic legitimation by the citizenry. These internal constraints upon the legitimate use of violence are then carried into the international arena, where sovereign states bind themselves to limit their use of violence through entering into pacts and associations, signing treaties, etc.

The end of the bipolar world of the cold war brought with it not just multiplurality but a global society in which nonstate actors have emerged as players possessing the means of violence but who are not subject to usual constraints of international law and treaties. All treaties which have hitherto governed the nonuse and proliferation of biological, chemical, and nuclear weapons have been rendered irrelevant: those who will deploy them have never been their signatories. Furthermore, not being recognized as legitimate political entities, these groups have no responsibility and accountability toward the populations in whose midst they act and which harbor them. Suppose Osama bin Laden and his group possess Scud missiles with nuclear warheads, which they may have obtained either from Iraq or from the Russian Mafia or other weapons smugglers. What would prevent them from firing these missiles against population centers in Afghanistan, Pakistan, India, or Israel if this would serve some purpose? Since they are accountable to no one, the collateral damage which they may cause even to their own allies and sympathizers is of no concern to them. Whereas terrorist groups like the Basque ETA and the IRA still have to be governed by some sense of proportion in the damage they inflict and the violence they engage in, in order not to lose all sympathy for their cause in world public opinion, these new terror networks are not motivated by foreseeable political goals analogous to the independence of the Basque land from Spain and France, the removal of the Irish Loyalist population and unity with Catholic Ireland, and the like. Nor are these groups fighting for hearts and minds in the West by seeking the conversion of the population to Islam and to Islamic ways of life. When it was practiced by Islamic armies in the centuries after the death of Muhammad (632 A.D.), *jihad*—which can also mean the struggle of the soul with itself to lead the virtuous life as dictated by the Qur'an[5]—aimed at the conquest of the land of the "infidels" in order to force their conversion to Islam. People of all races, colors, ethnicities, and tongues could convert to Islam and become "good Muslims." It is this option of conversion which has made Islam into the biggest Abrahamic religion of the world; ironically, it is the very absence of this conversion mission that is striking in the new jihad.

The new jihad is not only apocalyptic; it is nihilistic. A Taliban spokesman's statement that his people love death as much as the Americans love life is an expression of superb nihilism. The eroticization of death, as evidenced on the one hand by the frequently heard vulgarisms about *huris,* the dark-eyed virgins who are to meet the warriors in the afterlife, but on the other hand and more importantly by the destruction of one's own body in an act of supreme violence which dismembers and pulverizes it, is remarkable. Human beings have died throughout the centuries for causes they believed in, to save their loved ones, to protect their country or their principles, to save the faith, to exercise solidarity, and the like. But the emergence of "suicide bombings" among Islamist groups on a mass scale is astonishing. As many Qur'anic scholars have pointed out, there is no theological justification for this: it is one thing to die in war and yet another to make the destruction of one's body along with those of others the supreme weapon. In order to quell such waves of suicide bombings, the Israeli authorities resorted to an atavistic practice: they made it publicly known that they would bury the remains of suicide bombers in shrouds of pigs' skin (an animal that is considered "*haram*"—taboo—by Jews and Muslims alike) in order to prevent their ascent into heaven in accordance with Islamic faith. It is of course hard to know whether men of the sophistication and worldliness of Muhammad Atta and others, who have lived in the capitals of Europe and the West and who have attended universities as well as bars, movie houses as well as brothels, believe in the afterlife. I personally doubt it. Not only is it clear that the very strict version of Islam—Wahhabism—which Osama bin Laden follows is not shared by all even within his own group, but the Egyptian Brotherhood which was the original organization for many Islamist philosophies in the 1950s had its own version of things, as do members of the Algerian terror network. These networks of young militants who trot the globe from Bosnia to Afghanistan, from Paris to Indonesia, and back to Baghdad, Hamburg, or New York, are like Islamic soldiers of fortune, in search not of riches but an elusive and decisive encounter with death. In this regard they bear more resemblance to chiliastic sects among all world religions than to the Muslim armies of the Umayyad, the Abassids, or the Ottomans. While using friendly Muslim governments and their hospitality for their own purposes, these groups pose a clear threat to any established form of authority—which may have been one reason why the Saudis renounced Osama bin Laden's citizenship and rendered him an international fugitive.

As in the past century, faced with a novel form of totalitarianism, democracies confront unique challenges. The presence of an enemy who is neither a military adversary nor a representative agent of a known state creates confusion as to whether police and other law enforcement agencies or the military should take the lead in the investigation and the struggle; the lines between acts of crime and acts of war get blurred. The concept of an "internal enemy," which is now being promoted against "suspect groups" through surveillance, wiretapping, and stricter immigration controls, is not one that democracies can live with. The category of the terrorist as an "internal enemy," as one who is among us, even if not one of us, strains the democratic community by revealing that the rule of law is not all-inclusive and that violence lurks at the edges of everyday normalcy. Our thinking about foreigners, refugees, and asylees becomes colored by the image of others as potential enemies; the "other" becomes the criminal. We may be at a point in history when the state-centric system is indeed waning: global terrorism and the formation of a global economy and civil society are part of the same maelstrom. Yet our laws as well as institutions, practices as well as alliances, are governed by state-centric terms which presuppose the unity of territoriality, the monopoly over the use of the means of violence, and the attainment of legitimacy through representative institutions. It is of course supremely ironic that President Bush, who advocated a new version of American unilateralism and isolationism and who denounced "nation building," now finds himself supporting multilateral actions with allies like Pakistan, Saudi Arabia, and Syria, whose democratic legitimacy is highly questionable, but also reconstructing a post-Taliban government in Afghanistan. Can we find responses to this new challenge that will break the vicious cycles of violence, incomprehension, and repression at home and war abroad?

Although the attacks have so far been directed against the U.S., and although the U.S. is justified under international law in invoking the right of self-defense to justify the current war,[6] the U.S. and its NATO allies have resorted to the clause of collective security and Article 5 of NATO, which guarantees the security of each member of the alliance. I support this course of action, and I would further endorse the call by UN President Kofi Annan to declare terrorism a "crime against humanity," and to try the terrorists, if and when they are captured, before an international tribunal. Furthermore, the UN General Assembly should condemn the Taliban regime for committing crimes against humanity not only for harboring Osama bin Laden and his men, but for the way the Taliban have trampled upon the human rights of their own women. There is no reason why the human rights of women to work, to be educated, to walk on the street, to dress as they wish, etc. should be considered any less sacred and any less in need of defense than the rights of ethnic minorities. In response to the events of September 11 and to future threats, multilateral responses that enjoy cross-cultural legitimacy and reflect some of the new norms of international law—like crimes against humanity or genocide, as defined under the Statute of Rome of the International Criminal Court—should be invoked. Unfortunately, the current actions of the Bush administration tend exactly in the opposite direction: the captured Taliban and al Qaeda soldiers have been declared "non-military combatants" and will be tried by military tribunals, held in the extra-territorial space of Guantánamo Bay, which is not subject to U.S. constitutional protections. As with the abdication of the Kyoto and Salt II agreements, around this issue too the Bush administration preaches internationalism but practices unilateralism.

Of course—and this cannot be said clearly enough by the citizens of western democracies—a radical revision of U.S. and NATO policy vis-à-vis the Arab world and south-central Asia is needed. The U.S. and its allies have to stop propping up military dictatorships and religious conservatives in these areas in order simply to secure oil supplies. Democratic movements within the burgeoning civil societies of countries like Egypt, Turkey, Jordan, and the new Iran must be supported. A general UN conference must be convened to deal with the rights of nations, eth-nicities, and other minorities without states in this region, like the Kurds in Turkey, Iraq, and Iran; the Shi'ites in Iraq; and the Baha'is as well as the Azeris in Iran. Efforts analogous to the Marshall Plan in postwar Europe or the Soros Founda-tion in Eastern Europe must be developed and furthered for entire regions. But even if all these things are assumed, I believe that a more daunting cultural struggle and civilizational malaise is unfolding before our eyes.

II

As many have noted (including former Prime Minister of Pakistan Benazir Bhutto), the events of September 11 at first seemed to offer a belated con-firmation of Samuel Huntington's famous thesis of the clash of civilizations. Huntington wrote:

> It is my hypothesis that the fundamental source of conflict in this new world will not be primarily ideological or primarily economic. The great divisions among humankind and the dominating source of con-flict will be cultural. Nation states will remain the most powerful actors in world affairs, but the principal conflicts of global politics will occur between nations and groups of different civilizations. The fault lines between civilizations will be the battle lines of the future.[7]

Proceeding from a holistic understanding of cultures and civilizations—terms which he at times conflated and others distinguished—Huntington was unable to differentiate one "civilization" from another, with the consequence that, apart from "the West and the rest," he could not specify how many civ-ilizations there were and how they were to be differentiated.[8] Edward Said pointed out that Huntington made civilizations and identities into:

> shut-down, sealed-off entities that have been purged of the myriad currents and counter-currents that animate human his-tory, and over centuries have made it possible for that history not

only to contain wars of religion and imperial conquest but also to be one of exchange, cross-fertilization, and sharing.[9]

It is precisely this history of crossfertilization—exchange as well as confrontation—between Islamic cultures and the West that we must pay increasing attention to. One of the principal thinkers of the Islamist[10] movement, Sayyid Qutb, an Egyptian who studied philosophy in France and briefly visited the United States, developed a civilizational critique of the West for its corruption, coldness, heartlessness, and individualism. His critique resonates with themes from the works of Nietzsche as well as Heidegger, from Adorno and Horkheimer as well as contemporary communitarians.[11] Describing the current condition of the West as one of "*jahiliyyah*," a lack of knowledge and a condition of ignorance, the Islamists advocate a return to Qur'anic law—the *shariah*—and Muslim precepts to combat the corruption of the western way of life. To combat the condition of *jahiliyyah*, it is necessary to rebel and establish a countercommunity (*jama'a*) and spread it through *jihad*.[12] Very often, the Islamists' struggle against *jahiliyyah* takes the form of a struggle against established authorities in their own countries and their 'corrupt,' westernizing policies.

This clash within Islamic countries between Islamist religious forces and modernizers like Kemal Ataturk in Turkey, Habib Burgiba in Tunisia, Gemal Abdel Nasser, Anwar Sadat and Hosni Mubarek in Egypt, the deposed Reza Shah Pahlavi in Iran, and even Saddam Hussein in Iraq, is long, deep, and powerful. The modernizers in these countries have usually come from military rather than civilian backgrounds, and by transforming one of the few intact institutions of the old regime—namely the military bureaucracy—into an instrument of political power and hegemony, they have consolidated their authority, often with limited popular support and democratic institutions. All over the Islamic Arab world this *military modernization* paradigm, in which Syria and Iraq had participated through the Ba'ath regimes in the 1970s, has lost ground. The defeat of the Egyptian armies in the hands of Israel during the Six Day War and the Israeli occupation of the West Bank are reminders to the military elite of these countries, less of the plight of the Palestinians, whom they have massacred and oppressed when it suited their interests (remember Black September in Jordan in 1970, in which Palestinians were killed by the thousands, or the persecution of the Palestinians by the Saudis because of their support for Saddam Hussein during the Gulf

War) than of the failure of their own truncated projects of modernization. Israel is a thorn in the side of these regimes, whose very presence is a reminder of their own failure to modernize in military, technological, and economic terms.

The revival of Islamist movements is best understood in the light of the failure of most of these societies to succeed in combining a prosperous economy *with* political democracy and a Muslim identity.[13] Islamism emerges as a plausible civilizational project not just against the West, but against the failure of westernizing elites who have managed to import only a truncated modernity into their own societies. Some of these modernizing elites had considered themselves "socialists" of sorts. The Ba'ath regimes in Syria and Iraq, and even the kind of pan-Arabism envisaged by Nasser in the early 1960s, advocated strong redistributionist economic measures, built up huge public sectors (in state-owned utilities, for example), and practiced what could be called "statist modernization" from above. The demise of the Soviet Union has left these states with no patrons. Need we remind ourselves that the mobilization of the Islamist *mujahedeen* in Afghanistan began against the Soviet invasion of the country in 1979—an invasion the Soviets engaged in to support their own backers, the leftist *fedayyeen*?

The collapse of really existing socialisms and the failure of state-guided modernization from above have created an enormous vacuum in the ideological life of these societies. And into this vacuum have rushed Islamist fundamentalists. Osama bin Laden is the most spectacular member of a long chain of critics in the Islamic world, who, more often than not, have directed their local struggles against their own corrupt and authoritarian regimes (Nasser banned the Islamist Muslim Brotherhood and hanged some of its leaders) toward the outside, toward the external enemy.

III

I want to end with Max Weber's question: Which directions do religious rejections of the world take and why?[14] There is a fundamental conflict between secular, capitalist modernity, driven by profit, self-interest, and individualism, and the ethical worldviews of the world's religions. The religious worldviews preach various forms of abstinence, renunciation of riches, the pursuit of virtue in the path of God, the exercise of solidarity among members of the faith, and the disciplining of everyday life to do the work of the Lord. What is it, Weber asked, that enables some religious interpretations of the world to make their peace with the new world of modernity? For Weber the Protestant ethic exhibited its "elective affinity" to capitalism by transforming the abstinent and methodical pursuit of one's vocation in the service of God into the methodical, predictable, disciplined pursuit of work and profit in this world. This process took several centuries and not all early modern Christians accepted its logic: Millennarian movements which rejected the capitalist control of everyday life for the sake of disciplined labor and profit accompanied the rise of western modernity.

The Protestant—and more narrowly Calvinist—transformation of religious salvation into an earthly vocation of hard work in the service of an unpredictable God is one among the many paths that the religious accommodation with the world can take. It is also possible to split the religious and mundane spheres in such a Way that one altogether withdraws from engagement with the world; the religious abnegation of the world remains an option. A third option—besides engagement or withdrawal—is to *compartmentalize* by separating the spheres of life which come under the ethical dictates of religion from those like the public spheres of the economy in which more flexibility and compromise are possible. Throughout the Islamic world, such a strict separation of religious observance (in the domain of family life and everyday practices of prayer, cleanliness, food, and sexuality) from the sphere of the economy in the "bazaar" (the marketplace) was practiced. This separation of the home from the market was made possible by the practice of Islamic tolerance toward the other Abrahamanic religions, like Judaism and Christianity. The Ottomans adopted this "separate spheres" model, and permitted the wide array of ethnic groups and peoples whom they dominated to govern themselves in their own communal affairs according to their own religious and customary traditions (the so-called *millet* system.) Global modernization is destroying the fragile balance between these separate spheres; this may explain in turn the obsessive preoccupation with controlling female sexuality which all Islamist groups exhibit.

Technical modernization, which brings along with it the gadgets of modernity like computers, videos, DVDs, cell phones, and satellite dishes, is no threat to the Islamists.[15] In fact, there is a ruthless exploitation of these new media to convey one's message to believers. Neither is finance capitalism as such problematic from an Islamic perspective. Attempts exist all over the Muslim world to reconcile the *shariah* with modern financial institutions. Whether it is the *hawale* method of money transfers, which bypass modern banks and rely on personalized contacts among money lenders, or the obligation of the rich to share 5 percemt of their wealth with the poor, as dictated in the *Qur'an* (a practice that is partially behind the founding of the *madrassas*—institutions of religious learning—for war orphans in Afghanistan by wealthy individuals all over the Islamic world), institutional innovations to make Islam compatible with global capitalism are taking place. The threat to the separate spheres model is primarily a threat to family and personal life.

Global capitalism is bringing images of sexual freedom and decadence, female emancipation and equality among the sexes, into the homes of patriarchal and authoritarian Muslim communities. It is Hollywood which is identified as America, and not the Constitution, the Supreme Court, or the legacy of Puritanism and town meetings. These fast circulating images of sexual liberty and decadence, physical destruction and violence, sell very well globally because their message is blunt and can be extricated from local cultural nuance.

In a global world, it is not only images that travel; individuals all over the Islamic world are part of a large diaspora to the West. Sizeable Muslim communities exist in every large European and North American capital. These migrant communities attempt to practice the separate life-spheres model in their new homes. But the children of Muslim migrants are caught between worlds; be it through educational institutions or the influence of mass culture, they are torn between the authoritarian and patriarchal family structures from which they emerge and the new world of freedom into which they enter. There is a continuous renegotiation of clashing moral codes and value orientations in the minds of this younger generation, particularly regarding women. If we want to understand why so many educated, relatively well-off Muslim males who had lived in Hamburg and Paris would participate in the actions of September 11, we have to understand the psychology of Muslim immigrants in their encounters with secular liberal democracies of the West. Given the failure of their own home-grown versions of modernity like Nasserism and the Ba'ath movement, given the global entertainment industry's profound assault on their identity as Muslims, and given the profound discrimination and contempt which they experience in their host societies as new immigrants who are perceived to have "backward" morals and ways of life, many young Muslims today turn to

Islamism and fundamentalism. Commenting on *l'affaire foulard* (the head-scarf affair) in France, in which some female students took to wearing traditional headscarfs less as a sign of submission to religious patriarchy than as an emblem of difference and defiance against homogenizing French republican traditions, the French sociologists Gaspard and Khosrokhavar capture these set of complex symbolic negotiations as follows:

> [The headscarf] mirrors in the eyes of the parents and the grand-parents the illusions of continuity whereas it is a factor of disconti-nuity; it makes possible the transition to otherness (modernity), under the pretext of identity (tradition); it creates the sentiment of identity with the society of origin whereas its meaning is inscribed within the dynamic of relations with the receiving society. . . . [I]t is the vehicle of the passage to modernity within a promiscuity which confounds traditional distinctions, of an access to the public sphere which was forbidden to traditional women as a space of action and the constitution of individual autonomy. . . . [16]

We can intervene in this process of complex cultural negotiations as dialogue partners in a global civilization only insofar as we make an effort to understand the struggles of others whose idioms and terms may be unfamiliar to us, but which, by the same token, are also not so different from similar struggles at other times in our own cultures; through acts of strong hermeneutical generosity, we can still extend our moral imagination to view the world through the others' eyes.[17] While I believe that at this stage of the conflict the use of force against the Osama bin Laden network is inevitable and justified, the real political task ahead is to engage in a dialogue with millions of Muslims around this globe—beyond vengeance and without apocalyptic expectations. Democracies cannot fight holy wars. Reason, compassion, respect for the dignity of human life, the search for justice, and the desire for reconciliation are the democratic virtues which are now pitted against acts of apocalyptic hatred and vengeance.

Notes

1 See Susan Sontag, *New Yorker*, September 24, 2001; Fred Jameson, *London Review of Books* 23, no. 19 (October 4, 2001); and Slavoj Zizek, "The Desert of the Real: Is this the End of Fantasy?" *In These Times*, October 29, 2001.

2 The analogy is not quite accurate, for the French colonizers eventually left

Algeria. Despite all theories to the contrary, the Jewish population of Palestine are not colonizers in the traditional sense of the term. They are not there to exploit the indigenous population or their resources, but to establish a "Jewish homeland"—however problematic and tragic this vision may be. The refusal of much of the Arab world to understand the uniqueness of the dream that motivated the Zionist enterprise makes it easy for them to assimilate Israel to the model of the western oppressor while presenting themselves as the colonized and the oppressed. Israel was not established to be a colonizing force; it has become so increasingly since the occupation of the West Bank, and since its growing dependence on Palestinian labor to run its expanding economy.

3 "However, the monopolization of legitimate violence by the political-territorial association and its rational consociations into an institutional order is nothing primordial, but a product of evolution." Max Weber, *Economy and Society,* vol. 2, ed. Guenther Roth and Claus Wittich (Berkeley: University of California Press, 1978), 904–905.

4 Hannah Arendt, *The Origins of Totalitarianism* (New York: Harcourt, Brace, Jovanovich, 1979 (1951)), pt. 3.

5 Roxanne Euben, "Killing (for) Politics: Jihad, Martyrdom, and Political Action," lecture given in the Political Theory Colloquium, Yale University, October 16, 2001. Forthcoming, *Political Theory* (February 2002).

6 For a lucid elucidation of the current situation from the standpoint of international law, see Richard Falk, "A Just Response," *Nation,* October 8, 2001.

7 Samuel Huntington, *The Clash of Civilizations and the Remaking of World Order* (New York: Simon and Shuster, 1996), 2.

8 See my forthcoming *The Claims of Culture: Equality and Diversity* (Princeton: Princeton University Press, 2002). I discuss the conceptual and explanatory difficulties of Huntington's theses in the Introduction.

9 Edward Said on Samuel Huntington, in *al-Ahram Weekly On-Line,* <http://www.ahram.org.eg/weekly/standard/aaw.gif> no. 555, October 11–17, 2001.

10 Roxanne Euben observes that "'Islamism' is another, slightly less controversial way of referring to Islamic fundamentalism." ("Killing (for) Politics")

11 See Roxanne Euben's excellent book, *Enemy in the Mirror: Islamist Fundamentalism and the Limits of Modern Rationalism* (Princeton: Princeton University Press, 1999).

12 Euben, "Killing (for) Politics," 8.

13 See Sayres S. Rudy for an in-depth social theoretical analyses of some of these

issues, "Subjectivity, Political Evaluation, and Islamist Trajectories," in Birgit Schaebler and Leif Stenberg, eds., *Globalization and the Muslim World* (Albany: SUNY Press, 2002).

14 Max Weber, "Religious Rejections of the World and their Directions," *Economy and Society,* vol 1.

15 At the end of the 1980s, when I first visited Germany as a Humboldt fellow in Munich, I was taken aback by the sale of cassettes and videotaped versions of chants from the Qur'an in big shopping centers. Recorded by well-known *Muezzins* (cantors), these tapes permitted the faithful to utilize the technology of the society around them while remaining true to themselves. The irony is that the chanting of the Qur'an, like the reading of the Old Testament, and unlike the reading of the Bible, is supposed to be a communal and collective act of chanting, telling, and recalling. The medium of Western technology threatens this communal fabric. The result may be "religion à la carte," as this phenomenon has been called, for many Muslims as well.

16 Françoise Gaspard and Farhad Khosrokhar, *Le Foulard et la République* (Paris: Découverte, 1995), 44-45. My translation.

17 I deal with the ethics of communication and multiculturalism in *The Claims of Culture,* ch. 5.

Women's Human Rights and Security in the Age of Terror[1]

Charlotte Bunch

From *The Nation*, September 23, 2002

When I talk with feminists from other countries, whether from Europe or the third world, I am repeatedly asked: "Where are the voices of the U.S. women's movement against what the Bush administration is doing globally, using the excuse of 9/11?"

While I know that many feminists are concerned with these issues, it is clear that our voices are not being heard much—outside, or even inside, this country. The perception created by the Western media is that virtually all Americans support Bush's militaristic threats, his "you're with us or against us," "Evil Axis" rhetoric, and his unilaterialist positions against global treaties from the Kyoto Protocol on the environment to the newly created International Criminal Court. When I mention activities like the weekly Women in Black vigils in New York against U.S. policy in the Middle East or feminists working to change the composition of the U.S. Congress, where only Barbara Lee—a brave black woman—spoke out against the Bush madness immediately after 9/11, they are somewhat relieved.

But the point is clear and we must address it—feminists in the United States do not have much impact on U.S. foreign policy, which is military- and corporate-driven. Even when it was convenient for Bush to use women's rights in Afghanistan to drum up support for his war, this did not lead to a sustained commitment to women in that situation. It is puzzling to many outside this country how a women's movement that has had such profound influence on U.S. culture and daily life could have so little effect on, or seemingly even concern for, U.S. foreign policy and its impact on women worldwide. The consequences of this are disastrous for

413

women in many places around the world, and increasingly threaten the advances that the global women's movement made in the 1990s.

Current U.S. foreign policy makes women's international solidarity more difficult to build in a number of ways. I have seen personally the change from the widespread sympathy that the world offered the U.S. at the time of 9/11 to the rise of anti-Americanism and rage at what the U.S. is doing in the name of that event. On the day of the attacks, I was still in South Africa following the UN World Conference Against Racism held in Durban the week before. I experienced overwhelming concern from people everywhere, especially when they learned that I lived in New York. And this came in spite of the great frustration that most felt about the inexcusable disdain for other countries that the Bush administration had just exhibited during the world conference. But some six to eight months later, the atmosphere outside this country has changed dramatically, and there is great resentment and anger toward the United States. Even some feminist colleagues elsewhere tell me that they are now asked how they can really work with people in the U.S., given how little opposition to Bush's foreign policies they see happening here.

This resentment stems in part from the fact that 9/11 is *not* seen as the defining moment for the rest of the world—at least not in terms of what happened that day. In many places, people have long lived with terrorism and violence and death on a scale as great or greater than 9/11. So while they agree that this was a terrible and shocking event, they see the U.S. obsession with it, including the assumption that it is the defining moment for everyone, as self-indulgent and shortsighted.

Of course, September 11 has been a defining event within the U.S. But how we understand it in a global context is important. First, we must recognize that our government's responses to it were not inevitable. This event could have taken the country in other directions, including toward greater empathy with what others have suffered, toward more concern for human security and the conditions that give rise to terrorism, and toward recognition of the importance of multilateral institutions in a globally linked world. But that would have required a very different national leadership. Instead, it has become the rationale for an escalation of the regressive Bush agenda domestically and internationally, including more unrestrained exercise of U.S. power and disregard for multilateralism. Other governments have also used this occasion to increase military spending and to erode support for human rights within their countries. In that sense, it has become a defining moment because of how it has been used. But the issues highlighted by 9/11 are not new and have been raised by many other events both before and after it.

Indeed, 9/11 has raised the profile of many of the issues feminists were already struggling with globally, such as:

- Growing global and national economic inequities produced by globalization, structural adjustment, privatization, downsizing, etc.;
- The rise of extremist expressions of religious and/or nationalistic "fundamentalisms" that threaten progress on women's rights around the world (including in the U.S.) in the name of many diverse religions and cultures;
- The escalation of racist and sexist violence and terrorism in daily life and the growth of sexual and economic exploitation and trafficking of women across the globe;
- An increase in militarism, wars, internal conflicts, and terrorism that are affecting or targeting civilians and involving more and more women and children in deadly ways.

Since 9/11 has been used to curtail human rights—including freedom of expression—in the name of "national security," it has added both a greater sense of urgency to these concerns and made it more difficult to address them effectively from a feminist perspective.

Human vs. National Security

The call for redefining security in terms of human and ecological needs instead of national sovereignty and national borders was advancing pre-9/11 as an alternative to the state-centered concept of "national security," rooted in the military security-defense domain and academically lodged in the field of international relations. For feminists this has meant raising questions about whose security "national security" defends, and addressing issues like the violence continuum that threatens women's security daily, during armed conflict as well as so-called "peacetime."

The concept of human security had also advanced through the UN—first defined in the UNDP Human Development Report in 1994 and later taken up by Secretary General Kofi Annan in his Millennium Report in 2000, which spoke of security less as defending territory, and more in terms of protecting people.

While the concept of human security emerged out of discussions where women are active—from the peace movement and the debate over development—we know how easily feminist perspectives on such concepts can get marginalized as they become more mainstream. For example, a Proposal to Create a Human Security Report that emanated from Harvard University's Program on Humanitarian Policy and Conflict Research, in conjunction with the UN University in May of 2001, outlined an ambitious plan to create a report that would map key systemic causes of armed conflict and violent crime as well as a human insecurity index. Yet, while no group lives in greater insecurity than females, the proposal never once mentions women, gender, masculinity, rape, violence against women, or any other concept that has emerged out of several decades of feminist work. It makes one wonder whether men will ever learn to read what feminists write.

But in any case, efforts to advance the concept of human security and global sustainability over national security, and to make sure a feminist perspective was included in that work, were set back by 9/11, with its resurgence of the masculine warrior discourse. The media has been dominated by male "authority" figures and a few female clones—providing a rude reminder that when it comes to issues of terrorism, war, defense and national security, women, and especially feminists, are still not on the map.

Yet it is women who have been the major target of fundamentalist terrorism, from Algeria to the United States, over the past several decades. And it is mostly feminists from all parts of the world who have led the critique of this growing global problem—focusing attention not only on Islamic fundamentalism but on Protestant fundamentalism in the U.S., Catholic secret societies like Opus Dei in Latin America, Hindu right-wing fundamentalists in India, etc. Nevertheless, only when it became convenient for Bush's military and public relations purposes did the issues of women and fundamentalism surface in the U.S. media. And even this discussion has been largely confined to Afghanistan, and not extended to the rights of women in other conflicts, especially not to non-Islamic fundamentalist attacks on women's rights.

The events of 9/11 should have generated attempts to address the very real threats to women's human rights posed by fundamentalism, terrorism, and armed conflict in many guises. Instead the occasion was used to demonize the

Islamic Other and to justify further militarization of society and curtailment of civil liberties. Growing militarization, often with U.S. support and arms, has brought an increase in defense spending in many other areas, from India and Pakistan to Israel, Colombia and the Philippines. Meanwhile the Western donor countries' pledges to support economic development at the recent UN International Conference on Financing for Development (March 2002), fell far short of what would be needed to even begin to fulfill the millennium promises made in 2000 for advancing human security.

Thus, while human security is a promising concept, it is far from being embraced as a replacement for the nationalist security paradigm to which governments remain attached and have made vast commitments.

September 11 and Human Rights

The excuse of 9/11 has been used not only to curtail human rights in the U.S.—which some here are challenging—but also around the world, something not enough people in the United States see. We know we are in trouble when the U.S. government pulls out of global treaties and says it is not bound by international commitments made by previous administrations at events like the Beijing women's conference, because all international treaties and human rights conventions depend on the assumption that a country is bound by previous agreements and cannot simply jettison them with every change of administration. This erosion of respect for human rights in the U.S. also appears in the media, where some mainstream journalists have suggested that the selective use of torture may be justified and have defended the Bush administration's defiance of international norms regarding political prisoners as a necessary part of the war on terrorism. These are the kinds of arguments put forward by governments that torture and abuse rights and are contrary to the most accepted tenets of human rights.

Indeed, the erosion of the U.S. commitment to human rights helps legitimize the abuses of governments that have never fully accepted or claimed these standards. For while the U.S. government has often been hypocritical in its human rights policies, open disregard for international standards goes a step farther and thus strengthens other fundamentalist governments and forces who seek to deny human rights in general, and the rights of women in particular.

Ironically, even as public discourse demonizes Islamic fundamentalists, the unholy alliance of the Vatican, Islamic fundamentalists, and right-wing U.S.

forces is still working together when it comes to trying to defeat women's human rights. Feminists encountered this alliance in full force at the International Conference on Population and Development in Cairo (1994) and at the World Conference on Women in Beijing (1995) as well as during the five-year reviews of those events in 1999 and 2000. One need only look at the allies of the Bush administration at the UN Children's Summit in May 2002—such as the Holy See, Sudan, Libya, Iraq, and other gulf states—to understand that this alliance is still functioning globally after 9/11. Still, feminists need to do more research on the connections among various antifeminist "fundamentalist" forces, not only at the UN, which has begun to be documented, but in other arenas as well, such as in the making of world health policies, or even in the passage of anti-women's rights national legislation in some countries where outside forces have played a key role.

A high-profile example of how the Bush administration is assisting the agenda of those seeking to make the UN less effective in relation to human rights is its effort to ensure that the UN High Commissioner for Human Rights, Mary Robinson, would not get a second term in that office. She was among the first to frame her response to 9/11 from the perspective of international law, by suggesting that these acts of terrorism be prosecuted internationally as crimes against humanity, rather than by issuing a call to war, but she was quickly sidelined. Because of this, along with her efforts to make the World Conference Against Racism a success in spite of the U.S. contempt for it, the Bush administration adamantly opposed her reappointment. This opposition dovetailed with that of a number of other governments unhappy with her attention to their human rights abuses. Robinson is only one of the UN officials that the Bush administration has targeted in its efforts to purge the institution of its critics and anybody else promoting policies not to its liking.

Many governments see 9/11 and the Bush administration's policies as an opportunity for them to jettison even a rhetorical commitment to certain human rights in the name of fighting terrorism or providing for national or public "security," or simply to label issues like racism and violence against women as lower priority concerns. This has a particular impact on women because it reverses the broadening of the human rights paradigm, which had begun to encompass issues like violence against women and to focus more on socio-economic rights in the eighties and nineties.

Women's rights advocates are still seen as the new kids on the human rights block, and the recently gained recognition of women's rights as human rights is now jeopardized even before those rights had been fully accepted and mechanisms for their protection institutionalized. The need to articulate a feminist approach to global security that ensures human rights and human security, and recognizes their interconnection, is therefore more urgent than ever.

Challenges Ahead for Global Feminism

Women have transformed many aspects of life over the past forty years, and we all live differently because of it. Yet, looking at the world in 2002, we have to ask what went wrong. Why have feminists not had a greater impact on these global issues? How can we more effectively address current challenges like an increasingly militarized daily life, the rise in the political use of fundamentalism in every religion and region, and the widening economic gap between the haves and the have-nots?

Women in the U.S. need to think in a bigger frame and look at what strategies it will take at all levels to turn our government and the interests that surround this superpower around. Often what we must do to help women elsewhere is not to focus on their governments but to work to change ours so that U.S. policies and corporate forces based here stop harming women elsewhere. To do this, we need to pay more attention to foreign policy and to have more serious discussion that crosses both the local-global and the activist-academic divides.

If we look at women's movements over the past thirty to forty years, their strength has been in very rooted and diverse local bases of action as well as in the development of highly specific research and theory. There has also been a rich global dialogue and networking among women across national lines over the past two decades. But in the United States, these discourses rarely intersect.

The local/national/domestic and the global/international are mostly seen as separate spheres, and there is often little interaction and learning between feminists working in each of them. Therefore, we often have trouble determining what local actions will have the greatest impact globally. This has been illustrated in the lack of interest in the United States in using international human rights treaties like the Convention on the Elimination of all forms of Descrimination Against Women (CEDAW) to advance issues here. There is a tendency not to see the international arena as adding anything to causes at home, but only as a vehicle to assist women elsewhere. This needs to change.

Women's global networking and international solidarity has helped sustain feminist activists, especially when challenging the dominant nationalist or communalist discourse in their countries. Women have supported each other by keeping lines of communication open and accurate information flowing, by providing a sense that one is not alone, offering money and assistance in escaping difficult situations, compiling petitions aimed at governments, the UN, and other bodies. Feminists in the U.S. can benefit from the support of women in other countries, which we will need if we are to challenge what is now openly defended as the American Empire. Information and perspectives from women around the world can help us understand how the U.S. impacts their lives and give us new ideas for how to challenge the increasingly nationalistic parochialism of our media.

Women's activism in the U.S. must be both local and global simultaneously to succeed. We must continuously grapple with the dynamic tension between the universality and specificity of our work. Only through such a process can feminists address not only the needs of each situation but also the larger global structures creating many of these conflicts. Then we can move toward an affirmative vision of peace with human rights and human security at its core, rather than continue to clean up after the endless succession of male-determined crises and conflicts. This is our challenge.

Note

1 This is an adapted version of a speech delivered at the May 30, 2002, annual conference of the National Center for Research on Women in New York City.

About the Contributors

Betsy Reed is a senior editor at *The Nation* and the co-editor of *Homo Economics: Capitalism, Community and Lesbian and Gay Life*.

Janet Afary is associate professor of history and women's studies at Purdue University, West Lafayette, Indiana. She is the author of *The Iranian Constitutional Revolution of 1906-11: Grassroots Democracy, Social Democracy, and the Origins of Feminism*.

Leila Ahmed is a professor of women's studies in religion at Harvard University. She is also the author of *Women and Gender in Islam: Historical Roots of a Modern Debate*.

Karen Armstrong is one of the world's foremost scholars on religious affairs. She is the author of several best-selling books, including *The Battle for God, Jerusalem, The History of God*, and *Through the Narrow Gate*, a memoir of her seven years as a nun. She lives in London.

Ruth Baldwin is assistant editor at Nation Books.

Amrita Basu is professor of political science and women's and gender studies at Amherst College. She is the editor of *The Challenge of Local Feminisms: Women's Movements in Global Perspective*.

Margaret Lamberts Bendroth is the author of *Growing up Protestant: Parents, Children and Mainline Churches* and coeditor of *Women and Twentieth Century Protestantism*.

Seyla Benhabib is the Eugene Meyer Professor of Political Science and Philosophy at Yale University. She is the author of *The Claims of Culture: Equality and Diversity in the Global Era*.

Karima Bennoune is an assistant professor at Rutgers University School of Law, Newark. She formerly worked as a legal advisor for Amnesty International.

Angela Bonavoglia is a freelance journalist and author who covers social, health, religious, and women's issues. She is a contributing editor to *Ms.* and a frequent contributor to the *Chicago Tribune*.

Charlotte Bunch, founder and executive director of the Center for Women's Global Leadership at Douglass College, Rutgers, the State University of New Jersey, has been an activist, author, and organizer in the women's, civil, and human rights movements for over three decades. Previously Bunch was a fellow at the Institute for Policy Studies and a founder of Washington D.C. Women's Liberation and of *Quest: A Feminist Quarterly*. She is the author of numerous essays and has edited or coedited nine anthologies including the Center for Women's Global Leadership's reports on the Beijing Plus 5 process in 2000 and the World Conference on Racism in 2001. Her books include *Passionate Politics: Feminist Theory in Action, Demanding Accountability: The Global Campaign* and *Vienna Tribunal for Women's Human Rights*.

Amy Caiazza is a study director at the Institute for Women's Policy Research. Her forthcoming book, *Mothers and Soldiers*, examines women's and men's organizing, particularly around peace and military issues, in 1990s Russia.

Susan Muaddi Darraj is a graduate student at Johns Hopkins University. Her essays on Arab feminism appear in anthologies from Seal Press and Northeastern University Press, and her other work has appeared in *New York Stories, Mizna, Pages Magazine*, the *Johns Hopkins Magazine,* and elsewhere.

Barbara Ehrenreich is a columnist for the *Progressive* and the author of *Nickel and Dimed: On (Not) Getting by in America*.

Eve Ensler is an award-winning playwright, poet, activist, and screenwriter. Her many works for the stage include *The Vagina Monologues, The Depot, Floating Rhoda and the Glue Man, Extraordinary Measures,* and *Lemonade*.

Laura Flanders is the host of "Working Assets Radio" and author of *Real Majority, Media Minority: The Cost of Sidelining Women in Reporting* . Her "Spin Doctor Laura" columns appear daily on www.WorkingForChange.com.

Hillary Frey is *The Nation's* assistant literary editor.

Jan Goodwin is an award-winning journalist and the author of *Price of Honor*, which examines how Islamic extremism is affecting the lives of Muslim women.

Susan Friend Harding is professor of anthropology at the University of California, Santa Cruz. She is the author of *Remaking Ibieca: Agrarian Reform in Rural*

Aragon under Franco and coeditor with Charles Bright of *Statemaking and Social Movements: Essays in Theory and History.*

Amira Hass is the author of *Drinking the Sea at Gaza: Days and Nights in a Land under Seige.*

Homaira Mamoor graduated from St. Joseph's College. A native of Afghanistan and a devout Muslim, she is dedicated to raising awareness of the plight of her Afghan sisters back home. She lives in Long Island and is a board member of Women for Afghan Women.

Sunita Mehta is director of grants and programs at a feminist foundation in New York, The Sister Fund. She serves on the Board of SAKHI for South Asian Women, a New York-based women's anti-violence organization. Ms. Mehta cofounded Women for Afghan Women in April 2001. Originally from India, she lives in Brooklyn, New York, with her husband and two young sons.

Fatima Mernissi is the author of *Scheherazade Goes West, Islam and Democracy,* and *The Veil and the Male Elite: A Feminist Interpretation of Islam.*

Minoo Moallem is assistant professor and chair of women's studies at San Francisco State University. Her major areas of interest include gender and fundamentalism, women and globalization.

Valentine Moghadam is director of women's studies and associate professor of sociology at Illinois State University. She is the author of *Gendering Economic Reform: Women and Structural Change in the Middle East* and *North Africa and Modernizing Women: Gender and Social Change.*

Martha C. Nussbaum is Ernst Freund Distinguished Professor of Law and Ethics at the University of Chicago, appointed in the Philosophy Department, the Law School, the Divinity School, and the College. She is an associate in the Classics Department, an affiliate of the Committee for Southern Asian Studies, and a member of the Board of the Committee on Gender Studies. Her most recent book is *Upheavals of Thought: The Intelligence of Emotions.*

Rosalind Petchesky, professor of political science and women's studies at Hunter College and the Graduate Center, CUNY, is the author of *Abortion and Woman's Choice* and the forthcoming *Women and Global Power.*

Katha Pollitt writes the "Subject to Debate" column for *The Nation*. Her writings have been published in two best selling collections: *Reasonable Creatures: Essays on Women and Feminism* and *Subject to Debate: Sense and Dissents on Women, Politics and Culture*.

Arundhati Roy lives in New Delhi and is the author of *The God of Small Things* and *Power Politics* (South End Press). A longer version of her essay is forthcoming as "Democracy: Who Is She When She's at Home?" in a new collection from South End Press.

Rosemary Radford Ruether is the Georgia Harkness Professor of Applied Theology at Garrett-Evangelical Theological Seminary in Evanston, Illinois, and the Carpenter Professor of Feminist Theology at the Graduate Theological Union in Berkeley, California. She is on the board of directors of Catholics for a Free Choice and is editorial advisor to *Conscience*.

Alice Shalvi is a feminist and social activist. Born in Germany in 1926, educated in England (1934-1949), she has lived in Jerusalem since 1949. Professor of English literature at Hebrew University of Jerusalem (1950-1990), she was the founding chairwoman of the Israel Women's Network (1984-2000). Principal of Pelech Religious Experimental High School for Girls from 1975 to 1990, Ms. Shalvi was formerly the rector and is now executive chairperson of the Schechter Institute of Jewish studies, Jerusalem.

A graduate of Harvard College and Stanford Law School, Madhavi Sunder is an assistant professor of law at the University of California, Davis. She teaches and writes in the area of law and culture, intellectual property, and women's international human rights.

Meredith Tax, the author of *The Rising of the Women, Rivington Street,* and *Union Square and Families,* is president of Women's WORLD and vice-chair of the International Committee of PEN American Center.

Polly Toynbee is a columnist for the *Guardian* (London).

Ellen Willis directs the cultural reporting and criticism program at New York University and is a Freda Kirchwey Fellow of the Nation Institute. Her latest book is *Don't Think, Smile! Notes on a Decade of Denial.*

Permissions

Index